Europe in Conflict

A History of Europe 1870–1980

Europe in Conflict
A History of Europe
1870 — 1980

Alan Jamieson

Hutchinson

London Melbourne Sydney Auckland Johannesburg

Hutchinson & Co. (Publishers) Ltd

An imprint of the Hutchinson Publishing Group

17-21 Conway Street, London W1P 6JD

Hutchinson Publishing Group (Australia) Pty Ltd
16-22 Church Street, Hawthorn, Melbourne, Victoria 3122

Hutchinson Group (NZ) Ltd
32-34 View Road, PO Box 40-086, Glenfield, Auckland 10

Hutchinson Group (SA) (Pty) Ltd
PO Box 337, Bergvlei 2012, South Africa

First published 1967
Second edition 1972
Fifth impression 1978
Third edition 1982
Reprinted 1984

Maps by Denys Baker

Printed and bound in Great Britain by
Anchor Brendon Ltd, Tiptree, Essex

British Library Cataloguing in Publication Data
Jamieson, Alan
   Europe in conflict: a history of Europe 1870-1980.
   —3rd ed.
   1. Europe—History—1871-1918
   2. Europe—History—20th century
   3. Europe—Political events—1945-
   I. Title
   940.2   D424

ISBN 0 09 149301 3

Contents

Illustrations

Maps

Preface to Third Edition

The continuing use made of this book by students at all levels has led to several reprintings. This has allowed us to revise and update material in it. For this new edition an additional chapter has been added, covering the twenty years from 1960 to 1980. Other minor alterations have been made to adjust to the requirements of examination syllabuses on twentieth-century history.

Alan Jamieson
January, 1982

Preface to Second Edition

An increasing number of Examination Boards are widening the scope of their syllabuses to include a survey of European history from the end of the Second World War to the present day, and in addition more and more teachers are adding this period to their own schemes of work, whether or not they are preparing pupils for external examinations. For these reasons and to make the book more complete two additional chapters and three new maps on the period 1945–70 have been added to the new edition of this book, which has proved to be of some value to those studying the modern history of Europe.

Alan Jamieson
August, 1971

Acknowledgements

The author is grateful to the Radio Times Hulton Picture Library, Paul Popper Ltd, the Imperial War Museum and the Keystone Press Agency Ltd for permission to reproduce illustrations.

I

The European Scene

In the period of history covered by this book Europe experienced immense changes. Revolutions, two world wars, the rise and fall of dictatorships, and an economic boom followed by a collapse and a depression caused bewildering shifts in power. In 1870 Germany was the dominant European power: in 1945 she lay in ruins. In 1870 Russia was despised as a weak, backward state: in 1945 her victorious armies sprawled across eastern Europe. The USA, at last rejecting her self-imposed isolation, twice appeared on the scene as the champion of democratic ideals and assisted Europe to repair the ravages of war.

This book traces the major political and economic events of these years, relegating the history of ideas and of the arts to the sidelines, not on the grounds that they are any less important, but because of the limitations of space. The great scientific and technical advances are also touched on, together with the revolutionary changes in communications, warfare, and education. This chapter gives some indication of the innovations and ideas that have influenced the course of recent history.

Liberalism
The Europe of 1870 was in the process of assimilating new, dynamic ideas which were to change its character. Of these ideas, liberalism was the most potent. Simply, liberals believed that the community would benefit if each individual was allowed the greatest possible freedom to pursue his own interests and talents. The application of this theory can be seen in the development of religious liberty, capitalism and the extension of political power to representatives of the people.

Another important influence was the growth of nationalist sentiments. This began as an expression of the right of a people—Germans, Frenchmen, Hungarians—to decide for themselves how they should be governed. In the twentieth century nationalism developed into a more emotional and dangerous feeling that one nation was superior to or was threatened by another.

In 1870 liberalism reached its high-water mark. It had not solved the problems of poverty, overcrowding and disease in the huge cities of the industrial areas of Europe. Liberalism had flourished in the advanced countries such as France, Britain and Holland. In other areas, such as Spain, Italy, Russia and the Balkans, the peasants suffered from harsh exploitation by landowners, and industry was unorganised. Here, liberal ideas were supported by a small section of the community, the intelligentsia. In Britain, however, a large middle class, composed of shopkeepers, farmers, merchants and professional men, although largely conservative, nevertheless wanted to push their way towards greater wealth, and they saw in liberalism the individual freedom to exploit their own energy and ambitions.

In the more backward countries of eastern and southern Europe where there was a wide gulf between rich and poor, political power fell to the upper class. A propertyless working class had no love for liberal ideas. Within these countries revolutionary parties formed, prepared to seize power on behalf of the lower classes by violent methods.

Economics

Great Britain had been the first nation to develop the factory system and in 1870 she still had a considerable industrial lead over her rivals. However, in the last twenty-five years of the nineteenth century the economic boom spread to other states, such as Germany, Russia and France. Nations rapidly industrialised their economies, and Great Britain was eventually overhauled and passed. Railways led the field. Mileage was doubled in Germany in the 1870s, and France and Russia tripled their mileage in the twenty years from 1870 to 1890.

The railway boom, the greater use of steam-power, and the change to iron ships stimulated the iron, coal and steel industries. The Gilchrist-Thomas process of producing steel from the phosphoric ores of Lorraine enabled Germany to build up a large industry. As steel could be produced cheaply, more and more industries became mechanised. The combination of cheap steel and steam-power drove the sailing-ships from the oceans, to be replaced by uglier but faster rivals. The world tonnage figure for steamships rose from 2 million tons in 1870 to 17 millions in 1895. The development of refrigeration assisted the trade in foodstuffs, for fresh fruit such as pineapples and bananas, and meat and dairy produce, could be transported over large distances. Germany advanced fast in steel production and revolutionised the construction of everything from bridges to bicycles.

At the same time the chemical and electrical industries were making remarkable progress. In 1873 at the Vienna Exhibition, a dynamo was linked to an electric motor, eliminating the need for a battery. The telephone, electric light, wireless telegraphy, electric trams and hydro-electricity were all invented in the last years of the century. Daimler developed an engine which could run on petrol instead of coal-gas. A few years later this development led to the first motor-cars and aero-planes. By 1914 these inventions had radically altered the European scene, although the USA had risen to a pinnacle of economic power. In 1914 American steel production was twice that of Germany, and five times that of Britain.

This industrial boom was not matched in agriculture, for in the 1870s Europe was flooded by American wheat and later by Australian and Argentinian meat. Prices fell in Europe, where farmers had to change their habits and concentrate on growing what they could sell. Dairy farming and vegetables became more important. Rotation of crops and new chemical fertilisers helped to improve the quality of the crops, but the agricultural depression swept across Europe and had disturbing and dangerous effects.

The lower classes in the urban areas and in the countryside suffered from both the industrial boom and the agricultural decline. In the factories workers worked long hours in unhealthy conditions for small wages. The peasants could not understand why they could not sell their farm produce, but falling prices and profits soon made the problem all too apparent. More and more of the workers turned to socialism as a remedy for their grievances. Another effect of the agricultural depres-sion was emigration. Between 1870 and 1914 over 20 million people left Europe for the USA. Others settled in Australia, New Zealand and Canada. Millions of Russians moved east to build new towns in Siberia. Despite this population movement, the total population of Europe rose from 290 millions in 1870 to 490 millions in 1914. The increase coincided with the drift of people from the countryside to the towns, except in France and eastern Europe. Towns grew into cities, bringing fresh problems of food supply, housing and employment.

Protectionism

In the mid nineteenth century most states, persuaded by the example of Britain, had turned to Free Trade. In the optimistic, thriving world of business it was felt that a free economy would let trade find its own level. However, in order to save their industries and agriculture from the severities of foreign competition, such as the flood of cheap British

manufactured goods and American wheat, statesmen adopted pro-
tectionist policies. Politicians believed that by shutting out foreign
trade, and by introducing high tariffs, the government could assist the
economic development of a country. In addition, tariffs on imported
goods increased a nation's revenue. Between 1876 and 1878, Russia,
Spain and Italy raised their tariffs, to be followed by Germany in 1879,
France in 1881 and Austria-Hungary in 1882. Tariffs were low by later
standards, and Holland, Denmark and Britain remained loyal to Free
Trade. It was not until 1932 that Britain imposed a general tariff of ten
per cent.

Governments gave subsidies to encourage exports and backed railways and steel firms, on which they depended for the transport and
equipment of their armies.

The effects of higher tariffs did not please everyone. People had to
pay heavier taxes and higher prices. Some industries were able to
monopolise home markets but lost sales abroad. To placate the workers,
Bismarck established state insurance schemes for old age pensions, sickness and accidents. His example was followed in other European
states, although not until Britain adopted national insurance in 1911 did
any government compensate for unemployment.

Socialism and Trade Unions

With the industrial revolution in full spate labour was in demand, and
industrial workers, rapidly increasing in number, formed organisations
to fight for better wages and conditions. German trade unions multi-
plied rapidly after 1890. In France and Britain strikes were used more
frequently to force employers to grant concessions. Struggles were
bitter: the Taff Vale company sued a union for damages in Britain and
won the case; in France, Briand called up strikers to serve in the army.
The class war grew more violent and in the conflict socialist ideas
spread more rapidly.

Some trade unions turned to political action to assist their constant
struggle for higher wages and improved conditions. The British
Labour Party and the German Social-Democrats were supported
by trade unions. It was thought that electing working-class MPs
would bring social reform more quickly than reliance on the old
parties.

In the nineteenth century socialism was a persecuted and divided
movement. In 1889 the Second International was founded and a new
enthusiasm and energy gripped European socialists. But the optimism
did not last, for the differences which split the unity of socialism again
rose to the surface. After Karl Marx died in 1883 his ideas spread

rapidly, although there was considerable disagreement on the method of applying them. Marx taught that the capitalists exploited the workers and that the whole fabric of the capitalist system should be overthrown by revolution. For a time debate centred on how the revolution could be organised, then on the practical plans for the new society to replace capitalism. Some of the socialist parties co-operated with other parties, as in France. This did not prove to be too difficult for many socialists were middle-class intellectuals. The socialist movements in the western countries adopted programmes of gradual reform, except in Russia where Lenin and the Bolsheviks prepared for revolution.

It was in Russia and southern Europe that politics were more violent. Many of the revolutionaries in these parts of Europe aimed at the total destruction of the State and were named anarchists. They fed on the peasants' hatred of their landlords and the bitter resentment of factory and mine workers against their employers.

Militarism

The easy successes of Prussia's wars between 1864 and 1871 made many think that war could be more often employed as an instrument of policy. Prussia had seized huge territories at little cost either in men or money. Her victory had been the consequence of a highly trained army and the internal paralysis of her enemies. Consequently, it was believed that war would bring easy profits if a nation was militarily prepared. Russia, in 1904, and Austria-Hungary, in 1914, entered wars with little realisation of their terrible price.

To win in war one had to be ready to deal a swift knock-out blow. Nations spent huge sums to establish a superiority in armed strength. New and improved weapons might hold the key, so the chemical industry concentrated on making new explosives, and the firepower of artillery and rifles was increased. Generals realised that armies needed to be mobile, so railways and roads were constructed with an eye to the movement of vast armies. To be prepared meant that large standing armies had to be maintained, and reservists had to be ready for immediate recall.

No one nation could rival Britain's naval power, but France, Russia and Germany pushed ahead with the construction of battleships and other large vessels. Britain accelerated her building programme to keep ahead, and so a naval 'race' developed prior to 1914. A rapid increase in the size and armament of new ships was revealed in the famous *Dreadnought* of 1906, a super-battleship with ten big guns instead of four. To counter this advance in construction, the torpedo and the submarine were developed. Germany became Britain's greatest rival at sea, although the USA made quiet but fast progress and gradually overhauled Britain.

The 'arms race' was matched by a series of alliances between the major Powers, to give automatic protection in case of sudden attack or assistance in case of invasion. All this cost vast sums of money and a massive increase in military spending was made by all the Powers.

Imperialism

Another solution that appealed to some as a remedy for Europe's problems was imperialism. Faced by the domination of Germany in Europe, Frenchmen and Italians turned to other parts of the world for compensation. Bismarck encouraged this process, although Chamberlain in Britain, Crispi in Italy and Ferry in France needed little encouragement. Britain had been busily acquiring an Empire all through the nineteenth century, but in Africa especially she soon found her interests threatened by rivals.

Businessmen in all countries saw the advantages that might result from new markets and fresh sources of raw materials. Tropical products such as vegetable oils and rubber brought good prices in Europe. Yet there was more to imperialism than economic motives. Men wanted to spread the benefits of their own civilisation to the primitive peoples of other continents. Explorers, missionaries, soldiers, all made their own impact on tribal societies. Once the flag or the Bible had conquered, the traders were never very far behind.

In order to maintain order in their colonies or to protect them from jealous rivals, the Powers found themselves drawn more and more into military and political commitments. Yet imperialism produced few wars. The Germans, British and French found that on occasion they had to subdue native risings, but they settled differences between themselves peacefully. Only the Russo-Japanese war of 1904–05 disturbed the international peace. Despite this, imperialism helped to build up tension and instability. The crises of Fashoda and the Boer War almost brought about a major European war, and colonial rivalry contributed to the causes of the First World War.

Modern Science and Art

New ideas were not confined to economics and politics. The period 1870 to 1945 saw remarkable changes in the intellectual life of Europe. The new scientific discoveries made an immediate impact. From the discovery of X-rays by the German, Röntgen, scientists passed on to study radiation. About 1911 Ernest Rutherford and Nils Bohr began to work on the theories of atomic structure, although it was not until 1938 that scientists discovered the secret of splitting the nucleus of the atom and using the energy for practical purposes. Other 'miracles of science' were more readily seen: the Eiffel Tower in Paris, the Forth Bridge, the skyscrapers of New York, the Suez and Panama canals, Marconi's radio, and in 1909 Blériot's flight across the Channel in an aeroplane.

These engineering feats were made possible by great advances in mathematics. Some of the new ideas—Max Planck's quantum theory and Albert Einstein's theory of relativity—destroyed some of the basic ideas of science which had been held since the days of Galileo and Newton.

Before 1914 the ideas of Charles Darwin produced great speculation. The publication of *The Origin of Species* (1859) and *The Descent of Man* (1871) rocked Europe by asserting that man is related to animal life and has reached his present biological state by a series of changes stretching over thousands of years.

Darwin's theories at first horrified the churches although eventually they came to terms. But Darwin forced men to turn and look into themselves. Sigmund Freud and Carl Jung examined the psychology of man. Freud's major work, *The Interpretation of Dreams*, was published in 1899, and his theories about man's behaviour proved to be as startling to the general public as Darwin's statements on natural selection.

The novelists of the late nineteenth century had been preoccupied with social problems. Dickens, Tolstoy and Balzac had written about the perils and injustices of society. Later novelists turned to the scientific and psychological discoveries for their inspiration. In France, Emile Zola wrote a series of novels based on the laws of heredity. In England the science fiction of H. G. Wells gained a wide audience of readers, while on the stage the plays of Oscar Wilde and G. B. Shaw mocked the social habits of the day.

In the visual arts a revolt began against the cramping styles of the nineteenth century. In architecture structural ironwork (employed in the Crystal Palace in 1851) came into general use. In 1889 the first skyscraper was built in New York. In 1903 Hennebique built a house of reinforced concrete. Steel beams, cheap glass and the greater use of concrete revolutionised building. Once the break had been made with the nineteenth century, architects and builders experimented imaginatively with the new materials.

Between 1870 and 1914 painting and sculpture also experienced a revolution. The Impressionists considered that light, atmosphere and colour were more important than the subject. France still led the way. In 1874 Claude Monet exhibited a picture called *Impression, Sunrise*, which gave its name to the new art form. Later, Cézanne and Gauguin reacted against the cult of sensation and demanded that art should express both the outward form of the subject and also something of its inner quality. Van Gogh's experiments with colour were influential and then the Cubists, more restrained in the use of colour, went further in representing form, preferring to represent an object as the spirit rather than as the eye sees it.

After 1918, drama, sculpture and painting became more intellectual and more difficult to follow by the general public. The thirst for information and knowledge was exploited by newspapers and magazines, whose circulation figures ran into millions. New art forms, like the cinema, became popular. The action, spectacle and comedy of silent and then (after 1927) 'moving' pictures appealed to the masses. Charlie Chaplin created a universal type—the little man, pathetic and amusing at odds with authority.

In music the works of Stravinsky, Schoenberg and Bartok attracted the interest of a few, the intellectual élite. In the 1920s the jazz of the American negro crossed the Atlantic and made an immediate impact, both on popular and 'serious' music.

In painting most of the Cubists abandoned their wilder flights of fancy. The champion of the great revolution remained the Spaniard, Picasso, who experimented with all forms of painting. He worked in Paris which became the world capital of art, attracting artists from Russia, Italy and Japan. For a time Surrealism was popular. Freud was the inspiration as artists tried to depict delirium and hallucinations.

Not everyone welcomed these sweeping changes. The doctrines of the Roman Catholic church had been exposed by the scientific discoveries. In the *Syllabus of Errors* (1864) the Church denounced socialism, Darwinism, and liberalism. Pius IX refused to change the beliefs of the Catholic Church to suit changing opinions.

His successor, Leo XIII (1878–1903) tackled the problem. In 1891 in the encyclical *Rerum Novarum* he supported the claims of workers to fair wages, adequate leisure and better working conditions. He urged Roman Catholics to form political parties and to support trade unions. In Germany, Belgium and France they answered the call, taking political action on their own initiative. Leo XIII steered the Catholics into a position where modern scientific theories buttressed their Church and did not undermine it. He encouraged Roman Catholics to work with the new movements although in other encyclicals he stressed that the traditional beliefs of the Church had not changed.

EUROPE BETWEEN THE TWO WORLD WARS

The Depression

The safe, ordered existence of Europe ended with the First World War. The political upheavals that destroyed the Empires of Austria-Hungary, Germany, Tsarist Russia and Turkey had far-reaching effects. The political and economic strains of the war, and then the peace, forced liberalism into retreat. In Italy, Spain and Portugal, as in eastern Europe, dictators overthrew democratic governments, and state planning with controls replaced the free economies once practised in Europe. Europe had changed: the huge, sprawling Empires had gone and in their place smaller, more aggressive, more violent powers had arisen.

The USA, having made an effective entry into European politics in 1917, retired again into isolation in 1920, to enjoy a profitable economic boom, while the new Europe struggled to restore order and prosperity. American industry, stimulated by war needs, produced more and more goods. Businessmen hoped optimistically for even greater profits and invested in every enterprise. In the 1920s the European states produced more goods for themselves and cut down on American imports. When sales began to fall, the speculators who had invested huge sums in industry panicked. Share prices fell rapidly and in October 1929 the speculative boom on Wall Street, the American Stock Exchange, ended disastrously. Thousands of speculators were ruined, banks and businesses closed by the hundred. Share prices continued to fall as men desperately sold out.

The crash affected struggling Europe, for American financiers had done much to stimulate economic recovery by their wise investments. American loans were now called in. At the same time trade declined disastrously. The result was unemployment—3 million in Britain, 6 million in Germany, 12 million in the USA.

Falling prices, devalued currencies and the closure of banks were inevitable additional consequences. The Kreditanstalt of Vienna, a bank holding two thirds of Austria's assets, collapsed in 1931. This was the Great Depression. Capitalism had failed tragically: the Communists offered one solution, the Fascists another.

In an attempt to stave off worse effects, nations imposed higher tariffs. As this policy did not lead to trade recovery, governments began to insist on the restriction of imports from abroad. International trade was soon in chaos as one nation after another erected high tariff walls to protect its own industries. Physical controls over the movements of

goods, labour and currency spread from one country to another:
people accepted it as the price to pay for recovery.

The economic blizzard thrust Germany into a crisis from which the
Nazis emerged triumphant. The crisis assisted the dictatorships, for
they had the power to take immediate, harsh decisions without fear of
reprisal. From 1928 the Soviet planning agency, *Gosplan*, directed the
first Five-Year Plan. In 1933 Hitler inaugurated the Four-Year Plan and
in 1934 Mussolini adopted import and export controls. Long-term
planning and government controls seemed to offer the best chance of
recovery.

Recovery

Europe slowly recovered. The USA, encouraged by President Roosevelt's 'New Deal' policy, led the way. By 1938 the USA increased her
share to thirty-two per cent of world productive capacity. The USSR,
striving to increase industrial production at a fantastic rate of progress,
had acquired nineteen per cent. Below this level, Germany (eleven per
cent), France (five per cent) and Britain (nine per cent) had fallen out of
the race of the giants.

In Europe economic expansion began to move again after governments had abandoned attempts to balance their budgets. Heavy expenditure increased national debts, but once governments realised that
debts were inevitable, industry was given assistance. The expenditure
on armaments stimulated the recovery that was already under way in
1934. Production rose steadily in the late thirties: 1937 was the peak
year, and when war broke out Europe was in the middle of a recession,
soon ended by the massive spending on munitions of all kinds.

The Dictators

In the 1930s people found that governments increasingly interfered in
their lives. In Russia, the Communists drove millions of peasants into
collective farms; in Germany and Italy the Fascists imposed control
over trade unions, the press and transport. Inevitably, all political and
economic activities within these states were rigorously controlled by
governments.

Europe slipped into an apathetic acceptance of totalitarian regimes.
To many, Franco, Hitler, Mussolini, Salazar and the others were the
only answer to the breakdown of the social and political structure of the
state. If anything, the Depression aided the dictators: they had the
power to deal with crises, and opposition was swiftly crushed. Once in
power the dictators could demand absolute obedience, total confor-
mity. Through press and radio, these governments poured torrents of

propaganda at the people, crushing criticism and evoking national hysteria. The Nuremberg Rally of 1934, with 450,000 Germans carrying banners, shouting slogans and cheering the parade of troops showed how Germany came to accept display and violence.

Censorship was rigorously applied in the New Europe: France and Britain remained two of the dwindling number of states loyal to free speech. In Russia and Germany little escaped the control of the police and the government. The state organised writers and artists in its service. No longer was free expression allowed: Einstein, the scientist, and Brecht, the playwright, two of Germany's most famous men, left rather than face persecution.

Although the Nazi and Soviet regimes were the foremost examples of this sort of terror, they had many imitators. France and Britain, dismayed by the extension of tyranny, did not have the power or the nerve to challenge it. Only a few brave men spoke out and in many cases died for their courage.

2

France, 1870–1914

✷✷

The war of 1870 was one of the greatest disasters in French history. Unfortunately for the French, they stood in the way of a united Germany, and Bismarck had no compunction in trapping them into war. In June 1870 Prince Leopold of Hohenzollern, a distant relative of the Prussian King, accepted the vacant Spanish throne. The French Government protested, fearing German encirclement. Prince Leopold withdrew his acceptance and the whole affair appeared at an end. However, the French, stung by the diplomatic and military victories of Bismarck in the 1860s, demanded satisfaction. Napoleon III's prestige had steadily crumbled. At a low ebb in 1870, an outstanding triumph might restore his fame. Anti-Prussian fervour, whipped up to fever-pitch by the Paris press, gripped France. Nagged on by Empress Eugénie, Napoleon III demanded a formal guarantee from the King of Prussia that the Hohenzollern candidature would never be renewed. The Napoleonic government, already prepared to chase shadows, now committed suicide, believing that France could easily destroy Prussia. Napoleon gave little thought to the aims, the preparation, or the strategy of war. He raced into it with no more thought than that it would be popular.

Until July 1870 Bismarck had not realised the full significance of the situation. He had been more concerned to evade a crisis than create one. Now he saw that, by bringing in the South German states at the same time, war could be made to appear a matter of national honour. He recovered from his surprise at having a ready-made opportunity placed at his disposal. William I, disdainfully but politely, rejected the French demands. Bismarck followed this up with an insult. William sent a telegram to Bismarck who was at his estates at Varzin, explaining his actions. Bismarck edited the telegram and published it. From the revised version it appeared as if the French ambassador had been insulted. The famous Ems Telegram was intended to provoke France: it succeeded brilliantly. The telegram itself did not cause the war. That was the result of Napoleon's decision to have it out with Prussia, and equally, Bismarck's willingness to let him thrust France into a trap. On 19 July the French declared war, 'with light hearts'. The Paris mob yelled its delight. The French army might be totally unprepared, but honour had been satisfied. The French, deluded by Bismarck, lacked a friend in Europe. The British thought that France had sought war, and were worried about Napoleon's proposals to Bismarck that France might take Belgium.[1] Britain, pacific, stayed neutral, trying to play the part of a mediator. Russia was concerned for Poland, fearing its loss in a general war, and clung to neutrality, as Austria-Hungary did too. Austria had already felt the power of Prussia in 1866 and had no wish for another dose. Italy, grateful to Prussia for obtaining Venice in 1866, used the war of 1870 as an opportunity to seize Rome, formerly occupied by French troops. Everyone waited to see what would happen. In the event of a long war positions might be reconsidered. Thus the French were left to fight alone against a united Germany. Europe did not have long to wait for the outcome.

Early in August the French army mobilised and moved towards the Rhine. Behind the soldiers the organisation was chaotic. The General Staff had only vague ideas, their reserves were few, their provisioning and supply of arms and ammunition quite insufficient. Napoleon, suffering agonies from illness, took personal command. In eastern France he joined an army of 220,000 men. Together they edged forward into German territory, to be met by heavy counter-attacks that forced them into retreat towards Metz. Napoleon refused to withdraw his army any further after the halt at Metz. He left all his troops in the city, commanded by General Bazaine. Within a few days they were completely surrounded by the Germans. In Alsace, early French victories under General MacMahon did not last, and here too the French were thrust back.

Napoleon then decided to march to the relief of Metz. He linked up with MacMahon's army of 84,000 men and marched east. Paris, stunned and frightened, waited for news. MacMahon walked straight

1. Bismarck had published the 'secret' negotiations of 1866 between Prussia and France: the British Government took fright when they saw that Napoleon intended to seize Belgium.

into the trap set for him by the brilliant German strategist, Moltke, who
had planned for this war with scientific precision. Surrounded and
battered at Sedan, the whole French army, with its Emperor, surrendered. The war had been in progress for forty-six days. In Paris, the
mobs rioted. The Assembly deposed Napoleon. The Second Empire
collapsed with hardly a whimper. The Third Republic was proclaimed
amid enormous enthusiasm. Napoleon, carried off in triumph into
captivity inside Germany, seemed a bad dream. The newly formed
Government of National Defence decided to fight on. Men previously
in opposition to Napoleon, like Thiers, and the young lawyer Gambetta,
resolved not to surrender.

The Prussians advanced and in September surrounded Paris, happy
to starve the city into capitulation. In October, Bazaine at Metz surrendered his whole force. Paris refused to yield. A semi-armed rabble
put up an heroic resistance although reduced to eating rats and cutting
down trees in the Champs Élysées for firewood. Gambetta escaped
from the city in a balloon and organised new armies, which were untrained and no match for the Prussians. The Government under Thiers
retreated, first to Tours and then to Bordeaux. In January 1871, after
Paris had surrendered, Thiers completed his negotiations with Bismarck and on 28 January an armistice brought the war to an end. A few
days earlier in the Hall of Mirrors at Versailles the German Empire had
been proclaimed. Bismarck's triumph was complete.

The Treaty of Frankfort, 1871

It seemed as if French humiliation could not be worse, that is until the
terms of the Treaty of Frankfort were revealed. Harsh terms were imposed on France. Alsace and Lorraine were ceded to Germany. For a
time the town of Belfort hung in the balance. In the end the French
kept it, allowing in exchange a triumphant German march through the
streets of Paris. France agreed to pay an indemnity of five billion francs
(£200 million) and the German army of occupation would remain in
occupation of French territory in the north and east until it was all paid.
Not all France accepted the defeat. The Parisians made revenge (*revanche*)
one of their new political objectives. Men like Gambetta, who had indignantly resigned his position as Minister of War, voted against the Treaty
in the Assembly and campaigned for the continuance of the war. They
were in a minority. France, stunned, apathetically accepted the worst.[1]

The loss of Alsace-Lorraine proved a bitter blow to French pride.
The provinces had been French for over 200 years and the population
remained loyal to France, thousands emigrating rather than suffer

1. The Treaty, signed on 10 May 1871, formally ended the war.

German rule. The hope of their recovery played an important part in the policies of the Third Republic. The hatred of France for Germany was to dominate the next fifty years.

The Commune

In the elections for the National Assembly in February 1871, the Republicans, the war party, won only 200 seats. The Monarchists, in favour of peace, had 400. In this confused situation, Thiers, now seventy-three, but still an energetic and able politician, formed a Government. It did not seem likely that the Republic would last long. Previous attempts at Republicanism had failed dismally, and the present régime carried the burden of defeat and surrender. While the form of the new Constitution was being discussed, Thiers set about the problem of the indemnity. Money was subscribed with such speed that by September 1873 the whole sum had been paid and the last German troops had left France.

Before this, in March 1871, Paris had risen in a violent revolt. The causes were complex. Parisians had always passionately felt that they led France. In 1870 the siege had been a sign of their spirit but the provinces had ignored their courage and left them to the Germans. Paris, strongly Republican, disliked the Monarchists of the Assembly, and felt slighted when the Assembly moved from Bordeaux, not to Paris, but to Versailles. Neither could Paris endure the harsh Frankfort Treaty. The revolt expressed the passionate resentment against its terms and especially the German victory march. Parisians felt betrayed. In the city a group of determined men roused their tempers. The Assembly pushed these men into open revolt by demanding that household rents and commercial debts, suspended during the siege, should now be paid. As unemployment stalked the city, these fresh demands meant eviction and possible starvation for some. The Assembly ordered the disbandment of the National Guard, a sort of Parisian defence force. This action hit both pockets and pride, and when Government troops entered Paris to remove the guns on Montmartre hill, the mob turned on the soldiers in a rage and murdered them.

For two months, Paris, controlled by the Communards, held out. It is difficult to understand what they hoped to achieve. It was not a Communist rising in the Marxist sense. The revolutionaries set up their own municipal government, the Commune, and seemed to aim at a sort of national federation of self-governing town councils, but their ideas were never fully worked out. They certainly demanded wider powers of local government for Paris than the Assembly were prepared to grant. Its 'communist' aspect was limited to taking some factories, abandoned by their owners, into public ownership. A Committee of Public Safety, reminiscent of the first Revolution of 1789, hunted down those who disagreed with the Communards. In some ways it was an insane outburst of the Paris mob against the legal government—a sort of anarchy.

Thiers put Paris under its second siege. The French army mounted an assault and the National Guard, with courage but little hope, retreated, fighting bitterly from one barricade to another. Some of the most famous buildings, the Tuileries Palace, the Palais de Justice and the Hôtel de Ville were burnt down. Both sides shot innocent hostages, including the Archbishop of Paris. Finally, Thiers had to face the humiliating task of asking the Germans for permission to strengthen his army to a total of 80,000 men. While German troops grinned in derision, the French entered Paris in a last savage onslaught in which prisoners were indiscriminately shot. The killings continued after the rebellion had ended, for the Government was determined to restore order quickly and by the sword. During the rising, about 20,000 died. Another 13,000 were later imprisoned, executed or exiled. The wounds to the spirit of proud Paris bit deep. Her pretensions to home rule vanished, the National Guard was disbanded and her leaders were ruined.

Never again did Paris exert the same primacy and leadership over France as it had in the past: the provinces now restored the balance. Abroad, the Commune damaged French prestige and gave fright to the comfortable, propertied middle class. Karl Marx used it as an example of revolutionary technique, a failure but one with lessons for the future. In France the socialist movement was ruined for some time, although the workers never forgot the cruelty meted out to them by a middle-class government. Lastly, many who had voted for monarchism now turned to the Republicans as the party of law and order: Thiers could at last begin the work of reconstruction.

THE CONSTITUTION OF 1875

Having weathered the storm of the Commune, the Assembly was able to proceed with the details of the new Constitution. The Monarchists still dominated affairs, but they weakened their position by their differences over the candidates. One group, the Orleanists, supported the claims of the Comte de Paris, the grandson of Louis Philippe, a former King. The Legitimists favoured the Comte de Chambord, grandson of another King, Charles X. A third candidate was the Prince

Imperial, son of Napoleon III. None of the three had inspiring personal qualities, and Chambord was childless.[1] Unfortunately for all three the French people began to turn away from the Monarchists. In 1870 the only thing they had to offer was peace: in 1875 they had not advanced much beyond this, and by then the other parties offered peace too. Not only that, but the Republicans had become quite respectable and were winning more and more support.

Thiers personally favoured a constitutional monarchy, but 'as the Republic is the government which divides us least' he joined the Republicans, who helped him in his task of national recovery. The French, working with vigour and enthusiasm, built new roads and railways, repaired the ravages of the war, restored financial stability and rebuilt parts of Paris, destroyed in the Commune. In 1872 a limited form of conscription strengthened the army, and a new Committee of Defence planned and constructed a series of fortresses on the eastern borders. Despite these achievements, Thiers was not popular with some politicians and in 1873 he was forced to resign. The new President, General MacMahon, represented the Army and the Legitimists, although he was more involved in keeping order than in restoring the monarchy. The nearest France came to a restoration was in October 1873, but the Comte de Chambord ruined his chances by stubbornly refusing to accept the tricolour: 'a symbol of revolution', he called it. The Monarchists could stall for time no longer and by 1875 the Republicans forced them to accept the new Constitution. By a majority of one the Assembly decided that the head of the Government should be a President of the Republic and that he should be elected by a majority of the two Chambers for a period of seven years.[2] He was eligible for re-election. It transpired that the President's office was nothing but a pale imitation of the British system of constitutional monarchy, without the frills and prestige. Although it lasted until 1940 the Third Republic became notorious for its weak leadership.

The President nominated a Prime Minister, and presided over meetings of the Cabinet. Like MacMahon, later Presidents had to rely on the political parties in the Assembly to force through Government measures. The parties, not the President, held the key to power. The Royalists despised the office, for it looked to them like a monarchy without the crown.[3]

In the National Assembly the Senate consisted of three hundred mem-

1. They also differed on inessentials. Chambord would have nothing but the white flag of his ancestors, the Bourbons. The Comte de Paris wanted the tricolour.
2. 352 deputies voted for a monarchy: 353 for a President of a Republic.
3. It became accepted in French politics that no strong statesman would be elected as President. His duties, it was said, were to wear evening dress in daytime.

bers, all at least forty years of age. Seventy-five were appointed for life
by the Assembly and the rest were elected for a term of nine years.
A third of the Senate was elected every three years by an Electoral
College, made up of deputies and members of district councils and
Communes. The Senate tended to have conservative leanings and provincial, rural interests. The other house of the Assembly was the Chamber
of Deputies, with six hundred members, elected by all adult males over
twenty-one years of age. It sat for a term of four years, and the candidates had to be twenty-five years of age to be eligible. In an emergency,
the President had the right to dissolve the Chamber before its term
expired. In the elections of 1876 a strong Republican Chamber was
elected. MacMahon, who disliked the legislative plans of the Republicans, dissolved the Chamber and forced another election in 1877. The
protests created such a crisis that subsequent Presidents did not repeat
the experiment. In any case, MacMahon's tactic failed, for another
strong Republican Chamber was returned in the elections. The General
lasted until 1879, when, angered by some particularly bitter criticisms,
he resigned. By then Monarchism was a lost cause.

The National Assembly had full legislative powers. It voted for war
or peace, negotiated treaties and raised taxes. But it did not have full
control over Ministers and in subsequent years French governments
achieved a certain notoriety because of their instability. In forty years
there were fifty changes of government. The fault for this does not lie
entirely in a vague Constitution and the lack of control by the Assembly
over Ministers. The vast number of parties, large and small, created
chaos. French parties had a habit of dividing up into splinter groups.
Governments came to depend on the support of a number of these
groups in the Chamber. One group's difference of opinion could easily
bring down a government.

THE REPUBLICANS IN POWER

Jules Grévy, 1879–87

The resignation of MacMahon in 1879 was a triumph for the Republicans. But they themselves were divided. Thiers died in 1877 and Gambetta, who had promised much but achieved little, died in 1882. Jules
Grévy, an elderly barrister, became President. He hated the Monarchists, but won no respect from within the ranks of his own supporters,
the Republicans. After 1879, the Republicans slowly worked their way

into power, not only in the Assembly, but also in the Civil Service, the local Communes, the judiciary and the army. They tried to heal old wounds by granting a pardon to the Communards and by moving the Assembly back to Paris. New laws tried to win over the working class. Trade unions were legalised, and a genuine attempt was made to improve working conditions and wages.

In the next few years the rural peasantry and the middle class voted fairly solidly for the Republicans. The Socialist vote, such as it was, centred in the towns. Socialism never really prospered; Gambetta had abandoned it to found a new radical group called the Opportunists, and the Socialists, leaderless, did not offer much of a threat to the Republicans. In the 1880s new laws extended civil liberties. In 1881 full rights of public meeting and of the press were established. In 1883 all municipal councils except Paris received the right to elect their own mayors, although the central Government still exerted considerable control over local affairs through the Prefects. In 1884 the Life Senators disappeared, and entry into the civil service was to be determined by open competition, not by patronage.

Other constructive work was achieved by Jules Ferry, the outstanding French statesman of the period. As Minister of Education at various times between 1875 and 1885, he sought to reform the whole system of French education. The French people felt that the key to the German victories of 1870 could be found in the schoolroom. But before new studies in sciences and languages could be introduced into French schools, the reactionary hold of the Roman Catholic Church had to be broken. With one law Ferry abolished the right of the Catholic Universities to grant degrees. Another prohibited most Catholic teaching orders, and in particular the Jesuits, from giving instruction. When the Jesuits objected, they were expelled. The Government took over control of primary education, charities and hospitals, and instituted civil marriage and divorce. In 1882 primary education between the ages of six and thirteen became free and compulsory. Training schools for teachers and new secondary schools, better equipped and staffed, were provided for boys and girls. New science colleges were built in Paris and other cities. In the space of a few years Ferry achieved a revolution, by establishing an extensive system of secular education under state control. These educational reforms reflected the wave of anti-clericalism[1] in Europe at this time, and the popular demand for more education.

1. Anti-clericalism was the policy of destroying the political power of the church and subordinating its non-spiritual functions to the state. The Roman Catholic Church was the major victim. Similar struggles took place in Spain, Latin America and Germany.

THREATS TO THE REPUBLIC

General Boulanger

After Ferry's fall from power in 1885, the Third Republic came under heavy pressure which threatened its very existence. Abroad, disputes with Britain over colonies and the perpetual threat of German attack built up a feeling of tension. Inside France, crises of confidence almost brought the Republic to collapse.

The Government of 1885 was a mixture of Opportunist-Republicans and Radicals. Against this weak coalition General Boulanger, a former Governor of Tunis, ranged himself. He cut a glamorous figure, parading around Paris, covered in medals and riding a superb black horse. To Frenchmen, he seemed the double of the great Napoleon I, come to recover Alsace-Lorraine and free them from the petty intrigues of politicians. He became an idol, enjoyed the feeling, and cultivated extravagant political ambitions. In 1886, he became Minister of War, and immediately won popularity by pressing for the release of a French border-police official called Schnaebele, who had been arrested by the Germans. The Germans let Schnaebele go, although largely as a result of Russian protests. Boulanger gained the credit, and, idolised and feted by the French people, he allowed power to go to his head. In April 1887 Jules Grévy resigned, owing to a scandal caused by his son-in-law, Daniel Wilson, who had been running a brisk sale in medals and decorations.

Boulanger now attracted to his side political adventurers and patriots disillusioned by Republican corruption. He left the Army and was elected to the Chamber of Deputies, where he formed his own party, the Nationalists. The Monarchists, Bonapartists and Catholics joined the bandwagon, hoping to weaken the Republican hold on power.[1] Boulanger then pressed for a revision of the Constitution, by which the President's powers would be strengthened and those of the Assembly weakened. France stood at the edge of a *coup d'état*, to be followed perhaps by a military dictatorship. At this crisis, the nerve of the Republicans held, and that of Boulanger broke. Grévy's successor as President was the insignificant Carnot: here, surprisingly, he acted with resolution. In April 1889, while Boulanger hesitated to use violence to seize power, the Senate proposed that the General should be tried for 'plotting against the safety of the state'. Rather than fight a civil war, Boulanger fled to Brussels. Six months later his 'revisionist' group won

1. In 1888 Boulanger won in six by-elections. In French law he could stand for election in more than one constituency although he could only represent one in the Chamber of Deputies. In January 1889 he won in Paris, a former Republican stronghold.

only twenty-three seats in the elections. He committed suicide in Brussels in 1891. France had been near to revolution, but by quick thinking the Republicans had averted the danger. For a time, everyone rallied to the defence of the Constitution, but before long new quarrels and intrigues ruined any chance of political stability.

The Panama Scandal

The French people were all too willing to think evil of their political representatives, and the Panama affair seemed to justify their suspicions. Ferdinand de Lesseps had become another popular hero. As engineer in charge of building the Suez Canal he had brought fame to French science. In 1881, together with Eiffel (who built Paris's famous Tower) and a group of financiers, he formed a company to build the Panama Canal. This proved to be a most difficult technical problem. The engineers had to contend with hilly country, malaria, and an inadequate labour supply. More and more money was poured into the scheme, most of it by public subscription. As the news of one disaster after another reached Paris, investment fell off, and the Company came to rely increasingly on loans. In 1888 the Government gave a subsidy, which was insufficient. In order to prevent the disaster from being made public knowledge, politicians were bribed to keep quiet.

By 1892 the facts could no longer be concealed. The Company went bankrupt and thousands of French investors found they were ruined. In the inquiry into the accounts, corruption was revealed. De Lesseps and eleven Deputies were prosecuted, but because of lack of sufficient evidence only one who confessed went to prison. The others were fined or acquitted, which convinced the general public that those in authority had again swept some official dirt under the carpet. A hundred Deputies and Senators were rumoured to be implicated. Certainly over 750,000 Frenchmen lost money in the unhappy venture.

The inquiry also linked a German-Jewish financier, Herz, with the bribes. His complicity was not fully discovered but he fled to England to avoid investigation. Suspicion of corruption among politicians became linked in the public mind with anti-Jewish hysteria. Frenchmen refused to believe that honesty and unselfishness existed among their politicians and were willing to believe any nonsense about them. In the elections of 1893, the Socialists increased their number in the Chamber to fifty, but a general disillusion, rather than any new enthusiasm, marked the end of the Panama Scandal.

The Dreyfus Case

Anti-Semitism gained fresh ammunition in the startling events of 1894.

A leakage of military information from the French War Office embarrassed the Army. French spies discovered proof of treason in a letter smuggled from the German Embassy. The letter came from an unknown French officer who was obviously selling secrets to the enemy. On the basis of the most scanty evidence and a vague similarity in writing, Captain Dreyfus, a Jewish staff officer at the War Office, was accused. He became the scapegoat for others, and as a Jew had plenty of personal enemies. General Mercier, the Minister of War, convinced himself that Dreyfus was the traitor. A quick court-martial followed in which the defence was seriously hampered and had no chance. Dreyfus was found guilty, degraded, and sent to Devil's Island, the French penal settlement off the coast of French Guiana, for life.

The affair hardly made a stir. Although Dreyfus's family and friends continued to press for a re-trial, no one seemed interested. The Jews wanted the episode forgotten, the War Office shared their desire, and the politicians did not know the true facts. The Head of French Intelligence, Colonel Picquart, was not entirely satisfied, however, and followed up the case. Other documents continued to disappear from the War Office although Dreyfus was far away on Devil's Island. By 1896 Picquart had not only discovered that Dreyfus was innocent, but he had pinned the blame for the leakages on another officer, Esterhazy. Rather than admit their mistake, General Mercier and his officers hushed up the scandal. Picquart received an urgent posting to the fighting line in Tunisia. Before he left he communicated his findings to Clemenceau, a rising and ambitious young politician, and Emile Zola, the famous novelist. The scandal now became public knowledge, and Esterhazy was brought to trial in a secret court-martial in 1898. The French Army continued to bluff its way. Finding Esterhazy not guilty, it acquitted him. The court was told that 'fresh evidence' (undisclosed) had unquestionably proved Dreyfus's guilt. The Army dismissed Picquart. The Generals stubbornly persevered with their injustices rather than admit their error. So Dreyfus chipped stones on Devil's Island for two more years.

Clemenceau then published in his newspaper an open letter, headed 'J'Accuse', written by Zola. In it, leading officers of the French Army were named and accused of rigging the trial. The affair became a public sensation with France divided into Dreyfusards and Anti-Dreyfusards. The Roman Catholic Church, the Army and a large number of politicians found themselves uneasy allies in the gang to discredit the Jews and protect the prestige of the Army.

Almost in desperation the unscrupulous Colonel Henri, Picquart's successor as Head of Intelligence, produced 'fresh' evidence. Revealed as a liar, Henri committed suicide, after admitting he had forged the new evidence. Eventually, Dreyfus was brought home to face a new trial. Incredibly, the generals, still trying to protect the Army, found him guilty 'with extenuating circumstances'. His sentence was reduced to ten years. The violent public outcry against this decision created panic among the politicians. Dreyfus was grudgingly given a pardon for an offence he did not commit. Not until 1906 did he manage to prove his innocence, when a new court reversed the previous verdicts. Dreyfus obtained the Legion of Honour and he and Picquart were reinstated in the Army and promoted. A medal and a pardon had to compensate Dreyfus for five years on Devil's Island.

The fate of Dreyfus had been bound up with the survival of the Third Republic. In the course of the scandal the Army and the Catholic Church had been discredited and France had been on the verge of a civil war. The Republicans had again rallied to save it from a worse fate at the hands of the Army.

THE PERIOD OF REFORM, 1899–1914.

In January 1899 a Republican cabinet under a distinguished lawyer, Waldeck-Rousseau, began the recovery. Himself a vigorous leader, he chose a strong ministry. The result, in contrast with previous apathy, was a series of decisive measures, the restoration of stability and a sense of achievement.

First, under a new Minister of War, the Army had to be purged. The old guard retired, and the control of promotion, now dependent on merit, was transferred from the Army High Command to the War Minister. This ensured that in future the politicians would control the Army. The Republicans felt that their other enemies, revealed in the Dreyfus case, were the Clericals. The religious Orders (the Holy Fathers in particular) had been running a sort of religious crusade against the Republic. The Government struck: some of the Orders were dissolved, others were forced to apply for legal recognition and were thus brought more closely under state control. Waldeck-Rousseau resigned in 1902, to be succeeded by Combes, a vindictive man with an ardent anti-Clerical bias, although he had been educated in a Roman Catholic seminary. The attack mounted. The religious Orders found their applications for legal recognition rejected. One law prohibited them from teaching. This stimulated Pope Pius X to enter the struggle, but his intervention only served to increase the bitterness, and the attack widened, for in addition to the monastic Orders, the whole Roman Catholic Church now came under attack.

In 1904, the Republicans decided to cancel the famous Concordat, negotiated by Napoleon I and the Pope in 1801. In the Statute of Separation, 1905, the Republic ceased to recognise or pay the Church. Religious instruction was to be excluded from the state schools—'les écoles sans Dieu', as one observer put it. In 1905 all Church property including buildings fell to the ownership of the local authorities, the Communes. The clergy were allowed to use the churches but their property stayed in the possession of the state.

The separation revealed deep and bitter feelings in France. The Church, possibly because of its old-fashioned ideas and its link with the Dreyfus affair, suffered a considerable defeat. The poverty which in the next few years fell more and more on the village curés made recruitment more difficult, but it did mean that only those with a true religious vocation joined the Church. Another result of the struggle was that with less clerical interference in politics the tension and aggression against the Church died down.

The period from 1900 to 1914 proved to be one of economic progress and social reform. The Socialist Millerand became Minister of Industry in Waldeck-Rousseau's government, and largely because of his influence a Labour Board was set up, the working day restricted to ten hours and a Public Health Act provided state grants for housing. In 1905 the Socialist groups joined forces in opposition and demanded faster and more sweeping reforms. Old age pensions in 1910, then further reductions in the working day, failed to placate them. Violence increased. The French trade unions, or *syndicats*, turned to strikes and riots to overthrow the capitalist system. In 1909 Clemenceau, using tough measures, called out the Army to combat a railway strike, but he fell from power and the unrest continued. Briand, the new Premier, infuriated the Socialists by his ruthless measures, such as conscripting strikers into the Army. Briand's attempt to unite all parties in defence of the Republic failed and he too resigned in 1911. In the next three years there were seven governments, reflecting the French difficulties in working the system of parliamentary government.

Why was it so ineffective? The Constitution, in which the weakness of the President's powers paralysed the executive, was partly to blame. The fatal fault in the electoral system, by which control fell into the hands of local associations who tended to choose local and loyal party men as candidates, did not help matters. These men, as Deputies, often concentrated on local concerns or vote-catching policies, and able, ambitious men turned in disgust to other careers. The unstable and numerous ministries resulted from the multitude of parties in the Chamber and therefore the need for coalitions. Deputies often acted irresponsibly by bringing down governments on unimportant issues. A series of scandals led to popular distrust and lack of faith in politicians. Strong leaders like Waldeck-Rousseau and Clemenceau were feared and distrusted, and did not last long in power. Therefore France had to suffer weak and constantly changing governments as the price of the Third Republic at a time when the enemy, Germany, was building up her strength both at home and abroad.

FRENCH COLONIAL POLICY

The petty intrigues of French politicians contrasted remarkably with the stirring deeds of her empire-builders. The French had always been interested in colonies and before 1870 their soldiers had established bases in Algeria (1842), Tahiti (1844), and Indo-China (1860). After 1870 the pace of expansion quickened, largely through the efforts of explorers, as in South-East Asia, where the French widened their empire from Saigon to take in Annam in 1874 as a protectorate.

Jules Ferry was the chief architect of the French advance. He used French energies in the colonies to divert attention from Alsace-Lorraine. The Government stood behind the explorers, traders and soldiers who established the Empire. Emigration was encouraged and roads, canals, and harbours were built with state money. By 1914 forty million Frenchmen ruled an Empire of sixty millions.

North Africa became the main area of expansion. In Senegal the French had a small base dating from the days of the slave trade and in Algeria a larger colony had been established in the 1830s. In 1881, owing to attacks on Algeria from Tunis, the French invaded and occupied the country, to the great annoyance of the Italians who had been contemplating such a move themselves. The Italians, offended, signed a treaty (the Triple Alliance) with Germany and Austria-Hungary. France, not disheartened, looked beyond Tunis towards Egypt. In 1882, however, the British established a military occupation of Egypt, after the French Government, in one of their frequent periods of political paralysis, had refused to join in the bombardment of Alexandria. The French were unwilling to involve themselves in what they thought might be a dangerous Egyptian war. Many French politicians believed that the arch-intriguer, Bismarck, was creating a trap for France and so advised caution. In fact, Egypt collapsed into British hands very easily and the French, irritated by their own inaction, drifted into a period of colonial rivalry which almost brought them to war with Britain over the Fashoda incident in 1898.

By 1885 the French had moved into and established military control over Madagascar (annexed in 1896). The explorations of De Brazza led to the conquest of the French Congo in 1885. Generals Galliéni in Senegal, Bugeaud in South Algeria and Lyautey in Morocco carried on the policy of military advance. To their African possessions the French added the Ivory Coast (1893); the huge Saharan area of French West Africa (conquered by 1898); Dahomey (1894); and Chad (1899); and by 1911, after a series of crises, a French protectorate over Morocco rounded off their gains.

In Indo-China, the French were involved in wars against the Emperors of Annam, who resented foreign intrusion and took revenge on traders and missionaries. In 1882 the French captured Hanoi, thus extending their control further to the north. This annoyed the Chinese who attacked the French in 1883, only to lose the war and be forced to retreat from Tonkin, Cambodia and Annam, where the French then firmly established themselves. By this time, some people in France, Grévy among them, thought that the empire was becoming unwieldy and expensive. Ferry, on the other hand, wanted to maintain the pace. In 1896, a new Governor, Doumer, took over in Indo-China and by his vigorous reforms the country came to enjoy a wiser and more peaceful administration.

1   The Franco–Prussian War, 1870

3

Bismarck's Germany, 1871-90

✳✳

Otto Karl von Bismarck (1815–98) was the son of a wealthy Prussian landowner or *Junker*. He went to school in Berlin, briefly entered the civil service, followed this up with a period in the army, and, finding neither to his taste, returned to his estates as a gentleman-farmer. Bored by this life, he entered politics in 1846 as a champion of aristocratic privileges and royal absolutism. In 1851 he became a diplomat as Prussian Ambassador first at Frankfort, then at St Petersburg and Paris. In 1862 King William I appointed him Minister-President and Foreign Minister of Prussia, beginning a long partnership which lasted until 1888.

Bismarck's first problem was to solve the crisis which had brought him to power. The issue concerned the Army, but the principle in the dispute turned on the question of whether the Prussian Parliament or the Prussian King was to be the supreme power in the state. Bismarck solved it with speed and ruthlessness, qualities he revealed time and again during his career. The Prussian Parliament, ignored and humiliated, never quite recovered from the blow.

In his first eight years of power, Bismarck united Germany, fighting brilliantly successful wars against Denmark in 1864, Austria in 1866 and France in 1870. He believed that a strong Army held the key to most questions of diplomacy. His famous statement: 'the great questions of the day will not be decided by speeches and the resolutions of majorities ... but by iron and blood' was readily applied in his foreign policies.[1]

Bismarck stunned the men of his time and has amazed historians ever since. As a landowner, he owned vast estates at Varzin and Friedrichs-ruh. He lived on these estates for months at a time, like a recluse, con-

1. This for some reason became reversed and is now popularly known as 'the blood and iron speech'.

ducting his policies through a steady stream of state papers. His houses were ugly and uncomfortable. At Friedrichsruh he continued to use oil-lamps, despising modern aids like electricity. He was not interested in modern literature or ideas. He despised science, and dismissed Wagner, the greatest musician of his day, as a 'monkey'. He ignored visiting statesmen and royal personages, treating princes and people alike with the same curt lack of respect. When the King of Saxony arrived twenty minutes late for an interview, Bismarck rebuked him. He rarely made any appearances in public.

He was a large man, powerfully built, with huge appetites for food and drink. He suffered from indigestion, brought on by heavy beer drinking, heavy smoking and large suppers. He grew a moustache, and for one period of his life, a beard to hide a facial twitch. He gave the impression of strength and power, but in fact he admitted to being nervous, and flew into rages and tantrums. Few friends visited him, for he trusted no one and people found it difficult to break through the fierce, gruff barrier he presented, although he could charm when the occasion demanded it.

His beliefs were conservative, but not with the conservatism of inertia. The revolutions of 1848 had shocked him and he thought that peace and stability could only be obtained when Europe was organised into her national groups, or 'tribes', as he called them. In German history he has become the champion of nationalism which he regarded as an inevitable and dynamic force. In the years 1862 to 1870 he presided over the creation of the German Empire. In 1871 he felt that the great tasks were done. 'I am bored, the German Reich is made': Peace-making, conserving the Empire appealed to him less, yet for twenty years this remarkable personality dominated Europe and preserved peace.

THE GERMAN EMPIRE

In the 1860s Bismarck's plan had been to increase Prussian influence in Germany and oust Austria from positions of power. Austria was silenced by the war of 1866. Prussia had then created the North German Confederation, in which elaborate arrangements gave the small states in the north control over local issues but kept real power in the hands of Prussia. Two men, the President (King William) and the Chancellor

(Bismarck), with control over the Army and foreign affairs, ruled the Confederation.

The South German states of Baden, Württemberg, Bavaria and Hesse-Darmstadt remained suspicious. All had a tradition of independence and two of them were kingdoms. Faced with a powerful and dangerous Prussia they agreed to economic and military co-operation with the northern states, but nothing more. Consequently, when the Franco-Prussian War began in 1870 they joined in to fight the common enemy, France, for Bismarck revealed to them Napoleon III's plans for an increase of territory along the Rhine. Even so, their entry into the war was made reluctantly. Success blunted their suspicion, and while the war raged Bismarck opened up negotiations with these southern states, playing off the jealousy of one against the greed of another. He calculated that if he could only get the princes to enter a German Empire, he could handle them easily afterwards.

Once, by December 1870, the defeat of France was assured, the new Empire took shape. Bismarck had to reconcile different ideas and opinions. Some thought that he should sweep away all local rights and privileges and create a centralised state like France. Even if Bismarck had wanted to do this, it would not have been possible, for the South German states were too jealous to surrender all their powers. William thought that there was no higher office than King of Prussia and disliked the idea of being handed the title of German Emperor as a gift from a German Parliament. He was prepared only to accept it from the princes. The King of Bavaria was acutely sensitive about his loss of power and prestige. The National-Liberal party favoured a system similar to a constitutional monarchy. Bismarck, however, had no intention of being hamstrung by an opposition he could not control. He wanted a strong executive with himself at its head, but he gave way on minor points to the kings and the princes, to purchase their support.

The Constitution of 1871

Bismarck faced these problems at Versailles in 1871, with the French war still on his mind. Prussian arms had won in 1866 and 1870 and as a result, Prussia dominated the new Germany, just as he had forecast. Yet he had to make some concessions to persuade the princes to enter the Reich. The result was a federal state, rather like an enlarged North German Confederation. The new German Empire consisted of twenty-five states. Prussia, covering some two-thirds of the Empire, dominated it. The states surrendered control of foreign, commercial and colonial policy, but retained their own rulers, and their administrative, religious, parliamentary and taxation systems. This meant they could levy state taxes, but also had to pay federal taxes and obey federal laws.

The details were thrashed out in succeeding years with Bismarck having to make further, but insignificant, concessions. Bavaria and Württemberg obtained special privileges over their postal, railway and military (in peacetime) systems. The parliaments of the states never sank to the level of inept provincial councils. The great cause, however, was won. When, in April 1871, the King of Bavaria, acting for his colleagues, handed the imperial crown to William, he indicated that victory was complete and the states had entered freely into the new Empire. German power now existed, whatever the states might claim. National sentiment got to work and by 1914 Berlin overshadowed all other cities, as the 'German' voice became more strident and the provinces more prussianised.

In the new Constitution, the German Emperor (the 'Kaiser') found himself in a strong position. He appointed the Imperial Chancellor and controlled the armies of the states as commander-in-chief of the Prussian Army and Warlord of Imperial Germany. He had the power to make war and negotiate peace. In 1871 William I was seventy-five, and although he retained an alacrity of mind, he delegated more and more of his duties to his Chancellor (nevertheless he is said to have lamented 'it is not easy to be Emperor under such a Chancellor'). Not surprisingly, the next twenty years are known as 'the age of Bismarck'.

The Federal Council or Bundesrat represented the states, its members allocated proportionately according to population. There were fifty-eight members, including seventeen from Prussia, the leading and largest group. As fourteen negative votes were sufficient to check any constitutional change, and as the Imperial Chancellor was President of the Bundesrat, Prussia dominated the proceedings. The Bundesrat appointed committees and drafted new laws, which were then sent down to the Reichstag, as legislative proposals had to pass both Houses. In fact so great was the Prussian influence that no measure to which they objected ever became law.

The *Reichstag* was elected for five years at a time. Bismarck, to win over the Liberals, agreed that the vote should be extended to all men over twenty-five years, and exercised in a secret ballot. This made the German Parliament the most democratic in Europe. However, Bismarck kept real power in his own hands, for although the Reichstag's consent was necessary for the passage of laws, it had little opportunity to initiate laws or control the Chancellor's actions. The Reichstag could reject a law or a budget, but its debates were restricted to measures put before it by ministers. Again, Prussia, with 236 of the 397 deputies, had the major voice. Bismarck had the power to keep the

Reichstag at bay, and as the Chancellor was responsible only to the Emperor, and other ministers to him, he could act independently of Parliament. The animosity of the Reichstag could take effect in holding up legislation, in creating financial difficulties and even in open hostility, but it could not bring about Bismarck's overthrow. Only the Kaiser could do that.

The new Constitution did have its flaws. The enormous powers wielded by the Chancellor depended on the Kaiser's whim, and a future Chancellor might find a new Kaiser uncontrollable. In addition, the Prussian army and Junker class extended their power beyond Prussia into Germany, clashing with the National-Liberals, who found that, under its impressive front, Parliament was a weakly thing. Although Bismarck had paid lip-service to the ideas of democracy, he had never considered giving up power to a Parliament. In fact, from 1871 to 1888, two men, the Chancellor and William, ruled Germany. Behind the façade was as autocratic a state as had existed in Europe since the seventeenth century.

THE STRUGGLE WITH THE OPPOSITION

Prussia's military conquests raised new problems. The Danes of Schleswig-Holstein never took kindly to their new German masters; Bismarck's policy of petty persecution did not help. In opposition, they were joined by dissatisfied Polish and French minorities. From Alsace-Lorraine 50,000 people emigrated to France, alienated by Bismarck's schemes for the germanisation of the border lands. All in all, about a tenth of the Reichstag was made up of these discontented national minorities. To combat this opposition, Bismarck would have liked a special party of his own on whose support he could always rely. He found this impossible except for a few loyal Conservatives. Therefore he worked at different times with different groups, according to his policies. In the 1870s Bismarck relied on the National-Liberals who in 1871 had 120 deputies in the Reichstag. Much of the Kulturkampf was due to his surrender to National-Liberal sentiment.

In its early stages, the new Germany seemed calm enough. The fears of French recovery and Russian ambitions held opposition in check. Before long, however, new forces made themselves felt. Although the Liberals were won over by Bismarck's honeymoon period of reform, they could not swallow his plans for the Army. In 1871 an Army Bill proposed to extend Prussian military legislation to the Empire, making every adult German liable to serve.

The National-Liberals threw out the Bill. They wanted to authorise the change for only three or four years at a time but, in the end, the agreement was fixed for seven years. The number of trained men was gradually raised to 2½ million. Bismarck had healed a dangerous breach with the Liberals, the biggest group in the Reichstag, but they had revealed to the Chancellor that they had a mind of their own and were no subservient lackeys. Nevertheless, the Liberals missed an opportunity to bring the Army under parliamentary control.

The Kulturkampf

Bismarck and the National-Liberals co-operated in the struggle known as the Kulturkampf, or conflict of civilisations, between national Germany and the Roman Catholic Church. The quarrel can be traced in many deep causes, with faults on both sides.

The Church itself was in a fighting mood against most modern ideas, feeling itself to be challenged by the new creeds of nationalism, liberalism and socialism. In 1864, in the 'Syllabus', these and other modern ideas were roundly condemned. Some Germans felt that by denouncing nationalism, the Pope was by implication having a tilt at the new Germany. In 1870 the Ecumenical Council at Rome supported Pius IX in proclaiming the Infallibility of the Pope. This phrase has led to a great deal of misunderstanding, for it is difficult for anyone who is not an expert on Roman Catholic doctrine to understand its meaning. It appears to claim that when the Pope speaks officially as Head of the Catholic Church on points of doctrine his views are to be accepted and not questioned. To some, this seemed an old theory restated, and innocuous. To others, it appeared an issue in which, as in the Middle Ages, the Papacy claimed the right to depose and excommunicate rulers.

Some German Catholic theologians were unwilling to accept the new Vatican decrees. Dr Dollinger, leader of the Catholic liberals, or 'Old Catholics', condemned the claim to infallibility. The loyal Catholic bishops, under orders from the Pope, then dismissed Dr Dollinger and the Old Catholics from their positions in the Church, the Universities and the schools. The German Government refused to allow this to happen. The battle was on.

The aggression was not all one-sided. Bismarck in his creation of a national Germany could find no place for ideas such as these, and backed the Old Catholics to the hilt. He aimed at a national, not an international, Church. He and the National-Liberals resented interference from Rome in the affairs of Germany. Bismarck declared, 'it is a struggle for power as old as the human race . . . between king and priest'. Controversy centred around education in general, particularly the control over schools. Bismarck wanted a national, Prussian education system. He disliked the idea of priestly Italian meddling. The situation was complicated by the religious divisions within Germany. Bismarck, a devout Lutheran, turned from Rome with revulsion. Yet, in Bavaria, in the Rhineland and in the Polish borderlands, Catholicism was strong. Unfortunately, the Clericals of these areas tended to side with defeated causes, opposing unification in 1871 and the creation of a large Army. So Catholics became linked with anti-Prussianism, and were denounced as disloyal. The Clericals formed their own political party, the Centre, led by Windthorst, and won support from all those who disliked Bismarck's Reich in any way.

The campaign against the Centre party lasted nearly eight years. Fought largely in Prussia, it began in 1871 with the suppression of the Government department dealing with the Catholic Church. The Jesuits, the champions of the Papacy, were then expelled from the Empire. The pace quickened when Falk, the Prussian Minister of Education, applied the famous 'May Laws' of 1873–75. All religious orders in Prussia, except those in nursing, were dissolved. Civil marriage was made compulsory to weaken the Church's hold on family life. Priests were forbidden to interfere in politics. The inspection of schools, withdrawn from clerical control, passed into the hands of government officials. No priest could hold an office in the church unless he was German, had studied at a German university, and had qualified by passing examinations in German history and literature. Finally, all appointments to the clerical ranks had to be approved by the Government. If priests did not submit within six months, the payment of their salaries, controlled by the Government, ceased.

The bitter quarrel aroused deep passions, for in its martyrdom the Roman Catholic Church gained new strength. The Catholic priests did not succumb easily: by 1876 only thirty out of 10,000 had submitted. The rest faced fines, imprisonment and dismissal. There were murmurings against Bismarck. William and the Empress expressed their distaste at the schism. In the elections to the Reichstag in 1874 the Centre party increased its representation to ninety seats. In face of these pressures and new dangers abroad, Bismarck, making no admission of defeat, dampened down the persecution. He blamed Falk who was dismissed and in 1879, when the more conciliatory Leo XIII succeeded Pius IX, he opened negotiations. In the course of the next few years, most of the May Laws were repealed or modified, except that Bismarck retained control of education, the Jesuits remained exiled until 1917, and civil marriage stayed compulsory.

Bismarck suffered a rare defeat by underestimating the fervour and tenacity of his opponents, but he had asserted the demands of a national Church. In the 1880s he concentrated on winning over the Centre party, and in face of a common danger from Socialism, they more often voted with the Chancellor than against him.

The Liberals: Conflict over Tariffs

Between 1871 and 1914 German industry proceeded so rapidly that Germany became one of the leading manufacturing nations in the world. The industrial revolution came late, but once new methods and techniques had been absorbed, progress became almost meteoric. Germany developed great coal, iron, steel and chemical industries. Textiles and electrical plants did not lag far behind. In 1870 Germany was mining twice the amount of coal produced by France and the seizure of the Lorraine iron-ore deposits and the Alsace potash works added a new impetus to the productive capacity of the Ruhr and the Saar. By 1890 Germany was a major exporter of iron, steel and machinery to all parts of the world, and a dangerous rival to Britain.

This expansion brought its problems. Following the example of Britain who had based her industrial lead on free trade principles, Bismarck had applied similar policies. By 1879 a series of trade crises forced him to reconsider. Faced by Austrian, French and Russian tariffs, German trade began to suffer. Bismarck could see that protective tariffs had become inevitable. Once he saw that the revenues from these duties would make him less dependent for financial supply from the Reichstag, he did not hesitate. He had become irritated by the National-Liberals, who would not obey his instructions. Here was an opportunity to solve several problems in one trial of strength. In 1879, protesting that he aimed to save German industry from the flow of cheap goods from overseas, he imposed the new protective tariffs. The move proved popular with his own class, the junker-landlords, who had been worried by the agricultural repercussions of cheap American and Russian wheat. The captains of industry, who also benefited, put their weight behind the Chancellor, and despite angry Liberal opposition the measures became law. The National-Liberals never recovered from this blow, and their representation in the Reichstag gradually fell.

The Socialists

Another consequence of industrialisation was the rapid spread of socialist ideas. The German Working Men's Association had been

founded in 1863 by Ferdinand Lassalle, who advocated peaceful tran-
sition to socialism by constitutional means. The Marxists, on the other
hand, preached violent revolution. A third group, the German Social
Democratic party, founded in 1869 by Liebknecht, aimed at the improvement of conditions in the factories. They attracted little support
until 1875 when, pooling their resources, the different branches of
socialism joined forces to fight Bismarck and the industrialists on a
common front. In 1877 they polled 498,000 votes and had twelve
deputies elected to the Reichstag. Their programme demanded higher
wages, improved working conditions and shorter hours of work, but
the revolutionaries among them did not forget the ultimate aim of a
socialist society, to be accomplished by a revolution if all else failed.

Bismarck hated and feared these doctrines. He knew that if power
passed to the Socialists he would be cast out. He regarded them as
dangerous men who must be crushed. In 1877 he was alarmed more by
the potential threat than by their real strength and proceeded to deal
with them as he had the Catholics, by tough measures of repression. In
1878 two attacks on the Emperor's life by fanatics, conveniently
labelled socialists by Bismarck, gave him his opportunity. The Excep-
tional Law outlawed the Social Democratic party. Its leaders, Bebel and
Liebknecht, were thrown into prison. Its meetings and newspapers were
suppressed and all agitators deported. This policy was continued
throughout the 1880s but it failed to smash the Socialists who held their
meetings in secret, or abroad, and smuggled newspapers to their
supporters. The deputies in the Reichstag continued to speak fearlessly
in the one place where free speech could not be silenced.

Bismarck's repressive measures, although renewed four times in ten
years, were no more successful than they had been against the Catholics.
He turned to more subtle and statesmanlike methods, calculating that
by putting into practice some of the Socialist proposals for constructive
reform, he might steal their thunder. He moved into the field of state
socialism in 1883 with a compulsory sickness insurance scheme. In 1884
an accident insurance plan followed. Finally, in 1888 an old age pension
scheme was begun, with contributions payable by employer and em-
ployee, supplemented by a Government subsidy. These reforms were
unique and set a pattern later copied throughout Europe. However,
between them repression and bribery did not defeat the Socialists. In
the elections of 1890 the Social Democrats polled 1½ million votes and
gained twenty-four seats; by 1914, their strength in the Reichstag had
risen to 110.

CONSTRUCTIVE LEGISLATION

While struggling with the complex problems of the Constitution, the Kulturkampf, the Socialists and relations with the princes, Bismarck was quietly carrying out a series of internal reforms, aimed at strengthening and making more efficient the new state. Much of the legislation was planned to carry further the 'prussianisation' of Germany, and he did not always succeed.

In 1871 new Codes of civil and criminal law were issued, replacing the different sets of state laws, although some local variations were still allowed. In the same year a common currency, based on the mark, was established for the whole Empire. In 1873 an Imperial Bank, the Reichsbank, was set up and in 1875 a Banking Act legalised a uniform system of banking.

The various railway systems were co-ordinated, although the Chancellor had to surrender his plan to bring all the state railways under the control of the Prussians. He did ensure uniformity of gauges and agreement on other details of organisation.

So prussianisation was slowly imposed on the army, education, industry, agriculture, the civil service and finally, on thought.

THE FALL OF BISMARCK

In March 1888 William I died. Despite occasional quarrels, Bismarck had always been able to rely on his close personal loyalty. Frederick III succeeded, but, after a reign of only ninety days, he died of cancer. The new Emperor, William II, was an ambitious, high-spirited young man of twenty-nine. Within two years he had ousted Bismarck. The old Chancellor strongly disapproved of the vain, impetuous William; in his turn the Emperor disliked the cautious, interfering old man. A clash of personalities and wills led to frequent quarrels. It was a struggle for power, the power to rule Germany.

They differed over policy too. Bismarck wanted more stringent laws to crush socialism; William favoured relaxing the laws and granting further instalments of social reform, to win the loyalty of the German working class. Serious differences arose in foreign policy. The Kaiser favoured closer co-operation with Austria, Turkey and Bulgaria. If this meant the end of the Reinsurance Treaty with Russia, it seemed to him no great loss. Bismarck wanted to hang on to Russia as long as possible, to prevent Russia from turning to France. In the past, the Chancellor had always followed policies designed to placate, not anger, Britain. The Kaiser had no such intent. For him a large German navy and a vigorous colonial policy had priority; he was all for twisting the lion's tail. On these major issues the two men clashed with increasing anger. Bismarck treated the young Emperor's ideas with contempt, feeling he himself was too indispensable to be ever in danger of dismissal.

The final break came in March 1890 when the Emperor demanded the reversal of a cabinet order of 1852 by which the Minister-President was the sole intermediary between the king and the other ministers. The Kaiser intended that Bismarck should become merely a departmental head like any other minister, and the overall control of German policy would pass into William's grasp. After a violent row, William demanded Bismarck's resignation. When given, it was accepted. The old man lived until 1898 bitterly criticising, from retirement, the conduct of German policy but his fall in 1890 marks the end of an age.

4

Bismarck's Foreign and Colonial Policies

✳✳

OBJECTIVES AND DANGERS

After the successful wars of 1864, 1866 and 1870 Bismarck's policies became more conservative, less daring. His main objectives were to preserve the European peace, to allow Germany to digest her territorial gains and promote her internal development. The great danger to peace was France, for whom the immigrants from Alsace-Lorraine, the draped statue of Strasbourg in the Place de la Concorde, and until 1873, the German army of occupation, were constant reminders of her humiliation. France might at any time fight a war of revenge for the recovery of her lost provinces: Bismarck glanced uneasily over his shoulder at the danger across the Rhine. Yet, although French national pride had been deeply wounded, and Germany remained the hated hereditary foe, France did not take any active steps towards a war. Even in 1914, when at last the French gained their opportunity for revenge, their policies did not overtly drive Europe to war. Bismarck always suspected the French of planning war; his policies had to ensure that they stayed weak and isolated.

France in 1871 was on her knees but in the next few years staged a remarkable recovery. The indemnity of £200 million was cleared by 1873, when the German army withdrew. French newspapers kept up a barrage of patriotic fervour, and French politicians, to curry popular favour, called constantly for a war of revenge. The 'French problem' occupied much of Bismarck's thinking in these years. He had to prevent them from gaining a favourable opportunity to attack. This meant keeping Germany clear of any foreign wars, undermining French confidence, and building up a pro-German block of friends and allies.

He achieved this with most remarkable success.

He deliberately intrigued in French politics, encouraging the establishment of a republican form of government because he thought it
would be weaker and less militant than a monarchy. His chief task was
to isolate France from potential allies, for the French were unlikely to
attack alone, being weaker in manpower and heavy industry than the
Germans. Without allies, France was powerless; with allies, a real
threat. Bismarck suffered from perpetual nightmares that France would
find powerful friends. To prevent this, he bent his remarkable energies
to achieving domination over European politics.

Bismarck took care to secure the support of Russia and Austria. He
put a close friendship with these Powers first on his list of priorities. He
frequently spoke of Germany as 'a satiated state', free from further
ambitions, and devoting her energies to peaceful purposes. He refused to
be drawn into colonial rivalry or naval building, because Britain
might be annoyed. At his elbow he had always the power of the
German Army, ready to coerce reluctant allies or potential foes.
Another danger, however, was that the German generals had become
so confident and aggressive as a result of their victories that they
desired to extend the new German Empire. Bismarck had to hold them
on a tight rein, and damp down the nationalist press playing on the
emotions of the German public.

The first success in achieving an anti-French coalition came in 1872
with the *Dreikaiserbund* (the League of the Three Emperors). This was
no alliance or formal treaty but a rather vague agreement between
Austria-Hungary, Russia and Germany that they would preserve the
status quo in Europe, crush socialist movements, honour existing
borders and work for peace. The understanding, which was verbal,
arose from a joint meeting of the three Emperors at Berlin. Further
meetings took place in the next few years. None of the three Powers
really trusted the others, and in 1875 the deficiencies of the Dreikaiserbund were revealed.

Bismarck, alarmed by a new French law of 1875 which strengthened
her army, deliberately fanned the flames of a 'war-scare'. The *Berlin
Post* published an article headed 'War in Sight'. It seemed possible that
German troops might march against France as they had in 1870.
Britain and Russia this time leapt to France's support for they had no
wish to see France humbled again and Germany achieve a new mastery
in Europe. Bismarck hastily climbed down. Danger was averted, the war
scares blew over, but Bismarck saw that his allies in the Dreikaiserbund
could not be trusted in a crisis.

In 1887 a frontier incident in Alsace again raised fears of a war, especially as French public opinion was whipped up to fever pitch by a political adventurer, General Boulanger, who saw himself as another Napoleon. Again, Russia came to the rescue and peace was saved. It is not likely that in either of these two crises Bismarck seriously intended trouble: he used the situations as a threat to thrust Europe into a general war if France grew too ambitious.

The Eastern Question

The Dreikaiserbund, which had been found wanting in the French crisis of 1875, was soon to be tested again. In the same year a rising against their Turkish masters by the people of first Herzegovina and then Bulgaria resurrected the vexed problem of the Eastern question.

During the previous fifty years, the forces of nationalism, which had assisted the unification of Italy and Germany, spread into the Balkans. Here the Turks ruled with a mixture of inefficiency and cruel oppression. Greece had won her freedom by 1830 and after the Crimean War the new state of Rumania appeared on the map. The Slav peoples of the peninsula became restless, fired by patriotic enthusiasm for a war of liberation, and urged on by Russia and Austria whenever their interests dictated action. Russian leaders had a dream of domination in which the Russian Empire would extend to Constantinople. Their attempt at this in 1854 had been thwarted by France and Great Britain, who had no wish to see Russian troops at Constantinople: this would give Russia control over the entrance to the Black Sea and a valuable base for Mediterranean domination. Russia, turned aside by the Crimean War, still hoped for gains in the Balkans but made a subtle shift in policy in face of British opposition. Russia championed the Slav rebels against the Turks, hoping that she would acquire an overwhelming position, military or diplomatic, in the new and weak states erected out of the ruins of the old Turkish Empire. Today they would be called 'satellite' states. Russia had nothing to lose: therefore her hands could often be detected behind the rebel movements.

Austria-Hungary had a great deal to lose. This ramshackle empire contained people of many nationalities: Hungarians, Germans, Poles, Czechs, Slovaks, Rumanians, Serbs, Croats, and Italians. Nationalism to Austria spelt danger to her own Empire: in 1867 the Hungarians had insisted on a certain degree of independence and the Empire, divided into two parts, was ruled by the Hungarians from Budapest and by the Austrians from Vienna. It was known as the 'Dual Monarchy', under the same Emperor, Franz Josef, who spent his reign sitting on the bubbling forces of nationalism in other parts of his huge Empire.

Austria-Hungary had no wish to assist the spread of revolution to her own territories, for the contagion would bring ruin. The Serbs, one of the most militant and high-spirited of these subject peoples had already, in the mountains of Dalmatia, formed two little states, Serbia and Montenegro, free from Turkish rule. The Serbs hoped to assist their compatriots living in the Austrian and Turkish Empires and form a large all-Slav kingdom, and it was they who sparked off the crisis of 1875. Austria therefore did not share Russia's attitude to the Eastern Question. Austrian policy aimed at subduing nationalism and preventing Russian infiltration and annexation. The Austrians, however, looked to their own advantage. If they could utilise the situation to acquire further additions to their Empire, they would not miss the opportunity.

Bismarck disliked having to choose sides in these disagreements between Austria and Russia, and tried to avoid doing so. He had no wish to be dragged into the Balkan issue, for he could see no German advantage. However, he did not want to allow Russia to gain any further influence in south-east Europe, and if pushed, he favoured Austrian ambitions more. He had treated Austria with generosity in 1866 after her defeat at Sadowa, and he realistically wrote that Austro-German interests were closer than both nations would admit. He might announce that 'the Balkans are not worth the bones of a single Pomeranian grenadier', but he knew that if a war occurred German troops might easily be drawn into it. The Eastern Question therefore had to be brought under control.

In the summer of 1875 the Serbs of Bosnia, smarting from Turkish humiliations and heavy taxation, rose in revolt. The unrest quickly spread and Turkey appeared unable to stop it. The Great Powers took fright. When the Bulgarians rose in rebellion in May 1876 the Russians saw it as the opportunity they had been awaiting since 1856. In April 1877 they went to war; their armies swept the Turks aside and they came to within a few miles of Constantinople. The Turks gave in and signed the humiliating peace of San Stefano. These fast-moving events caused deep apprehension in Europe. Lord Beaconsfield, the British Prime Minister, made common cause with Austria. They both made warlike preparations to reverse Russia's gains.

With dismay, Bismarck had watched the situation get out of hand. He tried to halt the war by suggesting that a conference be held at Berlin. The Tsar, who had no wish to fight a European coalition, agreed. Bismarck later declared that at the Congress of Berlin he had played the part of 'an honest broker'. This was not a particularly honest view on his part for he sided with Austria and Britain against Russia, forcing the renegotiation of the Treaty of San Stefano. Bismarck had been forced into this decision by events, for he went to the Congress with the intention of keeping the Dreikaiserbund in existence. He had hoped that the Congress would allow both Austria and Russia to make gains, so that friendly relations could be preserved. Russia did not see things in this light and regarded the German attitude as base ingratitude. The Dreikaiserbund was shattered. Russia, resentful and humiliated, turned away from Germany.

The Congress of Berlin was a watershed in the history of European diplomacy, for it can be said to mark the origin of the sympathy between France and Russia which was to lead to their eventual alliance, some years in the future. Bismarck had struggled not to make a choice between Austria and Russia. He had failed, but soon recovered his nerve, and with typical thoroughness took what advantage he could from the wreck of the Dreikaiserbund.

The Dual Alliance, 1879

Negotiations between Austria and Germany followed in 1879. Bismarck, intent on his juggling act, tried to maintain good relations with Russia while secretly tying himself to Austria. The terms of the Dual Alliance finally agreed on by Bismarck and the Austrian Minister, Andrassy, were that either state would support the other if attacked by Russia, but if either was attacked by another Power, the other would remain neutral. Austria was therefore not bound to support Germany if the latter was attacked by France alone, although no doubt in these circumstances Austria would remain friendly. Bismarck felt reasonably safe for he calculated, correctly, that France would not attack single-handed.

Why did Bismarck choose Austria, a weak, sprawling Empire with dozens of major problems of administration, communication, and race rivalries? In the first place, German and Austrian ambitions in the Balkans coincided: both feared and opposed the extension of Russian power in this area. Bismarck also calculated that with a common German language and sentiment and closer sympathies he could control Austrian policies, whereas Germans cut no ice at St Petersburg or Paris. In addition, Bismarck was playing with grandiose ideas of German power in the Danube, south-east Europe, and possibly the Near East. Austria would be a useful channel for those ambitions.

The Dual Alliance was the firmest feature of the diplomatic scene until 1914. For Bismarck, it had not been easy. William I had been dubious, disliking the breach with Russia, for the two royal families had close ties. Bismarck kept the alliance secret, although rumours leaked out. He felt safer, but worked to strengthen the alliance. In 1881, Italy, angered by the French seizure of Tunis on the North African coast, territory they had had an eye on for some years, turned to Germany.

Italy had no love for France, for the Tunisian acquisition (which, incidentally, had been inspired by that arch-intriguer, Bismarck) was the latest of a series of slights the Italians had suffered at French hands. The French had in the past supported the Papacy and until 1870 their troops had kept the Italians out of Rome. The French had also extended their Empire along the North African coast, despite Italian protestations. Italy, on the other hand, felt drawn to Germany, for it had been Bismarck, after all, who had forced Austria to cede Venice to the Italians after the war of 1866. Germany was a strong, industrialised Power; it soothed Italian pride to think that this colossus sought their alliance. By a complicated series of agreements in 1882 the Dual Alliance became the Triple Alliance. Italy's understanding with Germany was defensive: Italian statesmen did not lose their heads. They specified that the alliance did not commit Italy to go to war with Great Britain. By the terms of the Triple Alliance, all three Powers promised to fight if one of them suffered an attack by any other two Powers. It guaranteed Italy against attack by France and freed Austria from fears of a stab in the back in the event of a war.

Although Italy's understanding with Germany was defensive, Bismarck congratulated himself. The value of this alliance to Germany can be seen on the map: the large block of the Central Powers lay across Europe, dividing France from her potential ally, Russia. France had again been isolated; Italy, neatly tied in, could be used to further German ambitions in the Mediterranean area. In 1883 Bismarck gained a fresh friend when Rumania signed alliances with Austria and Germany, and with Italy in 1888. Altogether, Bismarck, by his masterly juggling, had created a strong bastion of power.

The New Dreikaiserbund (1881) and the Reinsurance Treaty (1887)

Even now, Bismarck did not rest. The remaining danger was the possibility of a Russo-French pact. Bismarck accordingly reopened negotiations with the new Tsar, Alexander III, who succeeded his murdered father in March 1881. The bitter memories of the Berlin Congress were not forgotten but were subdued because of the Russian need to come to an agreement with the Germans. In June 1881 the old Dreikaiserbund came up for discussion; never completely a dead duck, it now gained fresh life. In a new, formal secret treaty of 1881 it was agreed that if one of the three Powers were involved in a war with a fourth, the other two were pledged to a benevolent neutrality. This meant that if Germany were at war with France, Russia would now remain neutral. Bismarck was delighted. As Russia at that time considered Britain to be her great rival, German neutrality in the event of a Russo-British war delighted the Tsar. Another clause called for joint consultation in the event of further trouble in the Balkans. The treaty was renewed again in 1884.

Another Balkan crisis, that of 1885–87, put the new Dreikaiserbund to the test. It ruined Bismarck's chessboard pattern of political manoeuvre. In 1885 the people of the Turkish province of Eastern Rumelia, separated from Bulgaria by the Great Powers in 1878, lost their patience with the Turks and proclaimed their union with Bulgaria. Once again, Europe was thrust into a dangerous situation, except that former roles were reversed. Russia, once the champion of Slav freedom, opposed the union of Bulgaria with Rumelia, for the new Bulgarian state had shown an annoying tendency to cold-shoulder Russia. Britain and Austria-Hungary, on the other hand, saw a strong and enlarged Bulgaria as an effective barrier to further Russian advances and supported the union. Bismarck's quandary had to be faced. He had to support his ally, Austria, yet he hated annoying Russia. At all events, following a successful anti-Russian revolution in Bulgaria, a new prince ascended the throne in 1887, Ferdinand of Saxe-Coburg, a German, educated at Vienna. Bulgaria kept Eastern Rumelia. This indicated another triumph for Bismarck, clouded only by the danger of increased Russian hostility to which the Chancellor now bent his considerable will. In 1887 the Dreikaiserbund lapsed and Alexander III refused to renew it. Bismarck then persuaded Alexander to come to Berlin to discuss their differences. Convinced that he had been misinformed about German policy in Bulgaria, Alexander agreed to enter a treaty. The result was the last stage of Bismarck's complicated intrigues, the Reinsurance Treaty of June 1887. In the Treaty was contained the promise of benevolent neutrality if one of the two Powers, Russia or Germany, was involved in a war against a third.[1] Bulgaria was recognised as being 'within the Russian sphere of influence' although this was something of a dead letter after July 1887 when Ferdinand became King. Germany was to be consulted if any change of territory occurred in the Balkans.

The Reinsurance Treaty, kept a close secret, did not last long. Bismarck hoped to control Russian policy as he had Austrian. He had a shock, for Russia, neither intimidated nor placated, kept interfering in Bulgarian affairs much to everyone's annoyance. In February 1888 the

1. This meant that (a) Germany would stay neutral if Austria attacked Russia; Russia would remain neutral if France attacked Germany.
But (b) if Germany or Russia were the aggressors, against France or Austria, these terms would not apply.

two allies came near to blows over the Bulgarian question and again Bismarck had to choose between Austria and Russia. He took the remarkably open step of publishing the terms of the Dual Alliance of 1879, and in a speech in the Reichstag challenged Russia, by calling for an additional 700,000 soldiers. Bismarck, the great manipulator of alliances, put his trust, as he always had, in the German Army. The Russians gave way with reluctance and ceased their attempts to secure the expulsion of Ferdinand of Bulgaria. The Tsar saw Bismarck's faithlessness and began negotiations with France. Even at this late stage, Bismarck, in his last two years of power, tried to patch up his differences with Russia. He also approached the British, trying to draw them into the Triple Alliance. He failed on both counts. Neither Russia nor Britain would be tempted: the spider spun his web in vain.

GERMAN COLONIAL POLICY

Germany lacked a strong fleet, and Bismarck made no attempt to strengthen it, for he had no wish to arouse British hostility. Only after his fall from power was the Kiel Canal built and the Navy League formed. For the same reasons he rejected demands that Germany should enter the scramble for colonies. He said on one occasion: 'colonies would only be a cause of weakness' and as late as 1884 announced: 'I am not a colony man.' Germany for him was a European power; he saw more disadvantages than advantages in a colonial policy. A vigorous policy of imperialism would necessitate a larger navy and greater expense, and would lead to rivalry with Britain.

Events conspired to change his opinion. In 1882 the German Colonial Society was founded at Frankfort. The Society put forward demands for a German stake in Africa and elsewhere. Bismarck may have turned an attentive ear to public opinion, although he normally ignored it. A more cogent reason for a change of heart may have been the approaching Reichstag elections of 1884. German electors had in the past turned to Bismarck in time of danger. In 1884 Europe was quiet, but if a colonial dispute with Britain blew up, the electors might turn to the old Chancellor, as a strong figure, able to meet the danger face to face. Whatever the reasons, Germany moved quickly into Africa. The trail had been blazed by explorers, but in 1884 the German flag was officially hoisted in South-West Africa, in Togoland, the Cameroons, and in 1885, German East Africa (Tanganyika). German traders and soldiers moved in. The expected dispute with Britain did not immediately materialise, although by 1890 conflict in these areas forced the Germans to negotiate African frontiers with Lord Salisbury, the British Prime Minister. The colonies, valuable as sources of raw materials and as markets for German goods, were largely an embarrassment to Bismarck in his diplomacy.[1] Bismarck's policy was to leave colonial development to chartered companies, protected by the Government. He would not accept direct personal responsibility for them and no separate German Colonial Office existed until 1907.

BISMARCK AS A STATESMAN

In his twenty years as Chancellor of Germany Bismarck dominated the European stage. As he had hoped, he had avoided war, kept France isolated, and created a confident, formidable German state. His tortuous, tricky diplomacy had kept Europe on a tight rein, for behind him lay the threat of the invincible German army. Yet, although he succeeded time and again, there were weaknesses and failures. The whole system depended on his personal skill and his ascendancy over the Emperor. The Chancellor had never been able to reconcile the differences between Austria and Russia and by 1890 Russia was turning towards France, something Bismarck had always striven to prevent, although it is difficult to see how he could have stopped it. Outside his complicated, close-knit alliances lay the British, whom he had never succeeded in entangling.

He had bound Germany close to Austria: this connection dragged the Germans into Balkan affairs and rivalry with Russia. Bismarck had, as in the Reinsurance Treaty, made agreements with Russia which were inconsistent with his promises to Austria. His actions have led historians to charge him with double-crossing and plain duplicity. The Russians eventually saw him in this light and therefore Bismarck was instrumental in throwing France and Russia together.

There is no doubt that he revealed great diplomatic skill; he gave the impression of juggling Powers like a puppeteer with marionettes. His

1. In the Pacific, colonies were acquired in the Marshall Islands (1886) and in North New Guinea (1884). It was hoped that the 200,000 annual German emigrants might be diverted to the colonies instead of the USA and South America.

skill revealed ruthless and unscrupulous opportunism—making the best use of events for Germany's benefit. He had little time for rights and liberty. He used repression ruthlessly against Socialists and Catholics and he handed over to William II an absolute system of government which had great dangers for the future. Some historians have argued that Bismarck, by leaving great power to the irresponsible William II and by nursing the cult of German militarism, helped to cause the First World War.

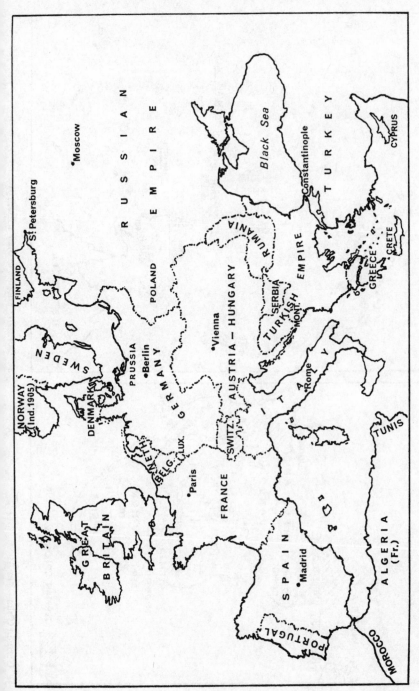

2   Europe in 1871

3 German Colonies in Africa, 1914

GOLD COAST
NIGERIA
TOGOLAND
CAMEROONS
FRENCH CONGO
BELGIAN CONGO
UGANDA
KENYA
GERMAN EAST AFRICA
NYASA-LAND
MOZAMBIQUE
RHODESIA
ANGOLA
GERMAN SOUTH-WEST AFRICA
UNION OF SOUTH AFRICA

GERMAN COLONIES

4 German Colonies in the Pacific, 1914

CHINA
Kiau-chau
JAPAN
MARIANAS
CAROLINE ISLES
MARSHALL ISLES
BISMARCK ARCHIPELAGO
NEW GUINEA
NAURU
SAMOA
AUSTRALIA

5

Imperial Russia, 1855-1917

✳✳

ALEXANDER II, 1855–81

In 1855 the stern and autocratic Tsar Nicholas I died, leaving Russia struggling with a disastrous war against Britain and France in the Crimea. Alexander II brought the war to an end quickly in the Treaty of Paris in 1856 and then set out to investigate, analyse and repair the faults in Russian administration that the war had revealed. The new Tsar was a mild, well-intentioned man: not quite of sufficiently strong and dynamic character to force through the radical reforms that Russia needed. In later years he became bitter and disillusioned by his failure. Curiously, Alexander, who tried to bring about liberal reforms, ended up by being assassinated, while other harsher, intolerant Tsars died peacefully in their beds. We have to examine Alexander's career to understand this paradox of a reformer hated by his people.

The Emancipation of the Serfs
Faced with a rising tide of peasant unrest, Alexander decided that, as the first step towards the modernisation of Russia, the serfs were to be freed. Discussions on possible emancipation had been held since 1800 but the nobles had always prevented any action. The army, the system of taxation, the landowners, and the nobility all depended on serfdom. To sever the shackles of the serfs meant revolutionary changes, but Alexander himself was willing and the peasants looked to him to give a lead. It took time, for great questions had to be decided. If the serfs were given their freedom, would they leave the land untilled? Would they demand land ownership? How would they be able to pay for their land? In 1856 one committee suggested emancipation by degrees.

Alexander rejected this plan, overruled the landowning nobles, and signed the Act of Liberation in 1861.

The terms of the Act, which ran to 300 pages, were that after a period of two years' bondage, the serfs were to be liberated from all services, payments and obedience to their former masters. A peasant was free to marry, to own property, and to engage in his own business. Serfdom was at one stroke totally abolished. But the land remained the property of the landowners. To stave off the threat of social revolution, the Government allowed the peasants to buy land from the nobles by a series of redemption payments over a term of forty-nine years. The Government gave the landowners financial compensation for the land they had surrendered to the peasants. So generous was the Government to the landowners that in most cases they were better off than they had been before Emancipation.

The big problem of how much land should be made available to the peasants varied from province to province. In practice, the landowners sold off their poorest lands and kept the best. All in all, about fifty per cent of the area of cultivated land passed into peasant ownership, and 22 million peasants in private ownership were set free. The 18 million serfs working for the Government had to wait until 1866, but eventually they too obtained their freedom.

There were grave defects and weaknesses in the Act of Liberation. Most serfs, with less land than they had before 1861, were worse off. Others had only tiny plots, with soil of poor quality. The land they wished to purchase was vested in a village Commune which controlled the legal and financial sides of the transactions. Peasants still had to obtain the permission of the Commune to leave their villages. Again, the peasants wanted more than half of the cultivated land surrendered by the nobles, and to them the decision to enforce payment over forty-nine years would mean that a son or a grandson would eventually pay off the debt. Only the serfs who actually worked on the land were able to buy their own plots: the domestic serfs when set free had no land. They were entitled to wages if they stayed in their old posts. Many drifted into the towns to work in the factories. Their social condition was little improved for they held the bottom rung in the social scale. The peasants and workers still had to carry internal passports, were liable to corporal punishment and had to beg favours from the village Communes. Forced service in the army was still required and invariably they did the heaviest and poorest paid jobs in the factories or on the land. Emancipation was for the peasants only the first step towards eventual freedom. They hoped that Alexander would continue to help them to achieve a better economic and social position. Many would not wait; in the first four months after the publication of the Act of Liberation there were 647 cases of peasants rioting in their disappointment. When the Tsar did nothing to carry the Act further, the peasants rejected him and took to rioting or joined the revolutionary parties, which promised to give them land, education and political power.

The position of the nobility in Russia was weakened by the Act. Few of the nobility were interested in agriculture and they were often deeply in debt. The compensation, though generous, was only a temporary relief. Once the repercussions of the loss of their former slave (serf) labour were realised, the more incompetent nobles suffered from the competition of able farmers and industrialists. Cut off by their pride from working with their hands, or indeed with their brains, the Russian nobility led a spoilt and frivolous existence in the cities until they were swept away by the Revolution. In many ways the Act proved to be a turning point in Russian history, marking the end of the old aristocratic tyranny and the beginning of revolutionary activity.

Local Government Reform

The Act of Liberation forced the freed serfs under the control of the village Communes. In 1864 the Tsar made a further surrender to those who demanded more local control over local affairs. A new law set up *zemstva* (elected councils) in each district. Three separate groups of voters—the nobles, the townsmen, and the peasants—elected representatives. The nobles, because of their influence, education and experience largely dominated the zemstva. Their functions were limited to the maintenance of prisons, roads, hospitals, schools, poor relief, and public health. The zemstva officials collected taxes, both local and national, but had no control over police and the army: the Tsar kept these powers in his own hands. In 1870 the towns were granted similar privileges to elect a town council or *duma* with equivalent powers.

As the zemstva spread to more and more provinces, they acquired a curious popularity. They employed the influential class of intelligentsia[1]—the doctors, teachers, engineers and administrators. These men gave the zemstva a radical, liberal outlook, made them critical of Tsarist bureaucracy and corruption, and created in the councils a debating chamber on subjects of all kinds.

Education

As a reformer, Alexander insisted on better education. The town and district councils were encouraged to build primary schools, censorship

1. A small section of the Russian people, largely members of the nobility or the middle class, who had been converted to liberal or socialist ideas at universities.

of books was at last relaxed and the universities obtained greater freedom for their students. In 1864 an edict ordered that secondary education should be available to anyone who passed the examinations. There seemed a new life and zest in the air, but progress was slow for illiteracy was widespread. Years of neglect could not be overcome by an edict.

The Army and the Courts

In 1861 a Commission studied the legal system and suggested sweeping reforms. In 1864 the procedure in the law courts was simplified, punishments were made less severe and public trials replaced secret ones. Judges were no longer to be at the mercy of an irate Government and were to be properly paid. Trial by jury was introduced. It was intended that peasants would have an equal place in the courts with any other class, but in fact the nobles and the middle class, again because of their education, had the advantage. For instance, the zemstva appointed the local justices and drew up the rules of the court. The justices were drawn from the same class that was represented in the zemstva. But despite these reservations, the reforms were most important, for they allowed more freedom and impartial justice than Russia had ever known.

After the disasters of the Crimean War, the Army needed radical reform. Milyutin, as Minister of War, reduced military service from twenty-five to fifteen years and ceased to use the army as a form of harsh punishment for criminals. The general efficiency of the transport, food supply, munitions and engineering branches was improved and new arms and equipment issued. In 1874 conscription was extended to all Russians to bring the Army up to strength.

The Russian Empire

Alexander faced a growing demand in Poland for independence and a return to the frontiers that had existed before the partitions of the 18th century. At first the Tsar offered concessions and reform to the Poles, but resisted their nationalist demands. In 1863 he lost patience and tried to crush the revolutionary clubs. Risings then occurred in many parts of Poland, hopeless, despairing risings, for 10,000 students and rebels faced a vastly stronger army of 80,000 Russians. Once the rebellion had been ruthlessly crushed, Alexander abandoned all his liberal policies. A Russian governor-general took over, Russian became the official language, and thousands of suspects were deported to Siberia.

Defeat in the Crimea had made the Tsar determined to give Russia a period of peace. For twenty years the initiative in expansion passed from the Russian Government to thousands of Russian soldiers, merchants and explorers who quietly extended Russian borders. Their activities brought Russia into Central Asia, to the borders of India, and deep into the Far East, all without war.

Alexander encouraged his merchants to extend their influence into China, and assisted Russian settlement in Eastern Siberia and in Korea. In 1860, by the Treaty of Pekin, the Chinese were forced to recognise Russian possession of huge territories along the river Amur and the port of Vladivostok. The grant of trade privileges allowed the Russians to exploit China's weaknesses. Further north, Russian explorers reached Alaska, where their activities so alarmed Britain and the USA that in 1867 Russia was persuaded to sell her rights in Alaska to the USA for seven million dollars.

In Central Asia the provinces of Khiva, Bukhara, and Turkestan were conquered, adding new and valuable extensions to the Empire. The expansion of Russian power southwards into the Caucasus was successfully completed by 1864. Persia lay across the new frontier, a weak, tempting bait. Russia gained economic advantages in Persia and seemed all set to annoy Britain in this area too. Russian ambitions in connection with the Eastern Question have been dealt with elsewhere: the Tsar, carried along by a wave of patriotic sentiment, smashed the Turkish armies in the war of 1877–78. What had started with such high hopes ended in the humiliation of the Treaty of Berlin, despite the Russian annexation of Batum, Kars, and south Bessarabia. Nevertheless, the war added to the general disillusionment which followed Alexander's change of heart from energetic reform to shaky ineptitude. The war also added to the hostility felt by Britain towards Russia over their clash of ambitions in Central Asia, Persia and the Far East.

Repression and Opposition

In addition to his other reforms, Alexander pardoned political prisoners at the beginning of his reign, ended religious persecution for a while, and encouraged free and open discussion. Much of this liberalism had been the result of the promptings of others. By 1862 Alexander could see the dangers involved in relaxing the reins. As his political enemies emerged from Siberia or secret hideouts, a wave of unpopularity rose. The peasants wanted further land reform, the workers demanded improved factory conditions, the intelligentsia wanted a free Parliament. Violence and disorder increased and in 1866 after an attempted assassination by a fanatic, Karakosov, had only just failed, Alexander clamped down. Count Tolstoy, the Minister of Education, withdrew many of the privileges previously granted to schools and universities, the courts were forced to try political cases without a jury, and censorship restrictions were again imposed on the press.

The zemstva suffered too. In 1868 their taxing powers were reduced. Local Tsarist agents, governors or civil servants, took over control of zemstva activities. By 1870 the Tsar had few allies in Russia. Opposed to him were the liberals, who demanded an end to repression and further constitutional reform. The peasants felt disillusioned, and the revolutionary societies plotted for the day they would overthrow the whole unjust Tsarist regime. To add to Alexander's difficulties, a series of disastrous famines revealed the ancient and inefficient agricultural system to be quite inadequate to deal with modern demands.

By 1875 criticism of the Tsar reached a new peak. Heading the attack were the intelligentsia but they had so little contact with the peasants, town workers or indeed the Tsar, that although loudly vocal, they were ignored. Political parties, like the Narodniks or Populists, subscribed to liberal ideas and won support from students and university teachers. These parties felt it was the duty of this minority, who had obtained their education at the expense of the downtrodden, to awaken the masses. They felt that they had to lead the people to a new order. In 1874 over 2,000 donned peasant dress and went out to spread the word to the peasants, but they awakened little response. The peasants wanted land, not oratory and vague promises. The Government treated the exodus to the peasants as a revolutionary action. 1,500 were arrested and, after mass trials, served various terms of imprisonment. The beaten Populists retreated from their earlier public fervour into frightened grumbling, in private.

Some of the reformers turned to more violent methods. Secret societies, like *Narodnaya Volya* (the Will of the People) were formed in the larger cities. Another group, the Anarchists, led by Michael Bakunin, advocated terrorist tactics to destroy the Tsarist state entirely. Fanatical students murdered the Chief of the Secret Police in 1878 and the Governor-General of the city of Kharkov in 1879. In 1880 four attempts were made to assassinate the Tsar, using dynamite. These clumsy failures were matched by the inept efforts of the police to catch the culprits. Alexander realised that terrorism and revolution would only end in the complete collapse of the state, and so in March he agreed to a plan of reform put forward by one of his ministers, General Loris-Melikov. The reforms pleased the liberals but dismayed the terrorists, who profited from a harsher regime. On 13 March 1881, Alexander signed a decree announcing the formation of a committee to consider reforms, including a plan to allow elected representatives some part in the machinery of law-making and government. The anarchists wanted a complete revolution, not reform. On the same day, a bomb was thrown at the Tsar's carriage, wounding his Cossack guards. As the Tsar alighted, unharmed, from his coach, a second bomb blew off his legs. He died two hours later in the Winter Palace, St Petersburg.

ALEXANDER III, 1881–94

The new Tsar was a dull, uninspiring man, fond of his family and Church. His only unusual quality was enormous physical strength, for he bent horseshoes with his bare hands to amuse his guests. He had thought his father's reforming ideas quite wrong, and felt that assassination was the inevitable price one paid for softness. Alexander III made no such mistake. During his brief reign he put tough men in power, like his old tutor, Constantine Pobedonostev, who despised western reforming ideas. The ministers who had served Alexander II were put into cold storage and replaced by harsher men. Count Tolstoy was recalled to office as Minister of the Interior and repression soon followed.

Alexander III aimed first at destroying the revolutionary movements. The killers of his father were caught and executed and the Chief of Police, Plehve, aided by horrified public opinion, hunted down and crushed the terrorist gangs. One of the victims was Lenin's brother. Subsequently, Alexander hoped to strengthen Russian autocracy by revising his father's reforms, and win over the nobility to the Tsarist ranks. In education, strict supervision held the universities in check, strangling liberal ideas at their roots. Pobedonostev excluded sons of peasants and workmen from secondary schools, and government inspectors saw that the zemstva schools were kept strictly under control.

The press was muzzled by the issue of temporary licences, conditional on good behaviour, and by a rigid censorship. In 1889, Land Captains, selected from the nobles by the Minister of the Interior, replaced elected Justices of the Peace as officials in the provinces. They controlled the law, the police, the zemstva, and all local officials. In 1890 a new law made the Land Captains members of the zemstva. This action which reduced the powers of the zemstva and their appeal to the intelligentsia showed how far Russia had returned towards autocracy. Power, as earlier in the century, rested in the Tsar, the Orthodox Church and the nobility.

In the 1890s a deliberate policy of Russification was forced upon 40 million non-Russian peoples of the Empire. In Poland, no Pole or

Roman Catholic could hold a government office and the use of the
Polish language in schools was forbidden. Similar policies were applied
in Finland, the Ukraine, Armenia, and central Asia. The Orthodox
Church was forced on all. Members of other faiths, like the Jews,
Protestants, and Moslems were cruelly and often murderously crushed.
The Jews had to undergo the worst excesses. Thousands were forcibly
concentrated in an area known as the Pale of Settlement where they
lived in misery, easy targets for Tsarist anti-semitism. A Jewish girl had
been implicated in Alexander's assassination. The Government took
revenge, and terror, murder and outrages annihilated nearly a third of
the Jewish population. A climax was reached in 1891 when in the
midst of a bitter winter, thousands of Jewish workers were evicted from
Moscow and hustled into ghettoes in the interior. Alexander III and his
ministers hoped that by an enforced loyalty to Tsarism and Orthodoxy
they could defeat the revolutionaries.

Alexander's reign saw an economic revolution, but not as the
socialists hoped. State investment and foreign loans assisted a massive
development in industry. Railways stretched out from Moscow to the
Caspian and the Pacific. Coal production doubled in ten years and in
the oil, cotton, and iron industries Russia made equally fast progress.
Most of the industrial centres were concentrated in the Donets region.
Under the control of Sergius Witte, Minister of Finance from 1892,
Russia's more stable financial position attracted other foreign investors,
particularly the French.

Together with this vast expansion went the hazards and poverty of
the new industrial society. The Russian workers had to contend with a
long working day, poor wages and horrible conditions, both at work
and in their hovels. The industrialists exploited the workers to wring
every penny of profit from their mines and factories. The Government
did pass a series of labour laws, controlling hours of labour for women
and children, fining the worst owners, and making strikes illegal, but
the laws were largely ineffective. Later, government inspectors were
appointed to see that the laws were observed. But they could not offer
any protection against exploitation, and socialism found a rich seam of
discontent in the squalid slums of the new industrial towns.

Some concessions were made to the peasants. In 1882 their redemption payments for land were reduced and the unpopular poll-tax
abolished, and in 1884 a Peasants Bank was set up to loan money to
help them buy land. Despite this, peasant opposition grew. In 1891–92
a serious famine caused great hardship and the poverty of the peasants, if
anything, grew worse. To escape their wretchedness, many moved
voluntarily to Siberia or central Asia, or into the cities and industrial

centres. Alexander no more succeeded in winning their affection than he had with the liberals and workers. When he died in 1894 Russia had a police state as harsh as any in her history.

RUSSIAN SOCIALISM

Marxism

The Revolution of 1917 was a victory for a few dedicated, determined men, who seized their chance to exploit a revolutionary situation and so create a new political order. It was a turning point not merely in Russian history, but for the whole world. Marxism revolutionised politics, philosophy and economics and has had a tremendous influence on the world in which we live. We must study briefly the history and ideas of Marxism to understand this vast transformation.

European socialism has many forms and varies widely in aims and means to achieve a socialist state, but there are common factors. The Russian Communists drew most of their inspiration from the work of Karl Marx, adding their own peculiarly Russian ideas.

Karl Marx (1818–83) was born at Trier in Germany, of Jewish parents. He studied law and philosophy at Berlin, earning his living as a journalist. His paper criticised the Prussian Government and Marx was forced to flee to Paris where he mixed with other socialists, such as Frederick Engels. By 1848 Marx had worked out his new political system based on his studies of law, economics and philosophy. He published the *Communist Manifesto* in which the fundamental Marxist ideas are stated:

a) that the history of mankind has been based on class struggles between oppressed and rulers

b) that the proletariat (workers) will rise in revolution against the oppressors, the capitalists

c) that this revolution will be followed eventually by a socialist state in which the right to hold private property will be abolished, together with all rights of inheritance

d) that the state will take into public ownership all banks, transport, industry and land

e) that free education and opportunities for all will be available.

The Manifesto ended with the famous words, 'the proletariat have nothing to lose but their chains. They have a world to win. Workers of the world, unite.'

In 1849 Marx fled to England and studied in the British Museum. He spent the remainder of his life in great poverty, writing and studying. In 1864 he formed the First International Working Men's Association and in 1867 he published the first volume of his great work, *Das Capital*. In this work he explains the economic justification for his ideas. He died in 1883 and is buried in Highgate Cemetery, in London.

Marx believed that the proletariat would strike first in the rich capitalist countries like France and Germany. He did not anticipate that agricultural states like Russia and China would move towards revolution. Marx also left vague his ideas on the machinery of the Communist society that would follow the upheaval. Consequently his theories are open to 'interpretation'. Communism in Russia today is a mixture of Marxism and the practical answers Russia has applied to massive problems of organisation and production.

Lenin

One man who adapted the Marxist theories to fit Russian conditions was Vladimir Ulyanov who took the pseudonym Lenin to hide his identity from the police. Born in 1870 in Simbirsk in the Volga region, Lenin was the son of a school-inspector, a cultured, intelligent man. After his elder brother had been executed for revolutionary activities, Lenin joined the socialist movement. He went to Kazan University to study law, was expelled after a student riot and finished his studies in St Petersburg. He was arrested in 1897 and sent to Siberia where he continued writing on Marxist ideas. He married another revolutionary exile, Krupskaya. In 1900 Lenin was released but fled to Switzerland to work on the socialist newspaper, *Iskra* (the Spark). Copies of the paper were smuggled into Russia. He became a leader of the Social Democrats and waited for an opportunity to return and lead a revolution.

The Revolutionary Parties

Lenin was only one of dozens of potential leaders. The Socialists were divided into several rival groups. The Social Revolutionaries (SRs) formed in 1902 a party programme designed to divide land among the peasants and setting up a democratic republic. Some of the more fanatical SRs broke away to form terrorist groups.

In 1898 Gregory Plekhanov and eight others formed a party called the Social Democrats (SDs). Lenin joined them and became the editor of *Iskra*. They concentrated their attention on the Russian working class, operating in secret to avoid the police. The two leaders quarrelled over whether there was to be a rising by the masses or a seizure of power on their behalf by a few audacious men. At the Second Congress of the Social Democratic Party, in a rat-infested warehouse in Brussels, this question was discussed. The delegates fled from the Belgian police, to settle in London, hardly halting for breath. Lenin wanted the party limited to a small restricted élite of organisers. He put the issue to the vote soon after many of his opponents had left a party meeting, and had a majority of two over those who wished to make the party wider and more democratic. Lenin seized on his victory and called his supporters the Bolsheviks (majority) and his opponents Mensheviks (minority). He lost control of *Iskra* but later started up his own newspaper, *Pravda* (Truth). Henceforth, the SDs were badly split and despite Lenin's trick, the Bolsheviks were very much the minority group.

NICHOLAS II (1894–1917)

Nicholas had spent his youth on tours of the Far East, India and Egypt and was attracted by the idea of the Tsar ruling over a large Empire in the East. He considered himself well qualified to rule such an Empire, but he was quite wrong. Although he possessed the Romanov charm, he revealed qualities of indecision, weakness of will and even stupidity that dismayed his ministers. He could not be relied on for firmness or resolution: his habit of changing his mind for the most foolish of reasons often caused chaos. His wife, the Empress Alexandra, was a rather silly, hysterical woman, a religious fanatic and devoted to her husband. Her meddling in politics hampered Nicholas and had disastrous effects. Their son, Alexis, suffered from a grave disease, haemophilia. The rulers of Russia spent their reign struggling for two objectives—to keep Alexis alive, and to ensure that he succeeded to an intact, autocratic Empire. This, at a time when Russia demanded wholesale, sweeping reforms, was catastrophic. Despite all advice, Nicholas persisted in marching resolutely towards his ruin.

The reign began, as it was to end, in tragedy. A crowd, assembling for the traditional gifts which were distributed at a coronation, stampeded like wild cattle when a rumour spread that the presents were insufficient. 1,300 were killed, crushed to death. That night, Nicholas and his wife gaily attended a ball.

The new Tsar decided to carry on his father's policy of crushing all opposition. The same ministers, Plehve, Pobedonostev and Witte directed operations, employing thousands of government agents to spy and interfere throughout Russia. The civil service grew larger and more inefficient. The liberals who now formed their own political party, the Cadets, despaired of any changes. The peasants and workers turned more and more to socialism, strikes and terrorism, culminating in the murder of the hated Plehve by the SRs in July 1904.

Disregarding the signs of disorder, Nicholas persevered. The Russification of his Empire continued, particularly in Finland. The Jews suffered even more terribly. A flood of political prisoners moved out to Siberia. Witte, meanwhile, continued to promote Russian economic expansion. By 1900 he had brought sixty per cent of the railways under state control. He signed a commercial treaty with Germany and helped to erect new factories and banks with government money. The Tsar prevented any further reform. In 1895 in a speech the Tsar said that schemes of cooperation between him and his people were 'senseless dreams'.

The Russo-Japanese War, 1904–05

In 1890, on a tour to Vladivostok, Nicholas had been impressed with the opportunities open to Russia in the Far East. Traders, adventurers and speculators urged him on, and pointed out that Russians had been edging into Manchuria for some years. By 1901 the Trans-Siberian railway had reached Vladivostok and the Chinese had been persuaded to allow the Russians to build part of the line through Manchuria, to avoid the difficult Amur valley. The line had also been extended south to link Mukden and Port Arthur. China's weaknesses were ruthlessly exploited, but in doing so, Russia ran up against a tougher foe, Japan.

Serious differences over Korea between China and Japan had led to war in 1894. The Japanese gained easy naval and military victories over the disorganised Chinese and captured the valuable base of Port Arthur. In the Treaty of Simonoseki in 1895 China lost to Japan the Liao-Tung peninsula, Formosa and Port Arthur, and paid an indemnity. Russia protested vigorously. The Tsar had his eyes on Port Arthur as a valuable ice-free port, and, backed by France, Russia threatened war. Japan, feeling unable to resist, returned the Liao-Tung peninsula and Port Arthur to China. Russia had gained the gratitude of China and this helped in acquiring concessions for railway construction. The Tsar went further, securing his hold on Manchuria. China allowed Russian troops to garrison Port Arthur and fortify the Liao-Tung peninsula. In 1878 Port Arthur was leased to Russia for twenty-five years and in 1900, taking advantage of the Boxer Rising, Tsarist forces occupied Manchuria.

Japan waited patiently. She strengthened her army and navy and gradually moved forward in Korea. In 1902 Japan signed an alliance with Great Britain, ensuring that she would not face a group of foes alone. In October 1903 Russian troops crossed into Korea. For Japan, incensed by Russian ambitions in Manchuria, this proved to be the last straw. Japan asked Russia to remove her troops and announced Korea to be an area of Japanese interest. The Tsar rejected Japan's demands. In February 1904 the Japanese launched a surprise attack against Port Arthur with 180,000 men. The Russians had only 100,000 men in the Far East, and the Trans-Siberian railway, which the Tsar had boasted brought Moscow to the threshold of Manchuria, proved unequal to the task of reinforcement and supply. After several hundred Russians had been rushed east, the single-track and incomplete railway collapsed under the strain.

Japan could not fight a long war and so hoped for quick successes. Admiral Togo bombarded Port Arthur, damaging the Russian fleet and achieving an early ascendancy at sea. In April the Russian Pacific fleet put to sea from Vladivostok and after several running battles lost most of its ships. The garrison at Port Arthur, cut off and demoralised, surrendered in January 1905. A force of 47,000 men and vast stores of ammunition fell into Japanese hands: it was a disgraceful disaster which shocked the Russian people. Worse was to follow. In the next month the Japanese defeated the Russians in a desperate battle, lasting two weeks, at Mukden. The Russians lost 90,000 men and evacuated Manchuria and Korea.

Nicholas gambled everything on one last desperate throw. The Baltic fleet had received orders in October 1904 to sail to the Far East. Threading through the North Sea, the Russians thought they sighted Japanese torpedo-boats and opened fire. Their targets were fishing fleets of British and Norwegian trawlers. Two sailors were killed. Hastily, Nicholas apologised and paid a large sum in compensation. The Baltic fleet sailed nervously on, to reach the Far East in May 1905. Admiral Togo led the Japanese fleet into battle at Tsushima. Twenty-three Russian ships were sunk: only four limped away to port. The Japanese did not lose a ship; their total casualties were 110 men killed.

Nicholas, horrified by these disasters to Russian military prestige, agreed to American mediation and sent Witte to negotiate peace terms. By the Treaty of Portsmouth (USA) in 1905, Russia renounced all claims to Korea, and gave up all rights in the Liao-Tung peninsula including Port Arthur and the southern half of the island of Sakhalin, all of which were annexed by Japan. Russia evacuated Manchuria. In 1907 and 1912 there were further agreements by which Russia and Japan divided

Manchuria into spheres of influence. Japan annexed Korea in 1910. Altogether, the Tsar's war ended in derisive sneers abroad and revolution at home.

The Revolution of 1905

The incompetence of the Tsar and his generals in a war considered unnecessary by the people pushed Russia into revolution. In July 1904 the feared Minister, Plehve, was assassinated, and the opposition came out into the open. The Zemstva Conference, meeting in St Petersburg, demanded an elected national assembly, freedom of speech, religion and press, equality in law, and the end of all repression. In December 1905 Nicholas issued an edict promising some measures of reform, but rejected any idea of a national assembly. However, as usual nothing came of his glib promises. In despair the opposition returned to terrorism, strikes and murder.

Earlier in 1905 strikers in St Petersburg had organised a peaceful procession of 200,000 poor workers and their families. Led by a priest, Father Gapon, the crowd moved slowly through the streets intoning hymns and bearing portraits of the Tsar. The march ended at the Winter Palace where the workmen intended to deliver a petition, asking the Tsar to consider the zemstva demands. The guards at the Palace panicked and fired indiscriminately into the crowd: over a thousand were killed or wounded. 'Bloody Sunday', as it was called, destroyed all chance that the people might break through the circle of ministers to appeal direct to the Tsar.

The answer to this crime was a wave of strikes throughout Russia. The universities closed down; Tsarist policemen disappeared in large numbers, especially in the Jewish Pale. In February 1905 Grand Duke Sergius, Governor-General of Moscow and the Tsar's uncle, was killed by a bomb thrown in the Kremlin. In Poland and the Caucasus the army ruled mercilessly but even so could not subdue terrorism. The SRs led the wave of unrest demanding 'all land to the peasants'. In the countryside the peasants needed no second invitation. Landlords were murdered, estates seized, records burnt and land subdivided among the peasant families. Local zemstva announced far-reaching reforms. Even the professional intelligentsia joined in. Lawyers, doctors and teachers formed unions to press for reform and formed a 'Union of unions' to provide a common cause.

Morale was low in the Russian navy after the recent disasters. The battleship *Potemkin* put to sea with a load of maggot-ridden meat for the crew. Led by a revolutionary, Matuschenko, the men refused to eat the meat and when threatened by the lash, rebelled. They threw their

officers into the sea, using them as floating targets, and sailed triumphantly through the Black Sea towards Odessa where other revolutionaries had seized control of the town. From Odessa to St Petersburg,
where a soviet, or workers' council, was formed, Russia was in turmoil.
Trotsky, Lenin and other rebels hastened back to Russia thinking that
the long-awaited revolution was at hand.

It is remarkable that the Tsar could save anything from the ruins, but
he did, and the revolution collapsed. For once, properly advised by his
ministers, Nicholas issued an edict announcing that a Duma, or Parliament, elected by popular vote, would be allowed to meet. Otherwise
the Government dealt severely with disorder. The Army remained
loyal to the Tsar; the Cossacks entered Odessa and crushed the rising.

The battleship *Potemkin* sailed aimlessly in the Black Sea until its
crew scuttled it in a Rumanian harbour. Lenin fled from St Petersburg to escape arrest, but the soviet were arrested and thrown into
prison. In November the general strike petered out and although unrest
continued into 1906 the disorders were gradually suppressed by the
execution of peasants and violent reprisals by the army against whole
villages.

The revolution failed, but not fruitlessly. A Duma had been won.
Autocracy was cracked. The revolutionaries learnt from their failure
and planned more thoroughly for the next rising. The SRs and the
SDs created a network of underground organisations, workmen's
soviets, and terrorist cells, to prepare for the next attempt.

The Dumas

The Dumas were cheated from the start, for Nicholas never intended
them to have any real power. The elections were heavily weighted in
favour of the nobility. When elected, the Duma could initiate laws,
but the Upper House, nominated by the Tsar, the Church, the nobles
and commercial organisations, could outvote the Lower House.
Ministers were responsible to the Tsar, not to the Duma, and as a last
resort, Nicholas could veto any of their decisions. He kept foreign
affairs and control over the armed forces in his own hands. In May 1906
the First Duma met. Most of the Socialists, recognising and despising
the weakness of the assembly, boycotted the elections. Even so, it was
almost totally hostile to the Tsar. The Cadets (the liberal party) were
the largest single group with 150 members in the Lower House. They
immediately presented Nicholas with a plan of moderate reform. When
it was rejected, the Duma passed a vote of censure on the Government.
The Tsar turned to a new Prime Minister, Peter Stolypin, who in July
dissolved the Duma. About 200 members indignantly left for Finland

where they issued a Manifesto urging the people to pay no taxes. Their appeals fell on deaf ears.

Stolypin took precautions before he called another Duma. An outbreak of terrorism was followed by strict repression. In twelve months, 3,000 were executed and 35,000 banished to Siberia. Stolypin tried to ensure that the second Duma would be loyal to the Tsar by manipulating the elections. He changed the Electoral Law and revised the registers so that large numbers of people lost the right to vote. Voting papers were mislaid and priests were told to order their congregations to vote for Government candidates. The attempt failed. The Cadets who had issued the Manifesto were not allowed to seek election because of their previous opposition. Socialists replaced them. When the second Duma met in March 1907 the Cadets numbered 123, but there were now fifty-four SDs and thirty-five SRs. Again, demands for reform and criticism of the Government forced Stolypin's hand. Three months after the Duma met it was dissolved.

Before the elections to the third Duma, Stolypin pruned the voting registers even more drastically. The press was rigidly censored and the right of public meeting limited. The Government was able to turn the third Duma, when it met in November 1907, into a loyal chamber of industrialists and landowners. Only fifty-four Cadets and a handful of socialists remained of the once huge opposition. The Duma lasted its full allotted span of five years and passed a few moderate reforms. In 1912 a fourth Duma replaced it and was still in existence when the revolution broke in 1917.

The Dumas achieved little, in terms of practical legislation or popular approval. The Cadets and the socialists, disillusioned with Nicholas's broken promises, turned to terrorism in order to destroy Tsarism completely. As a result parliamentary government was despised, associated with Tsarism and weakness. This proved fatal in 1917 with Lenin and the Bolsheviks waiting for an opportunity to impose their own form of government.

In the years before the Great War Russia passed into a period of relative tranquillity. Stolypin had won over many peasants by his land reforms and had brought efficiency to Tsarist administration. The police handled revolutionaries with an iron fist and the last two Dumas ambled along inoffensively. But Stolypin had many enemies: in 1911 one of them assassinated him. Nicholas did not waste Stolypin's advice. In 1912 schemes of accident and health insurance were introduced, educational facilities were improved, and by 1914 further land reforms had given one in four peasant households their own land. Lenin and other exiles were in despair, their hopes shattered. The war altered everything.

1914–18 War

In July 1914 Russia mobilised to go to the aid of her ally, Serbia. Within a few weeks war was declared against Germany and Austria. The Government was totally unprepared. The army lacked modern weapons and ammunition. Transport, medical and supply facilities were inadequate. The only resources Russia had in abundance were men, but, largely untrained and badly equipped, they were mown down by the superior German armies. At first, the Russians were successful, but under General Hindenburg the Germans rallied and in the battle of Tannenburg (August 1914) drove the Russian soldiers from East Prussia with the loss of 160,000 men. In the south, Russian armies moved into Galicia but in 1915 were forced to retreat. The Tsar left his capital to take personal command of confused, incompetent officers, and crushed, apathetic troops. In 1916, Nicholas promised his allies that he would mount an offensive, although some regiments had no rifles and his gunners were rationed to four shells a day. Nicholas threw his weary men forward but gained little ground. By the end of 1916 the Russian troops were deserting the front in thousands, throwing down their rifles and as Lenin put it, 'voting with their feet' for the end of a terrible war.

In Russia itself the outbreak of war had brought a surge of enthusiastic national unity. Defeat after defeat killed all spirit for war and Russia sank into apathy.

Rasputin

When Nicholas left for the front, his wife, Alexandra, took over the reins of government. She fell under the spell of Rasputin. Gregory, the 'Mad Monk', is one of the monsters of Russian history. The son of a Siberian peasant, he had acquired a questionable reputation as a holy man, with powers of healing and mind-reading. He seems to have been more adept at drunkenness and lechery. He was recommended to the Tsarina as a healer and he succeeded where doctors had failed in curing the haemophilia of the young Alexis. His secret still remains a mystery — drugs, hypnotism or coincidence may be the answer. The filthy, coarse, uneducated peasant whom Alexandra called 'the man of God', took his revenge on a society he despised by insulting and reviling it. As the war proceeded Rasputin became more ambitious. He began to make prophecies about the war, usually pessimistic, usually correct. His dissolute eyes ranged over the ladies of the court, and one word of disapproval from him led to the dismissal of ministers. From September 1915 he reigned in triumph. The loathing against him increased until in December 1916 Prince Yusupov and a group of nobles decided to murder him. Rasputin was invited to an aristocrat's house and plied with poisonous food and drink. The rascal ate with relish before the terrified eyes of the conspirators. Prince Yusupov ran for his pistol and fired several shots into Rasputin, who chased them, until, riddled with bullets, he collapsed. His body was bundled into a curtain and dropped in the icy water of the river Neva. A few days later he was washed up. Incredibly, he was declared to have died by drowning. Alexandra went into deep mourning: the rest of Russia celebrated. The episode hastened the demise of Tsardom. If the rulers of Russia were stupid enough to accept the nonsense of Rasputin, they had surely surrendered all right to rule.

By 1916 Tsardom was in its death-throes. Deserting troops joined the strikers. The German blockade brought trade to a halt and famine to the Russian people. The economy collapsed through lack of transport and proper organisation. Fuel shortages and bread rationing stimulated riots, strikes and more violence. Nicholas was quite deaf to all warnings. Among his soldiers he was happier than at any time in his life: events in Russia could await his return.

THE REVOLUTION

The revolution began in a small way, almost spontaneously, in Petrograd (formerly St Petersburg). Food riots, strikes and mutinies kept the city in ferment. On 8 March troops and police, sent to crush the demonstrators, joined them. In a wave of enthusiasm public buildings were seized, prisoners released and the Duma dismissed. In March, a committee of ten of the old Duma formed a Provisional Government. The Tsar hurried back from the front, to be seized and forced to abdicate in favour of his brother, Grand Duke Michael. He refused the throne so the royal family were all arrested. While the Provisional Government struggled to restore order, the Petrograd Soviet of Workers and Soldiers issued orders as if it was the rightful government. Similar soviets were formed in barracks and factories in Moscow and other towns. In this confused situation, with two rival governments in Petrograd, and the provinces ignoring both, the socialists quietly moved in.

The Provisional Government, with Prince Lvov as Premier and

Alexander Kerensky as Minister of Justice, were all middle-class liberals with the exception of Kerensky (an SR). The new Government abolished repressive laws, promised the Finns and Poles their freedom and planned a series of land reforms. This programme was not sufficiently revolutionary for the peasants who began to seize land, or for the workers who continued to strike.

In April 1917 Lenin and thirty-one other exiles were smuggled by the German High Command in a sealed train across Europe to Petrograd.[1] A huge mob greeted Lenin's return with slogans, songs and cheers. Lenin shocked his supporters by demanding the complete overthrow of capitalism, an end to the war, and the destruction of the Provisional Government. He was thought a madman but gradually won the Bolsheviks over to his support, adopting the slogan, 'All Power to the Soviets'.

Kerensky battled desperately to save the Government. He replaced Prince Lvov as Premier and promised further reforms. He was ambitious and patriotic but made the great mistake of insisting on loyalty to Russia's allies and a continuation of the war. A Russian offensive in the summer turned into a rout: the soldiers were too war-weary and disillusioned to obey orders. Armies dissolved overnight as soldiers shot their officers and left for home. The Bolsheviks calmly prepared for a coup. Lenin had to flee to Finland to escape Kerensky's police, but Trotsky stayed to direct operations in Petrograd. Kerensky was now ruling as a dictator in a deteriorating situation which he could not control.

The November Revolution

General Kornilov, Military-Commander of Petrograd, realised the danger of a Bolshevik coup and tried to crush the soviets. Kerensky resented his action and feared a rival. He had Kornilov arrested. The effect was to weaken Kerensky's military power and leave the Bolsheviks intact.

On 7 November Lenin acted. A secret meeting of the Bolsheviks decided on an armed rising. The Petrograd Soviet organised a military committee which ordered the Red Guards to the key points in the city. They met with little resistance. In the space of a few hours the railway stations, Post Office, barracks, banks, and power stations were occupied. The Ministers of the Provisional Government were seized: Kerensky fled, first to the countryside and eventually to America. In Petrograd, the Bolshevik seizure had been almost bloodless. A new Soviet Govern-

1. The Germans calculated that these revolutionaries would undermine Russian strength and morale, and so assist a German victory.

ment was proclaimed with Lenin as its chairman. With apparent ease, a small group of desperate men had seized control of a huge Empire. In the next three years the Bolsheviks had to fight a bloody war to maintain their power, but November 1917 had proved a victory for Lenin's determination to keep his forces a disciplined and tightly organised little group. Brilliantly led in the hour of revolution by Trotsky and Lenin, who had studied the mechanics of exploiting a revolutionary situation, and promising simply 'Bread, Land and Peace', they made an emotional and inspiring appeal to the Russian people.

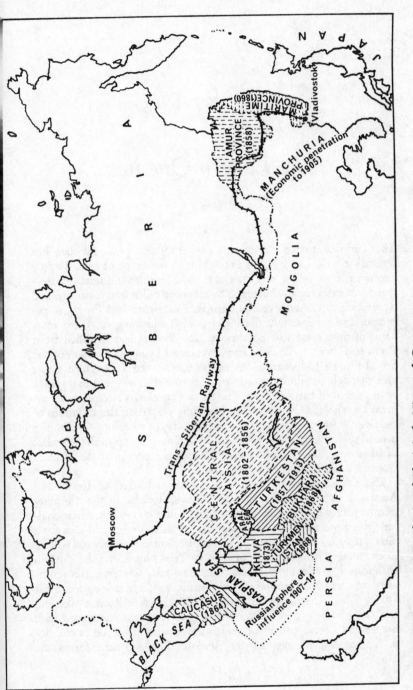

5 Russian Expansion in Central Asia and Siberia in the Nineteenth Century

6

The Eastern Question

※※

The Turkish Empire was once a dangerous and powerful state but internal misrule had by 1870 brought it to the verge of ruin. Turkey became known as 'the sick man of Europe', for under a series of dissipated and extravagant Sultans its finances had fallen into confusion and its administration into chaos. European statesmen had for years expected it to collapse but, obstinately, the Turks hung on to the remnants of their once vast possessions. The Empire had stretched from Persia to Gibraltar. With its army weakened by neglect, however, the proud Empire had shrunk. Yet in the Balkans the Turks ruled a vast area through an administration that alternated easy-going indulgence with periods of harsh cruelty. The Sultans checked all demands for reform by wholesale massacres, and skilfully played off the ambitions of the Great Powers in order to postpone the day of partition. The Empire needed speedy and drastic reforms for it to measure up to the demands of its peoples. This would mean reducing the power of the Moslem Church, a plan unacceptable to the Sultan.

The Christians who lived in the Balkans looked to Russia and Austria to defend them against the Turkish tyrants. In the late nineteenth century the religious crusade fused with the emotions of nationalism: the subject races of the peninsula began to dream and plot for a 'Slav' state, or states, in place of the Empire. Russia was only too willing to encourage them to rebel. Successive Tsars hoped that the Turkish withdrawal would allow Russia to expand her own territories southward towards the Danube and eventually to Constantinople and the Straits. The Tsars hoped to make the Black Sea a Russian lake and establish a base on the Mediterranean. They constantly intrigued with the Greeks, Serbs, Rumanians and Bulgars, who had to be careful not to replace Turkish tyranny by Russian. The Austrians feared the

6   The Russo–Japanese War, 1904–5

Russian advance, but were themselves anxious to keep Turkey weak, to further their own territorial expansion. They also feared that the Serb revolts might spread to their own dominions, where thousands of Serbs looked to tiny Serbia to free them from Austrian rule. This was the Eastern Question, a complex problem arising out of Turkish collapse, complicated by national revolts, and providing a battleground for the ambitions of the Great Powers.

Each of the Great Powers had her own ideas for solving the problems of the Balkans. Britain demanded that the Turks should overhaul their Empire by financial and administrative reforms and grant further concessions of religious freedom to the Christians. This would keep Turkey sufficiently strong to provide an effective barrier against Russia. The Turks glibly agreed with Britain to pacify her, but rarely did anything, fearing that these concessions to their Christian subjects would inflame Moslem opinion, and make the Slav peoples think the Turks were getting soft. A second suggestion was that the Turkish Empire should be partitioned. Austria and Russia would divide the Balkans between them while France, Italy and Britain would share out Turkey's North African and Arabian possessions. Russia favoured this policy: Austria was suspicious, fearing Russian influence on her borders. Britain and France were actively hostile, for they had no wish to see the Russians dominating the Eastern Mediterranean, threatening their interests in Egypt. Nor did the peoples of the Balkans care much for this solution; they had their own—the creation of independent states, free from Turkish or Russian control. By 1918 the final solution incorporated all three possibilities, but in the course of the nineteenth century Russia seemed to hold the advantage.

By 1870 cracks had appeared in the Turkish Empire. The tiny state of Montenegro had never been defeated by the Turks. Sheltering in their mountain fortresses of Dalmatia, the Montenegrins had clung to their independence and kept alive the spark of freedom. In 1817 another small state, Serbia, had emerged to acquire some degree of self-government. The Greeks had rebelled and with British assistance had by 1830 become an independent state. In the Crimean War the Russians had swept across the Danube before the joint efforts of Turkey, France and Britain had stopped them in their tracks and forced them to retreat. The war had indicated Russian intentions, but Austria's panic allied to British and French hostility made the Russians realise the strength of the opposition to their aggressive Balkan policies. After the war was over, in 1862, a new state, Rumania, obtained a considerable measure of self-government.

Consequently, in 1870 there were in the Balkans four states, Serbia,

Greece, Montenegro, and Rumania, with varying degrees of freedom. There were also thousands of fellow Serbs, Greeks and Rumanians still living under Turkish rule, inflamed by religious and nationalist emotions. In addition, all the Bulgar race suffered under Turkish tyranny, although in 1870 the Sultan, at Russian insistence, allowed the Bulgars to have their own religious leader, the Exarch. This stimulated their national passions, making them hopeful of further Turkish retreats. South-eastern Europe was a powder-keg: it needed only a spark to set it alight.

THE REVOLTS OF 1875–77

In July 1875 the angry peasants of the provinces of Bosnia and Herzegovina rose against the Turks. On top of bad harvests they had had to suffer heavier Turkish taxes. Serbia assisted them, intending to use the rebellion to form a larger Serb state. At first the Turks did nothing, hoping that the revolts would die down. But no crisis in the Balkans was ever allowed to rest. Austria was afraid that the Serbs living in her own southern provinces would join the rebels, so tried desperately to end the fighting. In December 1875 Count Andrássy, the Austrian Foreign Minister, took the initiative and despatched a Note to the Turkish Government, demanding that a list of reforms should be immediately put into effect. The other Great Powers, Russia, Germany, Italy, France and Britain, approved the peace-making move and put their agreement to the Note. The Turks, unafraid and irritated by foreign interference, accepted the Note but did nothing to implement it. The Great Powers, at first unanimous, then began to think what advantage each could gain from the revolts. The British Government, encouraged by its ambassador at Constantinople, Sir Henry Elliott, thought that Turkey should be preserved as a barrier to Russian penetration and was rather suspicious of Russia's moves. The Turks gained the impression that in the event of war, as in 1854, Britain would leap to their support. The Sultan therefore defiantly snubbed the other Powers.

In May 1876, Russia, Austria and Germany combined to draw up another plan of reforms, the Berlin Memorandum, which they presented to Turkey with a sting in the tail, that if the demand for an armistice were rejected, 'effective measures' might have to be taken. This confirmed British suspicions about Russian intervention and Disraeli, the

British Prime Minister, turned down the Memorandum firmly, refusing to sign. A British fleet was moved to Besika Bay, near the Dardanelles. If the Dreikaiserbund Powers were planning secretly to trick Britain, they would have to face the navy.

The Turks themselves had not been satisfied with the part played in this by the Sultan, Abdul Aziz, and in May 1876 he was deposed. His successor, Murad V, proved equally incompetent and only lasted three months in power. With Turkish administration paralysed by these palace intrigues, the situation worsened. The Bulgarians now rose in revolt, and throwing caution to the winds, Montenegro and Serbia declared war on Turkey. As the Great Powers had suspected, the situation was getting out of hand. Austria and Russia made their last attempt to end the revolts amicably; they still clung to the idea that peace might be restored and the status quo maintained. But the surge of nationalist passion in Bulgaria and Serbia, and the grim determination of the Turks, made nonsense of peace moves. In August 1876 Murad V was deposed and the throne passed to Abdul Hamid II. Under this terrible new leader, the Turks found a new energy and struck back.

Abdul was determined to crush the Bulgarian rebels and he stepped up the campaign of repression that was being waged by the Turkish army. A force of irregular troops, the Bashi-Bazouks, were let loose on the Bulgarians. Within a few weeks Bulgaria was a blood-bath, for thousands were slaughtered in cold blood and horrible atrocities were committed against the civilian population. These horrors had been going on all through the summer of 1876 but they reached a terrible peak when Abdul became Sultan. Sir Henry Elliott informed Disraeli that the reports of atrocities were exaggerated. But in September the true story became known to the *Daily News* and by the end of the month Disraeli had to admit the appalling truth. These events destroyed all sympathy for the Turks in England. Gladstone, the Liberal opposition leader, who had been in retirement, re-entered public life in a blaze of publicity to denounce the Turkish atrocities and British policy. His pamphlet, 'The Bulgarian Horrors', sold 40,000 copies in three days and it contained the sentence that the Turks in Bulgaria 'should carry away their abuses . . . one and all, bag and baggage, from the province they have desolated and profaned.' The popular revulsion against Turkey which this aroused made it impossible for Disraeli to prop up the cruel Turkish Government, and weakened Britain's moral position should the Russians attack.[1]

Tsar Alexander II demanded action, especially as the invigorated

1. Disraeli was created Earl of Beaconsfield in August 1876. For the purposes of accuracy he will now be referred to as Beaconsfield.

Turkish armies were driving the Serbs into retreat and damping down the fires of revolt in Bulgaria. Consequently, the Great Powers sent their representatives to the Constantinople Conference (January 1877) at which far-reaching reforms were proposed. Bulgaria was to become largely self-governing and Turkish administration elsewhere made less harsh. If Turkey had accepted the reforms there is no doubt that war would have been avoided. In fact, the wily Abdul Hamid deliberately wasted time and eventually tricked the Powers. He appointed as Vizier a man known for his liberal views, Midhat. Abdul also granted a new constitution to his empire and thus claimed that the Powers' reforms were unnecessary. He still believed that in a crisis, Russia would not chance war and in any case Britain would again rally to Turkey's side. The Conference broke up with nothing substantial accomplished. It had served its purpose for Abdul: it had fooled Europe. After the Conference dispersed, Midhat was dismissed and the new constitution scrapped.

THE RUSSO-TURKISH WAR OF 1877

Russia, tricked, now made active preparations for war, moving troops to the borders and buying off the other Great Powers. Austrian suspicions were placated by the promise of gains in Bosnia-Herzegovina. Informed that Russia had no ambitions towards Egypt, Suez or Constantinople, which would be entirely ignored, Beaconsfield proclaimed Britain's neutrality.

In April 1877 the Russo-Turkish war opened. Rumania gave free passage to the Russian armies which were soon in Bulgaria. Their advance then slowed down, to come to a halt at Plevna, where for five months an able Turkish general, Osman Pasha, held the Russians at bay. In Britain the defiance of the Turks revived the old dislike of Russia as a barbaric and aggressive foe trying to elbow into areas of British interests. Even Queen Victoria thought that Britain's duty was to go to war in the defence of the gallant Turks. The Bulgarian massacres were quite forgotten. In December 1877 Plevna was starved out and Osman surrendered. The Russians swept on.

At the end of January 1878 Russian troops entered Adrianople. The road was open to Constantinople. The British Cabinet now ordered the Mediterranean fleet to sail to the Dardanelles and asked Parliament to

vote £6 million for military purposes. These measures stopped the
Russians at the very gates of Constantinople and a week later they
signed an armistice with the Turks. Even so, the war fever still held
Britain in its grip and the famous music-hall song,

> 'We don't want to fight,
> But by Jingo, if we do,
> We've got the men; we've got the ships,
> We've got the money, too'

reflected the spirit of confident aggression which caught popular
imagination. For some months war seemed a real possibility but Russia
was exhausted by her efforts. Beaconsfield, who felt sure that Russia
could be stopped by diplomatic means, strove to avert bloodshed.

The Russians acted quickly to take advantage of their success. In
March 1878 peace was negotiated in the Treaty of San Stefano. Its
terms reflected the Russian victories. Serbia and Montenegro were to be
rewarded for their support of Russia by small territorial gains at
Turkey's expense. Rumania was to give up the province of southern
Bessarabia to Russia and in exchange would acquire the Dobruja. All
three of these Balkan states were to be fully independent of Turkey.
The most galling feature of the Treaty lay in the creation of a huge
Bulgarian state, stretching from the Black Sea to the Aegean, reputedly
independent, but plain to everyone a Russian satellite. Bulgaria would
depend on Russia for protection and be a useful spring-board for
Russian influence in the whole Balkan area. Russia also gained territory
in the Caucasus—the towns of Batoum and Kars—and the right to
supervise Turkish reforms in Bosnia. The terms, so strongly in Russian
interests, astonished and horrified Austria and Britain. Count Andrássy
mobilised Austrian forces and insisted on a conference. Britain called
up her reserves and moved 7,000 Indian troops to Malta. The danger of
war revived but Bismarck, who had been sitting uncomfortably on the
fence, now backed Austria. The Tsar, faced with a strong European
coalition, reluctantly had to agree to discuss peace terms at an international conference at Berlin.

THE BERLIN CONGRESS, 1878

Before the Congress met, Lord Beaconsfield negotiated secret terms
with Russia, Turkey and Austria. At Berlin the last details were ham-

mered out with Lord Beaconsfield and Gortchakov, the Russian diplomat, the chief adversaries. The British were assisted by Count Andrássy, and with Bismarck finally joining the Austrian camp, the Russians had to accept the cancellation of the Treaty of San Stefano and fresh dictated terms. The Berlin Treaty finally agreed to was:

(a) The 'Big' Bulgaria of San Stefano was to be divided into three parts:

1. Bulgaria—an independent state
2. Eastern Rumelia—returned to Turkey but to be administered by a Christian Governor chosen by the Sultan
3. Macedonia—returned, without limitations, to Turkey.

(b) Great Britain was to annex Cyprus. (The island was the price Turkey had to pay for Britain's support.)

(c) Austria obtained the right to occupy and administer but not to annex Bosnia-Herzegovina, and the province of Novibazar. Both of these areas were to remain nominally under the suzerainty of the Sultan.

(d) The full independence of Serbia, Montenegro, and Rumania was recognised by Turkey. These three states received small additions of territory though not as much as had been promised at San Stefano.

(e) Russia annexed southern Bessarabia from Rumania and Batoum and Kars from Turkey. Rumania had to be satisfied with the Dobruja, a barren coastal area.

(f) The French were compensated by the suggestion that they might move into Tunis. Italy and Germany gained nothing.

(g) Turkey guaranteed full religious liberty to all her subjects and promised reforms in other parts of the Empire.

The Congress of Berlin had its crises and critics. Lord Beaconsfield had to threaten to return home before the Russians agreed to leave Eastern Rumelia. Gortchakov had to swallow his pride and accept a far weaker role for Russia in the Balkans than he had hoped. It was felt by Britain and Austria that the Bulgars would be dogged by Russian influence and therefore had to be kept within tight limits. Consequently, thousands of Bulgars, Greeks and Serbs were forced back under Turkish rule, not a very wise or liberal decision. From the British point of view, the Russians had been checked, the navigation of the Straits safeguarded and Turkey forced to reform her administration. One side-effect of blocking Russia was that the Tsar turned towards Afghanistan and China, so creating threats to Britain's position in India and the Far East. As explained elsewhere, at the Berlin Congress Bismarck failed to retain the friendship of Russia. The Dreikaiserbund lay in ruins and the Russians never again trusted Germany as they had in the past.

Lord Beaconsfield made a triumphant return to Britain bearing, as he said, 'peace with honour'. But the Congress left many problems unsolved—the need to force Turkey to reform; the return to Turkish misrule of the subject races, especially in Rumelia; and the problem of Turkey's African Empire. In the years before 1914 the Berlin Treaty was amended again and again: it did not last nor did it reveal much wisdom. Its value in 1878 proved to be purely as a temporary check to Russian ambitions: the Congress certainly did not solve the Eastern Question, it only postponed the solution. After 1878, the Balkan peoples, disgusted with the Great Powers, took the initiative themselves. Despite Beaconsfield's phrase, the settlement brought neither peace to the Balkans nor honour to Britain.

THE BULGARIAN CRISIS OF 1885

Almost immediately the Treaty of Berlin had to be revised. In 1881 the French moved into Tunis, their share of the prize money. At the same time, Greece, who had noisily and unsuccessfully demanded territory at Berlin, now seized the Turkish province of Thessaly and part of Epirus. Turkey protested, but to no avail.

A more serious problem arose in Bulgaria. The new state had a most unhappy start. Under young Prince Alexander of Battenburg, the Tsar's nephew, everyone expected Bulgaria to be excessively pro-Russian. The Bulgars themselves had no such intentions and a patriot, Stambulov, led a nationalist rising. He made himself President of the Sobranje (Parliament) and began to expel Russian advisers. For a time Bulgaria's independent existence hung in the balance. In this situation, in September 1885, the people of Eastern Rumelia rose in revolt, expelled the Turks, and proclaimed its union with Bulgaria. On Stambulov's orders, Prince Alexander agreed. The previous roles of the Great Powers were now reversed. Russia, having failed to make a satellite out of Bulgaria, opposed the union. Britain and Austria, who could see an enlarged Bulgaria as a more effective barrier to Russia, viewed events with approval. The other Balkan states were not as keen: Serbia and Rumania recognised a dangerous rival in the offing. While the Great Powers hesitated, Serbia struck, demanding territorial compensation. The result was a complete surprise. The confident Serbs moved into Bulgaria, but were routed and their own country invaded.

To save Serbia from complete destruction, Austria compelled the Bulgars to withdraw. Peace followed in 1886 and the union of Bulgaria and Eastern Rumelia was recognised by the Great Powers.

No one now wanted Prince Alexander. The angry Tsar held him responsible for the decline of Russian influence. In August 1886 a group of army officers kidnapped the Prince, forced him to abdicate and hustled him across the border into Russia. Stambulov had no love for the unhappy Prince but this act insulted Bulgar pride. He insisted on Alexander's recall. War seemed likely but the Russians held their hand, unsure of the attitude of the Great Powers. Eventually Alexander reappeared in Bulgaria, but now without a friend in any camp he was expelled from Bulgaria for good.

In August 1887 a new prince, Ferdinand of Saxe-Coburg, became the ruler. The Tsar, horrified that Russian influence had been replaced by German, refused to recognise the election. By now Stambulov was something of an expert in insulting the Russians and he triumphantly continued to crush all traces of Russian influence, ruling Bulgaria with an iron hand until he was assassinated in 1895.

The crisis had petered out. Russia, humiliated again, had no wish to become involved in a war for the sake of Bulgaria. In 1888 Bismarck had published the terms of the Dual Alliance, so indicating that in the event of war he would choose Austria rather than Russia. Britain, Italy and Austria had signed a vague agreement to maintain peace in the Near East and Mediterranean areas. France was paralysed by the ambitious intrigues of General Boulanger. Alone, Russia would not fight. Bulgaria kept both Rumelia and Ferdinand, and in the Balkans war was again narrowly averted.

In the 1890s the situation changed. In 1889 Kaiser William II paid a visit to Constantinople. As a result German money, arms, soldiers and technical advisers replaced British. Plans were made for a railway linking Berlin to Constantinople and eventually Baghdad too. Britain was gradually elbowed out, and in 1914 Germany took over the defence of the Turkish Empire. A new balance of power emerged in the Balkans. Austria-Hungary became the dominant power there, hoping to use Bosnia as a base for further conquests towards Salonika and, linking up with the Kaiser, extend German power even further. Russia abdicated interest, transferring her ambitions to Persia and Afghanistan where gains were easier and more valuable. Only after Britain had blocked Russian expansion in these areas did the Tsar return to Balkan intrigues. Austria's one-time protégé, Serbia, now saw the danger. Both nations hoped to enlarge themselves in the Macedonian region: both were rivals for Balkan leadership. The increasing rivalry between Austria and Serbia formed one of the major causes of Balkan conflict and the eventual world war.

THE ARMENIAN MASSACRES, 1894

By the Treaty of Berlin Abdul Hamid promised to grant religious toleration to his subjects, and to introduce reforms into Armenia. In 1878 Britain and Russia undertook to see that these reforms were implemented. The Sultan ignored his pledges and indeed persecuted the Christians, keeping Balkan hatreds at boiling-point. Armenia, a province fringing the Russian Empire, held about two million Christians. The Armenians enjoyed a reputation as intelligent and successful businessmen. They aroused the envy and positive dislike of the Turks. In 1890 a revolutionary committee began to agitate for a national government for the Armenians, but without success. Abdul Hamid was determined to crush their ambitions before the Great Powers could interfere. In 1894 he despatched Turkish regiments and called up the Kurds, the hated enemies of the Armenians, to assist. A series of murderous attacks were made against villages and towns. When the Armenians protested a second wave of assassins moved in, and 50,000 died. The British people, horrified as they had been at the time of the Bulgarian massacres, demanded action. But rivalries among the Great Powers gave Abdul a free hand. William, hoping for some German advantage, sent the Sultan a birthday present. The Tsar, who deplored the atrocities, was nevertheless so committed in the Far East and at home that he did nothing. Austria feared a loss of influence and prestige. Britain would not act alone. Therefore, Abdul was able to take a horrible revenge on the Armenians. In August 1896, following an attack on a Turkish bank, 6,000 Armenians living peacefully in Constantinople were in three days rounded up and massacred. Again, as before, the Powers were made powerless by their own jealousies. Nothing was done and a fresh crisis, in Crete, turned embarrassed European eyes away from the bloodshed.

CRETE

Crete, peopled by Turks and Greeks, was racked by religious rivalries. In 1896, sporadic riots turned into open rebellion. Greece leapt to the defence of her own people and sent ships and troops to the island. The Moslems took a terrible revenge, massacring Christians living in the Turkish towns.

The revolt was transformed into a bitter war in which the Turks gradually captured the initiative and inflicted heavy defeats on the Greeks. At this stage the Powers decided to intervene and in 1897 British and French fleets blockaded the island and then landed troops. The fighting ended, but the Turks foolishly murdered the British Vice-Consul in retaliation. The British forces then expelled all Turkish troops and officials from Crete.

The Four Powers, Great Britain, France, Russia and Italy invited Prince George of Greece to govern. Although Crete remained officially within the Turkish Empire, it was to all practical purposes an independent state ruled by the Greeks. Again, a major war had been narrowly averted, but Turkey, furious with Britain and Russia for a further loss of territory, turned more and more to listen to German advice. In 1898 the Kaiser on another visit to Constantinople gained further trade and railway concessions and assured the Sultan that, 'the Kaiser will be their friend at all times'.

THE YOUNG TURKS AND THE 1908 CRISIS

In 1908 the Berlin Treaty came in for a fresh battering. What sparked off the crisis was a successful revolt within Turkey. A patriotic party calling itself 'the Young Turks' seized power. Their liberal ideas, which aimed at parliamentary government, freedom of religion and all manner of reforms, were almost immediately abandoned once they were in power. The Young Turks became as gruesomely adept at racial persecution as their predecessors. They were supported by the Army and the new National Assembly and when, in 1909, Abdul Hamid attempted to recover his authority the Army seized Constantinople, deposed him and elected his younger brother as Sultan with the title of Mahommed V.

This successful revolution of July 1908 had a number of side-effects. The Great Powers became alarmed, for a vigorous, aggressive Turkey was the last thing they wanted. Their various policies hinged on Turkey remaining in a weak position. Many of the Powers took immediate steps to safeguard themselves. Only two months after the Young Turk coup Ferdinand of Bulgaria shook off the last remnants of Turkey's suzerainty and declared himself Tsar of Bulgaria. He wanted his hands free for any eventuality. The people of Crete demanded union with Greece. Austria and Russia came to a common conclusion— to take advantage of Turkey's condition. Austria struck first, in October 1908, by annexing Bosnia-Herzegovina, provinces she had occupied in 1878. The Tsar, who for twenty years had been fishing in Far Eastern waters, now returned to the Balkans to seek the prestige that would bolster his tottering Empire. Russia hoped to gain some advantage like the free use of the Straits for her warships. The Tsar and Britain both demanded that these issues should be discussed at an international conference. Serbia, whose ambitions to annex territory and form an All-Slav state had been frustrated, agreed. Such was the feeling that a war seemed possible. It was only just avoided. Austria poured oil on the waters by paying £2,200,000 compensation to Turkey. William II made it known that in the event of war he would support Austria. At this threat, Russia gave way and agreed to Austria's annexations. Only the Serbs persisted and increased their army. But on the edge of war they wisely reconsidered, and accepted the situation. The bitter resentment in Serbia was nursed throughout the next few years. For the peoples of the Balkans, Austria had now appeared as the new danger, and Russia, as of old, their protector.

THE BALKAN WARS OF 1912–13

After 1908 Russia aimed at the impossible—the formation of a league of Balkan states as a military barrier against any further Austrian moves. A first step was the Russo–Bulgarian alliance of 1909. The Russians then struggled for three years to bring the other nations together. The old suspicions and antagonisms died hard: the only issue that could unite the states was the possibility that together they might fight a successful war against Turkey. Italy set the pattern in 1911 by invading and annexing Tripoli, in North Africa. Venizelos, the man who had been behind Crete's revolt, rose to become the Greek Prime Minister. He more than anyone smoothed over the difficulties. In August 1912 the Balkan League, composed of Bulgaria, Serbia, Greece and Montenegro, was formed, although jealousies were by no means forgotten. Having originated the League, Russia saw her own influence disappear.

Macedonia, the large and last section of the Turkish Empire in Europe, was the objective of the League. Bulgaria and Serbia made a secret agreement about their expected gains as the result of war. They promised scraps to the other two. As a pretext for war, in October 1912, the Balkan League insisted on immediate and radical reforms in Macedonia. The Powers tried to restrain the allies by forbidding the League to fight and demanding the maintenance of existing frontiers in the Balkans. On the very next day Montenegro, without consulting her allies, ignored the order and threw her armies against Turkey. Almost immediately the other three followed suit. Within a month, the Turkish armies had been defeated along all fronts. The Turks fell back to fortified defence lines only thirty miles from Constantinople.

In December, the Great Powers insisted on a conference and an armistice. Austria was alarmed by the growing strength of Serbia, and Germany did not like to see its new ally, Turkey, humiliated. The Conference was held in London in May 1913. By the terms of the Treaty signed there the Turks were forced to cede all their Macedonian territories to the victors, except for an area lying between Adrianople and the Straits. This tiny foothold was the sole remaining part of the once great Turkish Empire in Europe. Austria demanded the creation of a new state, Albania, to stop the extension of Serb power. Serbia and Montenegro had to evacuate the Albanian territory they had occupied. Demanding compensation elsewhere Serbia was allowed to annex northern and central Macedonia, Greece took southern Macedonia, including the valuable base of Salonika, and Bulgaria annexed Thrace and a stretch of the Aegean coastline.

The settlement at London pleased no one. Quarrels almost immediately resulted. Serbia had wanted a port on the Adriatic or on the Aegean coasts: she had neither, and blamed this on the Austrians who had forced the creation of Albania. Bulgaria held Thrace which was not particularly useful, and wanted central Macedonia, which was, although it now belonged to the Serbs. Bulgaria had done the lion's share of the fighting, and felt inadequately rewarded. Altogether it was a mixture of frustrated ambitions and envy, ingredients of a fresh conflict.

During 1913 the quarrels intensified and in June led to war. Bulgaria suddenly launched her armies against Serbia, who was rescued by Greece and Rumania. Faced by three foes the Bulgars retreated, and the Turks then moved in to try to recapture some of their territories lost earlier to Bulgaria. After only two months the defeated Bulgars sued for peace. The Treaty of Bucharest of August 1913 settled Bulgaria's fate. Rumania annexed southern Dobruja. Serbia and Greece forced the Bulgars to agree to their gains in Macedonia. Turkey recovered the city of Adrianople. The Treaty reflected Bulgaria's humiliation, but it was not a wise solution, for national aspirations were disregarded and all of the Balkan states had one grievance or another. The other states had made a bitter enemy out of Bulgaria, whose statesmen now turned to Austria-Hungary and Germany to help them obtain their revenge. Tension increased as each of the victors looked for further gains. The Balkan Powers were like a pack of hungry wolves greedily eyeing their weakest members.

Serbia had emerged as the leading power in the peninsula, and now eyed Bosnia where many Serbs lived unhappily under Austrian rule. Austria became convinced that Serbia had to be destroyed if the German powers were to continue with their policy of *Drang nach Osten*. In any case a possible Serbian invasion had to be nipped in the bud. On 28 June 1914, Archduke Francis Ferdinand and his wife were on a visit from Austria. At Sarajevo, the capital of Bosnia, they were assassinated by a group of Serb fanatics. In this tragedy lay Austria's golden opportunity to crush Serbia.

7   The Balkans in 1870

8 The Balkans by the Treaty of San Stefano, March 1878

9   The Balkans by the Treaty of Berlin, July 1878

10 The Balkans by the Treaty of Bucharest, 1913

7

The New Imperialism

During the course of previous centuries five of the European nations had built up large and powerful empires overseas. By 1870 Spain and Portugal, who had lost their colonies in South America, held a fraction of their formerly extensive acquisitions. Holland had only her possessions in the Dutch East Indies. The other two, Britain and France, had added steadily to their Empires. France had colonised most of Algeria, in the 1840s claimed Tahiti and the Marquesas in the Pacific, and under Napoleon III had established interests in Indo-China. Britain had not been idle. Natal, Singapore, New Zealand, Hong Kong and Burma had been added to an already extensive collection of territories.

1870 marks a dividing line between the old empires and a new, almost hysterical, grab for colonies. Suddenly, the European Powers began to see the possibilities of territories in the recently charted areas of the world. Even those who had been hostile were drawn along by the tide. Disraeli, the British Prime Minister, had declared that the colonies were 'millstones around our necks', and Bismarck regarded them as expensive and dangerous toys. Yet these two men became leading protagonists in the 'scramble' for colonies.

The dramatic seizure of Africa, spread out over a period of thirty years, would not have been possible without improved medical knowledge and new scientific inventions. Europeans learned how to live for long periods in the tropics and discovered that a few white soldiers armed with rifles or machine guns could overcome the resistance of the natives. Improved communications by sea, river and road made exploration easier. Although the advances in scientific knowledge may have assisted the Europeans they do not explain the impetus to conquer.

The reasons for the annexations were varied. In the first place, newly united nations such as Italy and Germany wanted colonies for prestige reasons. The German Colonial Society won the approval of public opinion and forced Bismarck to enter the race. Bismarck hoped that he would distract France from European affairs and stir up trouble between Britain and France. Europe was too small a stage and diplomats could manoeuvre and negotiate over the large expanses of Africa, without the restrictions of the strangling alliances that held Europe in a grip. Statesmen realised the potential strategic and economic value of a far-flung empire. Visiting the colonies became a royal duty, reflecting the increased interest. Queen Victoria and King Edward VII gloried in their positions as rulers of a great Empire. Edward, when Prince of Wales, toured India in 1875–76, and the young Tsar Nicholas II visited his dominions in the Far East in 1890. Empires became popular, objects of admiration, evoking a sense of power. It was felt in Europe that 'greatness' in a nation was reflected in the size of its empire, so envy and jealousy drove statesmen to compete for territories from Hawaii to Cyprus.

Empires also added to a nation's strength in terms of population. France trained Algerians and other Africans, like the famous Senegalese soldiers, to fight in her armies. Britain raised, trained and equipped Indian, Egyptian and African armies, which, officered by the British, went on to further imperial conquests, as in 1898 when Kitchener led a predominantly Egyptian army to the conquest of the Sudan.

Colonies were invaluable as bases. Britain, having acquired financial control of the Suez Canal, found it necessary to invade and occupy Egypt in 1882 to protect her strategic and commercial interests. The ports seized by the Powers in China in 1898 were needed as coaling stations for their iron-clad ships patrolling in Far Eastern waters. Once any Power had seized a base or territory it became imperative for the others to follow suit, otherwise they would be at a strategic or economic disadvantage.

Possibly, the most important reasons were economic. Industry in Europe was developing so fast that it needed fresh markets and new sources of raw materials. The new colonies provided rubber, cotton, silk, rare minerals and tea, and were used as dumping grounds for European goods. Traders were very often the first men into an unknown region. After them came the soldiers and the politicians. In the 1870s many of the European nations set up tariff barriers to protect their own industries from foreign competition, so the need to find new markets became more and more pressing. The population increase in

Europe created a greater demand for more foodstuffs and encouraged people to emigrate to the open spaces of Africa, to areas suitable for white settlement.

The scramble for colonies was criticised, first by a British economist, J. A. Hobson, and then by Lenin. In *Imperialism, the Highest Stage of Capitalism*, published in 1916, Lenin stated that imperialism was one of the last, most despairing stages in the development of capitalism. He argued that the bankers and industrialists of Europe, having vast fortunes at their elbows, invested in the colonies with the intention of creating subordinate economies. This makes imperialism a base, greedy affair, a grab for raw materials, easy markets and vast profits, all for the benefit of a few capitalists. Lenin went on to write that the exploited natives would eventually rise in revolt and overthrow their masters. He also expected the Great Powers to destroy themselves in a bitter struggle for colonial supremacy.

Lenin's explanations have been popular, especially within the colonies where they are used to explain their lower standards of living compared with Europe. Lenin's arguments also seem to point to 1914–18 as a war between capitalist Powers, bent on each other's destruction. The theories, however, do not fit the facts. The scramble for colonies and the causes of the 1914–18 war are a great deal more complex than this. For instance, although Great Britain's overseas investments rose from £785 million in 1871 to £4,000 million in 1914 more than half of the latter amount had been invested in non-colonial areas like South America and the USA. In any case empires existed before the glut of capital investment which Lenin mentions. France, one of the least industrialised nations, led the way in the search for colonies by her annexations before 1870 in Indo-China. Very often the men who opened up Africa and the Far East were not traders but explorers like De Brazza, for France, or Karl Peters, the German, and missionaries like David Livingstone. Some men spent their lives in Africa not for profit but to help the Africans or extend their knowledge of the continent. Economic motives are no doubt important. Africa and Asia provided the raw materials and the markets and attracted European settlement, although more people emigrated to North and South America. Besides these political and commercial factors, there were other considerations. Men went to Africa prompted by curiosity for scientific and geographical knowledge. There were adventurers like H. M. Stanley, who explored the Congo basin, and intrepid explorers like Burton, Speke and the Bakers who hazarded their lives to search for the source of the Nile. Livingstone was sent out by the London Missionary Society to spread Christianity, and the Catholic 'White Fathers' were equally inspired by religious and humanitarian zeal. There were soldiers like Marshal Lyautey who transformed the administrative chaos of Morocco into order and efficiency, and bureaucrats like Lord Cromer who performed a similar service in Egypt. Cecil Rhodes, who had made a fortune in diamonds, professed an imperialism which was a blend of patriotism, cash and personal power. He, like the other colonisers, defies Lenin's analysis: their motives were too complex to be explained simply in terms of investment. The story of African and Pacific colonisation is the story of adventurous and daring men, whether they were traders, explorers, missionaries, politicians or soldiers.

The Partition of Africa

In 1870 Africa was still the 'Dark Continent', unknown and unexplored. Within the space of thirty years the continent had been both explored and annexed. Although the coasts had long been plotted, it was not until the 1870s when the explorers burrowed deep into Africa that European interest was really aroused. The slave trade had kept Africa's peoples in servitude. Disease and poverty retarded their advance. Livingstone, who was able to move about without interference, was horrified by the backwardness of the natives and made a stirring appeal to Europe for medical and missionary aid. Livingstone made several journeys into Central Africa and on one of these, in 1872, Stanley met him on the shores of Lake Tanganyika. They both denounced the evils of slavery and in 1873 the British Government closed down the slave market at Zanzibar and called on other nations to co-operate to stamp out slavery, disease and paganism.

The 'scramble' itself may be said to start in 1876. Stanley's approaches to the British Government had been ignored, so he went to Brussels at King Leopold's invitation and helped the King to form the 'International African Association'. Leopold then sent Stanley on several expeditions to the Congo. By 1883 Stanley had established a land and water transport system stretching from the mouth of the Congo to Stanley Falls, a thousand miles away, the site of the modern city of Stanleyville. Leopold fooled the other Powers by developing the Congo as a commercial proposition under the cloak of an 'international' regime. The Belgians were quickly followed into action by the French. De Brazza had by 1881 effectively claimed a large area, called French Congo, for his country. Leopold's activities in the Congo sharpened the suspicions of Germany, and in 1884 Bismarck made a move. With an approaching election and a chance to make trouble between Britain and France he suddenly gave support to German traders and explorers who had been operating in East and West Africa.

Within two years Germany had become the ruler of vast territories in both areas of Africa. In April 1884 Bismarck annexed South-West Africa (except for Walfish Bay, a tiny British foothold), and quickly moved in to seize Togoland and the Cameroons. In East Africa, Karl Peters had obtained vague and dubious treaties from frightened native rulers and Bismarck backed him up by claiming for Germany in February 1885 a large region called German East Africa (Tanganyika).

While these events had been taking place in Africa, a conference had been meeting to draw up the rules. Fourteen Powers met at Berlin in 1884–85 to regularise the confusion in Africa. The result was the Berlin Act of 1885 whose principal points were:

(a) the Great Powers agreed to suppress the slave trade and slavery and to allow free trade between their colonies

(b) the natives were not to be exploited in the interests of the European Powers

(c) the Congo Free State was established, to be controlled by an international organisation on a free trade basis

(d) if any power 'effectively occupied' any territory, it could be claimed as a possession ('effective occupation' became difficult to define).

The well-meaning resolutions of the Conference were ignored in the race for advantages. King Leopold used the Congo to carve out a huge personal fortune for himself by setting up a trade monopoly in rubber and ivory. The friendly atmosphere of the Berlin meeting was forgotten in the swift, ruthless partition. Lord Salisbury, who handled the British side of the negotiations, was worried about possible threats to Egypt, the Nile and British interests in East Africa. Negotiations with Germany led to an Anglo-German Agreement in 1890 by which the British obtained Zanzibar, Uganda and Kenya, in return for the recognition of German claims to Tanganyika. As a make-weight, Heligoland, a small but strategically valuable island lying off the German North Sea coast, was ceded to Germany.

The French had not wasted time. Following their entry into Tunis in 1881, their soldiers had been gradually extending the empire within the western bulge of the continent. They advanced along the river Niger, reaching Timbuktu in 1893. Expeditions drove into the open spaces of French West Africa and into the forests of the French Congo. By 1895 the French army had added Dahomey, Senegal, Guinea, and the Ivory Coast, linking up the French territories in one vast block stretching from the Atlantic to the frontiers of the Sudan.

The British had been in some danger of missing the boat, for South Africa occupied their attention at first. Bechuanaland was hastily annexed in 1885 to forestall the Germans and Boers. Cecil Rhodes, who had made a vast fortune in diamonds at Kimberley, became interested in the territories north of the Limpopo river and in 1889 the British South Africa Company was formed to exploit the possibilities of the region. Within the space of little more than a year Northern and Southern Rhodesia and Nyasaland had been firmly pocketed by the Company for Britain.

In West Africa Britain used much the same methods, granting trade concessions to the Royal Niger Company, backed by the diplomatic support of the Government. Disputes with France led to an Anglo-French Agreement in 1890 by which the two Powers agreed to demarcation lines in West Africa. The borders of the British territories of Nigeria and the Gold Coast were agreed upon, and Britain recognised the existence of the French protectorate over Madagascar. Nevertheless, tension did not altogether disappear, for the French pushed towards the Sudan, and in 1898 when Captain Marchand appeared at Fashoda to claim the territory for France the two nations came near to a colonial war. After averting trouble in the Sudan, Britain became involved in a war against the two Boer states in 1899. By 1902 the Boers sought peace and in 1910 the Union of South Africa was created.

Italy, worried by a slow start in the race, made valiant efforts to catch up. Disappointed over Tunis, the Italians turned to Eritrea and Somaliland, which were first infiltrated by traders and soldiers and then annexed. In 1896 they attacked one of the few remaining independent states, Abyssinia, but suffered a humiliating defeat at the battle of Adowa and were forced into an ignominious retreat. The Italian Government recognised the independence of Abyssinia, and turned elsewhere to look for easier spoils. In 1911 Italy forced the weakened Turkish Government to cede the North African territories of Tripoli and Cyrenaica which were formed into the Italian colony of Libya.

The Portuguese had used the coast of Angola for many years as a trading area. They calmly proceeded to annex the interior and laid claims to Mozambique. Britain recognised both colonies in an Agreement of 1891.

By the end of this hectic period, it became apparent that the British had seized the most valuable share. Their colonies were more suitable for white settlement and they controlled bases from Simonstown in South Africa to Alexandria in Egypt. In no area of the continent were the British without territory or influence. France had collected the largest share. Her North African lands were useful economically and strategically but the same could not be said of her gains in the Saharan region and Madagascar. The Germans suffered disappointment, for their colonies were a drain on manpower and money. As markets for

German goods they proved inadequate and provided only small exports of raw materials.

The Pacific

A 'scramble' also took place in the islands of the Pacific, although not on the same scale as in Africa. By 1870 the Dutch had already established a secure claim to the East Indies and the British had bases at Singapore, Hong Kong and New Zealand, useful assets in the steamship age. The French, securely pivoted in Tahiti, exploited the possibilities of trade in copra and pearls. However, there were still islands free from European control and with considerable value as trading centres or bases.

In 1874 Britain added the Fiji Islands to her Empire and so sparked off the struggle. The Germans, again coming in late, in 1884, made strenuous efforts to rival the other empires. Missionary and merchant activities prepared the way for annexation. In 1885 the Germans moved into north-east New Guinea, the islands of the Bismarck Archipelago and Samoa, claiming them for the Kaiser. By 1899 they had purchased the Marianas and the Carolines from Spain, and seized the Marshalls as bases. They quickly discovered that the islands lacked resources and their climates took a heavy toll of Europeans.

The Americans soon arrived on the scene and disputed the German claim to Samoa. In 1889 warships of Britain, the USA, and Germany threatened each other, but a violent hurricane dispersed the fleets and probably cooled tempers. Eventually in 1899 Germany and the USA divided the Samoan Islands between them. The Americans turned to annex Guam, the Philippines and Hawaii, which were all taken by 1900. In the meantime, Britain had not been inactive, setting up protectorates over North Borneo and Sarawak, where a remarkable Englishman, Rajah Brooke, had made himself sovereign over the native peoples. By 1899 Britain had taken over the Gilbert and Ellice Islands, Tonga and the South Solomon Islands. France occupied the Society Islands, New Caledonia and several small islands surrounding Tahiti.

The Far East

The Chinese Empire under the Manchu rulers had been steadily sliding into decay. After the victorious Opium War of 1839-42 the British had forced the Chinese to cede Hong Kong to them and to open several ports to foreign traders. Following on British heels came other Powers, exploiting and humiliating the Chinese. In 1860 Russia captured the province of Amur and the port of Vladivostok. This act seemed to encourage the Powers to think of territorial as well as commercial gains.

In the next twenty years the French made great advances in Indo-China, sweeping into Cambodia, Tonkin, and Annam, finally defeating the Chinese armies in a bitter war in 1885. The French colony in Indo-China was larger than France itself and had a population of over twenty millions.

Burma passed under British rule and, by forcing China to cede further rights in 1860, Britain came to control two thirds of China's overseas trade. Other Powers looked jealously at the British advantages and began to elbow in. Russia edged into Turkestan and Manchuria. In 1895 Japan went to war and defeated the Chinese, and although Japan gained little for her pains the Great Powers took alarm. In 1898 Russia acquired a lease to the Liao-Tung peninsula and the right to build a railway link to Port Arthur. Hastily, France followed suit, obtaining a lease to the base of Kwang-Chow. Germany took a lease of Kiao-Chow and the Shantung peninsula and Britain, not to be outdone, took the port of Wei-hai-wei and made the Yangtze valley her sphere of influence. The ports were used as commercial centres for trade with the interior and as coaling-stations. In 1898 China was in some danger of being partitioned. What saved China was the American demand that the 'Open Door' policy should continue. This was a plan by which all Powers had an equal opportunity to exploit trade possibilities. The USA had no intention of being denied the golden goose. In addition, the Powers were content to trade in China, without the fag of having to govern.

Japan had been secluded from European influence until 1854 when Commodore Perry and his American naval squadron visited the country. Japan then felt the full influence of the traders, and accepted the western ways with enthusiasm, where China had rejected them. In 1867 Japan went through an internal revolution. A Parliament, with Lords and Commons, was set up. Industrialisation, western educational methods, copies of the German army and British navy appeared in the space of twenty years. The traditional Japanese way of life and the new western methods did not mix easily, yet Japan's population, trade and naval power developed at great speed, and before the end of the century the Japanese began to make their mark in international politics.

Adapting western ideas of imperial expansion to their own purposes, the Japanese went to war with China in 1895. Within a year the Chinese were defeated and had been forced to cede Port Arthur, Formosa, and Korea to the Japanese. This proved too risky for the interests of the Great Powers who forced Japan to return the conquests of Port Arthur and Korea. Russia, as the prime mover, was blamed by Japan for her setbacks. Within the next ten years the Japanese strained every muscle to strengthen their armed forces. Eventually, in 1904-05 they dealt Russia some shattering blows and triumphantly regained Port Arthur and Korea in the Treaty of Portsmouth (USA).

The Chinese had realised that defeat would always be theirs until they too copied the industrial techniques of the western powers. In 1898 Emperor Kwang Hsu issued edicts ordering reforms in education, the army and government. The hotheads among the Chinese people would not wait. In 1899 patriotic revolts against the hated foreigners threw the country into savage turmoil. A secret society called 'the Fists of Righteous Harmony' (nick-named 'the Boxers') made attacks on foreign legations and missionaries, killing over 300 people. At Peking, the embassies were beseiged by the 'Boxers' and an expeditionary force representing Japan, the USA and the European Powers marched in to crush the revolt. The Chinese suffered heavy fines and further invasions of their independence as a price of their rebellion. After 1900, the spirit of nationalism, far from being crushed, prospered. Even so, the Chinese could not prevent the Japanese making further gains in Manchuria in 1905. In 1908 the reforming Emperor, Kwang Hsu, died and for the next three years the revolutionaries waited their chance. In 1911 Sun-yat-sen overthrew the empire and set up a Republic. Unfortunately this did not see the end of China's troubles. Sun-yat-sen's party, known now as the Kuomintang (National People's Party) faced revolts against its authority from rival revolutionary governments in the north. A group of war-lords (aristocratic bandits) terrorised the countryside and in 1914 virtually eliminated the Kuomintang from power. Japan, taking advantage of the civil war raging in China, occupied Shantung and demanded increased trade and military rights. Abjectly, the Chinese Government gave in. The Chinese revolution against foreign control did not succeed until the Communist triumph in 1949.

Colonial Policies

By 1914 almost all of the native areas of the Pacific and Africa had succumbed to white rule. Liberia and Abyssinia in Africa, and China in the Far East managed to maintain a precarious independence. The Boer Republics had been swept under the British mat. Over all Africa from the Cape to Tangier the white man ruled. Remarkably, the process had been accomplished without a general war between the Powers, although they had come near to it. China, Japan and Russia had fought a struggle for supremacy in the Far East which had ended in a Japanese triumph. In Africa large empires had been carved out with distinctive European cultures transplanted to them. For better or worse huge areas of the globe felt the impact of alien civilisations.

South America had also attracted the Europeans as a market for their goods. A heavy proportion of investment found its way to the continent, but the USA prevented European annexations. Europe also provided skilled labour, for Italians, Greeks, and other nationalities flocked to the Argentine and other states.

Each of the colonising Powers regarded its empire in a different light. The British varied their administration from self-government in the larger dominions like New Zealand and South Africa, to direct rule by British administrators in most of the African colonies. In West Africa, the British lacked both sufficient trained administrators and sufficient funds to provide direct rule by British officials. After 1900 in Northern Nigeria, Sir Frederick Lugard made the local emirs responsible for the administration of justice, tax-collection, and the application of laws, under the supervision of a British Resident attached to their courts. Lugard's system of indirect rule won the confidence of the natives and enabled Britain to control vast areas of land both cheaply and effectively. Indirect rule was widely adopted throughout British territories in tropical Africa after the 1914–18 war.

The French, with their indifference to colour, followed a policy of 'assimilation'. This meant that Algeria or Tunisia were looked upon as parts of France, controlled and governed from Paris but with certain rights of citizenship and self-government. The French language and way of life, transferred to Africa, was a mixture of French and African influences. With the more backward areas, like the French Congo, the natives could not be treated as full citizens because of their obvious lack of education. The French soldiers and administrators ruled these areas as conquerors.

The Portuguese, Germans, Dutch and Belgians ruled through their own administrators, giving the natives little opportunity to learn the techniques of government.

8

William II and European Tensions

❋❋

William II opened up a new era in German policy. Instead of the shrewd calculations of Bismarck, the Germans had to suffer the theatrical gestures and emotional tantrums of their neurotic Emperor. Instead of the sure touch of the old master, the inept and nervous bravado of the pupil characterised the diplomacy of these years. Yet William expressed the vigour and bluster of German nationalism; he was popular at home and his popularity increased in proportion to the anger and embarrassment he caused foreign statesmen. He posed as the maker and breaker of politicians; no Chancellor ever achieved the control that Bismarck had enjoyed. The danger to Europe lay in his picture of Germany as a virile, militant force, powerful on land and at sea, with a colonial Empire to rival Britain's. He favoured politicians who supported his plans for expansion; the German people, whipped up by a nationalist press, followed his lead with admiration.

A sign of the times was William's choice of Chancellor. The first was General von Caprivi, an honest and competent administrator. William let him handle home affairs, leaving the Kaiser free to make his mark in diplomacy. Even then, Caprivi only lasted four years and of the other Chancellors who succeeded him, only Bülow dared oppose William's wishes. Others came and went: none approached Bismarck in character or ability.[1] Yet William did not have the talent or concentration to handle the complex problems of government: as a result German policy became flabby and inconsistent.

---

1. Chancellors: 1890–94 Caprivi; 1894–1900 Hohenlohe; 1900–09 Bülow; 1909–17 Betmann-Hollweg.

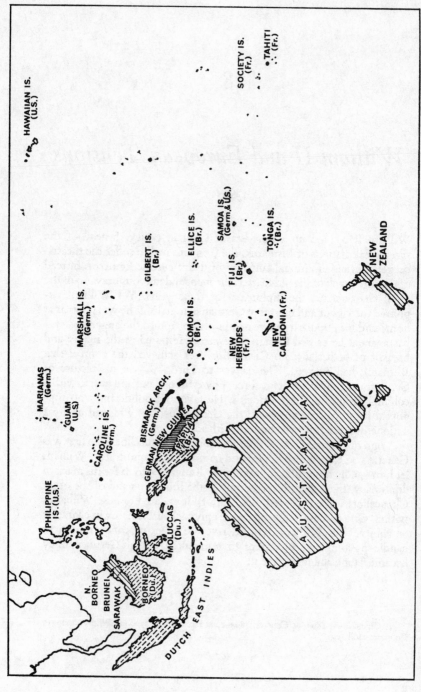

Home Policies

At first the Kaiser followed liberal policies. The repressive laws against the Socialists and racial minorities such as the Poles were relaxed. New regulations limited the hours of work in industry, and an Army Law of 1893 reduced the term of service in the infantry to two years. A series of commercial treaties (1892–94) introduced lower tariffs. But the Kaiser found that opposition, instead of being won over, increased. The Junkers were critical of the new tariffs, and in the elections to the Reichstag in 1893 the Socialists collected forty-four seats. William did not have to worry unduly about the strength of the opposition in the Reichstag, which was powerless to check him. It had no real political strength: Bismarck had seen to that. However, the Kaiser took the warning and halted. The superficial liberal honeymoon was abandoned and until 1914, although a few slight extensions to the social insurance laws were made, conservatism became the guiding policy. The Junkers, the landowners and the industrialists bolstered the Kaiser at the expense of the German working class. The Socialists increased their vote until in 1914 it stood at $4\frac{1}{2}$ millions, but the Kaiser's policies scarcely altered to take heed of the new rising forces.

GERMAN FOREIGN POLICY

The ambitious plans of William II found plenty of supporters. The Navy League, backed by the great shipping firms, and the iron, coal and steel magnates, like Krupp and Stumm, agitated for an increase in German armaments. The Pan-German League, a violent propaganda machine, represented the aggressiveness of large sections of the German people. William listened intently to all these groups. He aimed to make Germany the most dominant country in the world, not only in Europe but in other continents too. He planned to dominate the Atlantic, push German influence beyond the Danube to Turkey, and establish bases and colonies in the Pacific. His actions increased tension, aroused the enmity of England, France and Russia and helped to create the situation in which Europe went to war in 1914. Yet the Kaiser had no real intention of fighting any country. He thought that by his personal friendship with Tsar Nicholas and with Victoria and Edward VII of England he could avoid any dangerous clash of arms. Unfortunately, he was wrong.

The Franco-Russian Alliance

Bismarck had not succeeded in placating Russia, while remaining a close ally of Austria. He had, in 1888, made it clear that Germany's true interests lay with Austria, but he had tried to postpone the break. The Kaiser had no such scruples. He did not renew the Reinsurance Treaty when it expired in 1890.

The Russians distrusted William II even more than they had Bismarck and so, in 1891 and 1893, visits were exchanged by the French and Russian fleets and in December 1893 the entente was translated into a firm alliance. It provided for united action by both Powers if either came under attack by Germany or Austria. The Tsar followed this up with a visit to Paris in 1896. The treaty marked the end of French isolation and the division of Europe into two armed camps, with Britain as yet standing outside.

Yet the new Tsar, Nicholas II, had his pride and his snobbishness. He did not enjoy the link between aristocratic Russia and the plebeian Third Republic. He anxiously fostered good relations with William II in a series of personal meetings. Had William seriously put his mind to it he could have tempted Russia back into the German camp. He did not, and the French, profiting from his failure, loaned Russia large sums of money to finance new railway systems, like the Trans-Siberian and Trans-Caspian railways. French self-confidence increased and there were less bursts of hysteria such as had almost brought General Boulanger to power. The British at first regarded the Franco-Russian alliance with ridicule, quickly followed by fear, when the danger of a link between Britain's traditional enemy, Russia, and one of her greatest colonial rivals, France, was realised.

The Isolation of Britain

Europe, now divided into two armed camps, turned greedy and resentful eyes on Britain's huge Empire. The complicated history of these years reflects an anti-British feeling, largely composed of envy for Britain's prosperity and security, industrial strength and naval power. British policy had been what Lord Salisbury called 'splendid isolation', that is, Britain would keep herself free from any foreign commitments, relying on the Navy to keep out of trouble. The British system of parliamentary democracy meant that secret agreements could not be entered into: all alliances were discussed openly in the House of Commons. Lord Salisbury, like most of the British people, considered that an island position, a large and feared navy and a strong economy made alliances unnecessary. Lastly, foreign agreements might commit Britain to involvement in a European war: most politicians wanted Britain's hands to be free.

In the 1890s this attitude became more closely questioned in Britain as hostility from Europe increased. The French, the Germans, and the Russians all at various times clashed with British interests.

Anglo-German Rivalry

In 1897 Admiral Tirpitz became secretary to the German Naval Department. Given the Kaiser's enthusiastic support,[1] and backed by the propaganda of the German Colonial League and Navy League, the age of naval building began. The Kiel Canal was finished in 1895 and provided a link between the Baltic and North Seas. The Naval Law of 1898 provided for an ambitious expansion of German naval power. In 1900 the Germans flung restraint aside and doubled their construction plans. At first, Britain was not alarmed, but in 1907 the first German *Dreadnought*, a heavy, long-range battleship, was built. In the next year plans were announced for a force of six new cruisers and more Dreadnoughts.

Britain was startled and feared that her own naval shield might now be insufficient. After the German rejection of British suggestions for naval disarmament, put forward at the Hague Conference of 1907, the British retaliated by increasing the number and dimensions of their battleships. The Cabinet added to the strength of the British Dreadnought fleet and kept Britain's nose in front in the race for naval supremacy which continued until 1914.

The rivalry grew bitter in Africa, too. After five years of disputes, Caprivi and Salisbury eventually co-operated in a treaty which drew the borders between German and British territories in East Africa together. In 1890 Britain ceded Heligoland to Germany in exchange for a free hand in Uganda and Zanzibar. Although differences had apparently been patched up at a high level, the bitterness felt over Africa by both Germany and Britain filtered through to the newspapers in both countries, keeping up the feelings of bitter hostility.

The acquisition of Kiao-Chow in 1898 gave the Germans a naval base in China and a foothold for trade. Russia and Britain followed suit with their own bases, and although all three co-operated to crush the Boxer risings in 1900, the rivalries lay just below the surface, for German expansion of bases and trade in the Pacific and China led to direct confrontation with British interests.

In 1898 the Kaiser paid a friendly visit to Constantinople. After him

1. In a speech the Kaiser said, 'our future lies on the sea; I will never rest until I have raised my Navy to a position similar to that occupied by my Army.'

came engineers, soldiers, and merchants to modernise the Turkish railway, military and commercial systems. The construction of the famous Berlin–Baghdad railway was planned and the Turks granted Germany trade concessions. Again, German ambitions seemed to threaten British positions. Turkey, once Britain's ally, now seemed to be turning into a potential enemy, and at a time when British public opinion was horrified by the massacres of the Armenian Christians. In general, by 1907 the German Empire had vastly increased. Huge territories in Africa, bases in the Pacific, new friendships with the Turks, the extension of her trade and navy—all appeared to threaten British interests from Suez to Australia.

These vaguely realised dangers were brought into the open by the Boer War. In 1895 the rivalry between British and Boers in South Africa turned to violence when Dr Jameson, the impetuous lieutenant of Cecil Rhodes, Prime Minister of Cape Colony, launched his ill-planned attack on the Transvaal in the inglorious 'Raid'. Jameson had expected a simultaneous rising by the non-Boers working in Johannesburg and the mines. The affair was mismanaged and Jameson ended up in prison. William II, acting almost as impetuously, and delighted with the reverse Britain had suffered, sent Kruger, President of Transvaal, a telegram in which the Boers were congratulated on expelling 'the armed hordes'.[1] An explosion of anger shook Britain and a naval force put to sea. For the moment William was conciliatory. In 1899, however, the British–Boer rivalry erupted into war. Unexpected passions seized Europe. Sympathy for the 'little Boers', who it was felt were being bullied by Britain, set off demonstrations in France, Russia and Germany. Berlin newspapers violently attacked British policy; Germans went off to volunteer in the Boer armies. Germany and Russia considered joint action but in the end did nothing, for their interests would not be extended by a war, and in any case the British navy controlled all approaches to Africa.

By 1902 splendid isolation had been put to the test. What had saved Britain had been the lack of a common policy between Germany, France and Russia, and their common wish not to become too closely involved in a colonial war. But isolation had been revealed as a threadbare and dangerous policy. Before long, Joseph Chamberlain, the Colonial Secretary, perturbed by the anti-British feeling, turned to Germany and on three occasions, in 1898, 1899 and 1901, tried to negotiate an alliance.[2] German and British interests did not seem

---

1. In fact, 470 mounted men, eight machine-guns, and three artillery pieces.

2. Bismarck had suggested on more than one occasion during the period of British isolation that Britain should join the Triple Alliance, but he had been rejected.

irreconcilable, since in trade and strategy they had common ideas. A combination of German power on land and British at sea seemed a natural alliance. The negotiations failed. In the first place, public opinion in Germany was so vehemently hostile in 1901 that the Kaiser and Bülow did not dare to challenge it. In addition, the differences over South Africa, over naval rivalry, over China, and the German demands for 'compensation', proved all too much. In short, neither country trusted the other.

THE NEW ALIGNMENTS

The Anglo-Japanese Alliance, 1902

Curiously, it was in the Far East that Britain found her first ally. The Boxer Risings, suppressed by the Great Powers in concert, left problems to be solved. In the Yangtse Convention of 1900 Britain and Germany agreed to maintain freedom of trade and to protect the territorial integrity of China, which meant that they hoped to keep Russia out. Germany in bad faith secretly encouraged the Russians to intrigue in North China, knowing that this would annoy Britain. The British found that the Japanese were willing to assist in keeping Russia excluded. Joint talks led to the Alliance of January 1902. Both countries agreed to maintain the status quo in the Far East. Each agreed to help the other if attacked by more than one foe.[1] Japan's objectives were to eject the Russians from Manchuria and consolidate her own hold on Korea. For Britain, it meant an end to a long period without allies. In Europe, however, splendid isolation still held good, with Britain as arbiter between the two armed camps. But not for long, for events soon moved Britain into a European partnership.

Anglo-French Rivalries and the Entente of 1904

Curiously, whereas the Anglo-German rivalry had prevented their alliance, the ill-feeling (much deeper and more dangerous) between France and Britain was overcome. France had been the traditional enemy, and although during the nineteenth century the two nations co-operated at various times, Napoleon's designs on Belgium had prevented the British from going to France's aid in 1870. Gladstone's policy of neutrality, considered a popular and wise move in England, aroused resentment in France.

1. In 1904 Britain was therefore not involved in the war between Russia and Japan.

Most of the bad feeling between the two nations originated in colonial disputes. The French had established colonies in the Pacific, Indo-China and in Africa. Salisbury had in 1878 agreed that France should have a free hand in Algeria and Tunis. Here and in the Niger and Congo regions, French explorers and soldiers claimed huge territories for their country. Clashes with Britain occurred in several of these areas.

The French had always regarded Egypt with keen interest ever since Napoleon I's invasion. In 1869 French money and technical skill had done much to build the Suez Canal. The ruler, the Khedive Ismail, got himself into financial trouble and in 1875 Disraeli purchased his shares in the Suez Canal for Britain. The sale did not save the extravagant Khedive, who was soon deposed by an agreement between Britain and France. The two nations set up a Condominium to take over the management of Egyptian finances, and institute essential reforms. In 1882 an Egyptian colonel, Arabi Pasha, led a national revolt against these foreign intrigues. Riots and murders were followed by an army revolt and soon the British residents were in danger. The two Governments intended sending a joint force, but the French withdrew at the last moment. The British army and navy sailed for Egypt, bombarded Alexandria, invaded and defeated Arabi's army at the battle of Tel-el-Kebir and in the space of a few weeks occupied Egypt. The French, discomfited, continually criticised British policy and administration in the country, feeling that Britain had stolen a march on them. Bismarck exploited this situation to make trouble.

In West Africa, by enlarging territories eastwards from Senegal and north from the Congo, the French effectively prevented the British from extending their line of coastal territories. In 1890 many of the major differences at issue between the British Royal Niger Company and the French colonists were solved in a treaty, but again in 1897 another dispute on the Lower Niger nearly brought the two nations to war. Two years later a convention settled their respective spheres of influence in West Africa.

Shortly after the French had shown their sympathy for the Boers at the time of the Jameson Raid, a trial of strength in the Nile valley again nearly ended in war. The British had found that Egypt presented many problems. In the south, a Moslem fanatic, known as the Mahdi, had unleashed a religious, nationalist rising. In 1884, General Gordon, sent to evacuate the Egyptian garrison in Khartoum, was brutally murdered. Gladstone decided to abandon the Sudan which the Mahdi then ruled peacefully until his death. Kitchener, who had been involved in the abortive rescue attempt of General Gordon in 1884, rose to command the Egyptian Army. He helped to persuade Lord Salisbury of the need to reconquer the Sudan. In 1898 Kitchener advanced southwards from Egypt and after the battle of Omdurman, the city of Khartoum fell into British hands. The Sudan appeared safe.

However, in July 1898 Captain Marchand and five other French officers emerged from the jungle after a heroic march of 3,000 miles from the French Congo. He hoisted the tricolour at Fashoda on the Nile. The British were most sensitive to any foreign influence near the Nile, regarding it as dangerous to their own Egyptian interests. Kitchener immediately marched south with 25,000 men and faced Marchand. The two men, courteous and polite as if they were being introduced in a London drawing-room, obstinately refused to withdraw. They both referred the dispute to their respective governments. In France the crisis reached fever-pitch. Paris newspapers ran headlines like 'War with England'. For six months they stood on the brink of war. Delcassé, the French Foreign Minister, discovered that neither Germany nor Russia would support him, and calculating that Fashoda was not worth a war, ordered Marchand to give way. The French explorers left the Sudan and an Anglo-French Convention (1899) fixed a demarcation line between French and British territories. The Sudan stayed in British hands. Although the two nations had been near war, this agreement and the Niger one in 1897 ended much of the bitter friction.

These disputes in Africa had been dangerous, but after Fashoda, relations steadily improved. Both sides were anxious to remove tension. In May 1903 King Edward VII visited Paris and scored a personal triumph. Boos and catcalls greeted his arrival; 'Vivent les Boers!' followed the next day, but by the time of his departure the French cheered wildly, 'Vive le roi!'. Paul Cambon, the French ambassador in London, worked steadily for an agreement and came to England in July for some hard diplomatic bargaining. On the British side, Lord Lansdowne, the Foreign Secretary, and A. J. Balfour, the Prime Minister, were ready to discuss terms.

The Entente Cordiale, as it was known, was finally agreed to by 1904 and settled most of the remaining difficulties. Britain, already well established in Egypt, gained when France gave up all her claims in this area. Britain in turn recognised the claims of France to influence in Morocco and ceded a scrap of territory in the Gambia region. Spheres of influence were defined in West Africa, Siam, and Newfoundland. The Entente removed the threat of war and settled ancient disputes. It was no military alliance but paved the way for one, although Britain refused to be drawn into military agreements until 1911.

Anglo-Russian Rivalries

During the nineteenth century the Russian bear had been Britain's
most stubborn enemy. In the Balkans, where successive British
Prime Ministers had striven to prevent the Russian advance towards
Constantinople, the hostility almost came to war in 1878. Checked,
the Russians transferred their attentions further to the east, threatening
British interests in India by their dangerous advances in Afghanistan
and Persia. In 1876 the British, to stop Russian penetration, established
military garrisons on the Afghan frontier. In 1885 the Russians returned to the area, seizing Pendjeh, a small town on Afghan territory.
Again, a colonial war seemed imminent and was only narrowly
avoided, although on this occasion at the expense of British prestige.
In the 1890s the Tsar began to extend Russian trade and military
interests in Persia. In the Far East Russia began to nibble at Manchuria,
forcing China to look to Britain for support. In 1904 the Russian
fleet sailing to the Far East accidentally fired on British trawlers in the
North Sea. From the Dogger Bank to Korea, Britain and Russia appeared inveterate foes.

Yet by 1907 they had worked out an amicable agreement. France
helped to smooth over the difficulties and the Russian defeat in the war
against Japan made it appear that Russia was no great military threat, to
India or anywhere else, as had been once imagined. What brought
them together was the growing threat of German military and naval
power. By 1907 they had similar policies with regard to the Balkans,
for Germany was now the favourite in the Turkish Empire. Both, too,
were allies of France. Therefore bearing in mind these factors it is not
surprising that when Sir Edward Grey, the British Foreign Secretary,
made overtures to Russia, his suggestions should be favourably received. In August 1907 the Anglo-Russian Entente was signed, settling
the major differences between them. In Tibet, both Powers agreed to
stop interference and end their search for economic advantages. In
Afghanistan, the British obtained a free hand: Russia promised in
future to leave the province alone. Thus the Russian threat to India was
at last removed. The main agreement concerned Persia which was
rapidly breaking up. It was agreed that Persia should be tri-sected. The
Russians were to have a large area in the north including Teheran as
their sphere of influence. The south-east was to be the British sphere
with the central third remaining independent and neutral under
Persian control. Not a happy arrangement for the Persians, but it satisfied the other two Powers.

By 1907 Britain had thus emerged from her isolation to sign

Ententes with France and Russia. The Triple Entente, as it was called, was not a military alliance but merely arrangements to end existing differences. However, serious crises occurred after 1907 and with Europe divided into two armed camps, the danger of war was never very far away.

THE CRISES, 1905–14

The Morocco Crisis, 1905

In March 1905 the Kaiser interrupted his Mediterranean cruise to land at Tangier. Here he made one of his boastful speeches in which he assured the Sultan of Morocco that Germany recognised the freedom and independence of his country. The Kaiser hoped for commercial gains in Morocco and deliberately chose to embarrass and hamper France. Germany had no real interest in Morocco except a vague hope of trade, but Bülow and William II wanted to test the strength of the Anglo-French Entente. The Kaiser followed up his visit with a demand for an international conference, and dismissed French offers of a joint solution to African problems.

France had been interested in Morocco as a strategical asset, to link up with her other North African territories, but faced by German hostility, thought twice about fighting for it. The French Foreign Minister. Delcassé, favoured defiance, but found that the Premier, Rouvier, and the entire Cabinet were against him, convinced that neither Britain nor Russia would come to the support of France. Delcassé resigned, a considerable victory for German pressure and bluff.

Before the conference met at Algeciras in January 1906, Britain came to the rescue of France. The British Government had no wish to see a German naval base established on the Atlantic coast of Africa. The General Staffs of the two armies held discussions on military and naval co-operation in the event of war. Thus the Moroccan crisis strengthened the Entente, whereas Germany had hoped to weaken it. At the Conference, Germany found herself outvoted, for Russia, Britain, the USA and Italy all backed the French. Only Austria-Hungary and Morocco supported Germany. The Conference decided that Morocco should remain independent, but France and Spain were given a joint responsibility over police and customs. Germany had been given a rude and unexpected rebuff. The Triple Alliance had proved a sore disappointment to the Kaiser, for Italy had rejected her allies, and the Entente drew closer together. The Kaiser looked for a diplomatic counter-attack elsewhere to recover his dwindling prestige in Germany.

Naval rivalry

In the two years after 1906 the Anglo-Russian Entente added to the Kaiser's difficulties. Almost in pique, the Germans stepped up their naval armaments. The Navy League warned the Kaiser that lack of seapower would lead to further snubs by the other Powers. In 1906 the British launched the *Dreadnought*, the first of a new class of battleships which out-classed other ships in speed and firepower. These Dreadnoughts were expensive but they made older ships obsolete and so the British felt they had to build some to maintain their naval supremacy. The Germans copied the design and in 1907 Tirpitz published an ambitious naval programme with the Kaiser's blessing, making provision for a German Dreadnought fleet.

In 1908 the *Daily Telegraph* published an interview with the Kaiser, in which he claimed to have restrained France and Russia from intervening in the Boer War and said he had devised the military tactics which the British had used to win the war. Few people in Britain believed him, taking it as an indication of the Kaiser's unscrupulous methods of causing suspicion among his enemies. This was confirmed in 1909 when Germany began to catch up in the Dreadnought race, rejecting all British proposals for naval disarmament. The Liberal Government in England preferred to spend money on social reform, but had to bow to popular hysteria. When it was announced that six more Dreadnoughts were to be built, the refrain, 'we want eight, and we won't wait', forced Lloyd George to increase taxes to pay for the additional ships. In fact, by 1912 Britain had built a force of eighteen Dreadnoughts to Germany's nine so Germany still lagged behind. But the naval race which no one but the Germans wanted had heightened the rivalry between the two countries.

The Agadir Crisis, 1911

Almost every year brought a fresh crisis, a fresh danger of a European war. In 1908 the Young Turk revolution in Turkey provoked Austria into annexing Bosnia-Herzegovina. The Serbs protested and tried to persuade Russia to fight the Austrians. The Tsar, worried by Russian weakness shown in the Russo-Japanese war, surrendered to what virtually amounted to a German ultimatum.

In the same year, the French occupied Casablanca and arrested several German deserters from the Foreign Legion. Germany demanded a French apology and in 1909 the dispute was referred to the International Court at the Hague, which announced that France had acted legally, in line with the police powers given in 1906. As a sop to German pride the French Government allowed equal economic opportunities for German traders in Morocco. The French had no intention of letting the country slip from their grasp, and in April 1911 French troops occupied Fez, the capital city. The Germans decided to force the issue, possibly for colonial or economic gains, possibly to try to split the Entente again. In July 1911 the German gunboat, *Panther*, entered the harbour of Agadir. The action aroused the latent suspicions of Britain: here seemed direct evidence of the German desire to create an east Atlantic naval base. Lloyd George in a speech at the Mansion House, London, made a challenging statement that Britain would strive 'at all hazards to maintain her place and her prestige'. The spectre of an aroused angry Britain deterred Germany. No one wanted war and the Kaiser announced that the *Panther* had only sailed to protect German interests. Both sides had again been at the brink of war, for during the two months of September–October 1911 the Great Powers had begun to mobilise their armies.

Late in October there was a panic among international bankers, especially those operating in Berlin, and this helped to bring the German Government to its senses. In November, Morocco became a French protectorate, with a special zone allotted to Spain. In return, Germany added some scraps of territory in the Congo to her colony in the Cameroons.

The Germans had made an error of calculation over Agadir. They had not anticipated the menacing repercussions in Britain, and like Russia in 1909, had withdrawn at the last moment. But hatred of Britain mounted in Germany, and heated speakers in the Reichstag demanded that next time Germany should stand firm. In a future crisis, if German interests and not just prestige were threatened, a retreat from the brink would be unlikely. There could be no repetition of the humiliation of 1911.

In 1912 Europe began to make preparations for war. Admiral Tirpitz stepped up German naval armament and had the Kiel Canal widened for the new Dreadnoughts. France increased the period of military service to three years and co-operated more closely with Britain on military strategy in the event of war. Russia improved her railways and overhauled her ramshackle army.

The Outbreak of War, 1914

In 1912 and 1913 the Balkan Wars created an electric tension in south-east Europe. At the end of 1913 Austria-Hungary and Serbia stood toe to toe. All that Austria needed was a favourable opportunity backed by German support and Serbia could be crushed.

On 28 June 1914 Archduke Franz Ferdinand and his wife were murdered by Serb revolutionaries at Sarajevo. Princip, the student who fired the fatal shots, had no connection with the Serb government, but Austria saw the episode as a chance to destroy Serbia. The Kaiser, in one of his more foolish moments, pledged German support, apparently not appreciating or perhaps ignoring Russian pledges to Serbia. A month passed, and then on 23 July Austria-Hungary delivered a ten-point ultimatum which demanded compensation and the right of Austrian troops to occupy Serbian territory. Serbia had forty-eight hours grace. She desperately agreed to eight of the points, offering to put the other two to arbitration. Austria ignored the peace offer and on 28 July declared war. The Kaiser and his Chancellor, Bethmann-Hollweg, worried by the turn of events, warned Austria against provoking a total war. However, the Austrian war machine had already begun to grind into action and in any case the Vienna government coolly calculated that Germany would support them.

It is hard not to argue that the Great Powers then drifted into war. On 30 July Russia mobilised her armies while France and Britain were still pressing for a peaceful settlement, perhaps by a conference. But the Tsar did not dare back out of his promises to the Serbs, as he had in 1909. Germany demanded that Russian mobilisation should be cancelled and when rejected, immediately swung into a general mobilisation. Russia, by quoting the agreement of 1893, persuaded France to mobilise. Brandishing their weapons the nations went to war. On 1 August 1914 Germany declared war on Russia and on 3 August, on France.

British Intervention

Great Britain had no agreement that brought her automatically into the war. The Foreign Secretary, Sir Edward Grey, had been striving to end the Serbian-crisis since the assassination. The Germans considered that Britain, having failed to find a peaceful solution, might stay neutral. Some historians have blamed Sir Edward Grey for the war, arguing that if he had warned Germany earlier that Britain would intervene, fighting would never have started. This is foolish, for Grey could not have involved Britain in that way without Parliamentary consent, and in any case the German High Command had already decided on a strike through Belgium and had chosen to disregard the British Army as a puny force which could not hold a swift German advance.

On 4 August German troops invaded Belgium. In the Treaty of London, 1839, Britain had guaranteed Belgian neutrality and independence. Grey, supported by Parliament, sent an ultimatum, asking Germany to withdraw. Britain declared war on Germany when the ultimatum was rejected.

It seems on the surface as if Britain went to war in a vain attempt to save Belgium. There was a great deal more to it than this, however. British policy had traditionally been to prevent any continental Power dominating the Channel coastline. In addition, by a Naval Convention signed in 1912 the British Navy was committed to defend the North Sea and Channel, while the French patrolled the Mediterranean. So, in fact, Britain did not have a free hand in 1914 at all; with either German troops in Belgium or German ships in the Channel Britain was bound to become involved.

In any case, Germany and Britain had a few scores to settle themselves. Since 1900, events in South Africa, Turkey and the Balkans, North Africa and the Pacific had brought the two countries into a head-on clash on several occasions. Naval rivalry had increased the tension; Belgium was the last straw.

THE CAUSES OF THE GREAT WAR

Ever since 1914 controversy has raged on the question of responsibility. Who was to blame? Within Europe, two great rival groups of Powers, linked by alliances and armed to the teeth, glowered at each other. But the alliances did not cause the war, and indeed did not make war inevitable. Not one of the Powers entered the war *because* of an alliance; they all had more specific reasons. The war was not necessary: it could have been avoided. Why, then, did it happen?

Some historians have blamed the arms race, pointing out that in a desperate situation like 1914 those nations at a peak of military readiness like Germany are inclined to act ruthlessly. Others point out that re-armament was only one aspect of the economic rivalry between the Great Powers. Germany and Britain, producing similar manufactured goods, were competing in the world markets. However, although there is evidence that the German High Command favoured a quick war in 1914, there is no trace of any businessmen, in any nation, putting pressure on their governments, unless it was to keep the peace.

Nationalism is another vague concept which has been blamed. It has been said that subject peoples living under German, Russian and Austrian rule erupted into revolt against their oppressors in 1914. The only evidence of this lies in the Serb-Austrian rivalry. Austria-Hungary was anti-nationalist, and blamed Serbia for stirring up trouble among the Slavs living in her southern provinces. Austria faced the alternatives of destroying the Slav menace or giving her own eight million Slavs a share in government. The Austrians chose the former course. Otherwise, nowhere else in Europe did nationalism lead directly to war, unless it contributed to the German passion to play the part of a world power, and the French patriotism which bled at the thought of Alsace-Lorraine.

The answer, like the problem, is complex. All these factors—nationalism, economic and colonial rivalry, the system of alliances, the arms race, and dreams of grandeur and prestige harboured by statesmen of all nations—they all contributed in their various ways to causing the war. But in the last resort it was the ambitions of the politicians and soldiers, in command in 1914, which led directly to the battlefields. Russian intrigue in the Balkans, Serbian support for Slav nationalism, the desperate Austrian attempt at recovery, German militarism and French hopes of recovering Alsace-Lorraine all helped to create an explosive situation. Mixed together and brought to the boil, these varied factors created political tension, needing only a spark to cause an eruption into war.

Another factor was the arms race. Germany had led and dominated the race, alarming and stimulating the other nations into following her example. By July 1914 effective control of German policy had fallen into the hands of the generals. The Kaiser complained of 'encirclement' by the Entente but his own aggressive policies had helped to create the circle of foes which surrounded Germany. Not only that, but he listened more and more to the advice of his generals who suggested an early war, while Germany had the advantage of readiness. The only answer to this problem lay in disarmament, but talks at the Hague conferences had broken down.

Each nation has at one time or another been pilloried. Some historians have written that the French started the war to recover Alsace-Lorraine. This is difficult to believe, for the French knew that a war, which they would be more likely to lose than to win, would be fought on their soil. They feared a repetition of 1870.

Britain and France argued that they entered the war to defend themselves. If France was destroyed, the Russians and the British could only expect further German aggression, so all three Powers of the Entente fought to prevent German domination of Europe.

Russian policy had been ambitious and dangerous but after the fiasco of the war against Japan in 1905 she stood revealed as militarily weak. Yet Russia still interfered in the Balkans, supported Serbia and mobilised first. The Tsar must bear some of the responsibility. He thought a short, victorious war might solve his difficulties within Russia and therefore he did not draw back as he had in 1909. Austria has been accused of striking the match. Arrogant and desperate, her statesmen provoked the Serbian war, regardless or careless of the consequences.

Finally, what of Germany? In 1919 in the Treaty of Versailles the victorious Allies fixed the war-guilt firmly on German shoulders. It is true that the Kaiser by his delusions of grandeur had provoked a series of crises, but William II did not deliberately plan for a war in 1914. Yet he seemed powerless to stop it, for he lost control to the German General Staff. If a real villain is wanted, Moltke seems the man, but this is to distort history. All the Powers and their statesmen must bear the shame of thrusting Europe into a terrible war.

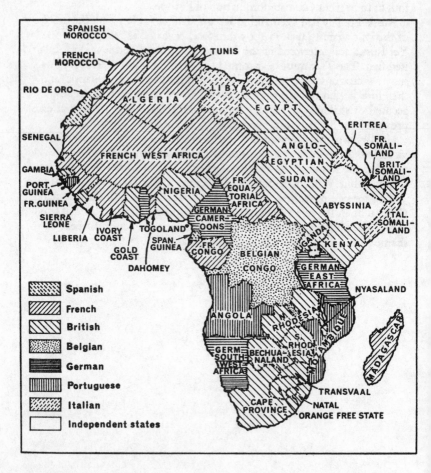

12   The Partition of Africa

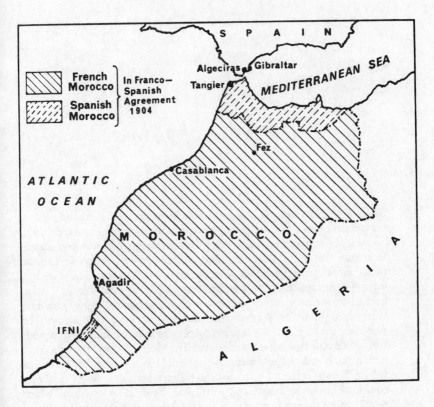

13   The Partition of Morocco, 1904

9

The War of 1914-18

❈❈

Seven European nations began the war in August 1914. At the time of the armistice in November 1918 thirty nations were involved in the fighting. New recruits joined, other Powers staggered away, exhausted. Germany was in 1914 the strongest military power, with two million men under arms (doubled after peak mobilisation). The German infantry, equipped with Maxim machine-guns and Mauser rifles, backed by artillery and supplied by a highly organised railway system, were thought to have twice the efficiency of any other army. The Austrians mustered half a million men in 1914 but suffered from poor staff work and lack of national unity. The German-Austrian officers in their army could not be understood by their Hungarian or Czech soldiers.

The French army of a million men (later increased to six million), equipped with the famous 75 mm. gun, boasted of an 'élan' which would carry them to victory against superior odds, but they were led by elderly cavalry-conscious generals. Russia in 1914 mobilised one and a half million hardy, brave men, the 'steam-roller' of legend. In action deficiencies of artillery, ammunition, and supplies, and the incompetence of officers meant that the infantry suffered as helpless cannon-fodder, until they broke and fled in 1917. Britain had a small army, for she had put her trust and her money in a large navy, but, by the end of the war as a result of conscription and volunteers from the Empire, nearly six million men served in her armies.

All of these forces relied on the horse for transport: motor transport and aviation had not yet been harnessed. Aeroplanes were unreliable contraptions of wire and wood, capable of speeds up to 70 m.p.h., but of little use apart from reconnaissance. Tanks were virtually unknown. The generals of 1914 expected the heavy gun and the cavalry to be the decisive factors: in fact, the machine gun proved to be king.

THE WESTERN FRONT

1914

On 1 August 1914 Germany declared war on Russia, and two days later, on France. No one expected it to be a long war. The wars of 1866, 1870, and 1912–13 had been short. The Germans therefore thought the first campaigns would be decisive. In 1905 General von Schlieffen had prepared for an early victory. Although he had died in 1912 his spirit continued to infect the German General Staff. The 'Schlieffen Plan' envisaged war on two fronts. Germany's task was to deal a knock-out blow to France in the west before Russia mobilised her vast armies in the east. The French defences from Belfort to Verdun were considered impregnable, with no possibility there of a quick victory. Schlieffen therefore advocated a thrust through Belgium to outflank the French fortifications, followed by a massive sweeping advance west and south of Paris, trapping the French armies and destroying them between the two German armies, one advancing from Lorraine and the other like a scythe sweeping from the west.

The Plan was modified by von Moltke, in 1914 the Chief of the German General Staff. Worried by the promised French tactics of 'toujours l'attaque' he had strengthened the German forces in Lorraine and during the course of the first few weeks of the war moved troops to the Russian border to counter Russia's unexpectedly early mobilisation. The 'Schlieffen' divisions had been the losers.

On 4 August the German armies rolled into Belgium. Only the small Belgian army barred their way. After one or two reverses, it retired to the fortress of Antwerp, but valuable time had been gained for the Allies. Liège held out briefly: after an artillery bombardment General Ludendorff drove through the main gate of the city in a motor car to receive its surrender. The Belgians wrecked their railway lines which stopped the flow of German troops and supplies. Moltke's infantry pressed forward on foot. General Kluck, commander of the First Army, marched his men at a terrific pace, up to thirty miles a day, covered by 17 inch howitzers. Brussels fell on 20 August.

Earlier, on 14 August, the French had launched their counter-offensive. One army struck at the flank of the Germans advancing through the Ardennes and another moved into Lorraine. Both attacks were disastrous: the French lost heavily, for their best officers and soldiers died in a headlong rush against German machine guns. The French fell back, in confusion. In Belgium Moltke's juggernaut rolled on.

The 160,000 men of the British Expeditionary Force landed in northern France and by 22 August had advanced north to Mons in the direct line of the German advance. Kluck's First Army blundered into the British who fought bravely, but after several days had to fall back. Now French and British armies streamed southward, handicapped by terror-stricken refugees swarming along the roads. The German impetus slowed, for their troops were tired after their long march.

At this point the character of the campaign changed. General 'Papa' Joffre reorganised the shattered remnants of the French armies. He dismissed dozens of incompetent generals, promoted men of ability and strengthened his forces to the east of Paris, along the river Marne. Joffre turned Paris into a military stronghold, commanded by a veteran of the colonial wars, General Galliéni. Sir John French, commander of the BEF, moved into position on the left of the Allied line. Paris proved to be the great flaw in the German strategy. If Kluck went west of the city while Bülow and the 2nd Army travelled east, the danger of a French wedge became all too obvious. Kluck therefore switched the line of his advance and linked up with Bülow to march on, east of Paris.

On 5 September Kluck, rash and bull-headed, crossed the Marne. He was largely out of touch with the commander in chief, Moltke, whose HQ was still in Luxemburg. At this point, Joffre stayed his retreat, turned, and counter-attacked. Galliéni moved his garrison from Paris to strike at the exposed flank of the German army. Parisian taxi-cabs and buses were seized to transport troops to the front. So began the battle of the Marne. The French discovered a gap between the two German armies and drove a wedge between them. The Germans grew increasingly anxious. On the eighth day of the battle General Foch sent Joffre a famous telegram:

'Hard pressed on my right. My centre is yielding. Impossible to manoeuvre. Situation excellent. I attack.'

The French were indeed close to a disastrous defeat. They were saved by German indecision. Moltke, nervous, kept asking 'where are the prisoners, the captured guns?' German reports indicated that the revised Schlieffen Plan had petered out and that the German armies were in danger of annihilation. The general retreat began. The German infantry retraced their steps over ground that had been occupied at heavy cost. The Allied advance lasted for five days, driving the Germans back to the river Aisne. Moltke reported to the Kaiser: 'We have lost the war.' As a reward he was replaced by General Falkenhayn.

By 14 September the German troops, exhausted by their retreat, had flung themselves to the ground, dug holes, and set up machine guns. The Allied armies halted at the Aisne, and also dug in. The war of movement had ended. Trench warfare had begun. The Allies tried to break through with massive artillery bombardments and by throwing in their reserves of infantry. The Germans dug more deeply and repulsed the infantry attacks. The generals gazed at the trenches and thought of the obvious solution—outflank the enemy. So began the 'race to the sea' although Falkenhayn's objective was not the sea but to outflank the French. The gallant Belgians still held out in Antwerp. Neither Joffre nor Kitchener, the British Secretary for War, would send help. Winston Churchill, then at the Admiralty, despatched 3,000 marines to Antwerp but too late to save the city which fell on 10 October. However, Falkenhayn's attention had been diverted, giving Joffre time to send his troops racing to the north-west. At Ypres the British and German armies slaughtered each other in the mud but made no progress. Ypres ended the big battles of 1914. Now both sides dug trenches, erected barbed wire barricades and mounted machine guns. Already the French had suffered over a million casualties and the majority of the BEF had fallen at Ypres. Germany had lost many of her best soldiers in the failure to reach Paris. The war was beginning to take its terrible toll.

1915

The Western Front stretched from the sea to Switzerland. The French hated the thought of Germans occupying their northern provinces and Joffre gave orders for offensives to be launched to probe for weaknesses and then drive through the enemy line by sheer force and verve. The French attacked in the Champagne area gaining yards and losing thousands of men in the process. At Neuve Chapelle, Sir John French lost over 3,000 soldiers an hour in a series of insensate charges. At Ypres the Germans used chlorine gas which choked and killed as it wafted down on the Allied lines. From February to September the killing continued, to end in deadlock and exhaustion.

The generals could not solve the impasse: the civilian governments of France and Britain, horrified by the slaughter, could do nothing but trust the generals. When they failed, like Sir John French, they were replaced. Sir Douglas Haig, the new British commander, could do no better. Churchill and Lloyd George thought that a back door could be found to Germany. A debate blew up between the 'westerners', those like Haig who thought the war would be won in France, and 'easterners' like Churchill who believed that from Turkey, or Salonika in Greece, or Italy, offensives could be mounted to knock out Austria and Turkey. A. J. P. Taylor has called these side-shows 'cigar-butt strategy'.

Politicians stuck their cigars at a map and decided to attack at this or that spot. These assaults only distracted attention from the Western Front where the French, suspicious of British designs elsewhere, had to bear the brunt of the fighting.

1916

The generals tried desperately to break the stalemate. New volunteer and conscript armies were raised and thrown into the battles. Industry worked at great speed to produce guns and shells. Massive artillery barrages blasted holes in enemy lines, and columns of infantry dashed forward in vain attempts to break through. All attacks finally petered out in failure. The shells churned up the battle area into a sea of mud and craters filled with water. The infantry floundered and were cut down by machine guns. As each side acquired gas masks, poison gas ceased to be decisive. The Germans used Zeppelins[1] and aeroplanes to bomb the trenches but damage was slight. The only way out of the impasse was for one side to wear the other down.

Joffre and Haig, however, still believed a break-through was possible. They chose the Somme and preparations began. Meanwhile, Falkenhayn had decided that the only way to destroy the Allies was by attrition, that is, to bleed the French army white by constant bombardment and attack. He chose Verdun at the head of a dangerous salient projecting into German lines. Verdun could have been evacuated but it became a matter of French pride to hold it. In February 1916 the Germans launched a series of terrible barrages, battering the French into insensibility. Pétain, the Commander at Verdun, coined the phrase 'They shall not pass'. Every inch was contested. French troops poured into the salient along a road named 'the Sacred Way' constantly under German fire. By June the French had suffered 315,000 casualties. But the Germans suffered too. The Kaiser thought the capture of the city a dazzling prize worth any price. The price was 280,000 casualties.

At the end of 1916 the French army had almost broken: regiments were on the verge of mutiny. But Verdun was held, and the French hailed it as a victory, one of the few they could celebrate. On the Somme, the Germans had dug into strong positions defended by barbed wire and iron stakes. In July, Haig battered these lines for five days, then sent in the infantry along a fifteen mile front. The German machine guns opened up on the British as they swarmed across 'No Man's Land'. 60,000 men fell on the first day of the battle but the attack continued. An advance of five miles encouraged Haig to send in the cavalry. The

1. Named after Count von Zeppelin, the inventor of the airship, a self-propelled balloon inflated with a gas lighter than air.

machine guns massacred them. The few tanks available were thrust forward, but as no infantry followed them, the advantage was lost. By November the battle petered out, a grim, dismal defeat.

The heads toppled. Kitchener, on his way to Russia in the cruiser *Hampshire*, died when the ship struck a mine and sank. The Kaiser moved Falkenhayn to the Rumanian front and brought in Hindenburg and Ludendorff who between them constructed the impregnable defence works known as the 'Hindenburg Line'. Joffre, too, lost power. General Nivelle replaced him as commander-in-chief on the Western Front. Sir Douglas Haig continued as British commander but under a new Prime Minister, for in December 1916 Lloyd George replaced Asquith.

1917

The new men promised knock-out blows. General Nivelle boasted that by a ruthless and violent offensive he could evict the Germans from northern France. Briand, the French Premier, in desperation swallowed Nivelle's promises. Ludendorff, meanwhile, withdrew twenty miles from the exposed Noyon salient to the new defensive position on the Hindenburg Line. The Germans left a desolate area—houses wrecked, wells poisoned, roads mined. Nivelle ignored the hazards and in April launched his offensive. The British and Canadians attacked at Arras, advanced two to five miles and captured Vimy Ridge. Nivelle mounted an 11 million shell onslaught but 120,000 of his men fell in capturing a few hundred yards. The attack ended and Nivelle was dismissed in disgrace. Pétain, the 'Saviour of Verdun' assumed command. He was faced with a mutiny in the French army, sick of the futile bloodshed. Pétain struggled to restore discipline by executing fifty-five of the ringleaders and by arranging more leave and better food. 1917 was spent by the French resting, recuperating. Britain, her conscript armies flooding into France, had to take over the burden of the war. At Ypres, Haig mounted attack after attack. The Messines Ridge was taken but in the terrible battle of Passchendaele the infantry had to advance into steady drenching rain. One Colonel wrote:

'Wounded men falling headlong into shell holes were in danger of drowning. Guns sank till they became useless; rifles caked and would not fire; even food was tainted with the inevitable mud.'

The assault failed and again the war settled into deadlock. In April 1917 the USA had entered the war. Unprepared, it took time for America's levies, commanded by General Pershing, to be raised, trained and transported to Europe. However, their arrival in Europe was to transform the war. The Germans, aware of the new threat, moved troops from the Eastern Front, where Russia had made peace in March 1918, and prepared for a new onslaught.

1918

Ludendorff made his last, desperate throw. Food supplies were running short in Germany; American troops were on their way; his allies were creaking. Ludendorff, however, had nothing new to offer Germany. He had neglected to build sufficient tanks and aeroplanes, and in terms of men the two sides in northern France were roughly equal. He decided to try new tactics. His artillery remained silent. Small groups of infantry made sudden attacks, probing for weaknesses, then when they found one, several divisions bludgeoned their way forward. The biggest assault came in fog, on the Somme. The Germans advanced fourteen miles in four days, astonishing by the standards of the war.

In this crisis all French and British troops were at last put under one unified command, that of General Foch. He threw in his reserves to hold the line. Lloyd George sent all available soldiers from Britain and appealed to the USA for more men. Ludendorff's offensive ran into stiffer resistance. He persisted, killing thousands of his men in the process. However, the Germans found another gap, held by a demoralised Portuguese division. Ludendorff drove south to a depth of thirty miles. To add to the horror, a giant German gun began to lob 8 inch shells a distance of sixty miles into Paris. In May 1918 the third sledge-hammer blow, on the Aisne, drove back the French. The Germans were almost through to Paris. 'Ils ne passeront pas' again became the rallying cry. The Germans were held at the Marne, with American troops assisting the Allies in a series of bitter battles.

In July came Foch's turn. The first blows were against the salients Ludendorff had driven into the Allied lines. German losses increased and morale began to weaken: recruits moving up to the front were met with shouts of derision from veterans and wounded. In August the Allies battered their way forward, recovering the ground lost earlier and advancing across the Hindenburg Line. By then the Americans had 500,000 men in the field. With new enthusiasm and a sense of victory they hammered at the Germans: the whole Allied line moved forward for the first time in four years. The advance accelerated across the Argonne Forest. Germany suddenly collapsed: Ludendorff realised that he could not stave off defeat and advised the Kaiser to make peace. He then resigned, on 22 October. Bulgaria, Turkey and Austria hastily asked for terms. On 11 November, in a railroad carriage at Compiègne, the German delegation signed an armistice of defeat.

THE WAR AT SEA

The responsibilities of the British Navy were world-wide. In 1914 the Grand Fleet immediately mounted a blockade, forcing Germany to trade through her neighbours, Holland, Sweden and Denmark. Most of Germany's shipping was swept from the seas, but to enforce the blockade the Royal Navy had to patrol from Norway to Gibraltar. Admiral Jellicoe had to keep the greater part of his fleet stationed at Scapa Flow, in case the powerful German North Sea fleet ventured from its bases at Kiel and Wilhelmshaven. German tactics were to make sudden forays into the North Sea and Atlantic to catch unwary detachments of the British fleet, or to bombard coastal towns. The British had to keep a large fleet in the North Sea on permanent watch. Besides these tasks, the Royal Navy ferried troops across the Channel, and to Egypt, Gallipoli and Africa; protected convoys; patrolled the Pacific and Atlantic Oceans and hunted for German submarines and surface raiders along the shipping lanes.

In August 1914 the British struck the first blow. A force of battle cruisers, commanded by the energetic Sir David Beatty, raided Heligoland Bight, surprised and sank four ships of a German patrol. The Russians acquired possession of a set of ciphers and passed them on to the British who, until the Germans changed their codes, were able to decode radio messages and plot enemy movements. The information failed to prevent a disastrous encounter between a German submarine, *U.9* and three old cruisers, *Aboukir*, *Crécy* and *Hogue*. All three British ships were sunk in an hour, for when the *Aboukir* was torpedoed, the other two ships stopped to pick up survivors. The *U.9* picked them off like sitting ducks. 1,400 seamen died and the Navy learnt a lesson: destroy the enemy before looking for survivors.

The Germans seized on the value of the submarine, although they possessed few in 1914. In October the dreadnought *Audacious* sank after hitting a mine laid by a submarine. In retaliation, Britain declared the whole of the North Sea to be a military area: neutral ships were stopped, searched, and if bound for Germany, diverted to British ports. To counter the British tactics the German High Seas fleet made its first move. A squadron left port, bombarded Hartlepool and

Scarborough, killing 120 civilians, and escaped unscathed.

Germany had several cruisers based in foreign waters. The *Königsburg* did some damage to Allied shipping in the Indian Ocean and was then trapped up-river in East Africa. The *Emden* sank many vessels in the Pacific before being caught and destroyed by the Australian cruiser *Sydney*. Admiral von Spee collected five remaining cruisers, *Nürnburg, Gneisenau, Scharnhorst, Leipzig* and *Dresden* and sailed for the coast of Chile, to re-coal. The British, in the Nelson spirit, but without his strategic skill, sent a hastily organised and inferior force under Admiral Cradock. Off Coronel, Chile, Admiral Spee out-manoeuvred the slow British ships. Cradock and his crew died on board the *Good Hope* which exploded in a sheet of flame. Another cruiser, *Monmouth*, capsized and sank. The Germans had two men wounded.

Churchill at the Admiralty authorised Admiral Sturdee to sail at once from England with the battle cruisers *Inflexible* and *Invincible* and concentrated other ships of the South Atlantic force at the Falkland Islands. Incredibly, Spee rounded the Cape and sailed into the trap. The British fleet, coaling and repairing, were surprised. Spee, missing the opportunity to attack, ran for the open sea. Sturdee gave chase, caught and destroyed the whole force. Only the *Dresden* escaped, to be caught and sunk three months later.

The German outposts, Kiao-Chow and the Caroline and Marshall Islands, were occupied by the Japanese, who entered the war for territorial booty. Their bases and fleet lost, the German threat in the Pacific ended.

In January 1915 a German squadron put to sea, to be intercepted by Beatty. In the battle of the Dogger Bank two large cruiser and destroyer fleets pounded each other at a distance of several miles, ending when the Germans ran for Heligoland. The Kaiser decided to keep his fleet intact in harbour, and use submarines to harry the British. On 7 May the *U.20* sank the *Lusitania*, an unarmed passenger liner. Over 1,000 died, including 115 Americans. The sinking horrified world opinion and raised a storm in America. Germany ignored the warnings and increased her toll of Allied shipping. Admiral Scheer, the new Commander of the German Navy, proposed a more daring policy and in 1916 took his fleet to sea.

Jutland, 1916

In May 1916 Admiral Scheer sent out his cruisers, under Admiral Hipper, to entice the British battlecruisers into action. He hoped to split the British fleet and destroy it piece by piece. Using the captured codes, the British followed every move. Jellicoe steamed south from

Scapa Flow to set his own trap. The North Sea was crammed with ships. Britain had superior forces; nine battlecruisers, 112 cruisers and destroyers and twenty-eight dreadnoughts to Germany's sixteen dreadnoughts, five battlecruisers, and seventy-eight cruisers and destroyers.

Beatty, sent ahead with a scouting party, opened fire on Hipper at 3.48 pm on 31 May. Hipper changed course to draw Beatty back on to the main German force. The British gamely gave chase and were mauled, losing two ships, when the *Indefatigable* blew up in a terrible sheet of flame and the *Queen Mary* disappeared after an explosion. Beatty then turned away, apparently in flight, but to tempt Scheer on to Jellicoe's ships. At 6.15 pm the two armadas joined battle at between 11,000 and 15,000 yards. Scheer saw the trap and veered off. Jellicoe, cautious, did not pursue. He thought it more important to preserve the British Navy intact than chance defeat. Suddenly, thirty minutes later, Scheer, who had gone to the assistance of a sinking cruiser, the *Wiesbaden*, again ran into Jellicoe's fleet. The guns crashed and Scheer turned to the south, launching a last defiant torpedo attack. The battle of Jutland was over.

Germany claimed it as a victory. Britain's fleet had been battered, with over 6,000 men killed and fourteen ships sunk. The Germans had lost 2,500 men and eleven ships. British gunnery had been inferior and British armour weaker. Jellicoe had been too cautious, Beatty too daring. Germany may have gained in terms of prestige but lost in terms of power. In effect, the real victory was Jellicoe's for Scheer did not again bring his fleet out to sea until the surrender of 1919.

Another consequence of Jutland was that the blockade tightened. Within Germany, Chancellor Bethmann favoured a negotiated peace. Ludendorff, on the other hand, wanted a tougher line, unrestricted submarine warfare. Bethmann calculated that this would bring the USA into the war. His attempts to find a peace settlement in December 1916 failed, and he could not prevent the introduction of unrestricted warfare on 31 January 1917. All shipping (including neutral) was to be sunk on sight in the War Zone of the eastern Atlantic, fringing Britain's shores. Several ships were sunk immediately. In addition, Zimmerman, a German Minister, offered to help Mexico in a war against the USA. The message was intercepted and stung the USA into a declaration of war against Germany on 6 April.

The Germans came near to defeating Britain at sea. One out of every four ships leaving British ports was sunk. In April 1917 alone over a million tons of shipping was lost. Lloyd George had a solution: convoys. He fought the obstinate refusal of the Admiralty, overruled their objections, and instituted convoys. Almost immediately, the rate of sinkings fell, eventually reaching only one per cent of the total shipping at sea. Allied destroyers and cruisers fortified by contingents of the American fleet formed a protective ring around the convoys. The 140 U boats patrolling the routes became more desperate as their casualties mounted and their victims decreased.

Even so, rationing of meat and butter had to be introduced into Britain in February 1918, when the danger was past its peak. To deal a blow at the U boat packs by blocking up their lairs, the Dover barrage, composed of nets and mines, and patrolled by destroyers, was erected at one end of the Channel. Another barrage from the Orkneys to Norway was planned but never fully laid. Admiral Sir Roger Keyes took five old cruisers filled with concrete, escorted by seventy other ships, sailed to Zeebrugge and sank the blockships in the harbour entrance. The passage was not quite closed, and in any case German submarines rarely used the harbour, but it was a brave and adventurous enterprise.

Throughout 1918 the submarine threat was gradually brought under control. Within the German fleet cases of indiscipline became more frequent, culminating in the mutiny of October 1918.

THE EASTERN FRONT

In the East, Russia launched an offensive before mobilisation was fully complete. Two armies crossed Poland and drove into East Prussia. The Germans had only one army whose commander lost his nerve and retreated. General Hindenburg, dug out of retirement, took over supreme command with a younger man, Erich Ludendorff, as his Chief of Staff. The Germans gave one Russian army the slip and destroyed the other at the battle of Tannenburg (August 1914). 90,000 Russian prisoners were taken. The offensive halted, turned and fled. Russian troops, harried by Germans, evacuated East Prussia.

To the south in Galicia the Austrian commander, Conrad, flung his armies at the Russians. The result was a confused struggle ending in Austrian retreat. The Ludendorff-Hindenburg combination moved into action, switching men in 750 trains to assist the Austrians and block a Russian attack on Silesia. Grand Duke Nicholas forced the Russian steam-roller forward, to be bludgeoned and halted again. By the end of 1914 a 'front line' stretching from the Baltic to Austria had been established, although it was never as solid as in the west.

In January 1915 the Kaiser reinforced his eastern armies, believing a break-through to be possible. Conrad launched his offensive in Galicia, advanced a few miles and stopped. Further north, in Poland, von Mackensen and Hindenburg fired 18,000 tear gas shells against the Russians in the battle of the Masurian Lakes. Panic-stricken, the Russians fell back, but a heavy snowstorm bogged down the German advance. To replace the thousands of men killed the Russians brought forward apparently inexhaustible supplies of men from their reserves. However, many had no rifles and relied on picking them up from dead soldiers. Guns were rationed to four shells a day. Behind them, the supply system was in chaos. In May, the Germans made another offensive and advanced eastwards a distance of a hundred miles. 200,000 Russians were herded, starving, into cages to be transported to prison camps. In August Warsaw fell. In desperation the Tsar, Nicholas II, removed Grand Duke Nicholas from command and took over himself. It was one of the gravest blunders of the war.

In 1916 the Western Allies asked Russia to attack. The Tsar entrusted General Brusilov, an impetuous, vigorous man, with the command. His offensive took the Austrian army by surprise. The Hungarian and Czech elements in the Austrian army deserted or joined the Russian units. Hindenburg collected every division that could be spared and moved them hastily to the front. Brusilov's frantic assaults failed: his infantry were mown down like corn. In all, another 500,000 Russians were killed, wounded or taken prisoner. Russia had reached the end of her endurance: Brusilov's offensives brought revolution nearer. Everything had to be sacrificed to the army. Peasants were dragged off to war, leaving their lands untilled. Food ran short and the administration was too inefficient to organise rationing. Hunger and disease mounted. In the Austro-Hungarian Empire too, 1916 proved to be a decisive year. In November, the aged Emperor, Franz Josef, died, with his Empire collapsing about his ears.

The revolution came first in Russia. In March 1917 food rioters in Petrograd were joined by soldiers, terrified that they might be sent to the front. The Tsar's government was overthrown and a liberal government led by Prince Lvov and Alexander Kerensky seized power. They intended prosecuting the war more efficiently but the Russian soldiers had different ideas. Thousands killed their officers, threw down their rifles and returned to their homes. With the loyal armies that remained Brusilov launched his last offensive in July 1917. A Russian advance of twenty miles ended when the Germans counter-attacked. The Russian army disappeared: the Germans rolled slowly forward meeting little opposition.

In October 1917 Lenin and the Bolsheviks seized power, determined to end the war. An armistice in December was followed by the peace of Brest-Litovsk in March 1918 after German troops had captured Riga and Kiev and had advanced deep into the Ukraine.

SERBIA, ITALY AND TURKEY

In September 1914, Conrad, the Austrian commander, deployed three armies against Serbia, but his attack crumbled in the mountains. Bitter fighting resulted, with Belgrade falling first to the Austrians and then to the Serbs. Falkenhayn became convinced that Serbia must be destroyed if only to keep open Germany's link with Turkey. In October 1915 Bulgaria was tempted to join Germany and Austria in a three-pronged assault on the Serbs. Belgrade again fell to the Austrians as the Serb troops retreated. The Allies hurriedly sent an expeditionary force to the neutral Greek port of Salonika, but they were hard pressed to hold their position and could give no assistance to the Serbs. In a grim, hungry march the remnants of the Serbian army escaped over the mountains to Albania, to be rescued and evacuated by the Allies to rest-camps. The Austrians quickly overran the remainder of Serbia, Montenegro and Albania.

Rumania was the next victim. In April 1916 Rumania joined the Allied side, hoping for territorial gains at Austria's expense. Von Mackensen, the German conqueror of Serbia, moved along the Danube, while Falkenhayn advanced from the north. The pincers closed on Rumania by January 1917 with Bucharest occupied and Rumanian resistance crushed. The Allied army, locked up in Salonika, tried to relieve the Rumanians but failed, prevented by the Bulgarian army.

In June 1917 Greece entered the war on the Allied side but made little contribution to the fighting until 1918, when Bulgarian morale was low and most German troops had been withdrawn. In a new Allied offensive the Salonika Force moved north, routed the Bulgarians, liberated Serbia and in the South put Turkey under severe pressure.

Italy entered the war in May 1915, hoping to seize territorial gains along the northern frontier with Austria. General Cadorna flung his armies, deficient in machine guns, supplies and modern equipment, against the mountain defences of Austria. A series of expensive and indecisive battles was fought throughout 1915 along the river Isonzo.

In October 1917 German divisions reinforced the Austrians and at Caporetto the Italians, exhausted and riddled with communist agitators, collapsed. The Italians withdrew seventy miles to the shorter defensive line of the river Piave where they held on. Cadorna was dismissed from his command. Orlando became Premier. In 1918 the Austrians tried a thrust towards Venice, failed and were forced to retreat after the battle of Vittorio Venuto in October.

Turkey had enlisted a German General, Liman von Sanders, to train and direct the army. He deployed Turkish troops in the Dardanelles-Bosphorus area together with the two German cruisers *Goeben* and *Breslau* to prevent Britain from supplying Russia by the Black Sea route.

Other Turkish forces attacked in the Caucasus, suffering heavy losses against the Russians. Turkey's ramshackle empire presented a host of problems. Forces had to be despatched to all corners of her territories from the Greek border to Basra to control the restless subject peoples and check British attempts to spark off rebellion against Turkey. In 1915 Winston Churchill, First Lord of the Admiralty, suggested that the Dardanelles could be forced without much difficulty. The rewards would be the opening of a supply route to Russia; the elimination of Turkey from the war; the reinforcement of Serbia; and an attack on the exposed southern frontier of Austria. Ministers, horrified by the killing on the Western Front, saw it as an operation likely to create a war of movement and allow the Navy to play a more prominent part in events.

The Navy optimistically agreed they could perform the task. From the start the expedition lacked careful planning. It was mounted too quickly, against the opposition of the French and Haig who refused to divert troops from northern France, and with insufficient imagination and forethought.

The Navy was expected to blast its way through. Ships had to sail through the Narrows, a difficult passage flanked by forts and guns on both sides and with mines and submarine nets fouling the channel. In February 1915 Admiral de Roebeck took twenty-two British and French warships towards the Straits. The outer forts were silenced, marines landed, and some mines cleared. Heavy gunfire prevented the minesweepers from dragging the whole of the Narrows, and the force withdrew. Three weeks later another attempt was made and almost succeeded but three battleships, the *Irresistible*, the *Ocean* and the French *Bouvet* struck mines and sank. De Roebeck would not risk losing any more ships and called off the attack. He asked the army to land and clear the guns from the surrounding hillsides. A force of 18,000 men was hastily assembled, commanded by Sir Ian Hami lton. A largeANZAC (Australian-New Zealand) contingent added to the strength. On 25 April landings were made on the Gallipoli peninsula in the teeth of heavy artillery and machine gun fire. The Turks, boldly led by Mustapha Kemal, pinned the British infantry to their beach-heads. Sir Ian Hamilton failed to break the stranglehold and on yet another front the war settled down to the grim business of fighting from trench to trench.

Each subsequent assault led to heavy casualties, increased by malaria and dysentery in the summer months. The Navy, patrolling outside the Straits, suffered losses to prowling U boats. Neither side would give way. In August Hamilton was reinforced with new divisions and fresh landings were made at Sulva Bay. 20,000 men landed almost without loss. General Stopford had a nap, his men a bathe. Hamilton cruised up and down the coast in a battleship. By the time the British troops had advanced inland, the Turks were ready for them. The dominating hills along the spine of the peninsula could not be taken. Lord Kitchener came out to see for himself and advised withdrawal. The evacuation, unlike the assault, was brilliantly planned and executed: the British escaped from the peninsula with few casualties. Gallipoli was a disaster: an imaginative enterprise bungled. It added another 250,000 dead and wounded to the Allied lists and tarnished the reputations of Churchill, Hamilton and other service officers.

MESOPOTAMIA

In Mesopotamia, a small British army assisted by Indian troops guarded the oil wells at the head of the Persian Gulf. General Charles Townshend, their commander, advanced northwards from Basra to Kut which he reached in September 1915. Foolishly, he pushed on towards Baghdad without a sufficient guard for his supply route. The Turks suddenly attacked and drove the British in retreat to Kut where they endured the hardships of a cruel siege. 10,000 men, riddled with disease, hungry and under constant fire hung on grimly, but their relief failed to arrive, Townshend surrendered in April 1916. During the rest of 1916 Mesopotamia was quiet as the new British commander, General Maude, built up the strength and supplies of his army. Early in 1917 he moved out of Basra, recaptured Kut and marched on up the Tigris to seize the city of Baghdad.

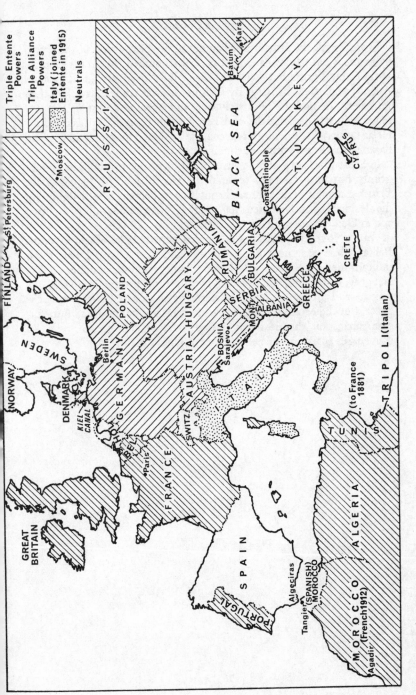

Triple Entente
Powers

Triple Alliance
Powers

Italy (joined
Entente in 1915)

Neutrals

FINLAND

St. Petersburg

NORWAY

SWEDEN

•Moscow

R U S S I A

GREAT
BRITAIN

DENMARK

KIEL
CANAL

Berlin

G E R M A N Y

POLAND

BLACK SEA

Batum

Kars

T U R K E Y

CYPRUS

•Paris

BEL.

SWITZ.

AUSTRIA–HUNGARY

RUMANIA

BULGARIA

Constantinople

F R A N C E

I T A L Y

BOSNIA

Sarajevo

SERBIA

MONT.

ALBANIA

GREECE

CRETE

S P A I N

Algeciras

Tangier

(SPANISH
MOROCCO)

Agadir (French 1912)

M O R O C C O

A L G E R I A

T U N I S

(to France
1881)

T R I P O L I (Italian)

PORTUGAL

14 Europe in 1914

From Egypt the British had begun the slow expulsion of the Turks from the Sinai peninsula. The British encouraged the Arabs to rebel against the Turks, but even so, made little headway until General Allenby took over in 1917. By October he was ready: Gaza fell, then Jerusalem. Behind the Turkish lines a young archaeologist, T. E. Lawrence, helped to organise the Arab revolt and harried the Turks along the Hejaz railway. As Allenby advanced, the Arabs fed him information and harassed the Turks with sudden raids.

In September 1918, the Turks, short of men and ammunition, fought grimly but unsuccessfully to hold the Holy Land. At Megiddo the British made a complete breakthrough with their cavalry, slaughtering the fleeing Turks. Damascus fell: Turkey had had enough of fighting and in October 1918 fell out of the war.

On 11 November 1918 the war ended. It had begun obscurely in the Balkans, had become a European war and then a world war. Eight million men had been killed and twenty million wounded. The savagery, the killing, had horrified the world: it became known as 'the war to end all wars'. Those who survived looked longingly at the peace, but the economic crises produced by the fighting had unfortunate effects on the post-war period. The exultation and relief of November 1918 soon turned to bitter disillusionment.

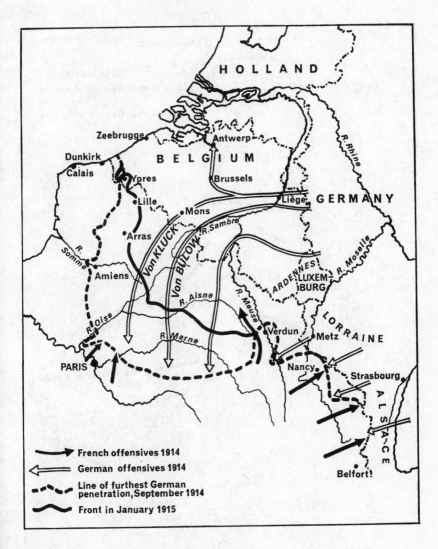

15   The Great War: The Western Front, 1914–15

16   The Great War: The Eastern Front, 1914–18

17   The Great War: The Italian Front, 1915–18

18   The Great War: The Balkans, 1914–18

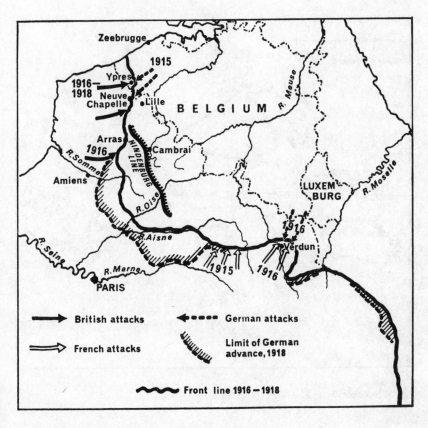

19 The Great War: The Western Front, 1916–18

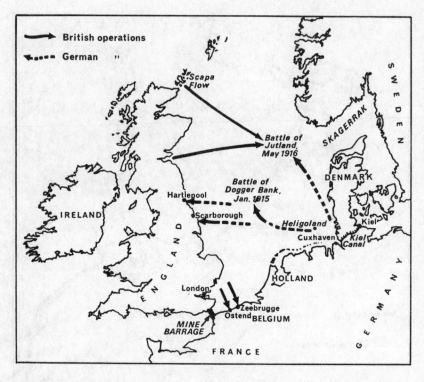

20   The Great War: The North Sea Campaigns, 1914–18

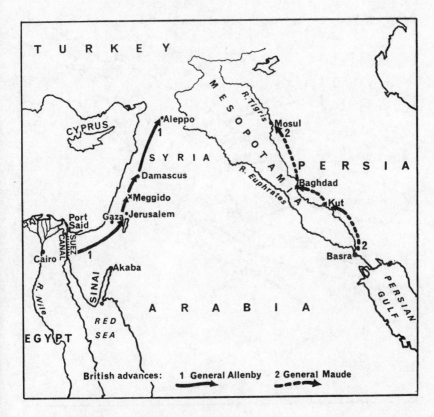

21   The Great War: The Middle East, 1914–18

22 The Great War: The Dardanelles Campaigns, 1914–18

IO

The Peace Treaties

THE ARMISTICE AND THE FOURTEEN POINTS

The Germans fought ruthlessly throughout 1918 until the armistice was at last signed on 11 November. While negotiations for a cease-fire were in progress the Germans torpedoed the *Leinster* off the coast of Ireland. 450 people, including women and children, drowned. At the same time, in their retreat through northern France and Belgium the Germans destroyed mines and factories and burnt towns and villages. These actions help to explain the bitterness felt against Germany, whose delegates, when called to Paris to sign the completed Treaty, had to be protected by police and steel wire from an angry mob.

On 11 November the armistice brought hostilities to an end. By its terms, Germany was to evacuate all occupied territory, retreat to the right bank of the river Rhine and surrender her navy and most of her military supplies. The Treaties of Brest-Litovsk and Bucharest were to be cancelled. The terms were reluctantly accepted but there was a real danger that, if a general such as Ludendorf seized power in Berlin, Germany might reopen the war to obtain better terms. This is one reason for the continuation of the Allied blockade, for which in later years the British and French were much criticised. The blockade was made much worse by the Germans' refusal to allow their merchant ships to ferry food supplies to Europe, or to allow more than one twentieth of their gold reserves to be used to purchase food. Not until March 1919 did the Germans relax these harsh restrictions which sentenced the German people to months of starvation. Then, under the direction of the American, Herbert Hoover, the Allies poured in supplies to a hungry Europe, the bulk of the food going to Germany.

The cease-fire conditions accepted by Germany were set out in a Note from President Wilson sent to the Germans on 5 November 1918. These conditions were based on terms stated in the President's speech to the American Congress on 8 January 1918. A summary of these proposals was called the Fourteen Points. Of the Fourteen Points dealing with Germany, the evacuation of Belgium and the transfer of Alsace-Lorraine to France were inevitable. The Points did not in January 1918 specifically mention reparations, changes in Germany's eastern frontiers or forcible disarmament, although they hinted at these things in a vague sort of way. The Fourteen Points stated general principles, not specific frontier changes. The most important principles were:

1. the freedom of the navigation of the seas
2. an end to all barriers preventing international trade
3. the reduction of all armaments by all nations
4. the adjustment of all colonial claims in the interest of the colonial peoples
5. the formation of a general association of all nations.

These were the optimistic views of President Wilson, which in the course of the peace conference were sometimes amended and sometimes ignored. As far as territory was concerned, the Fourteen Points indicated that the frontiers of states should be drawn as far as possible along the lines of nationality. The peoples of the former empires of Austria-Hungary and Turkey were to be given their independence, and a new state of Poland with access to the sea would be formed.

In October 1918 the German Chancellor, Prince Max of Baden, had asked President Wilson to open discussions for peace on the basis of these Points. The French and British were not altogether happy with them and insisted on two qualifications. The first virtually eliminated the 'freedom of the seas' clause, for Britain did not intend to allow any restriction on her power to establish a naval blockade. The second change, at French insistence, added another clause, that Germany must pay reparations in full for all damages inflicted on civilians and their property, as the result of land, sea or air attack.

The utter collapse of Germany in November 1918 changed the situation. The Allies indicated then that the Fourteen Points would be only a guide to the peace terms: they would not commit themselves to specific issues until the conference met. The Allies missed the opportunity to insist on unconditional surrender but to do so would have humiliated Germany and perhaps have prolonged the war. In later years the Germans argued that they had been tricked. They stated that, after surrendering on the basis of the Points, the Allies at Paris forgot their promises and inflicted a much harsher Treaty on Germany. As German delegates were not allowed to debate terms at Paris, the whole Treaty was seen as a gigantic swindle to punish Germany. This myth was fostered by Germans, swallowed by Hitler and to some extent believed in Britain. The argument does not bear close examination, for of the Points, only four dealt specifically with Germany and in any case were only statements of intent, open to a variety of interpretation.

Even so, in drawing up a peace treaty the Allies did not have an altogether free hand. Certain promises had been made to Italy in the Treaty of London (1915) which had to be honoured, despite the contempt felt by the Big Three towards the unhappy Italian Premier, Orlando, and his countrymen. In addition, there were the armistice terms agreed to by Germany. The German, Turkish and Austro-Hungarian Empires were in a state of collapse and in Central Europe the Czechs and Poles were eagerly taking advantage of the situation to create new states. Their claims to independence could not be ignored. In other parts of Europe, chaos reigned, and in this situation the Allies acted hastily to settle urgent problems.

THE PARIS CONFERENCE

On 18 January 1919 the Peace Conference opened in Paris, attended by the delegates of thirty-two states, accompanied by large advisory staffs. The major Powers, who had shouldered the greater share of the war effort, dominated the proceedings, but they had to contend with the demands made on them by dozens of other states. Powers like China, Cuba, Brazil, Panama and Liberia had entered the war late to gain a voice in the peace settlement. Their delegates mixed with pressure groups representing Jews, Egyptians, Armenians and White Russians, all hoping to gain some reward, some advantage. The enemy Powers, Germany, Austria-Hungary, Bulgaria and Turkey were not represented, nor were the Russians, locked in a bitter civil war. These omissions later proved to be major weaknesses, for Germany and Russia felt no loyalty to a humiliating settlement imposed upon them in their hour of defeat.

Control of the Conference remained in the hands of the major Powers. At first, a Council of Ten, made up of two representatives from Britain, the USA, France, Italy and Japan drew up the agenda and sent out the invitations. This Council split up into a Council composed of the five Foreign Ministers of these states, and another Council of Four, consisting of President Wilson, Clemenceau, Lloyd George and Orlando. The Japanese were only interested in the Far Eastern settlement and ignored other issues. Premier Orlando of Italy left Paris in April in protest at Wilson's refusal to allow all Italy's territorial demands. The remaining Big Three made all major decisions.

The Conference met hurriedly, only nine weeks after the armistice and while the blockade of Germany was still in operation. The delegates wanted to get the terms of the Treaties decided quickly, so that they could begin the work of reconstruction. Because the topics were so diverse and the Conference so large, fifty-eight committees and commissions were set up to deal with special topics. The committees reported their findings to the Big Three who decided on controversial points. The minor Powers grew restless, feeling that they were excluded from decision-making. No plan or procedure was clearly thought out beforehand. Overlapping and muddle resulted. Although the Treaty with Germany had been decided on by June 1919, discussion on the treaties with other states dragged on into 1920. The delegates grew tired of Paris, and hurried through decisions which ought to have been given longer consideration.

The Big Three

The 'Big Three' differed widely in political aims and temperament. President Woodrow Wilson came to Europe with the best of intentions. Sincere, well-meaning and religious he hoped to use the peace treaties to build a new Europe based on justice for all. In his view the frontiers of the new states should be based as far as possible on the wishes of the people, on the principle of self-determination. He had the vision and the idealism to hope that old hatreds would be forgotten and that in the League of Nations a new movement for peace could be forged. Unfortunately, he knew little of the complexities of European politics, of the countries whose frontiers he would decide, of the people who looked to him to solve their problems. His cold, aloof personality antagonised his colleagues. He resented criticism and was hurt by the vicious Paris press which poked fun at his seriousness. He did not appreciate the strong feelings in Britain and France against Germany and clung stubbornly to his own views. Nor did Wilson have the trust and backing of the American people. In November 1918 the Republicans, his adversaries, won control of both houses of Congress. Wilson's Democrats struggled to persuade America of their responsibilities in Europe but fought a losing battle, for Americans plainly preferred to forget Europe, which many had left as emigrants. Wilson had to anticipate that on his return to the USA he would have to fight to persuade the Senate to pass the Treaties with the two thirds majority required by the American Constitution. The growing isolation of his position in Paris made him increasingly lonely and unhappy. On his arrival he had been heartened by the vast, cheering crowds. The enthusiasm abated as he refused to give in to French demands for terri-torial changes on the Rhine, and Wilson grew increasingly disillu-sioned. He made more and more concessions to the British and French as a price for his passionate wish to have the League of Nations accepted. Yet Wilson was not totally naïve. He knew a political trick or two, and in some cases forced the hard-headed Allies to accept some of his views. On one occasion he threatened to return to the USA if Clemenceau did not surrender a point.

Georges Clemenceau was the chairman of the Conference. Now an old man of seventy-eight, tired and cynical, he said little, except to make caustic remarks on Wilson's idealistic opinions. He remembered the disasters of 1870, when as a young man, he had witnessed the German invasion and siege of Paris. He had seen German militarism strike twice at France. He was concerned to prevent it from happening again. Impassively, he fought for three objectives for France; repara-tions; Alsace-Lorraine; and security.

Lloyd George had led the British to victory. In December 1918 a general election had resulted in an overwhelming vote of confidence in his leadership. The election campaign had been fought on the slogans, 'Hang the Kaiser' and 'Make Germany Pay'. In the House of Commons J. M. Keynes saw 'hard-faced men who looked as if they had done well out of the war.' Lloyd George had to represent the tough, un-compromising opinion of Britain that Germany was guilty and must pay. In fact, Lloyd George did not have strong feelings against the Germans. He was much less vindictive than the British press at the time. Lord Northcliffe, owner of the *Daily Mail* and the *Times*, kept up a hysterical cry for a retributive peace. A headline, repeated daily, warned Britain that 'the Junkers will cheat you yet.' His political enemies meant to embarrass Lloyd George and keep him tied to his election promises. Lloyd George tried to steer a middle course at Paris between French and American interests. He was wise enough to see that a revengeful political settlement would not work, yet was unable to prevent Clemenceau from imposing harsh terms on Germany. Like

Wilson, the British Prime Minister hoped the Conference would plan for a just peace and a liberal, democratic Europe, but realistically he used his eloquent, persuasive political gifts to put the ideas into practical form. So these three men, 'the tired and contemptuous eyelids of Clemenceau, the black-button boots of Woodrow Wilson, and the rotund and jovial gestures of Mr Lloyd George's hands', as one eye-witness, Sir Harold Nicholson, described them, settled down to a vast and daunting task.

THE TERMS

Germany: The Treaty of Versailles, June 1919

Immediately after the armistice all German forces evacuated Belgium and France, and Alsace-Lorraine was annexed by the French. These changes had been promised in the Fourteen Points and were included in the terms of the Treaty of Versailles. Beyond that, Clemenceau wanted to strengthen France's eastern frontier even further. He tried to obtain for France the whole of the territory lying to the west of the river Rhine but the other Allies vetoed this plan on the grounds that the area was predominantly German and its annexation would cause another war. Clemenceau was bitterly attacked in the French press for his failure to achieve the Rhine boundary for France. The French Premier therefore squeezed all he could from Germany to gain the elusive security that France lacked.

Three frontier areas, Eupen, Malmédy and Moresnet were detached from Germany and ceded to Belgium, the first two after a plebiscite. The Rhineland was demilitarised permanently along a zone fifty kilometres (thirty-two miles) wide on the right bank and completely on the left bank. The industrial region of the Saar was taken from Germany and put under the control of the League of Nations for fifteen years. At the end of this period, in 1935, a plebiscite would be held to determine its status.[1] The coal mines of the Saar were given to France as compensation for war losses.

A plebiscite held in Schleswig resulted in the partition of the province. The northern area was ceded to Denmark and the southern remained in Germany. In eastern Europe, a small area of territory near Troppeau was transferred to Czechoslovakia. The port of Memel was taken from Germany and held by the League of Nations until annexed by Lithu-

---

1. From 1920 to 1935 France administered the Saar on behalf of the League. In 1935 the plebiscite resulted in a vote for return to Germany. France handed the Saar and its mines to Germany, receiving financial compensation in return.

The proclamation of William I as German Emperor at Versailles on
18 January 1871

Delegates at the Congress of Berlin, June 1878

Napoleon III

Bismarck

Clemenceau

Kitchener

The Franco-Prussian War: the Artillery Park at Montmartre, 1871

Rasputin

Nicholas II under guard at Tsarkoe Selo in 1917

The leaders of the Russian Revolution: Stalin, Lenin and Kalinin

The Great War: the German leaders in conference—Hindenburg, William II
and Ludendorff

The Great War: French soldiers passing through barbed-wire fences

The Great War: A transport column going up the line at Mihiel, France

The Dictators: *Left*, Hitler at a youth rally in 1935. *Right*, Mussolini making a speech in 1928

Chamberlain and Hitler at Munich, September 1938

Woodrow Wilson
F. D. Roosevelt
Winston Churchill
Joseph Stalin

The Second World War: British soldiers on the march in France

ania in 1923. To Poland went the provinces of West Prussia and Posen which made up the 'Corridor', Poland's access to the Baltic Sea. The city of Danzig was separated from Germany and made into a Free City, administered by the League of Nations, but with its foreign policy under Polish control. In Upper Silesia a plebiscite was held to decide on the question of the frontiers. The majority voted for inclusion in Germany. The Allies partitioned the province, about half of it going to Poland, the remainder handed back to Germany. All gains made by Germany in the Treaty of Brest-Litovsk were surrendered. The union of Austria and Germany was forbidden without the unanimous consent of the League of Nations. As a result of these changes, Germany's total losses of territory in Europe amounted to 28,000 square miles and 6 million people. The German Army was reduced to 100,000 men serving for twelve-year terms (to prevent the accumulation of a large reserve). Conscription was disallowed, and the General Staff dissolved. No tanks, aircraft, or heavy artillery were to be manufactured. An Allied Control Commission was set up to apply the provisions of the Treaty dealing with disarmament.

The question of reparations proved so complex and difficult to assess that a Reparations Commission was established and given the responsibility for determining the amounts of money and goods Germany would eventually pay. The principle that Germany would pay for damages inflicted on Allied civilians, including war widows' pensions, was decided on by the Allies. In the interim period, until the amount of Reparations was decided, Germany had to pay £1000 million towards the costs of the occupying armies. These forces were to remain in the Rhineland for fifteen years to enforce the payment of reparations and to fulfil the frontier clauses of the Treaty (by 1930, all Allied troops had left). Where the rivers Elbe, Niemen, Oder and Danube ran through German territory they were to be administered by an international organisation. The Rhine was to be administered by a Commission.

The German navy was not to exceed six battleships, six light cruisers, twelve destroyers and twelve torpedo boats and the naval base on the island of Heligoland was to be demolished. All merchant vessels of over 1600 tons had to be surrendered and for five years Germany had to build ships for the Allies, up to an annual tonnage of 200,000.

Germany lost all her overseas colonies, covering a total of one million square miles. These colonies were distributed among the Powers who were to govern them as 'mandates', responsible to the Permanent Mandates Commission of the League of Nations. The Germans denounced the mandate system as a disguised and dishonest method of seizing German colonies. Of the German African territories, South Africa took over German South-West Africa; Britain administered Tanganyika; and the Cameroons and Togoland were divided between France and Britain. In the Pacific, Japan took over the North Pacific islands and all German rights in the Shantung province of China. Of the southern Pacific colonies, Australia secured New Guinea; New Zealand, Samoa; and the smaller islands were divided between France, Britain and Australia.

Included in the Treaty as a sop to public opinion in Britain was the demand that the Kaiser should be brought to trial. He had fled into exile in Holland in 1918 and the Dutch refused to give him up. The Dutch saved the Allies the embarrassment of making a martyr of him. Other 'war criminals' were to be tried, but with the passage of time, the Allies quietly dropped their intention.

One of the more controversial sections of the Treaty of Versailles was Article 231. This stated: 'The Allies and Associated Governments affirm, and Germany accepts, the responsibility of Germany and her allies for causing all the loss and damage to which the Allies and the Associated Governments have been subjected as a consequence of the war imposed upon them by the aggression of Germany and her allies.' This was the famous 'war-guilt' clause, bitterly disputed by Germany at the time, and debated by historians ever since.

The French were still dissatisfied, and to placate them, Britain and the USA gave a joint guarantee to support France if she was attacked by Germany Clemenceau accepted this as an alternative to the French annexation of the Rhineland, for it seemed to give France some security. The bottom fell out of the guarantee when the United States' Senate refused to ratify the Treaty and with it, the guarantee. The British would not enter the commitment alone, and so the French ended up without the Rhineland or an alliance, and in some considerable dismay and disillusion with their former allies.

When the terms of the Treaty of Versailles were presented to the Germans, their chief, Count Brockdorff-Rantzau, complained bitterly of its severity. The Germans were allowed three weeks to prepare their protests. They complained of almost every clause, but the Allies ignored all but a few minor amendments. The Germans had no option but to accept. On 28 June in the Hall of Mirrors at Versailles the delegates signed. The legend of the 'Diktat', the dictated, unfair peace, was born.

Austria-Hungary

In 1918 the Austro-Hungarian Empire collapsed under the shock of military defeat. The Czechs led by Masaryk and the Poles inspired by

Pilsudski clamoured for their independence. These patriotic leaders encouraged their countrymen to set up provisional governments while the delegates at Paris solemnly debated the boundaries of the newly independent states.

On 10 September 1919 the Treaty of St. Germain settled the fate of the once powerful Austrian Empire. The Treaty of Neuilly, signed on 27 November 1919, dealt with Bulgaria, and the Treaty of the Trianon agreed on 4 June 1920 decided the fate of Hungary.

Austria was treated, like Germany, as a defeated foe, and her Empire was broken and distributed among the victors. Italy acquired the southern Tyrol, Trieste, Istria and the Trentino. To Czechoslovakia went the rich, industrialised provinces of Bohemia and Moravia; to Yugoslavia, the provinces of Bosnia, Herzegovina and Dalmatia; to Rumania, the Bukovina and to Poland, Galicia. No union of Austria and Germany was to be allowed in future. The Austrian army was never to exceed 30,000 men, and her navy was to be restricted to three police-boats to patrol the Danube. Reparations were to be paid. So Austria was reduced to a weak, tiny state, a shadow of the once mighty Empire. Struggling to establish a democratic government, Austria sank into bankruptcy in 1920, to be rescued for a brief time by Allied loans.

Hungary suffered too. Her neighbours, Rumania, Czechoslovakia and Yugoslavia, claimed and annexed various frontier districts. Hungary's most valuable province, Transylvania, was transferred to Rumania. By the terms of the Treaty of the Trianon, over three million Magyars were forced to live under the rule of foreign powers. Neither Austria nor Hungary had a coastline. Neither would again threaten the peace of central Europe. On the other hand, they were too crippled to oppose any possible aggressor, save one as weak as themselves.

Bulgaria did not escape the punishment. Western Thrace was taken from her and given to Greece and her frontiers pruned in other areas.

Eastern Europe

New states suddenly appeared on the map of Europe. Serbia, added to Montenegro and enlarged by her gains at the expense of Austria-Hungary, was re-named Yugoslavia. Poland, partitioned among the Great Powers in the eighteenth century, arose like a phoenix from the ashes of the defeated nations. Czechoslovakia, a multinational state, contained 1 million Ruthenes, 6 million Czechs, 2 million Slovaks and over 3 million Germans. Rumania doubled her size by the addition of territory from her unfortunate neighbours.

Germany, having defeated the Russians in 1917–18, had by the Treaty of Brest-Litovsk annexed immense areas of territory in Poland

and western Russia. Germany had to withdraw from her conquests in 1919, and three new states, Estonia, Latvia and Lithuania were established, bordering the Baltic Sea. The independence of Finland was recognised and the new state of Poland was treated most generously by the grant of large areas of formerly Russian territory. The Curzon Line, imposed on Poland by the Allies, fixed her eastern boundaries with Russia. The Poles refused to accept the Line and in 1920 attacked Russia to acquire more land. The province of Bessarabia, previously Russian, was ceded to Rumania.

President Woodrow Wilson's plea that frontiers should be drawn on the grounds of nationality and self-determination was not always observed. This purpose had to be balanced with two other objectives, to weaken Germany and her former allies, and to satisfy the demands of the triumphant Powers, such as Rumania, and new states such as Poland. In any case, national groups were scattered and intermingled. In the borderlands between Czechoslovakia and Germany or between Poland and Russia, to take only two examples, it was hard to say which nationality had a majority. The Paris Conference, aware of these difficulties, appointed a Minorities Commission, responsible to the League of Nations, to look after the interests of people forced by the Treaties to live under foreign rule.

Turkey

The settlement with Turkey proved to be more difficult to achieve. The Allies were embarrassed, as they had been in Europe, by wartime promises and by the conflicting claims of different national groups. The Allies tried again to balance these claims in the Treaty of Sèvres, signed in August 1920.

In Europe, Turkey was to cede Adrianople and Eastern Thrace to Greece. Constantinople would remain in Turkish hands, the last remnant of the once powerful Turkish Empire in Europe. The Straits from the Dardanelles to the Sea of Marmora were to be demilitarised and placed under the control of the League of Nations.

The Greeks, assisted by the Allies, had occupied Smyrna in Asia Minor in 1918. By the Treaty of Sèvres, they were allowed to keep this area. However, Turkey's defeat in the war sparked off an internal revolution. An army officer, Mustapha Kemal, seized power. Sultan Mohammed VI had accepted the Sèvres Treaty, but Kemal, setting up his revolutionary government in Ankara, rejected the Treaty and prepared to fight the Greeks.

Greece had been weakened by the death of King Alexander in October 1920 as the result of a bite from his pet monkey. Venizelos, their distinguished statesman, had been defeated in the 1920 elections. Kemal struck at the Greeks and by September 1922 expelled the last Greek garrison and recaptured Smyrna. A new treaty, signed at Lausanne in 1923, replaced the Treaty of Sèvres. Turkey no longer had to pay reparations. She recovered Adrianople and Eastern Thrace, Smyrna and full control over the Straits.

Palestine

The division of the spoils in Palestine proved no easier and no more popular. The Allies had to contend with both Arab and Jewish nationalism, and with conflicting promises made to both groups during the war. The Arabs, led by the Emir Hussein and his sons Feisal and Abdullah, had supported the British forces in Arabia, assisting T. E. Lawrence in campaigns against the Turks. Lawrence had led them to believe that Arab independence would be granted at the end of the war. However, in 1916 the British and French Governments made the Sykes-Picot Agreement, partitioning Syria and Iraq into spheres of influence—an arrangement which apparently contradicted some of the promises made to Arabs and Jews. In 1920 the Allied Supreme Council finally decided to set up mandates in Palestine and Syria although they allowed the states of the Arabian peninsula full independence.

Palestine, Iraq and Transjordan were placed under a British mandate, and Syria and Lebanon under a French one. These states were 'A' mandates, that is they could expect to be given independence by the Mandatory Power at some time in the future after a period of internal development. The Arabs were displeased with this arrangement and felt that their interests had been betrayed. No area was set aside as a Jewish national home although, again, the Zionists had been led by the British Government to think that, with peace, a Jewish home would be established in the Holy Land.

The other Arab provinces in the former Turkish Empire did become independent. Under a powerful ruler, Ibn Saud, the largest of these states, Najd, set out to conquer its weaker neighbours. Eventually Ibn Saud captured most of the Arabian peninsula, and created the extensive kingdom of Saudi Arabia. Only a few states fringing the Persian Gulf and the Indian Ocean managed to evade capture, largely because of British protection. Among them were Aden, the Yemen, Oman, Qatar, and Kuwait. Hussein became King of the Hejaz[1] until overcome by Ibn Saud in 1924.

1. The Hejaz was the holy land of the Moslems, and included the city of Mecca. It is now part of Saudi Arabia.

THE WEAKNESSES OF THE SETTLEMENT

Both at the time and subsequently the Peace Treaties, especially the Treaty of Versailles, have been bitterly denounced as unfair, unworkable and vindictive. Historians, politicians and economists have joined ranks to attack the settlement. Throughout the inter-war years Hitler exploited the weaknesses of the Versailles Treaty to criticise and embarrass the Allies, and to whip up German resentment to boiling point. What were the principal criticisms?

1. That having announced that they would be guided by the principle of self-determination, the Allies deliberately ignored their promises in order to punish their enemies. For instance, although plebiscites were held in some areas, in others like Danzig and the Polish Corridor which obviously contained a majority of Germans, plebiscites were not held. The wishes of the Arabs, of the colonial peoples of Africa, of the inhabitants of Russian Poland and other frontier areas in eastern Europe were all ignored. To be fair to the Supreme Council of the Allies and the Big Three in particular, they had said that self-determination would apply in the majority of cases but not in all. They had other objectives too; to secure France's eastern borders; to help the peoples of the former Austro-Hungarian Empire to seek independence; to punish Germany; and to reward the victors. In other cases, like the inclusion of the mountainous area of the Sudetenland in Czechoslovakia, the Allies chose to give the new states a defensible and clearly defined frontier. To give Poland access to the Baltic, essential for her economic development, meant depriving Germany of territory (Posen-West Prussia) largely inhabited by Germans. Geography, defence and economics forced the Allies to modify their principle of national self-determination.

2. That, arising out of the way in which frontiers were drawn, minority groups of Germans, Magyars, Russians, and Bulgarians were pushed under alien rule. Despite the efforts made by the Minorities Commission, the intrigues and disputes between the governments of the new states and their minorities contributed to the crises of 1938–39 in Czechoslovakia and Poland.

3. That the decision to make Germany pay, through reparations, was foolish and short-sighted. The French insistence on German repayments

raised countless difficulties. In 1919 the total amount to be paid was deferred. Eventually, in 1921 the sum of £6,600 million was fixed. J. M. Keynes, an economist and one of the British delegation to the Paris Conference, wrote a scathing indictment in *The Economic Consequences of the Peace*. He argued that the amounts to be levied were impractical, and would ruin German industry. In any case, if Germany was to supply Britain and France freely with industrial goods, raw materials and ships, the corresponding industries in the Allied countries would be ruined. This would then lead to unemployment and inflation. Keynes's answer was that the Allies should cancel the debts owed to each other, and fix a reparations figure within Germany's capacity to pay. The USA took a curious stand, announcing that they did not want reparations from Germany but demanding that all Allied debts should be paid in full. The French and British decided that they would pass on this debt to the Germans by insisting on reparations. France hoped that reparations would be a stranglehold to keep Germany permanently weakened.

Throughout the 1920s reparations caused several international crises. The French stuck stubbornly to their demands: the Germans insisted the amounts were impossible to pay. In 1929 the total payment was reduced, and finally by 1932 Germany refused to pay more. By then, Germany had paid out only £250 million in cash, but had received foreign loans totalling considerably more than this figure. The Germans had surrendered their merchant fleet, had scuttled their navy at Scapa Flow and had provided France with coal, iron, and other raw materials. Even so, Germany probably made a profit out of reparations. The important point about the payment of reparations was that the apparent injustice angered the German people and made Hitler's task easier. Reparations extended the bitterness felt against the Treaty of Versailles into the 1930s, and in the end benefited no one.

Consequently, by this process of reasoning, it is easy to argue that the Big Three, by their political decisions taken at Paris in 1919, paved the way for another war. It is true that the punishment meted out to Germany was also a provocation, but considering the difficult tasks facing the peacemakers, it is remarkable that they achieved anything of lasting quality. The European peoples were not arranged in neat parcels, fitting into clearly defined territorial limits. The intermingling of peoples in the borderlands of the new states could be solved by varying methods; sensible, kind policies by the various governments; the transfer of populations; or the destruction of one people by another. The Powers at the Paris Conference preferred and hoped for the exercise of the first method, but they could only advise, not force, governments to follow their lead. Unfortunately, their advice was all too often ignored.

4. That the Treaties were based entirely on political objectives and ignored economic considerations. President Wilson's determination to re-divide Europe into states based on nationality and language meant the break-up of closely integrated economic groups. For instance, the division of Silesia, part in Germany and part in Poland, weakened the industrial capacity of the area. In place of the large economic unit of the Austro-Hungarian Empire, the newly independent states set up tariff barriers to protect their own industries and agriculture. European trade was thus hampered at a time when world trade was in the doldrums.

Not all the provisions of the settlement were applied, and Hitler, who began by denouncing the Treaty of Versailles, ended by destroying it. Twenty years after the Paris Conference another war began. Were the Treaties so faulty that they produced another war? The answer lies not in the Treaties but in the nations themselves. With the USA retiring into isolation in 1920, few of the Powers could be relied on to defend Treaty provisions. Germany and Russia sought to change the Treaties; Britain had a guilty conscience; Italy felt cheated; alone, France felt too weak to enforce Treaties so universally denounced and derided.

It is easy to criticise the settlement. It was harsh to the defeated and contained the seeds of future trouble. To the extent that the Treaties did not bring a long period of peace to Europe, they obviously failed.

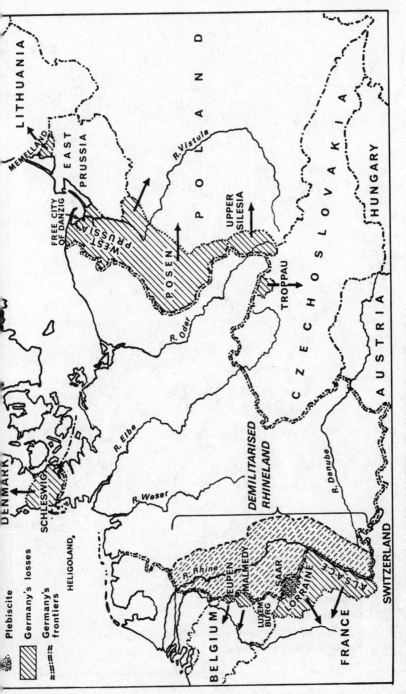

23 The Treaty of Versailles, 1919: Germany's Territorial Losses

Plebiscite

▨ Germany's losses

══ Germany's frontiers

24 The Balkan Settlement, 1919–23

25 The Peace Settlement in Central and Eastern Europe, 1919

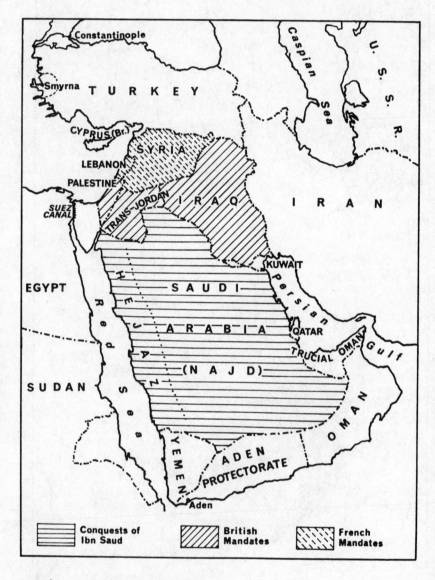

26 The Peace Settlement in the Middle East, 1919

I I

Italy, 1870-1945

UNIFICATION

For centuries Italy had been ruled by foreigners and despots. Spain, France and Austria had in turn imposed their alien regimes. Cruel monarchs like Ferdinand, the tyrant of Naples, had achieved an international notoriety. During the nineteenth century there was a spontaneous movement (called the Risorgimento) to rid Italy of these rulers and establish a united, independent state. Inspired by patriots like Mazzini, Cavour and Garibaldi, who led the famous Thousand to Sicily and conquered both the island and southern Italy as far as Naples, the Italians threw off foreign rule and exiled the tyrants. In 1861 at Turin a united independent state was proclaimed, but Venice and Rome still remained in alien hands. In 1866, with Prussian help Venice was recovered and in 1870, when French soldiers stationed in Rome were withdrawn to fight in the war against Prussia, the Italians triumphantly marched in. Rome became the capital city of the kingdom of Italy. A nation of 27 million people took its place among the major European nations.

After 1870, the inspiration, the dreams and the enthusiasm evaporated, to be replaced by disillusion and petty squabbling. The Italian politicians faced the practical problems of governing the new state. Men had to abandon the heroism of the Risorgimento and think about the everyday tasks of government, like taxation, education, trade and employment. The Italian people after years of neglect demanded progressive changes quickly and discontent arose when many felt that the achievements of the politicians did not measure up to the promises made in 1870.

PROBLEMS OF THE NEW ITALY

The men who came to power after 1870 were politically inexperienced, for only in Piedmont had a parliament existed before unification. Within the new Italian Parliament no dominant leader emerged. No outstanding personality took Italy in a firm grip. Instead, many politicians, nurtured on corruption in the south, carried their methods into the new Parliament, where bribery, unscrupulousness, and intrigue became the accepted means of doing business. Parliament became divided into factions, and effective party government became impossible. The three men who dominated Italian politics after 1870, Depretis, Crispi and Giolitti all held power by manipulating these factions. Elections were rigged (as in 1876), and by rewarding his followers with honours and bribes Depretis maintained a precarious hold on power. As only two per cent of the people had the vote, public opinion could be ignored. The parliamentary system was thoroughly discredited, for stable, competent government was rare.

Another problem was poverty. Agricultural methods were rooted in the past. Italy's peasants were largely illiterate and slow to accept new methods. The poor soil and dry climate of the south kept the region struggling in the depths of poverty, and brigands and secret societies such as the Mafia terrorised the countryside. The Government seemed unable to solve either the problem of poverty or of order and a stream of young emigrants left for the USA and South America.

Northern Italy enjoyed a higher standard of living. With better soil and climate, the major share of what raw materials there were, together with some industry, the outlook was not as bleak. The south looked to the north with envy and dislike, feeling the injustice of their position and fearing higher taxation and interference with their traditional ways.

Relations with the Roman Catholic Church remained strained. Pope Pius IX had been forced to surrender all his lands, and in 1870 suffered the humiliation of the assault and conquest of Rome by Italian troops. The Pope refused to recognise the kingdom of Italy, and so, ignoring his silence, the Italian Parliament in 1871 passed the 'Law of Guarantees' which recognised the Pope as an independent sovereign, left him in possession of the Vatican and Lateran Palaces, granted his little state exemption from taxation and promised him an annual income of £129,000. He was given the right to receive diplomatic missions from foreign powers and the freedom to come and go as he pleased. He could have his own postal and telegraph system. For its part, the Italian Government ensured that the clergy remained within the power of the state.

Pius refused to accept the annual grant and declared himself, 'a prisoner of the Vatican'. He ordered Roman Catholics not to vote in elections.[1] Friction continued for some years. In 1878 Pius IX died but his successor, Leo XIII, continued to protest against the loss of Rome. To the political disunity of Italy was added the bitterness of religious differences. The Law of Guarantees did not close the breach between Church and Government but by 1905 most differences were sensibly ironed out in private, and ill feeling slowly dissolved.

Depretis and Transformism

In 1876 the Chamber of Deputies in the Italian Parliament was divided into many antagonistic groups. Finally, Depretis formed a government of the left-wing members and, except for short breaks, he remained in power until 1887. His political methods became known as 'transformism'. Originally this meant that politicians adapted their policies to suit the times, but later it became interpreted even more cynically as 'every man has his price'. To establish the control and discipline necessary to carry on effective government Depretis offered bribes to any deputy who would support him. A dangerous opponent was bought off with a lucrative office. Sometimes a decoration, a government post, or a new school in a deputy's constituency were the rewards employed. Depretis pleaded as an excuse for his immoral methods the impossibility of forming a stable regime by any other means. But the system had other defects apart from the common factor of self-interest. Ministries and posts rapidly changed hands and fresh posts were created to bribe fresh recruits to the government ranks. Depretis carried his methods into elections, as in 1876 when bribery and threats gave him victory. In the long run, transformism added to the public contempt of politicians and made it easier for a dictator to sweep away the whole rotten system.

Depretis, once in power, faced squarely the problems of government. By heavier taxation and strict economies, he managed to balance the budget, and by a policy of industrialisation he improved Italy's trade figures.

Colonial Policy

Italy in Bismarck's phrase had 'poor teeth and such a large appetite'.

1. This was generally ignored by Catholics and was finally annulled in 1903 by the new Pope, Pius X.

Although her politicians thought that Italy's prestige in Europe would be improved by the acquisition of an empire, the army was not strong enough to win colonies by conquest.

Tunisia attracted Italian eyes, for it had been a magnet for settlers and would provide both a base for further African colonisation and for Italy's Mediterranean fleet. In 1881 France annexed the territory, enraging Italian public opinion. Italy hastened to enter the Triple Alliance in 1882, thinking that the friendship of Germany and Austria-Hungary would strengthen her colonial hand.

Italy then transferred her attention to the Red Sea, which since the opening of the Suez Canal held an important strategic value. Massawa was occupied in 1885 and the territory of Eritrea was explored, colonised and annexed. When Depretis died in 1887, Francesco Crispi, the new Premier, enthusiastically assisted the traders operating further south in Somaliland, eventually negotiating the borders of the territory with the neighbouring British. Crispi now looked to Abyssinia, and after a series of disputes over the extent of Italian influence, war broke out. At Adowa, in 1896, an Italian army of 20,000 (mostly natives) was cut to pieces by a force of 100,000 Abyssinians. The crushing defeat at Adowa and the subsequent recognition of the independence of Abyssinia led to Crispi's fall from power and a stain on Italian military history which Mussolini tried to expunge by his invasion in 1935.

Not until 1911 did Italy's statesmen dare to reopen the colonial wars. Turkey was attacked and by the end of 1912, the provinces of Tripoli and Cyrenaica had been captured and formed into the colony of Libya. At the same time, Italy held the Dodecanese Islands and Rhodes in the Eastern Mediterranean and refused to yield them up until all Turkish forces had been withdrawn from Libya. In fact, the islands remained in Italian possession and were eventually annexed.

Social Unrest

Socialism in Italy grew out of the disgust felt at the political corruption, out of poverty and out of colonial disappointments. By 1887 Italian Socialists were turning increasingly to the ideas of the Russian anarchist, Bakunin. King Humbert narrowly escaped assassination in Naples and bombs were thrown in other cities. In Pesaro, strikers tried to seize an armoury and disorders broke out in Sicily.

Crispi, a Sicilian, whose motto was 'energy', became Premier in 1887. Impetuously, he infused a new enthusiasm into politics. He gave the provinces a greater degree of self-government and enforced measures of public health. Dictatorially, he persecuted the Socialists, prohibiting their meetings and arresting some of their leaders. In 1891 he fell from power but returned again in 1893. He continued to deal firmly with the Socialists and when a revolt occurred in Sicily he sent troops who savagely put down the rising (which had been a protest against crushing poverty). Crispi's methods embittered the Socialists and horrified liberal opinion. Bomb throwing increased and after one outburst in Rome when Crispi himself was the object of the attack, the Premier in a rage dissolved all socialist societies and newspapers. Italy waited uneasily for repercussions but Crispi fell from power again in 1896 over the failure of his Abyssinian policies.

The Socialists themselves were divided into factions. Moderates hoped for peaceful reform but the extremists continued to throw bombs and earn the movement a bad name. In 1898 the Army was called out to deal with an outbreak of risings from Milan to Sicily. In Milan the troops patrolled the city and in Rome General Pelloux formed a military government. He could neither keep order nor solve the misery of the poor. In July 1900 King Humbert was assassinated. Shortly afterwards, in 1901, Giolitti became Premier. He remained in power until 1914, holding office himself or using figureheads from other factions.

Giolitti

Giolitti quite unscrupulously made terms with any party in the Chamber of Deputies and by the grant of offices and rewards skilfully maintained himself in power. The Socialists who increased their members to thirty-three in the Chamber in 1901 opposed him, but Giolitti stole many of their ideas and put them into effect himself. He improved conditions in the factories, introduced modest reforms in national insurance, old age pensions, and public health, abolished child labour, and in 1912 enlarged the electorate from $3\frac{1}{2}$ millions to 8 millions. Wages slowly rose as trade expanded and industry flourished. Socialism declined as the general condition of Italy improved, and Giolitti's task of maintaining himself in power became easier.

Although Italy no doubt benefited from the economic progress and reforms of the Giolitti era, his methods accelerated the decline of Parliament begun by Depretis. The Italian people despised their parliamentarians as greedy hypocrites. The politicians gave all their attention to local concerns or petty intrigues in the Chamber, losing sight of the major issues of Italian politics. When, after the war, the Fascists destroyed the parliamentary system, few wept its passing.

Foreign Policy

Although Italy had agreed to join the Triple Alliance in 1882, an uneasy friendship distinguished her relations with Austria-Hungary and Germany. Italy wanted to expand towards Trieste and Albania, boost her trade in the Balkans and acquire 'Italia Irredenta', the 'unredeemed' provinces of the southern Tyrol and the Trentino. All these objectives ran up against Austrian hostility. Italy in the 1890s found that her ties with France and England were closer than those with the Central Powers. In 1902 Italy renewed the Triple Alliance but hastened to assure France that this did not tie her to a war of aggression against France. Italy indeed recognised the claims of France in Morocco and in return obtained the concession of a free hand in Tripoli. On the other hand, relations with Austria worsened. Clashes occurred between Italian workers and Austrian officials in Trieste and the Trentino, deepening the bitterness between the two nations and making impossible any chance of Italy assisting Austria in a war.

When, in 1914, Austrian troops invaded Serbia, Italy, taken by surprise, declared her neutrality. As Austrian troops poured into the Balkans Italy asked for compensation in the Trentino. Her demands were curtly rejected.

Within Italy the politicians who favoured neutrality argued with the interventionists. France had many friends in Italy, and in addition the Socialists and the Nationalists pressed for action. A daily paper, *Il Populo d'Italia*, edited by Benito Mussolini, inflamed the fever by demanding an aggressive war. Very few men advocated fighting alongside Austria. The Italian government postponed a decision until 1915, principally because the army had been revealed as an inefficient force in the Libyan war of 1911, and more time was needed to reform it. Giolitti, fearing defeat, was pessimistic and pressed for peace. Others, like Mussolini, pressed for war. The Allies opened secret negotiations to bribe the Italians by promises of territorial gains at Austria's expense in the event of victory. In April 1915 the Treaty of London gave Italy all she asked for—the Trentino, Istria and Trieste, part of the coast of Dalmatia, special rights in Albania and a promise of gains in Africa. In May, Italy formally withdrew from the Triple Alliance which had never been regarded as binding and on 24 May King Victor Emmanuel III declared war on Austria.

Italy in the First World War

The promises of the Treaty of London still had to be fought for. In 1915 Italy was almost totally unprepared. Deficiencies in artillery, ammunition, and fully trained soldiers handicapped the plans of her commanders. Yet for the first three months General Cadorna advanced steadily across the river Isonzo and into Austrian territory. In the spring of 1916 the Austrians launched an offensive, forcing the Italians to fight grimly during the hot summer and severe winter. In 1917 the Italians began to buckle under the weight of better-trained troops. In October 1917 a renewed Austrian attack caused the Italians to break and flee after the battle of Caporetto. Six French and five British divisions were rushed to reinforce the front. On the river Piave, the Austrians (now assisted by German divisions) were halted. Under a new Premier, Orlando, Italian morale recovered. In 1918 a determined assault succeeded at Vittorio Veneto and when the armistice was signed on 4 November 1918 Italian troops were advancing. Victory had been costly, for apart from a huge National Debt, 680,000 men had been killed and over a million wounded.

Post-War problems

At Paris, the Italians found that their war efforts were not fully appreciated by the Allies. Italy's heavy losses and success in holding the Austrians for three years were ignored. The defeat at Caporetto was grossly exaggerated, and Woodrow Wilson, who refused to be bound by what he thought an excessively generous Treaty of London, had little sympathy for Italian demands. He classified the Italians as 'imperialists'. Orlando, who headed the Italian delegation, proved no match in diplomacy for Lloyd George or Clemenceau. The Allied leaders sacrificed Italian hopes in favour of new nations like Yugoslavia. Consequently, in the Treaty of St Germain of September 1919, Italy obtained Italia Irredenta—Istria and Trieste, the southern Tyrol, and the Trentino—but her claim to Fiume was rejected despite the evidence of a plebiscite which had resulted in a majority for union with Italy. Orlando returned to Rome to seek further parliamentary support. In his absence the mandates for the Middle East and Africa were settled. Italy obtained nothing, although in the Treaty of London specific promises of gains in the German colonies had been made. The Italians felt cheated, bitter towards the Allies and angry with Orlando, who fell from power. To the problems of 1919—demobilisation, unemployment, high prices, food shortages and an enormous budget deficit— was now added the bitter pill of international contempt for Italian fighting prowess.

With Fiume still in dispute, the poet Gabriele D'Annunzio and a group of fanatical volunteers marched on the city and occupied it. Italy applauded their defiance although the Government frowned on the episode, fearing Allied retaliation. D'Annunzio hung on in Fiume until in November 1920 the Premier, Giolitti, negotiated the Treaty of Rapallo with Yugoslavia by which the two countries settled their differences over frontiers. Fiume became an independent city with a joint commission of Yugoslavs and Italians to supervise its affairs. This necessitated the removal of D'Annunzio, a delicate and unpopular task performed by the army. In Fiume the Rapallo arrangement proved unworkable, and in 1924 the city passed under Italian control.

One effect of the failure of the peace manoeuvres was to turn Italians against their system of government. Crimes of violence increased. The extreme socialists organised a reign of terror. Strikes in the railway, postal and steel industries in 1920 brought the country to its knees. Greatly daring, the 'Maximalists' (Italian Bolsheviks) tried to seize control of factories by forming workers' councils. Ex-army officers were beaten up in the streets and the Government, quaking in its shoes, could only advise soldiers not to wear uniform. The socialists (who fought the communists and the conservatives with equal ferocity) lacked both strength and leadership to carry out a revolution. On the other hand, each successive Government lacked the resolution to deal firmly with the rebels. In effect, a civil war raged over all the country.

MUSSOLINI AND THE RISE OF FASCISM

Benito Mussolini was born in a village in central Italy in 1883. His father was a blacksmith, his mother a teacher. Hating school,[1] Church and work he wandered in Switzerland, living like a tramp, arguing and reading his way through socialist books. Fired by his visions of a new order, he proposed an Italian revolution, but preferred to lead it from Switzerland, safe from Italian military service. In 1905 he returned home and became in turn teacher, journalist and professional agitator. A forceful speaker, he held his audiences rapt with his wild eyes, unkempt appearance, violent gestures and ranting words. In 1911 he went to prison for the fifth time after tearing up the tramlines of his town with a pick-axe in a strike. Released, he became editor of the newspaper *Avanti*, but was expelled from the socialist party in 1914 because he demanded Italy's entry into the war.

Mussolini began to see himself as the leader of a new movement, patriotic and revolutionary but not tied to socialist dogma. He started his own newspaper, *Il Popolo d'Italia*, and in 1915 joined the army. After two years in the trenches an accidental mortar explosion badly

1. He left one school after stabbing a boy with a penknife.

wounded him. Never at a loss for effect, he used his crutches long after he had recovered from his injuries, and pressed in his newspaper for strong government representing the interest of the soldiers. In 1919, in Milan, the Fascio di Combattimento (a sort of ex-servicemen's union) was formed out of 150 discontented soldiers, ex-socialists and idlers.[1] At first Mussolini won little support but by September 1920 Italian industrialists and bankers were looking to the Fascists to save them from the communists, lawlessness and ineffectual government. Mussolini began to attract to his side hundreds of soldiers, deserters and even criminals who formed his force of black-shirted thugs, the Squadrists, who marched to fight the communists in the streets singing patriotic songs and shouting nationalist slogans. Mussolini posed as the national hero, with tough but necessary measures. He forgot his socialist origins and used revolvers and knives against his opponents. In the elections of 1921 the Fascists won thirty-five seats out of a total of 535 in the Chamber of Deputies. Mussolini stepped up his campaign of violence and promised all manner of reforms. In August 1922 the Socialists, to the fury of the public, called a general strike. The Fascists broke up the strikers' meetings and in October Mussolini decided on 'the march to Rome'. Fascist troops converged on Rome from several different directions. King Victor Emmanuel, fearing a civil war, advised the police to stand aside. Mussolini was asked by the King to form a Ministry. He arrived in Rome by train, clad inelegantly in bowler hat, black shirt, army trousers and spats. Vaingloriously he announced to the King, 'I come from the battlefield.'

FASCIST RULE

Once he had been called on to form a Government, Mussolini demanded full powers. Threatened by a force of over 300,000 Blackshirts, the Chamber of Deputies gave way and granted Mussolini the powers of a dictator. Criticised in the Chamber, he slowly destroyed the opposition. In 1923 a new electoral law ended the old party system which had paralysed Italian politics. By the law, the party which obtained the largest number of votes in an election became entitled to

1. The Italian word 'fascio' means a bundle, group or union. The 'fasces' were a bundle of rods and an axe carried by the lictors before the magistrates in ancient Rome as a symbol of their authority.

two thirds of the seats in the Chamber of Deputies. The other parties divided the remaining seats proportionately between them. In 1924 the Fascists polled sixty-five per cent of the votes and took control of the Chamber.

Mussolini set to work with energy and determination. Unpredictable, excitable and cunning, he had no political programme but to balance the budget, assist the workers, and keep order. The greatest danger to his position came from the more militant socialists. In June 1924 a socialist Deputy, Matteotti, was murdered. The Fascists were suspected, and Mussolini's position was for some time in danger. To prevent open criticism Mussolini drove his enemies into exile or submission. The press was gagged. Journalists' articles were censored, offices wrecked or closed and the defiant were forced to drink castor-oil. School and university teachers were dismissed if they did not praise the new regime, and text-books contrasted the vigour of the new government with the corruption of the old.

For a time Mussolini had observed the forms of the parliamentary system but in 1926 he strangled its last remaining vestiges. By new laws the Council of Ministers obtained permission to issue decrees which had the force of law. All ministers were chosen by Mussolini from the Fascist Grand Council. The King found himself an ineffectual figurehead, and Mussolini took the title of 'Il Duce' (The Leader). All members of the Senate were nominated by the Fascists, and with majorities in the two Houses, Mussolini was able to force through any legislation he pleased. In 1938 the Chamber of Deputies was abolished. Candidates for elections were drawn from the Party list to which only Fascists could belong. The electorate voted 'yes' or 'no' for the Party list published at elections. This procedure was used extensively at local and general elections to fill places with Fascist supporters. In the provinces local elections were eventually abolished completely, and the old councils replaced by Fascist officials controlled directly from Rome.

Children from the age of four entered youth organisations where they were given toy machine guns and black shirts. Regular instruction in the aims of Fascism prepared them for the youth corps which they entered at fourteen. Here, open-air camps, physical training and drilling were the main activities. From the corps the next step was the Army.

The arrival of Fascism in Italy did bring some beneficial results. Order was restored after years of misrule. The currency was at last stabilised. Enormous cuts were made in government expenditure, although by 1939 arms costs added vast new burdens to the Italian economy. With the end of strikes, industrial production increased. Rent and price controls pleased many. The main-line trains ran on

time, streets were cleaned, and municipal government reformed.
Bridges, canals, roads (the autostrade), hospitals, schools and railway
stations were built, adding to the picture of vigour and achievement.
The cold blast of the economic depression hit Italy as it did other states
but Mussolini rode the storm. In order to accomplish self-sufficiency in
foodstuffs, the 'battle for wheat' was begun, the Pontine Marshes were
drained and cultivated and trade pacts negotiated. Mussolini enjoyed
making visits to the countryside. Stripped to the waist he would make a
series of rousing, boastful speeches, or be photographed using a pitch-
fork. He made efforts to link Italy with ancient Rome by adopting the
Roman salute and aiding archaeological research with government
grants.

On the other hand, he never solved the problem of Italy's lack of raw
materials. His internal achievements tended to be superficial; no
amount of speeches could hide Italy's industrial weakness. Trains
running promptly and the ruins of Pompeii on display do not add up to
industrial power. To cover up Italy's essential poverty, Mussolini
promised war and conquest. If his regime was to be a second Rome, he
must have his empire. Meanwhile his propaganda machine built up a
picture of a Superman leading a virile and progressive Italy.

The Corporate State

To weaken the socialist hold on the working class the Fascists established their own trade unions and dissolved the original ones. In 1926
the Government ended the right to strike and abolished all political
associations that they considered anti-Fascist in character. The secret
police, the 'OVRA', hunted down opponents, and brought them to
trial in special new courts which could impose heavy penalties for
political crimes. There was no appeal against sentences.

To try to achieve economic unity between workers and employers
and to add a spark of originality to his regime, Mussolini introduced
his plan of 'the corporate state'. The idea seemed to be to replace
political institutions by bodies of economic experts. In 1926 unions of
employers and workers were formed and grouped into nine National
Confederations, four for employers, four for workers in industry,
commerce, banking and agriculture and the other representing the
professional classes. Through these institutions the Minister of Corporations could keep control of the economic life of the state.

In 1928 Mussolini allowed the Confederations to submit the names of
candidates for election to Parliament, although all nominees had to be
Fascists. The Fascist Grand Council, the real seat of power, made a
selection of names for the final electoral list. In 1934, twenty-two

Corporations representing other workers and employers were added to the Confederations. In 1938 the Duce decided that the Chamber of Deputies should no longer represent districts or constituencies, but trades, professions and employers. The Chamber of Deputies disappeared, to be replaced by a Chamber of Corporations and Fasces, a body representing the various corporations, but controlled like its predecessor by the party leaders in the Fascist Grand Council.

Mussolini was determined that Fascism would dominate every aspect of Italian life, and the achievements of the regime would echo round the world. An organisation called the Dopolavoro controlled all forms of sport and amusement even as far as the appointment of officials. Everything from football clubs to orchestras had to accept the supervision of a government department.

The Vatican Treaty, 1929

No Italian government since 1870 had succeeded in solving the differences which existed between the Pope and the state. Mussolini knew that if he could work out an agreement it would be of immense propaganda value, not only in Italy but throughout the world. Pius XI made it known in 1927 that he would welcome a new approach but negotiations ran into difficulties and it was not until 1929 that agreement was reached.

The Lateran Treaty ended the dispute which had existed since 1870. The Pope recognised the Kingdom of Italy. Mussolini in turn recognised the Pope as head of the Vatican State and declared that henceforward the Roman Catholic religion was the formal religion of Italy. Religion was to be taught in primary and secondary schools. In order to gain these concessions, the Church had to give ground too. Control over religion in Italy was conceded to the Government: in future, appointments of archbishops, bishops and even priests could be vetoed by Parliament. The agreement was received with great enthusiasm on both sides. The Fascists felt the Pope had given them the seal of respectability, and Catholics, who sent floods of congratulations to the Pope, were gratified that their religion was to be accepted and taught in schools. After 1929 the Catholic press came under censorship, but the bishops gave Mussolini almost unqualified support. Pius XI later came to doubt that his ties with Mussolini were for the greater benefit of the Church and increasingly spoke out against the tyranny he witnessed in Italy.

FOREIGN POLICY

The Duce's objectives in foreign policy were to gain territory and win prestige for Italy. His methods were composed of bluster, threats and the occasional use of force against weaker foes, like Abyssinia and Albania. Italy's lack of industrial resources weakened his hand, although he acted as if his country was powerful. By propaganda and his own personality he fooled Europe into believing in Italian strength.

At the Lausanne Conference in 1923 he scored his first success, by securing Rhodes and the Dodecanese islands, which had been in Italian possession since the defeat of Turkey in 1911 but had never been Italian-owned. To push Italian trade into Europe, Mussolini signed commercial treaties with Poland, Czechoslovakia, Spain, Greece and Yugoslavia. In 1924 he successfully reopened the Fiume question, bullying the Yugoslavs into giving up all claim to the city, which passed into Italian possession.

In 1923 an Italian General, Tellini, and three other Italians were murdered by Greeks while negotiating the frontier of Greece and Albania. An ultimatum was presented to the Greek Government demanding the huge compensation of 50 million lire,[1] payable within five days. When the Greeks hesitated, the Italian fleet bombarded and invaded the island of Corfu. The Conference of Ambassadors, meeting at Paris, supported Italy. The compensation was paid in full and Italian troops evacuated Corfu. The incident increased Italian prestige in the eyes of the Mediterranean Powers, but France and Britain were critical of the use of force. Mussolini intended Albania to become an area of Italian influence. In 1926 he negotiated a commercial treaty and helped to train the Albanian army, forestalling the Yugoslavs, who had similar intentions.

For ten years after Corfu Mussolini pursued a peaceful policy. He signed the Locarno agreements of 1925 and supported disarmament at the conference of 1930, declaring that Italy was prepared to reduce her armaments to any level. In the economic blizzard of 1931 foreign trade fell off, unemployment increased and the budget showed a deficit. Italy joined the World Economic Conference in 1933, hoping for a better world economic order. This, like the Disarmament Conference of 1933, broke up in failure. New pressures threatened Europe. Hitler withdrew from the League of Nations and increased German armaments. In July 1934 the murder of Dollfuss and the Nazi attempt to

1. Approx. £500,000.

seize control of Austria awoke Mussolini to the danger in the north.
40,000 Italian troops moved to the northern frontier to maintain the
independence of Austria, which Mussolini guaranteed. Hitler called off
his coup: not at sufficient strength to call Mussolini's bluff, he postponed the attack on Austria.

Impressed by Italy's determination, Hitler bent his energies to drawing the Duce into the German orbit. Mussolini responded, enjoying
the attention Hitler paid to him. However, German rearmament in
1935 re-awakened Italian fears and in April 1935 at the Stresa Conference representatives of France, Italy, and Britain drew up a joint
resolution condemning German rearmament. Although Italy was
openly planning an attack on Abyssinia, the other Powers said nothing
to annoy or distract Mussolini and so ruin the common front. Mussolini
in consequence felt he had a free hand and pushed ahead with his preparations for war.

The Abyssinian War, 1935

In January 1935 Italy and France settled their differences over Africa.
Mussolini dropped the old Italian claim to Tunis in return for a few
scraps of territory. After Stresa, the Duce felt sure there would be no
European intervention if and when he attacked Abyssinia. A quick
conquest would consolidate Italy's colonial territories, add to his
popularity at home, and be an instalment of what he optimistically
called 'the Second Roman Empire'. The defeat at Adowa in 1896 had to
be avenged. News of preparations for war leaked out and Anthony
Eden went to Rome to plead for peace. He was ignored and, in October
1935 after a frontier dispute had been deliberately engineered by the
Italians, Abyssinia was attacked. Poison-gas and bombers were used
against the tribesmen. As the Italian armies swept into Addis Ababa,
the action was condemned by the British and French press. Haile
Selassie, Emperor of Abyssinia, appealed to the League of Nations,
which declared that Italy was an aggressor and had outraged international
agreements, and asked that sanctions should be applied. Italy was
saved by the weakness of Britain, with her army demobilised and navy
reduced, and by France, worried by German strength and reluctant
to lose a friendly Italy. Pierre Laval, the French Foreign Minister and
Sir Samuel Hoare, the British Foreign Secretary, arranged a pact by
which more than half of Abyssinia would be annexed by Italy. An outcry in Britain forced Hoare to resign and the Government to enforce
sanctions. Even then, essentials like coal, iron, steel and oil were excluded and the Suez Canal was not closed to Italian shipping. Mussolini,
benefiting by these half-hearted measures, completed the conquest and

in May 1936 could announce from the balcony of a palace in Rome to a
hysterically applauding crowd that Abyssinia had been added to the
empire. As the months passed, the European Powers accepted the
inevitable, sanctions were dropped and diplomatic relations reopened.

The war had been a victory for violence, for the deliberate rejection
of international agreements. It was a fatal blow for the League, and revealed the disunity and weakness of the democracies. Hitler and Mussolini thought that the other Powers would not fight: therefore they
prepared for further aggression and conquest. Although the dictators
learnt their lesson from the Abyssinian war, the western Powers did
not: they were ready to undergo further humiliations in the vain
pursuit of peace.

The Berlin-Rome Axis Pact, 1936

The ignominy of having sanctions applied created bitter and angry
repercussions in Italy. Hitler on the other hand had been careful not to
embarrass Italy in any way. Mussolini, worried by his economic weakness, made plans to try to make Italy self-sufficient. Schemes to provide
Italy with oil, rubber, coal and iron proved impracticable. Mussolini was
forced to look abroad for supplies, and Italy and Germany collaborated
more and more on trade agreements.

When the Spanish Civil War broke out in the autumn of 1936, the
two new friends co-operated in assisting Franco's Fascist army. Italian
troops, planes and submarines joined the fight. In November 1936
Count Ciano, the Italian Foreign Minister, visited Berlin: after his
return both powers began to refer to the 'Axis'. The idea was that the
axis of power ran from Rome to Berlin, around which the lesser
states of Europe rotated. Mussolini copied Hitler's criticism of the
Russian Bolsheviks, strengthened his armed forces and hoped for further
victories in the Balkans.[1]

Yet German and Italian interests did not coincide. It had been Italian
policy to keep Austria independent, free from domination by any other
power. In 1937 when Germany began to put pressure on Austria, Italy
was powerless. 100,000 Italian troops in Spain and 25,000 in Abyssinia
seriously depleted Mussolini's strength in Europe. Hitler prepared the
ground by inviting the Duce to Berlin in September 1937. A calculated
display of power impressed Mussolini. Line after line of impassive
soldiers stood or marched in pouring rain. Massive crowds cheered his
every appearance. A month later Italy entered the Anti-Comintern Pact

1. A meeting followed between Hitler and Mussolini but the two men secretly despised
each other. The Duce thought Hitler .... 'a mad, silly little clown'. Later he changed his
opinion and came to admire the Führer.

with Germany and Japan, an agreement specifically directed against Soviet Russia. In February 1938 Germany invaded and annexed Austria. With German troops peering over the Brenner Pass into Italy Mussolini abjectly invited Hitler to Rome to congratulate him. A few months later, the depth of Mussolini's committment to Germany was revealed when the Fascist Grand Council issued a Jewish Code.[1]

These events caused criticism in England and France, driving Italy further into Germany's embrace. The agreement signed with France in 1935 was ended and Franco-Italian relations worsened. With the Duce playing the role of peacemaker, Hitler scored a remarkable diplomatic triumph at Munich in September 1938. Italy was now fully committed to the new ally.

The Second World War

By March 1939 German forces had not only occupied the Sudetenland, but had also entered Prague. Italy had not been informed of the plans for invasion, and Mussolini felt he must make a display of force to gather some of the garlands of fame and remind Germany that he was not to be ignored. The victim, King Zog of Albania, had shown far too independent a spirit. Mussolini calculated that another easy victory was likely. The gain would be a valuable strategic foothold on the Balkan coast and a stranglehold on Greece and Yugoslavia. Without warning, on Good Friday 1939, Italian troops landed and occupied Albania. As a check to Italian ambitions, Britain immediately guaranteed the security of Greece and Rumania but Mussolini was allowed to digest his new conquest.

In face of hostile European criticism, Mussolini drew more under Germany's protective shield. In May a ten-year treaty of alliance was signed with Italy's proviso that she would not be committed to war for two years. Hitler by now despised his ally and showed it by signing the Russo-German Pact in July and planning an attack on Poland without consulting Italy.

In September 1939 Mussolini wisely declared Italy neutral. He carried on his preparations for war but refused to be dragged along by Hitler. However, the German conquest of Denmark, Norway, Holland, and Belgium and the fall of France convinced Mussolini of the superiority of the German army. Germany was capturing all the glory while Italy waited. Mussolini could restrain his impatience no longer. He calculated the Allies would collapse before Italy's unreadiness became

1. Two startling results of Mussolini's admiration for Germany were the introduction of the goose-step into the army and anti-Semitism into public life. No Jew was permitted to become a teacher, lawyer, doctor, journalist or banker. The legislation was, however, applied haphazardly and without conviction.

apparent. On 10 June 1940 he declared war on Great Britain and France.

The war went badly from the start. Shamefully ill-equipped to fight a major war, Italian forces in Greece, North and East Africa suffered defeat. Hitler had to come to Italy's rescue: German divisions completed the conquest of Greece, Yugoslavia and Crete. Field-Marshal Rommel accomplished brilliant deeds in North Africa with limited resources. In July 1943, when the tide of the war had turned and the Allied armies were sweeping up the Italian peninsula, Mussolini was arrested and deposed. In September Hitler had him rescued and restored to a precarious sort of power in northern Italy. Until April 1945 he lived as a German puppet, sinking more and more into apathy and ill-health. Finally, as he tried to escape to Switzerland he was caught and shot by Italian partisans. His last public appearance was in a square in Milan, where his corpse, together with that of his mistress, Claretta Petacci, and two other Fascists, was strung up by the heels and jeered at by a bitter crowd.

I2

Soviet Russia

✳✳

THE REVOLUTION OF 1917

In October 1917 the Bolsheviks seized power in Petrograd. For the next three months they struggled to achieve control over the other major cities. Lenin, now Premier of the new Government, had promised the Russian people bread and peace. The machinery of government had collapsed under the strain of war and revolution. Food was difficult to obtain and almost impossible to distribute. Somehow the Bolsheviks organised the supply of bread and survived the first crisis. Faced with these desperate conditions, Lenin determined on peace at any price.

Trotsky, the Commissar for Foreign Affairs, was despatched to negotiate with the Germans. Horrified by their demands, he rejected the proposals, but as the German army again began to roll nearer to Petrograd and Moscow, Chicherin, who replaced the angry Trotsky, accepted the terms. In the Treaty of Brest-Litovsk of March 1918 Russia surrendered to Germany vast tracts of her former Empire. Eastern Poland and the Baltic states were given up, and the independence of Finland and the Ukraine was recognised. Above all, Germany saddled Russia with a huge indemnity. Lenin accepted these harsh terms for two major reasons. One, he thought that a Communist rising would soon occur in Germany, leading to the overthrow of the Kaiser and the return of the Russian provinces. Two, he was prepared to pay almost any price to gain a breathing space and give Russia the freedom to get to grips with her pressing internal problems.

Without pause, the Bolsheviks swept away the old order. All land formerly owned by the Tsar, the Church or the landlords was confiscated and transferred to Peasant Committees. Banks, industries and public transport were all taken over by the Government. All titles, including army ranks, were abolished. In future officers would be elected by their men. The alphabet and the calendar were changed. Peoples' Tribunals replaced the courts and a new police force, the Cheka, succeeded the old inefficient organisation. All government debts to foreign powers were cancelled and all nationalists within the former Russian Empire were promised self-government.

One result of these sweeping changes was the resignation of the Social Revolutionaries from the Government, leaving the Bolsheviks as sole rulers. In January 1918 the Constituent Assembly, in which the Bolsheviks were in a minority, was closed by troops. In July 1918 a new Constitution set up the All-Russian Congress of Soviets as the supreme law-making body. The Bolsheviks, now known as the Communists, dominated the Soviets, and so, in the space of six months, had established a one-party state.

WAR COMMUNISM, 1918–21

On seizing power Lenin found the industrial, agricultural and transport systems in ruins. He immediately applied full Marxist principles in a programme called 'war communism'. Russia became a vast military camp: factories were taken over by workers' soviets; peasants seized the land and administration was organised on military lines. Private trading was abolished; the People's Bank replaced the capitalist banks. As the workers took advantage of the confusion to loot their factories Lenin was forced, in December 1920, to nationalise all factories employing more than five persons. The sudden revolution paralysed Russia. Assured that they had the right to wages, men stopped work. The peasants produced enough food for their own needs and ignored the Government order to supply the state with all surplus food. Faced with starvation people fled from the towns to the countryside. In 1919 the population of Petrograd was but a third of the figure for 1917. The money system broke down, to be replaced by barter. In 1920 a severe drought increased the severity of the famine. Transport came to a halt, foreign trade almost ceased, even cannibalism occurred in parts of the country, with domestic pets an expensive delicacy. In the space of three years possibly as many as 3 million people died of disease and malnutrition.

Facing disaster, the Communists desperately tried to make their system work. Experiments and improvisations made the situation worse. By 1920 heavy industrial output was only thirteen per cent and food production fifty per cent of the figures for 1914. In 1921 Lenin came to his senses, and realised that although the Communists might control Russia, they could not hope to continue to do so with their present policies. In March 1921 sailors at Kronstadt mutinied. Lenin heeded this warning signal and dropped his grand schemes, replacing them with more sensible, workable plans.

The Civil War, 1918–21

By July 1918 a growing and dangerous opposition threatened the Bolsheviks. The Social Revolutionaries thought that Russia should continue the war against Germany and went as far as organising a plot against Lenin. Mass reprisals by the Cheka against the conspirators and their friends the Mensheviks drove the opposition into open rebellion.

As thousands were shot or murdered the situation deteriorated into civil war. The 'Whites' or counter-revolutionaries were a mixed bunch. Ex-army officers, nobles, landlords, liberals, embittered peasants and civil servants joined together in forming armies of adventurers prepared to overthrow the Bolsheviks by force. Many of the SRs and the Mensheviks allied with the 'Whites', who formed armies in the Caucasus, under General Deniken and in Siberia, under Admiral Kolchak.

The situation was complicated by the intervention of foreign interests. Britain, France and the USA were annoyed by the Russian refusals to pay war debts, and they feared the spread of communist ideas to their own states. Japan hoped to exploit the situation to gain territory in the Far East. Finns, Estonians, and Lithuanians in the Baltic area and Ukrainians and Georgians in the south joined in, hoping to gain their independence from the Russian state. The 'Whites' were conservative, but did not wish for a return to Tsarism. Taking no risks, the 'Reds' brutally murdered Nicholas II and his family in July 1918.

In the same summer the White Armies scored a series of victories which for a time reduced the area under effective Soviet control to a few hundred miles of territory around Moscow. In Siberia, a Czech legion of 45,000 ex-prisoners seized the industrial centres and began to march west. The bread ration in Moscow was reduced to an ounce a day. American troops landed in Siberia, joining the Japanese already there. British troops, stationed in Archangel and Murmansk to guard the vast array of stores sent to Russia during the war against Germany, now marched south. The French sent military help to the rebels in Odessa and to the Poles.

At this moment of great danger two men decided the destiny of

Russia. One was Lenin, who in Moscow directed the struggle. The other was Trotsky, the Commissar for War who set out in his armoured train to lead the newly raised levies of the Red Army, made up of volunteer workers and peasants, with a sprinkling of ex-Tsarist officers. In June 1919 the Red Army checked the advance of General Deniken at Tsaritsyn[1], preventing him from linking up with the rebels in Siberia.

The greatest danger came from the east where Admiral Kolchak gained control over all the various groups and centralised his forces into an army of 100,000 men. The Red Army, fighting with verve and strong resolve, defeated the Whites and drove them east. Kolchak was eventually overthrown, betrayed to the Reds and executed in 1920. The Red Army then turned on Deniken who was finally driven from southern Russia by March 1920. Britain and France recognised the hopelessness of the struggle and withdrew their forces.

Despite famine, civil war, foreign attacks and administrative breakdown, the Communists survived. The reasons for their success lie in the divided leadership, muddle and lack of coordination among their enemies, the Whites. The Red Army drove a wedge between the White armies in the Ukraine and Siberia and this military success, combined with the suspicion between the White commanders, paralysed the rebel forces. On the other hand, the surge of patriotism among the raw armies of the Reds gave Trotsky a considerable advantage. The Soviets controlled the interior lines of communication, especially the railways. Supported by the majority of the peasants and the urban workers who feared the return of landlords and industrialists, the greater numbers in the Red armies turned the tide. The ruthless purges of the Cheka, the Communist propaganda which denounced the Whites as traitors, and the half-heartedness of the Allied intervention were other important factors.

The Polish War, 1920–21

The Poles continued to believe they could exploit Russian weakness. In 1920 Marshal Pilsudski launched an attack in the Ukraine, hoping to seize more territory on Poland's eastern borders. France sent arms and military advisers to assist the Poles. In September 1920, in an attempt to end the fighting Lord Curzon, the British Foreign Secretary, suggested that a cease-fire line should be drawn along what became known as the Curzon Line. The Poles, who had penetrated deep into Russia, rejected the idea. At Kiev, the Poles suffered a decisive defeat and were driven back by the Red Army to Warsaw, where a desperate Polish recovery,

1. Later renamed Stalingrad, now Volgograd.

organised by the French General Weygand, saved the situation. The war again ebbed back across the Russian frontier and by the Treaty of Riga in 1921 Poland acquired a large area of White Russia, far greater than would have been theirs by virtue of the Curzon Line.

THE NEW ECONOMIC POLICY

Russia survived the civil war and the disastrous episode of war communism, but in a state of collapse. The whole industrial system was shuddering to a stop, and insufficient quantities of food were being produced to feed a starving people. A series of peasant risings and the sailors' mutiny at Kronstadt gave Lenin some indication of the dissatisfaction in the Soviet Union. Typhus, malaria, cholera and smallpox were rampant. Lenin called a halt, announcing in March 1921 a new plan, or 'The New Economic Policy'.

The objective of the NEP was clear—'everything must be set aside to increase production.' 'Gosplan', the department of economic planning, directed operations. Although the 'commanding heights of the economy', the heavy industries, banks, transport and foreign trade, remained in state hands, a limited form of capitalism returned to smaller industries. In place of the socialist dogma that workers laboured for the glory of the state, capitalist carrots like bonuses, piece-rates, extra rations and housing were introduced into factories and mines. The class war between rich and poor peasants was ended; the peasants, after paying a heavy tax or part of their produce to the government, were allowed to sell their surplus foodstuffs in open markets. A new taxation system, with concessions to foreign investors, and reformed currency and banking systems more along the old business lines also marked a return to more orthodox capitalist organisation.

With the stimulus of private gain, production and distribution increased. Food rationing and the forcible collectivisation of farms could be relaxed. The Russian people gave a sigh of relief as the oppression lifted. In Europe statesmen welcomed the NEP as an indication that the Communists were weakening, but Lenin, a realist, understood the need for compromise. The NEP strengthened the Communists, for they won the support of the people.

Foreign trade was resumed and the European countries jostled to gain entry into the lucrative Russian markets. In 1921 a commercial agreement with Britain started the rush. In April 1922 Germany and Russia signed the Treaty of Rapallo by which the two nations settled their claims for war damages and agreed on a plan for trade. The European governments still hoped to persuade Lenin to pay Russia's pre-war debts, but Chicherin, the Russian representative at the Genoa Conference of 1922, stalled for time. Eventually, the European Powers abandoned their claims and made what agreements they could with the USSR.

In 1922 Lenin had a stroke and did little active work until his death in 1924. In these years of the NEP more emphasis was thrown on the campaign against illiteracy. In 1917 some seventy-five per cent of western Russians were illiterate (eighty-five per cent in Siberia). The Communists concentrated on technical subjects, medicine and economics, encouraging the universities to accept more students and the schools to establish courses leading to the new technical universities. However, in the first years progress was slow: the Communists purged some of the ablest men in the universities because they would not conform. The period of experimentation came to an end in 1925, when greater emphasis was placed on discipline and the basic skills of reading and arithmetic. Physical education was encouraged because it proved a valuable introduction to military training. The crash programme of education in the USSR had remarkable results, for by 1939 illiteracy was rare, and the technical triumphs of Russia today owe much to the stress laid on science in the 1920s.

The Greek Orthodox Church came under severe attack. In 1921 the teaching of religion to anyone under eighteen was prohibited, except at home. The Communist youth organisation, the Komsomol, organised plundering raids on churches and issued pamphlets criticising the church and advocating atheism. Many of the church buildings fell into disuse, were turned into museums or put to other uses. Many priests, like the Patriarch Tikhon, were arrested and put on trial in 1922–23. The Communists thought that religion would wither and die in the course of time and have not mounted any bitter persecution of the churches in the USSR since the 1920s, but have always advocated Marxism as the only possible basis for education, morality and loyalty.

In 1924, Lenin died. He is still the great hero of the revolution, the philosopher, the organiser, the active revolutionary. He more than anyone had by his strength of will and vision of the future overcome the terrible disasters following the events of October 1917. The Russian people acknowledged their debt to him by making his tomb in Moscow a shrine, visited daily by thousands of worshipping followers.

JOSEPH STALIN

Joseph Djugashvili (later called Stalin) was born in Georgia in 1879. His father, a shoemaker, died when Stalin was a young boy. The young Stalin attended a theological seminary, intending to become a priest. He joined a secret socialist organisation and in 1899 was expelled from the seminary. He continued working for socialism until in 1901 he had to go underground to escape arrest. To dodge the police he used assumed names like 'Koba' and later 'Stalin' (man of steel). He moved to Baku where he was finally caught and sent to Siberia. He escaped and returned to Georgia where he organised raids on banks to obtain money for party funds. By 1912 Lenin recognised his worth and promoted him to the editorship of *Pravda*, the Bolshevik newspaper. Arrested again, Stalin spent another term in Siberia, playing no part in the First World War or in the early stages of the 1917 revolution.

When the revolution occurred, Stalin returned hurriedly to Petrograd where he joined the Central Committee of the Bolshevik party. He played an important part in the events of October 1917. Lenin made him Commissar for Nationalities in 1918, with the responsibility of negotiating with the different racial groups like the Georgians and Ukrainians. He combined this post with that of Commissar for the Workers' and Peasants' Inspectorate, established to root out inefficiency and corruption. Stalin travelled the country and became a national figure. In 1922 he was made General Secretary of the Communist Party, giving him control over the discipline and the personnel of the Party. When Lenin fell ill Stalin added to his hold on power. In 1923 he produced a new Constitution which created the USSR, composed of four republics, Russia, Byelorussia, Transcaucasia and the Ukraine, each with considerable rights of self-government, although effectively linked to Moscow by the Communist Party and an All-Union Congress of Soviets.

Trotsky, Stalin and the Struggle for Leadership

Son of a Jewish farmer, Trotsky, whose real name was Lev Bronstein, had been educated at the University of Odessa where he enlisted with the Marxists. Arrested in 1898, he spent four years in Siberia before escaping to England to join Lenin. Trotsky became a contributor to the party newspaper *Iskra*, and earned a reputation as a brilliant writer and orator. In 1905 he returned to Russia to lead the St Petersburg Soviet. When the revolution collapsed he fled to Vienna and then toured Europe until 1916 when he went to America. In 1917 he again returned to Russia to take up his old post as chairman of the Petrograd Soviet and helped to organise the October revolution. He became Commissar for Foreign Affairs and negotiated with the Germans to bring about an end to the war. He resigned from this office to become Commissar for War and led the Red Army in its struggle to defeat the Whites in the civil war.

Despite his brilliance, Trotsky had few friends among the Bolsheviks, who distrusted him. When Lenin died, the party set up a Triumvirate of Stalin, Kamenev and Zinoviev. Trotsky was excluded, and a deadly struggle for power soon developed. Trotsky's opposition to Stalin was a compound of personal and political motives. Trotsky was criticised for his lack of orthodoxy. He had been a Menshevik and even after he joined the Bolsheviks in 1917 he had criticised the party leadership and Lenin's policies. Yet he now shifted his ground and accused the Triumvirate of not being 'pure' communists. His acid tongue made him many enemies. His brilliance aroused the envy of his companions and his arrogance irritated them.

Stalin played a cat and mouse waiting game. Cautious, dour, he used his influence as Party Secretary to build up a clique of Stalinists in power and gradually ousted Trotsky's supporters.

The quarrel was also one of principle. In 1925 relations between the Soviet government and the peasants had become strained, for the peasants deeply suspected that the Communists would seize their land. The party gave in to peasant demands for financial help and guarantees of ownership. Trotsky (who was now joined by Kamenev and Zinoviev) denounced Stalin as a traitor to the purity of Lenin's ideas, but such was the strength of Stalin's hold on power that his policy was agreed at the party conference.

Trotsky made another serious error. He demanded that Russia must spread communism to other nations. His ideas were that by 'permanent revolution' Russia could spark off a chain of revolts in capitalist states. Stalin had travelled little outside Russia, despised the outer world, and wanted to concentrate on rebuilding his own country. He pointed out that communism had failed in Hungary and Germany in 1919 and to assist the communist parties in other countries would involve the Soviet Union in wars that the Russians were not equipped to fight. The USSR must first consolidate, by applying what Stalin called 'socialism in one country'. Then, in the future, the USSR could take up her role of crusader for world communism. Stalin's programme struck a responsive chord in the Russian people, weary after international and civil wars.

Stalin persuaded the party to force Trotsky's resignation from his post as Commissar for War in 1925; from the Politburo (central committee of the Communist Party) in 1926; and from the party itself in 1927. Zinoviev and Kamenev made humble apologies for their opposition to Stalin and were demoted. Trotsky found himself the victim of an implacable vendetta. He was sent to Siberia and then expelled from Russia in 1929. In exile he wrote a critical account of Stalin's part in the revolution, was pursued by Soviet agents and in 1940, in Mexico, had his head smashed with an assassin's axe.

By 1929 Stalin had triumphed over all his rivals. The contest for power had ended in the elimination of the Leninist 'old guard'. In Moscow and other cities huge portraits of Stalin covered every wall; statues, pictures were everywhere. His admirers shouted their leader's praises: he was the new, all-powerful dictator.

The First Five-Year Plan, 1927–32

In December 1927 the fifteenth Convention of the Communist Party, under Stalin's direction, adopted a new, revolutionary answer to Russia's economic problems. The NEP had been successful in restoring the battered economy to workable condition after the disasters of war communism, but it was not the answer to the rapid development of industrial strength that Stalin envisaged for Russia, so it was scrapped and replaced by the First Five Year Plan.

The new planning committee coordinated all the economic activities of the Soviet Union. It produced a Plan which aimed at destroying individual, capitalist techniques in industry and agriculture, replacing them by a planned economy. A new corps of technicians planned the exploitation of Russia's unharnessed resources. New factories, mines, power stations, roads, and railways were built, old industries forced to reorganise and increase production, giant labour forces moved to new centres of industry, and technical education given a boost. To increase productivity, quotas were fixed for factories and workers, and these quotas increased as the momentum of production built up.

New towns appeared in the industrial areas of the Urals, Donets and western Siberia. The frantic pace led to mistakes in planning and production. Valuable machinery was ruined by enlisting uneducated peasant boys and girls to work it. The quality of goods was poor: forty per cent had to be scrapped because of ignorance, lack of skill or sabotage. Long delays occurred because of the incompetence of petty officials. Foreign engineers recruited by Russia were too few or could not be trusted.

Despite the drawbacks, production soared. By 1932 the national income had risen from 27 billion roubles to 45 billion roubles in the space of four years. The last year of the Plan (which finished a year ahead of schedule) saw the completion of the great Dnieprostroi Dam, the Stalingrad tractor works, the Gorky motor works and the new railroad linking Siberia with Turkestan. In spite of terrible hardships, a great revolution had been achieved, for instead of being an agricultural economy, Russia's was now fifty per cent industrialised. Stalin had shown ruthless leadership and an iron will. He had been aided by the fanatic Komsomols and party members, inspired by the idea of building 'socialism in one country'. Discipline was cruel, mistakes punished, but the Russian people, inspired and coerced by turn, were the real heroes.

The Second and Third Five-Year Plans, 1933–41

So far, there had been little improvement in the standard of living for the ordinary Russian. 1928–32 had seen the foundations laid. In the Second Five-Year Plan Stalin concentrated more attention on education and consumer goods. Although the greatest weaknesses in the upheaval had been the result of lack of skill, the first Plan had been a massive experiment in practical training. In the Second Plan more schools and technical colleges were built and the quality of teaching improved.

In industry, the basic objectives of increasing production and creating a classless society remained, but more emphasis was placed on the quality of the products. Some old capitalist tricks were introduced, like piece-work rates and bonuses. A young miner named Stakhanov exceeded his production quota. He was made a national hero and a scheme was devised to reward similar 'factory heroes' (now called 'Stakhanovites') by giving them medals and by placing their names on Honours Boards in factories. Wages slowly rose, more food appeared in the shops, and greater efficiency in public transport made life a little easier for the people.

The objectives of the Third Plan were determined by the threat from Germany and the weaknesses of the previous Plans. Newer industries were placed further east, away from any European invader. More stress was thrown on the production of war materials, on housing and on education. Again, Stalin claimed that these two Plans had been completed in four years.

Agriculture: Collectivisation

Stalin was dissatisfied with Russia's food production. More food had to be grown to offer for export in exchange for machinery, and to feed Russia's people. 'War communism' had failed, and in the NEP the peasants had been allowed to keep the land and cultivate it as they wished in return for fixed quotas of goods or taxes paid to the Government. Stalin decided that this arrangement must be ended, for the town workers depended on the peasants for their food and they contrasted their communist society with the capitalist one in the countryside. Since the peasants would not work harder voluntarily, they must be forced to do so, or be destroyed. Food shortages every year until 1928 convinced Stalin of the urgency of his campaign.

The Russian peasants were roughly divided into two classes, the kulaks, the more prosperous group who produced the greatest amount of grain, and the muzhiks, or poorer peasants. Stalin attacked the kulaks on the lines of a military campaign, hoping to enlist the muzhiks in his support. The central objective of the new policy was to replace the thousands of small farms by large units called collectives. In 1929 the peasants were invited to transfer their land to the state. The government offered money and other inducements in exchange, and heavily taxed those who refused. When the kulaks resisted, the Soviet troops moved in, seized the land, and set up collective farms (kolkhozes), cooperative farms (artels), or state farms (sovkhozes). By the end of 1929, 57,000 collectives had been set up, but this proved to be too slow for Stalin. In 1930 a new law enforced wholesale collectivisation. Within a year half of the peasants were working in collectives. The peasants resisted and terror was used ruthlessly against them. The kulaks as a class disappeared, either into collectives, forced labour camps, or mass graves. In 1932 Stalin's wife, Nadia, horrified by the terror, committed suicide. Bitterly, the kulaks killed their animals and burnt their farms rather than surrender.

In the spring of 1931 Stalin called a temporary halt, but in 1933 further pressure was placed on the remaining kulaks to move into collectives. In the space of five years eighty-five per cent of arable land had been collectivised. Eventually, under the rigour of state direction and control, more efficient methods increased production. But the heavy price paid for the agrarian revolution shocked Russia and Europe.

The Treason Trials

In the 1930s bitter personal conflicts rocked the Communist Party. Out of these struggles Stalin emerged triumphant, having destroyed all his enemies and rivals. Since the disgrace of Trotsky, new men had risen to power. One was Serge Kirov, chairman of the Leningrad Soviet, who urged the abolition of all class distinctions and advocated changes in Soviet government to make it more democratic. Suddenly, in December 1934 Kirov was assassinated by a Komsomol member. Stalin, alarmed, ordered a vast investigation. Suspicion fell on the old Bolsheviks, Zinoviev and Kamenev, who were arrested. By inference the other associates of Lenin and those therefore potentially dangerous to Stalin came under suspicion. Here was Stalin's chance to rid himself of his critics. Aided by confessions alleging treason, fascism, counter-revolution, attempted assassination and negotiating with foreign powers, Stalin widened the net. Trotsky was blamed for much of the agitation and those who dared to criticise Russia were labelled 'Trotsky-ite', a term with the same meaning as traitor and earning the same grisly punishments. In a wholesale wave of arrests, public trials, and public confessions hundreds of the old Bolsheviks perished. In August 1936 Kamenev, Zinoviev and fourteen others were charged with plotting to overthrow the government and to murder Stalin. In 1937 Radek and sixteen others were tried as 'Trotskyites'. The distinguished soldier Marshal Tukhachevsky and some of his officers were accused of treason. All were shot. Even Yagoda, the head of the political police, the NKVD (the successor to the Cheka), was executed. Thousands of small fry went into labour camps or disappeared. Over a fifth of the Communist Party were expelled or shot. The 'Moscow Trials' attracted widespread publicity, for it was claimed that the plotters had made agreements with Germany to invade and overthrow Stalin. Trotsky denied any connection with the conspirators, but the 'evidence', composed of the lurid confessions of the accused, seemed conclusive. Loyal Bolsheviks openly admitted plotting against Russia. Were they the victims of torture, both physical and mental, threats against their families, or fear?

Whatever the reason, Russia suffered. With fear and suspicion everywhere, no one dared to act independently or with initiative. Everyone suspected everyone else within the Party. The reign of terror continued until 1939, with damaging effects on the Russian economy, until the greater dangers of the Second World War pulled the people together in another patriotic crusade. Another result was that Stalin had triumphed over all plotters, real or imagined. In 1937 he was in an impregnable position, the last of the old guard, surrounded by subservient party men.

The Constitution of 1936

Stalin was clever enough to alternate repression with liberalism. In 1936 he published a new Constitution. The Russians claimed it as the most truly democratic constitution in the world. The new Parliament, the Supreme Soviet, consisted of two parts, the Soviet of the Nationalities, elected by the republics, and the Soviet of the Union, representing the people on the basis of one deputy for every 300,000 people. All those over eighteen could vote, and the secret ballot replaced the show of hands, formerly used in voting. Although the new system of government might appear democratic, the dominance of the Communist Party in politics meant the dictatorship of a one-party state continued. In elections only those sponsored by the Party, trade unions or co-operatives were allowed to stand.

Within the Party, the Central Committee decided the main lines of policy, and as Secretary to the Party, Stalin was in supreme power. Presidents and Premiers came and went, but as long as Stalin controlled the Party, his voice and ideas dominated Russian life. Through the youth movement, the Komsomol, Stalin ensured that an elite of young dedicated Communists would bring new vision to the Party. Although the great majority of Russian people were excluded from political power, broadly speaking they agreed with the regime, for it brought them new hope for the future, if not for themselves, for their children.

FOREIGN POLICY

1918–30

The capitalist Powers were angered by the separate peace negotiated by Russia with Germany in 1918, by the Soviet cancellation of foreign debts, and by the announcement of Russia's intention to assist other communist parties to establish world revolution against capitalism. The abortive intervention of the Allies in the civil war was not easily forgotten in Russia and in 1919 Lenin set up the Communist International, or the Comintern, to organise communist revolutions throughout the world. Moscow became the headquarters of international communism. However, the failure of the communist plots in Hungary, Germany and China dismayed the Russians, and Lenin came to realise that for a time Russia was to be the only communist state.

Between 1922 and 1925 the European Powers gradually forgot their hostility as the advantages of trade became apparent. Commercial treaties with Germany, Sweden, and Britain in 1921 led to brisk negotiations with other states. Germany led the way with formal recognition of the Soviet Union in the Treaty of Rapallo (1922) which promised close economic and political links between the two countries. By 1925 most states (except the USA) had given official recognition to the USSR, but remained hostile to Soviet motives, for the Comintern continued its activities, with a barrage of propaganda and instructions to other communist parties.

After 1925 Germany and Poland cooled towards Russia, and Stalin drew back behind his frontiers, concentrating Russia's attention on the industrial and agricultural revolutions, only keeping links open with the West for essential imports of machinery and food. Stalin supported plans for disarmament and signed the Kellogg Pact in 1928 to outlaw war, although he did so to placate the West, still suspected of plotting against Russia. By 1930 the USSR had won grudging acceptance, but not trust, throughout Europe. Russia had no close friend, no ally. Germany, once a close contact, fell into Hitler's grasp in 1933 and became the leading state in the anti-Bolshevik group. Stalin, alarmed, made new efforts to gain allies.

The Far East

In the Far East the Red Army had first to reconquer Siberia. By the spring of 1920 Allied troops and the Czechs had left Vladivostok, but not until 1922 were the last Japanese troops expelled. The Chinese had taken advantage of Russian weakness to set up a protectorate over Mongolia, which Russia reluctantly recognised in 1924. Towards China, Stalin followed a double policy, of negotiating both with the official government and with the rebels, the Kuomintang, which had a strong communist section. A Chinese general, Chiang Kai-Shek, purged the Kuomintang of communist elements and Stalin withdrew his advisers and military aid. Diplomatic relations between Russia and China were severed for a time, during which the Chinese Communist Party became a small, uninfluential group. Relations steadily deteriorated. In 1929 the Chinese authorities raided the Soviet consulate at Harbin, and found evidence of communist plots in Manchuria. The Chinese arrested over 100 Russians and seized control of the Chinese-Eastern Railway, which ran through Manchuria to Vladivostok. An agreement signed in 1924 provided for the joint ownership of the railway by China and Russia. In retaliation, Soviet troops suddenly invaded Manchuria, defeated the Chinese and re-established their right to partial control of the railway.

In 1931 Japan occupied southern Manchuria. The League of Nations failed to evict the invaders who in 1932 occupied the northern province and set up a puppet state, Manchukuo. These moves threatened Russian interests but vigorous diplomatic protests did not dislodge the Japanese. Russia was not prepared for a full scale war in the Far East and acquiesced in the invasion. Stalin later sold out Russian interests in the

Chinese-Eastern Railway and waited for more favourable times.

The USSR and the German threat, 1933–40

In 1933 the USA at last formally recognised the Soviet government. A year later, the Soviet Union joined the League of Nations. Litvinov, the Commissar for Foreign Affairs, made frequent attempts to bring about partial or general disarmament at the talks in the Geneva Conference, with no success. While Russia was undergoing the pressures of collectivisation and the industrial Plans, war could not be considered. Litvinov redoubled his efforts to keep out of trouble, but faced with German militarism, advised rearmament within Russia.

In an attempt to find allies, the USSR abandoned her former isolation and tried to find security in pacts of collective assistance. The British and French governments, who had been very cool to Russia, now considered the possibility of an agreement. In May 1935 Litvinov negotiated pacts between the USSR and France and the USSR and Czechoslovakia, promising mutual assistance in case of war. However, when France, Italy and Britain formed the Stresa Front later in 1935, Russia was not invited to join. In 1936 when the Spanish Civil War occurred the Spanish Communist Party appealed to the USSR for help. Soviet 'volunteers' were dispatched to Spain to assist the Republican forces, but they failed to prevent the victory of the Fascist, General Franco. As collective security had meant little more than polite conversations in the Allied capitals, the Russians changed their diplomatic tactics in 1936. Litvinov suggested that all the non-fascist parties, Socialists, Communists, Radicals and Liberals, should unite together to form Popular Fronts. Only in Spain and in France did the scheme have any success. In Spain the Republican forces were eventually overcome by the Fascists, and in France the coalition of Radicals and Socialists under Leon Blum only lasted two years. In other countries Popular Fronts were not popular simply because the other parties distrusted the Communists. In addition, the purges inside the Soviet Communist Party had horrified world opinion and convinced Western statesmen that the Russian regime was on the verge of disintegration.

In 1938 Hitler's troops marched into Austria. Flushed with success, the Germans turned against Czechoslovakia, and the strength of the Czech-Russian-French agreements was put to the test. France, torn by internal quarrels and at a loss as to how to deal with the German problem, tamely followed the British line of appeasement. The Russians gave the impression that they would fight Germany for the possession of Czechoslovakia but the Czechs decided to trust the Western Powers in preference to the Russians. The result was Munich.

Stalin, Litvinov and the other Russian leaders were now thoroughly alarmed. Munich seemed to indicate that the Western Powers intended to give Germany a free hand in the East where Hitler had sworn to acquire 'lebensraum'. In April 1939 Litvinov was replaced as Commissar by Molotov, a tough negotiator. He immediately suggested a triple alliance of Britain, France and Russia, but in London a lukewarm reception greeted this plan. Chamberlain, the British Prime Minister, sent a delegation to Russia but the negotiations dragged on fruitlessly, for Stalin demanded the right to send Soviet troops through Polish territory and neither the Poles nor the British were keen on this arrangement. Stalin turned to Germany and in August signed a Soviet-German trade agreement. Ribbentrop, the German diplomat, flew to Moscow and signed a ten-year non-aggression pact. The pact shocked Europe but it gave Stalin time to prepare his defences.

Poland's death warrant was sealed, for the pact contained secret clauses dealing with her partition. In September 1939 Hitler invaded Poland and Britain and France went to war. The Russians pushed across the eastern frontier of Poland and partitioned the country with Germany. To safeguard her defences the Soviet Union seized bases in the Baltic states of Estonia, Latvia and Lithuania. In June 1940 these three states were swallowed up in the Soviet Union. In November 1939 the Russians had attacked Finland and in March 1940 negotiated a treaty which gave them a strip of territory north of Leningrad. Stalin knew the German attack would come and made desperate efforts to prepare the country's defences. On 22 June 1941 the expected invasion began and Russia entered another period of war and privation.

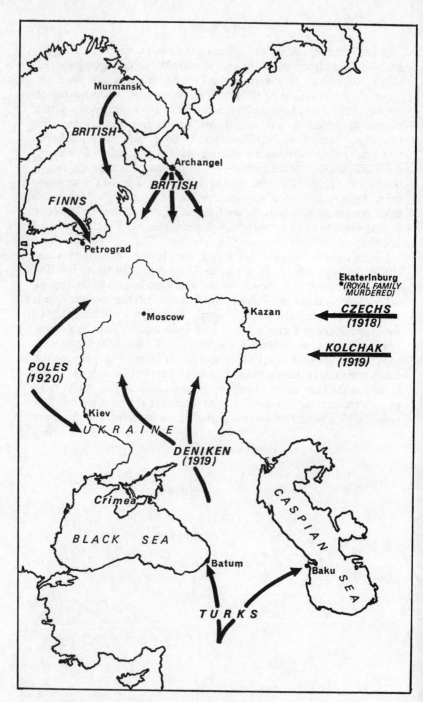

27 The U.S.S.R.: The Civil War, 1920–21

13

Turkey, Spain and France

❋❋

KEMAL ATATURK AND MODERN TURKEY

In 1881, Mustapha Kemal was born in the large seaport of Salonika, then a Turkish city, now Greek. He attended military schools in the city and elsewhere, and developed a profound distaste for the corrupt, inefficient rule of the Sultan, Abdul Hamid. Kemal joined revolutionary societies like the Vatan (Fatherland) and later the Young Turk Movement. Many young officers like himself impatiently awaited reform or revolt. Mustapha, a born leader, was hounded by the police and the authorities and was lucky to keep his army command.

In 1908 Kemal assisted Enver Pasha, the leader of the Young Turks, to overthrow the Sultan and set up a new government. Kemal quickly grew disillusioned with Enver Pasha, for the ambitious army officer did not obtain the high office he expected, nor did the German domination of Turkish life cease. 'Turkey for the Turks' became Kemal's rallying slogan.

In 1911 he fought in Tripoli against the Italians, in 1912 against the Bulgarians, and in 1915 against the British. His qualities as a commander raised him to high rank: with the German, Liman von Sanders, Kemal held the British at Gallipoli in 1915 and then forced them to withdraw from the peninsula. In peacetime, Kemal had been more dangerous to himself than to his enemies, dissolute, a gambler and a drunkard. In war, he revealed himself as a cool, shrewd, competent officer, purging himself and his men of all desires but the will to win.

Kemal moved to the Caucasus in 1916, where the Russians had earlier inflicted a crushing defeat on the Turkish armies. Success here led to his promotion to General but again he quarrelled with Enver Pasha and watched, inactive, as Turkey collapsed in November 1918.

Enver fled into exile. A new government excluded Kemal from power. He was too dangerous, too able, too unscrupulous to trust. He left for central Turkey and at Ankara, in the province of Anatolia, set up a rival government, challenging the Sultan Mohammed and the foreign invaders.

The Revolution of 1919

Kemal was joined by all those who had a grudge against the government, or who shared his hate for the Greeks, British and French. The country dissolved into a fury of murders, atrocities and civil war. The Sultan called on the priests to rouse the people against Kemal; the rebels slaughtered the priests and sacked mosques.

Meanwhile, in Paris, the Allies calmly signed the Treaty of Sèvres. Turkey was to lose Smyrna, Adrianople and Thrace to the Greeks, the Arab provinces as mandates to the Allies, and the Dardanelles were to be neutralised under international control. Kemal, now recognised in Turkey as the rightful leader of a national revolution, exploited the wave of passionate hysteria which broke on the heads of the Allies. Turkish troops advanced on Constantinople and confronted the British troops guarding the city. The British were too few to hold the Turks, but the Greeks saw an opportunity to increase their territorial gains and attacked the Turkish forces, driving them back towards Ankara. The National Assembly at last accepted Kemal and gave him full power to organise a last-ditch struggle. Kemal announced, 'Not one inch of Turkish soil will be surrendered until it is drenched in Turkish blood.' Throughout 1921 bitter fighting raged along the front but the Turks slowly began to push the Greeks westwards. Behind his troops Kemal took precautions to see that no rival would overthrow him, or the Assembly ever regain power. Officers were hanged, the Assembly purged and threatened.

In 1922 the Turks launched a surprise assault on the Greeks, driving them out of Smyrna and into the sea. Tens of thousands of helpless soldiers and civilians were murdered by the terrible Turkish cavalry. Britain feared that Kemal would now attack the Allied occupation force guarding the approaches to Constantinople. The British detachments at Chanak (on the Asiatic shore of the Dardanelles) were reinforced. The danger was averted by General Harrington and the Turkish commander, Ismet, who negotiated a settlement. In the Treaty of Lausanne (1923) the Greeks surrendered their 1919 gains in Adrianople, Thrace and Smyrna, and Turkey recovered full control over Constantinople and the Straits. Mustapha Kemal had fulfilled his boast and had freed Turkey from the foreigners.

Reconstruction

The task of reconstruction was a daunting one. Turkey lay in ruins, torn by war and revolution. Kemal refused to allow his country to lapse into her former apathy. He insisted that Turkey must be 'westernised', that it should try to copy the great scientific and technical achievements of the Western European powers. Ruthlessly, he forced the Assembly at gunpoint to abolish the office of Sultan. Turkey became a Republic, with Kemal as President and Commander-in-Chief of the Army. His capital remained in Ankara, where he issued order after order, thrusting Turkey into the modern world.

First he attacked the Islamic religion. In 1924 the office of Caliph was abolished. The ancient religious courts and codes were swept away and replaced by modern laws. Two million acres of the land belonging to the Moslem Church were distributed among farmers. In 1934 another law forbade the wearing of religious clothes in public.

Kemal threw caution to the winds and thrust Turkey into the twentieth century. The western calendar, alphabet and metric system replaced the ancient Arabic customs. English and French were taught in the schools, education was made free, and universities and training schools for nurses were opened. Agriculture, banking, industry and commerce were given state aid and direction and in 1933 a Five-Year Plan was put into effect. The abolition of some of Turkey's more trivial but passionately held customs aroused the greatest opposition. Harems and the distinctive Turkish headgear, the fez, were banned. The government forbade women to wear veils, and in 1934 gave them the vote and encouraged them to enter professions on the same terms as men. Polygamy became illegal.

For some years Kemal was the most unpopular man in Turkey. He had to be protected by squads of police. He divorced his wife and drove his mistress to suicide. Plotters ended up at the end of a rope. By 1930 the country was seething with discontent. Kemal made one compromise. He allowed an official opposition to be formed in the Assembly. The Turks took advantage of the situation; newspapers made harsh criticisms of the government; strikes brought the country to a standstill and in the Assembly the opposition carried revolvers to reinforce its arguments. Kemal ended the experiment in opposition, reverted to dictatorship, and called on the army to restore order. Kemal (who had now adopted the name of 'Ataturk', 'Father of the Turks') did not abandon his hope of transforming Turkey into a modern democratic state but waited for the hubbub to die down before he again allowed any rivals to his own People's Party to exist.

In the 1930s high taxation, the forcible conversion to western ideas and the sustained attack on the Moslem Church did not endear Kemal to his people. In 1938, worn out by overwork and debauch, he died, leaving his old military companion, Inonu, to continue his work. Although vast changes were made Kemal could not alter the habits of a lifetime in the space of a few years. He began the process of transformation but left it unfinished. His plans faltered for lack of technical education among the people, for lack of money and mineral resources, and his agricultural schemes were crippled by the constant problem of water shortage. The Turks have not learnt all the lessons Kemal sought to teach, but they have never returned to the old ways. As the years passed, they recognised the wisdom of their leader's vision.

In foreign policy the Turks cautiously kept the Western Powers at bay. Through the 1930s they rejected the advances made by Germany and Italy and joined the League of Nations in 1932. In the Second World War the Turks maintained their independence and neutrality.

SPAIN

In 1868 Queen Isabella's reign came to an end in confusion and revolution. After a period of civil war, in which the regional rivalries of Catalonia, Andalusia, Castile and Valencia defeated all attempts to establish stable central government, Isabella's son, then a cadet at Sandhurst, was thrust on the throne by a group of generals. A form of parliamentary government was set up, under the domination of cliques of politicians and army officers, who controlled government appointments and kept the young king, Alphonso XII, under a watchful eye.

In 1886 Alphonso XIII succeeded to the throne. During his long reign little reform was accomplished. In education, public welfare, industry, and agriculture the iron grip of the Church and the landowners did not relax. The peasants and the industrial workers in Barcelona were restless but lacked leadership. In 1890 the Government placated the growing opposition by extending voting rights. The peasants voted for their landlords out of fear and ignorance, as the Government had accurately predicted.

In Spain's colonies, unrest culminated in revolution. In 1895 a rebellion in Cuba, followed by a revolt in the Philippines, revealed the incompetence of Spanish administration. After a United States' battleship blew up in Havana harbour with the loss of 266 men, America inter-

vened in the Cuban rising. In the brief war of 1898 American fleets
destroyed two Spanish fleets off Manila and near Cuba. After eight
months of war a peace was signed in Paris in December 1898 giving
Cuba limited independence, for the USA controlled Cuban foreign
affairs and internal law and order. In the Philippines the Americans subdued a nationalist rising and granted conditional rights of self-government. The USA annexed Puerto Rico in the Caribbean and Guam in
the Pacific. The once great Spanish Empire had shrunk to the barren
wastes of the Rio de Oro on the edge of the Sahara, and Spanish
Morocco, a narrow strip of territory in northern Africa lying opposite
the Spanish mainland.

Within Spain, discontent ripened into bloodshed in 1909 when the
city of Barcelona rebelled against conscription for a Moroccan war.
After five days of mob violence in which forty-eight churches were
burnt and drunken workers danced in the streets, the Government
crushed the rising, executing over 400 people in the process. The
Socialists, who had protested against the war, rapidly increased their
share of the votes, but not sufficiently to upset conservative governments. In the 1914–18 War Spain sensibly remained neutral and
benefited from greatly increased trade.

Dictatorship

In 1919 the industrial boom of the previous years collapsed, and the
Socialists, inspired by the example of the Russian Bolsheviks, resumed
their struggle for social revolution. Strikes and brutal gang warfare
forced the Government to rule by military law. The Army was discredited, however, for in 1921 Spanish forces in Morocco suffered a
heavy defeat at the hands of the Moors.

By 1923 the Spanish parliamentary system had few supporters but
many enemies. When Primo de Rivera, landowner and General, overthrew parliament and ruled through the Army, few protested. King
Alphonso was alleged to have called Primo 'My Mussolini' but the
General was no Fascist. He had no powers of mass control nor an
ambitious foreign policy. He ended the Moroccan war, restored public
order and signed a friendship treaty with Italy. New roads and railways
were built and Spain enjoyed for a time both peace and a certain
measure of prosperity. The price was the loss of political freedom. De
Rivera set up an Assembly in 1927 made up of 350 men representing
commerce, labour and agriculture, but the dictator gave this new
Chamber very little power.

Spaniards grew restless at their loss of freedom and at the harsh
censorship imposed on the press. When the regime ran into economic

difficulties in 1930, made worse by the world depression, De Rivera took the curious step of asking all garrison officers throughout Spain if they were for or against him. To his surprise they voted for his retirement. He left for France where he died a few months later.

King Alphonso took Primo's place as a dictator, but few men now supported the monarchy. In December 1930 a group of Republicans attempted a coup d'état, issuing a manifesto which began, 'A passionate demand for Justice surges upwards from the bowels of the Nation . . .' The coup was suppressed, but in the elections of 1931 heavy Republican majorities indicated the declining popularity of the King. To prevent bloodshed Alphonso left Spain for exile.

The Republic, 1931–36

The new Government, dominated by Socialists and Republicans, had to tackle a wave of anti-clericalism in which churches and convents in Madrid and other cities were set on fire. A new constitution provided for a Cortes (Parliament), religious toleration, civil marriage, and divorce. The President, Zamora, a Catholic lawyer, intended sweeping reforms but first he had to restore order. Artillery had to be used to crush a strike in Seville, and again the press was placed under a trying censorship. A wave of arrests for crimes against the state swept up the Republic's enemies, at least for a time.

Many of the Republicans opposed the power of the Roman Catholic Church. In the new constitution, payments by the state to priests were to stop, religious education was to end and divorce would be made easier. By these actions, the Republicans, careless and confident, antagonised the Church, one of the most powerful institutions in Spain.

By 1932 the Republicans estimated the time ripe for social revolution. The Army came first on the list. The Government retired hundreds of officers from active service, brought the Army and Navy under the control of the ordinary courts, and closed the military academy for officers at Saragossa.[1] Many of these officers had fought together in the Moroccan wars. Their loyalty lay to the Army and its privileges. They hated the reforming Republicans and nursed their resentment, forming a secret organisation, the Spanish Military Union, to plot against the Republic.

The Government then turned on the landowners. By the Agrarian Law of 1932 most landlords were to be dispossessed and their lands transferred to peasant cooperatives. The Law, although totally inade-

1. The Spanish army was heavily overloaded with officers—15,000 commanding 115,000 men.

quate to deal with Spain's agricultural problems (only three per cent of the whole country was irrigated), ran into opposition from the landlords. The peasants took the opportunity to pay off some old scores. Murders, strikes, and church-burnings disrupted the food supply and the Government postponed the application of the Act, which remained a dead letter. Consequently, the landlords were suspicious and the peasants angry with the unhappy Government.

The Republicans also tried to deal with the sore problem of Catalonia and the other provinces which expected greater powers of local government. To placate the opposition the Republicans hastily agreed that the provinces would be guaranteed further rights in the new constitution, still being drafted.

One can see that although the infant Republic tried bravely to solve some of Spain's most pressing problems, it raised powerful interests against the Government. Nor was the Government at Madrid stable. Only by multi-party coalitions could a majority in the Cortes be guaranteed.

In 1933, despite a flood of legislation that included a new penal code, fairer labour contracts, and guarantees of minimum wages, the Socialist vote declined and the right-wing parties gained more support in the Cortes. Two new parties emerged, the Catholics led by Gil Robles, an ambitious young lawyer, and the Falange or Fascists, controlled by José de Rivera, son of the former dictator.

In the following three years Spain sank into violence, murder and finally, war. Neither a series of Governments nor any one man could prevent the disasters. One coalition after another watched helplessly as chaos increased. The various political groups—Anarchists, Socialists, Catholics, the trade unions, the Falange—were pulling Spain in different directions and each was convinced that it was right and the other parties wrong. The politicians had to fall back increasingly on the Army to maintain order. When the miners of the Asturias rebelled in October 1934 General Franco, the brilliant ex-commander of the Foreign Legion, used his soldiers to crush the rising, killing 1,300 men in the process.

After six Cabinet crises in one year, President Zamora finally suspended the Cortes and announced that new elections would be held in February 1936. The campaign was fought out between the Right (representing the landlords, the Catholics and the Army) and the Popular Front, a combination of left-wing parties including the Communists. The Popular Front won a narrow victory. Spontaneously, hundreds of Catholic churches were set on fire and in the south peasants seized land in anticipation of more sweeping agrarian reforms.

In Madrid, Zamora was removed. The new President, Manuel Azana (known as 'the Monster' because of his ugly face) appealed for

calm but he was ignored. Arson, murder and riot returned to plague
Spain. Azana had to mount a military campaign against agitators.
1,500 people were killed or wounded in six months. Largo Caballero,
the Socialist leader, fanned the flames when he announced that a revolution was near and that he, the 'Spanish Lenin', would lead it. In the first
two weeks of July 1936 Spain had clearly drifted into anarchy: it
seemed the Republic could not succeed against the powerful forces
bent on its destruction.

The Generals lost their patience. On 18 July 1936 an insurrection
succeeded in Spanish Morocco. Risings followed on the mainland.
Officers called on their men to follow them. Main buildings were
seized and known Communists and Anarchists rounded up. The Army
was not successful everywhere. In some districts soldiers shot their
officers and pledged support for the Republic. A junta of generals took
control of the areas loyal to the Army. Generals Mola and Franco
issued a declaration, stating that as public order had collapsed, the
Army's duty was to restore discipline.[1]

The revolt was violent. The Army (now referred to as 'the Nationalists') savagely slaughtered those who opposed it, partly to frighten the
working-class into submission. In retaliation, Republicans indiscriminately killed priests and nuns and burnt down churches and barracks.
The Government seemed paralysed. Azana was reluctant to issue arms
for he still hoped to avoid civil war. While he dithered, the revolution
gathered pace. In cities, towns and villages, soldiers fought Republicans
with increasing bitterness.

Within a few days there were two Spains. The loyal Republican
areas included Catalonia in the north-east, the Basque country, Castile
and in the south, Valencia and Andalusia. The Nationalists were strongest in Morocco and in northern and western Spain. In both Spains the
tide of assassination, confiscation and hatred flowed. In the Nationalist
areas the Communists were swiftly eliminated. In the Republican
provinces soldiers and priests were tortured, thrown down mine-
shafts or shot. The Spanish workers attacked the Catholic Church
with such ferocity because they believed it to be on the side of the
middle class and the capitalists.

In August General Francisco Franco returned from Morocco to lead
the rebellion. Born in 1892, son of a naval paymaster, Franco had made
a reputation as a courageous, thoughtful soldier in the Moroccan wars.
He proclaimed himself as 'Head of State' in October, after executions
and accidents had reduced the number of his rivals.

1. José de Rivera, a possible rival to the generals, was in a Republican prison, where he
was executed in November 1936.

The Civil War, 1936–39

President Azana was no man for a crisis and the Communist party, aided by Russian agents, took over more control of the Republican forces. Private wealth was confiscated, all right-wing organisations and newspapers were disbanded, all rents were reduced by half and government restaurants, giving rice and potatoes, were set up to feed the starving people of the Republican towns.

In August, the Nationalist armies advanced on Madrid. Caballero found himself defending the Republic instead of overthrowing it. He emerged as a man of decision, organised resistance in Madrid, and repulsed the attacks. Neither side took prisoners and doctors had to struggle to prevent wounded men being shot in their beds. For a time there was stalemate and both sides looked around for allies. Italy was the first to answer the call. Mussolini, anxious to prevent a communist state in Spain and ready to posture as a friend of the Fascists, sent planes, ammunition, guns, vehicles and by mid–1937 50,000 men. German 'volunteers', together with Heinkel fighters, also appeared in the Nationalist ranks. About 14,000 Germans served in Spain in the war. Later they were organised into the 'Condor Legion' of a hundred fighters and bombers, artillery and troops.

On the Republican side, Russia assisted, but more slowly. Eventually tanks, guns, and artillery were supplied. Political agents appeared and disappeared but the Russians sent few troops.[1] In western Europe, opinion was divided. Many volunteers travelled to Spain to fight, mostly for the Republicans. International Brigades were formed, containing French, British, American and eastern European volunteers. Among intellectuals of the Left, Spain became an inspiration. The fight against Fascism had come into the open, and young English writers like Stephen Spender, W. H. Auden and John Cornford (who was killed) fought on the Republican side. Ernest Hemingway, the American novelist, went to Spain as a reporter and stayed to assist the Republicans.

Faced with the threat to the peace of Europe France proposed a general policy of non-intervention. A Non-Intervention Committee composed of Britain, France, Italy, Germany, Russia and other countries was formed. The United States remained strictly neutral. Britain prohibited exports of war material to either side, and other nations followed suit, some with less honesty than others. By 1937 an Agreement had been worked out. No arms were to be sent to Spain; observers were to watch the frontiers, and warships would patrol Spanish

1. Russian troops never exceeded 500 at any one time.

waters. The Republicans were dismayed and cheated. Italy and Germany had already poured assistance to the Nationalists: now their ships were to patrol to prevent aid reaching the Republicans. The mockery was complete. Germany sent two battleships, the *Admiral Scheer* and the *Deutschland*. Attacked by Republican planes, the *Deutschland* retaliated by bombarding the port of Almeria.

In October 1936 the Nationalists again attacked Madrid. As the sounds of battle drew nearer, President Azana fled to Barcelona, as he put it, 'for an extended tour of the fronts'. This contrasted with the bravery of the Spanish workers and the foreign volunteers who managed to hang on. Throughout the winter an army of 20,000 Nationalists fought its way into the outskirts of the city. The Republicans fought bitterly, a women's battalion fighting alongside men, children building barricades. Overhead German and Russian planes fought for supremacy. The Republicans wore makeshift uniforms, ignored training and frequently ran short of ammunition, maps and food, yet they held the city. As the Communists gained more control over them the Republicans became more disciplined and effective, but throughout 1937 it was by resolution rather than military competence that they kept going.

In the south Italian forces landed secretly, linked up with the Moroccan army which had been ferried from Africa by German planes, and captured the town of Malaga. Non-intervention was a farce: while Britain and France earnestly kept to the Agreement, other nations flaunted it.

In March 1937 Franco changed his tactics. The Nationalists attacked in the north, hoping for a quick victory. 50,000 Spanish troops, assisted by Italian divisions and the Condor Legion, defeated the out-numbered Basques. During the campaign the Germans bombed the undefended town of Guernica for three hours, killing and wounding 2,500 people. Göring in 1946 admitted that Germany had used Guernica as a testing ground for massive bombing. The destruction of the town horrified the world. By June the Basque capital of Bilbao had fallen to the Nationalists and soon all resistance ceased in the north-west.

In the autumn of 1937 Franco launched fresh onslaughts on the Republican positions. Meanwhile Italian submarines attacked neutral shipping travelling to Spain. When a British steamer was sunk, British and French statesmen called a conference at Nyon and authorised a joint patrol to sink any belligerent warships operating off the east coast of Spain. The mysterious attacks on shipping ceased for a time. In 1938 they restarted when Mussolini realised that Britain would endure any slight to avoid war.

With defeats on every front the Republicans were reeling. Late in 1937 the Communists overthrew Caballero, made Dr Negrin leader of the Government, transferred headquarters to Barcelona and reorganised the Army. However, the Communists also brought in executions without trial and secret police, and suppressed non-communist views. The Republican army, for a time revitalised by its new leaders, nevertheless lacked fuel, food and aircraft. The Nationalists were better equipped. By March 1938 they had overrun Aragon and the Italians began to bomb Barcelona.[1]

In April Franco's forces reached the Mediterranean, cutting the Republican armies into two parts. Superior air power and artillery enabled the Nationalists to continue their advance. When both sides were exhausted in October 1938 Hitler reinforced the Condor Legion in return for Franco's promise to pay with iron ore, vital for Germany's industrial needs. In January the victorious Nationalist forces entered Barcelona. 400,000 refugees and soldiers fled north across the Pyrenees into France.

The Republicans still held a third of Spain, including Madrid and Valencia, but their cause was doomed. In the death throes of the Republic its leaders quarrelled among themselves. The Nationalists seized the opportunity to occupy Madrid, and within a few days overran Valencia. By the end of March the Republic was at an end, its leaders in exile, its soldiers in prison or hiding.

General Franco, whose persistence, patience and military ability during the civil war had done much to ensure a Nationalist victory, formed a new government with himself as Caudillo (Leader). He allowed only one party, the Falange, to exist and he filled the main Government offices with members of this party and with his own cronies. Although opposition was silenced and thousands of former Republicans were imprisoned, Franco's regime did not copy the graver excesses favoured by other Fascist dictators. Nor did Franco involve Spain in the Second World War.

After the civil war had ended Franco thanked Hitler and Mussolini for their assistance, paid his debts to them, praised them in speeches, joined the Anti-Comintern Pact, and even sent a division of 47,000 men to freeze on the Russian front in 1942. Hitler tried to tempt Franco into a more formal alliance and a declaration of war against the Allies. Franco, wily as ever, avoided the trap. The Führer met Franco at Hendaye in 1940 in a nine hour discussion in a vain attempt to move

1. Mussolini declared his pleasure that the Italians 'should be horrifying the world by their aggressiveness, instead of charming it by the guitar'. Aggressive perhaps but not accurate, for the Barcelona petrol depot was bombed thirty-seven times before being hit.

Spain out of cautious neutrality. Franco rejected Hitler's blandishments and kept Spain resolutely neutral throughout the Second World War.

FRANCE, 1919–40

In 1919, France returned to the normal processes of politics. New elections for the Chamber of Deputies resulted in a sweeping victory for Clemenceau's group, the Bloc National, a coalition of right-wing parties. Almost at once the new Government rid itself of its leader, Clemenceau, because he had not gained sufficient reward for France in the Treaty of Versailles.

Millerand, an ex-socialist, became President in 1920, and he sent General Weygand to Warsaw to assist the Poles against the Russian Bolsheviks. A Franco–Polish treaty (1921) was followed by interlocking agreements with other Powers, Yugoslavia, Rumania, and Czechoslovakia, in the Little Entente. However, the French gained no strength from these states which looked to France for protection and support against bigger Powers. The French realised that these agreements gave only limited security, so the Versailles terms had to be rigorously imposed on a weakened Germany. Patriotic demands for German reparations were reinforced by the internal problem of reconstruction. To rebuild the shattered towns of the north-east cost money and France insisted that German marks should pay. In January 1922 Poincaré, considered to be the strong man of French politics, took office with the task of collecting reparations. In January 1923 he sent French troops into the Ruhr to force Germany to pay. Passive resistance, strikes and sabotage destroyed the prosperity of the Ruhr and with it the stability of the German mark. In 1924 France ended her occupation of the Ruhr and accepted the Dawes Plan with an ill grace. French public opinion, disillusioned with the Bloc National, turned in the elections to the socialists. A coalition of the parties of the Left, called the Cartel des Gauches, took office with Herriot as Premier.

This Government, which signed the Locarno agreements in 1925, could not offer any solution to France's internal problems any more than the Right. A vain attempt to impose anti-clerical legislation in Alsace aroused more opposition than support, and as the financial situation worsened, the three major elements in the Cartel—Radicals,

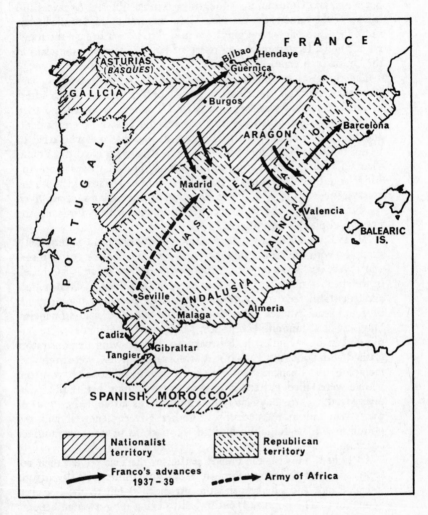

28 The Spanish Civil War, 1936–39

Socialists, and Communists—fought each other bitterly. As prices and taxes rose the value of the franc fell. Galloping inflation led to the break-up of the Cartel in 1926. Poincaré returned to power to save the franc. He formed a Government composed of France's leading politicians in the Union Nationale.

The threatening financial collapse was averted by revaluing and stabilising the franc, much to the relief of France's investors. International tensions were relaxed by Briand (Foreign Minister from 1926 to 1932) who persuaded France to accept the Locarno commitments and to admit Germany to the League of Nations, and who tried to bring about reconciliation with Germany. Briand accepted the Young Plan on reparations in 1930 and evacuated French troops from the Rhineland. Poincaré retired in 1928 and Briand had to struggle with the consequences of the Wall Street crash and the increasing support given to the Nazis in Germany, two developments which dismayed the French people and their governments.

When Briand died in 1932 a succession of ministers and governments grappled with the economic problems of the age. Salaries of civil servants were cut, government spending reduced, and taxation increased. In the space of just over a year four cabinets rose and fell. Communists and Fascists offered their solutions to replace the paralysed incompetence of republican politics. The climax came when a shady financier, Stavisky, shot himself. The police, Ministers, and Deputies were implicated in his swindles. In February 1934 right-wing demonstrators clashed with police in a Paris riot. Various fascist groups were involved, including one financed by Coty, the perfume millionaire. Fourteen people were killed and 200 injured in street-fighting before the rising petered out. Three days later the Communists attempted a coup of their own, no more successful. Another government fell and the politicians of the Republic shuffled the pack to produce yet another coalition.

To fight the fascists the French parties of the Left pooled their resources in 1936 to form a Popular Front government. Its slogan was 'bread, peace and liberty', and the premiership fell to the Socialist, Léon Blum. The Popular Front hoped to bring long-awaited benefits to the working class. Almost immediately an announcement promised a forty hour week, holidays with pay, and a twelve per cent wage increase. To find the money to pay for the reforms proved difficult but Blum fell back on government borrowing. Confidence in the franc suffered, and eventually Blum had to devalue. So at a time when German industry was booming, production in France fell. A recurrence of strikes revealed the failure of the Popular Front to bring industrial peace.

The slogan circulated 'Better Hitler than Blum', as French morale tumbled downwards. In June 1937 the Popular Front collapsed and France returned to the ineffectual rule of coalitions supported by small majorities in the Chamber.

None of the groups had any solution to the problems of foreign policy. In the 1920s French diplomats had thought security and reparations would solve France's difficulties. Later, Briand had hoped for a détente with Germany and had made concessions to Stresemann, the German Foreign Minister.

The coming of the Nazis to power in Germany altered everything. The initiative passed from France; Hitler called the tune and France danced to his music. In 1934 Pierre Laval held office briefly as Foreign Minister. He and his successors put their faith in the incomplete Maginot Line, in Hitler's promises of good faith and in vague hopes of an anti-German alliance. The high water mark of this policy came at Stresa in 1935 when a common front of Britain, France and Italy made brave protestations of their intention to defend international agreements.

With Mussolini's Abyssinian adventure the Stresa Powers fell out. The French uneasily followed the British policy of appeasement in 1938–39, not out of conviction but because of a despairing desire for peace and a massive hopelessness when faced with Hitler's triumphant diplomatic victories.

As the Czechoslovak crisis reached its climax in 1938 France was as usual divided. A mixture of pacifism and pro-fascist sentiments emerged as a powerful influence on policy. The Socialists, for instance, were split on the question of whether to resist Hitler or fight. Daladier, the French Premier, trailed behind Chamberlain at Munich and in 1939 drifted, almost listlessly, into war with Germany.

The war caught France unprepared. Daladier had refused to set up a Ministry of Munitions and other premiers had neglected to provide modern weapons for the Army. The French trusted the Maginot Line, assuming that the Germans would bleed themselves trying to breach its powerful defence works. No attempt was made to assist the Poles.

In May 1940 the German Panzer columns made a surprise attack, forced the French into retreat, and contemptuously ranged the countryside with their tanks. Gamelin, the defeatist French general, was removed and old Pétain was called back into power. With her army and morale shattered, France collapsed. By 22 June it was all over, the armistice was signed, and a pro-German government was set up at Vichy in central France with Pétain and Laval as its leaders.

14

The League of Nations

✳✳

In the later stages of the First World War statesmen in Britain, France and the USA were considering the best means to guarantee a future peace. Opinions differed on the form of the organisation to be set up at the end of the war. The French hoped to create a league of allies, bound to each other by rigid agreements, armed and prepared to use force to suppress any threat to their common security: a league to *enforce* peace. The British idea was for a wider membership, a permanent council of nations meeting regularly to discuss common problems, and to cooperate peacefully in negotiating settlements. President Woodrow Wilson of the USA enthusiastically supported the British scheme and made the establishment of the League of Nations one of the chief objectives of his policy at Paris in 1919.

Wilson and his advisers drew up the Covenant, a document of twenty-six Articles, explaining the objectives, powers and responsibilities of the League. The Covenant was incorporated into all the Treaties signed at the end of the war. By using the Treaties, Wilson hoped to remind the nations of the League and to encourage them to use it. By the same token, as the Treaties came under increasing criticism and were finally disregarded, so too was the League. By a quirk of fortune, the USA, by rejecting the Treaties, rejected the League too.

All the Allied and Associated Powers were included in the League from the beginning, and neutral Powers were invited to join. From forty-one in 1920 the number of members rose to fifty in 1924. Among the members were Latin-American states, the Scandinavian neutrals, and new states like Poland. The defeated Powers were at first excluded at the insistence of the French, for Clemenceau still hoped that the League would be used like the old war-time alliance to guarantee the French security from German attack.

The Covenant stated the rules the member-nations were to observe. 'In order to promote international cooperation and to achieve international peace and security', any fully self-governing state could join if its admission was agreed to by a two thirds vote of the Assembly. Any member state could withdraw from the League, giving two years' notice. By Article Ten, all states undertook 'to respect and preserve as against external aggression the territorial integrity and existing political independence of all members of the League.' They agreed not to go to war but to submit all disputes to the League. If negotiations were unsuccessful, states promised not to go to war until three months after the award of the arbitrators. The Council of the League had to make a decision on a dispute within six months. The Council or the Assembly were to hear political issues; judicial questions would be settled by the Permanent Court of International Justice. The members agreed to reduce armaments 'to the lowest point consistent with national safety'. The Council was to formulate plans for the reduction of armaments and the individual states were to exchange full information on the scale of their armaments.

THE ORGANISATION OF THE LEAGUE

The League of Nations worked through an Assembly, a Council and a permanent Secretariat. The Assembly, which consisted of representatives of all the members of the League, met annually to discuss general topics connected with international affairs. At these meetings each state had one vote.

The Council, which met three times a year, at first consisted of a Permanent Council made up of representatives of the Allied governments (USA, Britain, France, Italy and Japan) and a Non-Permanent Council elected for a term of office. With the USA's withdrawal, the other four Allies took over control of the Permanent Council with another four Powers as Non-Permanent members. The Allies had intended to be able to out-vote the others but the departure of the USA made numbers equal. Later, the Permanent members found themselves in a minority for by 1926 the Non-Permanent group numbered nine. Germany in 1926 and the USSR in 1934 joined the Permanent group. Although out-numbered, the Allies greatly influenced the League's policies and decisions. The main functions of the Council were to hear and decide on disputes submitted to it. In its work, Article Five (i) of the Covenant proved to be a major stumbling-block. It stated that 'decisions at any meeting of the Assembly or the Council shall require the agreement of all the members of the League represented at the meeting.' This fatal clause paralysed initiative and made the League little more than a debating-chamber for the nations. In the United Nations this difficulty has been avoided by allowing only the major Powers on the Security Council the power of veto, but in the League the smallest and weakest Power could prohibit action by a single adverse vote.

At Geneva, in Switzerland, the Secretariat, composed of the Secretary-General and an organisation of payment officials, looked after the daily affairs of the League. The officials and the expenses of running the League were provided by the members.

POWERS OF THE LEAGUE

To give the League of Nations teeth proved to be a difficult problem. Nations were reluctant to surrender their independence, their freedom of action, to an international organisation. People wanted the League to be strong and effective but were not prepared to give it the powers to ensure this, if it meant the loss of their own rights. In effect, the League only acted decisively when its members were unanimous in their agreement and this was a rare event.

In a political dispute between member-states the Council would sit in judgement. It was hoped the Council would end disputes by negotiation, by a just settlement of rights. If the Council failed to find a solution they could refer it to the Assembly.

If any member-state or even a non-League state resorted to war it was considered to have committed an act of war against the other member states. Then sanctions, the severance of all trade and financial links with the aggressor, would be imposed by the nations acting together. If this diplomatic and commercial isolation did not work the Council could then recommend that their members take military action. This cumbrous machinery proved difficult to put into effect. The League never had an army of its own; it relied on a common pool of armies provided by the nations, acting on the League's behalf.

To handle legal disputes between nations the Permanent Council of

International Justice was set up with its headquarters at the Hague, in Holland. The Court's fifteen judges, chosen from various nations, dealt with questions of maritime law, the interpretation of treaties, and legal disputes between one state and another. The members of the League agreed to carry out any decision of the Court without resorting to war. The Court could not compel a state to appear before it, nor enforce its verdict, once given. Like the League it depended on good-will and honest dealing.

THE COMMISSIONS

The political activities of the League won the greatest publicity but the most valuable part of its work was being achieved quietly and far more effectively. To deal with the former Turkish and German colonies, mandates were set up under a Mandates Commission. A mandate was not to be annexed by the controlling Power but had to be held 'in trust' for the native peoples until they were ready to take over the reins of government for themselves. The League forbade slavery and the exploitation of the native peoples and guaranteed religious freedom. The character of the mandates differed according to their varying stages of development. 'A' class mandates were those near to full independence (Palestine, Lebanon, Transjordan, Iraq and Syria). Here, the Mandatory Power had to give administrative advice and direction 'until such time as the territories were able to stand alone.' 'B' Class mandates (like Tanganyika, Togoland and the Cameroons) were at such a stage that the Power had to exercise stricter, more thorough control and had to safeguard religious freedom, maintain order and prohibit abuses like the slave trade and drug traffic. In 'C' class mandates (S W Africa, and the Pacific Islands), complete control was essential because of the backwardness of the native peoples. Each Power had to submit an annual report to the Council and accept the supervision of the Permanent Mandates Commission.

The League established other commissions to deal with social and economic questions. The control of drugs, the resettlement of refugees, the improvement of health and the fight against disease, the prohibition of forced labour, and co-operation in developing communications were some of the activities delegated to the responsibility of the Commissions. Other bodies were set up to administer Danzig, the Saar, Minorities and Disarmament.

Another quite separate body was the International Labour Organisation. The League hoped to end social injustice which in itself was felt to be a threat to world peace. The ILO tried to persuade nations to improve working conditions, raise wages above mere subsistence level, end unfair contracts between workmen and employers, and provide sickness and injury compensation schemes. A Labour parliament composed of employers and workmen and the various governments drew up a code of rights for the Labour movement.

In the 1920s the grim conditions of unemployment, hunger and low wages were examined by the ILO in a series of documents, but like the League, it could not force members to adopt its recommendations, and on occasions was ignored and humiliated. However, over the years the social and economic commissions and the ILO did make governments aware of the problems of the poor and under-privileged, and achieved lasting changes in many states.

The League gave people new confidence, new hope for the future. It could not guarantee peace, but at last nations were to co-operate to amend unfair treaties and discuss their disagreements openly. War could not be banished, but if nations really wanted peace, here seemed the opportunity to grasp it. The League fitted the feeling of revulsion against the slaughter of the war. The League, the International Court and the ILO reflected a new faith in 'internationalism' and 'collective security' by which nations would freely and voluntarily co-operate for common objectives. This idea depended on goodwill and friendship, but as the years passed it had to contend with the ambitions of the Powers, which after the honeymoon period of 1919–23 became as self-seeking and nationalistic as before. Through the combination of the Treaties and the League, President Wilson and his colleagues at Paris hoped they had solved the causes of wars. German militarism, the arms race, minority grievances, territorial claims, colonial disputes, secret alliances, even economic injustice—all seemed to have been catered for. Any loose ends could be tied up by the League. It was an inspiring picture, and yet it failed, disastrously.

THE SETTLEMENT OF INTERNATIONAL DISPUTES, 1920–25

After the Paris Conference had ended and the delegates had dispersed to their own states, Europe went through a period of uncertainty. Not everyone was satisfied with the decisions made by the peace-makers and some nations tried to extend their frontiers by force. At first, statesmen took little notice of the League. It received little publicity and politicians made it clear that they preferred swift action to slow negotiation at Geneva. Without the power to pass binding laws, without an army, the League could only appeal to and not punish belligerent nations. In any case, the war-time Allies liked direct consultation with each other. In Paris, France and Britain set up a Conference of Ambassadors, a body composed of the ambassadors of all the Great Powers, together with the French Foreign Secretary. This Conference's responsibility was to enforce the provisions of the Treaty of Versailles and the other Treaties. In the 1920s a series of conferences between the ambassadors, ministers and representatives of the Powers met at London, San Remo and Genoa. At these meetings, reparations, economic problems, frontier changes and disarmament were discussed. The conferences cut the ground from under the feet of the League, for the spotlight was concentrated not on Geneva but where important decisions were being taken.

Nevertheless, the League of Nations slowly gained in prestige, surviving the setback of the rejection of the Treaty and the League by the United States' Senate. The League had a few successes in minor disputes. Sweden and Finland quarrelled about the possession of the Aaland Islands, lying between the two countries, in the Baltic Sea. In 1917 the Finnish people had declared their independence from Russia and had seized the Islands, useful as a naval base. The islanders themselves preferred union with Sweden, who brought the dispute before the League in 1920. The League's decision, that the Islands were to be joined to Finland, but that they should be demilitarised and given self-government, seemed a sensible compromise.

The League carried out the plebiscite in Silesia, and on the basis of the result partitioned the provinces between Germany and Poland. In 1919–20 it arranged an international loan for Austria and helped to organise its banking and currency systems.

The next dispute ended in failure. The Paris negotiators found it difficult to decide on Poland's eastern frontiers. The Curzon Line was fixed as a temporary frontier but the Poles thought that the award of territory was insufficient. In 1919 they attacked Russia and seized the town of Vilna, which was predominantly Jewish and Lithuanian in character. Vilna changed hands several times during the fighting but eventually returned to Polish control. The League decided that Vilna ought to go to Lithuania but the Poles refused to surrender it, and the League could not evict them. To save the League from further humilia-

tion, the Conference of Ambassadors took the dispute into consideration in 1923 and acquiesced in the Polish annexation. Poland, like
Finland, had friends in Paris and London, where the western Governments felt that strong states on the Russian borders would deter the
Bolsheviks from trying to recapture Russia's lost territories or carry
their communist theories abroad. Sweden and Lithuania on the other
hand felt that injustice had triumphed, because Anglo-French interests
had been given priority.

ATTEMPTS TO STRENGTHEN THE LEAGUE

The League of Nations had tried to keep the peace by inviting all
nations to join in pacts of 'collective security' against aggressors. The
French, however, did not believe the promises that, if attacked, the
other Powers in Europe would necessarily leap to their defence. Nervously, they insisted on additional guarantees, including permanent
German disarmament. France rejected all proposals for her own disarmament: without the alliance of Britain and the USA, the French
felt defenceless. The French opposition to the general reduction of
armaments annoyed the British who believed that the arms race had
helped to cause the First World War, and in any case, protected by their
navy, the British did not sympathise with the French arguments for a
large army.

One attempt to end the dilemma came in 1923 in the Draft Treaty of
Mutual Assistance. This Treaty proposed general disarmament, and to
help the French in their search for security, regional agreements binding nations together for their common defence. To assist the League,
the Treaty proposed that within four days of the outbreak of hostilities,
the Council should brand the aggressor and all member states should
then take military action. France welcomed these suggestions, but
Britain and her Dominions rejected them.

To find a way around the British objections the Geneva Protocol
was drawn up and approved by the League Assembly in 1924. The
regional agreements were dropped. In a new plan which aimed at reducing the chance of war, the Protocol suggested general disarmament
coupled with compulsory arbitration in political disputes by the League.
If the League failed to achieve a unanimous verdict, the case would be
passed to a committee of arbitrators. If any nation still persisted in war,
sanctions would then have to be applied by all the nations. The Protocol

might have solved the League's difficulties but again Britain refused to accept, for the Dominions made it clear that they would not bind themselves to fight in another European war.

The failure to have the Treaty or the Protocol ratified was a set-back to the supporters of the League. Almost immediately new problems were thrust upon it. In August 1923 four Italians, including a General, all members of a frontier commission, were murdered on the Greek side of the Greek-Albanian border. Mussolini, intent on building up his international prestige, sent a violent ultimatum to Greece, demanding compensation of 50 million lire. The Greek Government, reluctant to provoke a war, agreed to pay compensation to the families of the four men but haggled over the price. Italian forces sailed to the island of Corfu, off the Greek coast, shelled and occupied it. The dispute was submitted to the League of Nations by the Greeks. In the Council, the Italian delegate vetoed action whenever he could. The Conference of Ambassadors again came to the rescue, took the case out of the hands of the League and promptly supported Mussolini. The Greeks were ordered to pay the 50 million lire indemnity and the Italians were asked to evacuate Corfu.

In 1925 sporadic fighting broke out along the frontier between Greece and Bulgaria. The Greeks, fearing that they might be suddenly attacked, seized the initiative and launched an invasion on an unsuspecting Bulgaria. The Secretary-General, Sir Eric Drummond, quickly called a meeting of the Council. The Greeks were ordered to retire and to pay a sum of £45,000 to Bulgaria in compensation for damage caused by their forces. The Greeks obeyed: a weak military Power, they did not dare to bluff a critical, united League.

Convinced by these events that the League must be given greater prestige if not greater powers, changes were made. The Conference of Ambassadors was disbanded, so ridding the League of a rival; membership was increased to fifty-two by inviting uncommitted states to join, and the British and French Governments gave more publicity to the affairs of the Council by sending their Foreign Ministers more regularly to its meetings.

REPARATIONS

The Reparations Commission, appointed to fix the total amount to be repaid by Germany, found its task difficult. The Commission had to

balance the demands of the Allies with Germany's capacity to pay.
Conferences called at San Remo and Spa in 1920 failed to decide on this
elusive total, and by April 1921 the Commission had discovered that
Germany had paid no more than the costs of the Allied army in the
Rhineland. In sudden agreement, the Commission fixed on the figure
of £6,600 million. Germany paid the first instalment later in 1921—
£50 million.

In 1922 France quibbled over the inadequacies of German deliveries
of coal and timber and in January 1923 the French Premier, Poincaré,
ordered troops into the Ruhr.

The Reparations Commission and its parent the League of Nations
were powerless. The passive resistance of the German workers led to the
French seizure of the Ruhr railways, factories and mines. Poincaré was
determined that the German commitment to pay reparations partly
in goods and raw materials should be met. Production in the Ruhr fell
by two thirds when the German workers refused to obey French
orders. Financial collapse followed quickly for Germany. Violent
clashes occurred between French troops and the workers. To try to end
the crisis, Stanley Baldwin appealed to the USA to cooperate with
Britain in an investigation into Germany's capacity to pay. A new
committee, with the American general Charles Dawes as its chairman,
drew up a Plan, published in April 1924.

Dawes suggested that German financial recovery with a balanced
budget and a stable currency was the first priority. A new Reichsmark
was recommended as a replacement for the worthless currency then in
use. With a return to stability, Germany could begin to pay reparations
by increasing instalments, from £50 million in the first year to £125
million by the fifth year. To set the wheels of German industry moving, a foreign loan of £40 million was raised and given to Germany.
The Dawes Plan was put into effect and by July 1925 a more conciliatory
French Foreign Minister, Briand, had withdrawn the last of the French
troops from the Ruhr.

The reparations problem was complicated by the war debts in-
curred by the Allies. The USA had loaned Britain 4½ billion dollars.
Britain had herself made loans of about 10 billion dollars to her Allies.
Since the USA demanded repayment from Britain and her other
debtors, France and Italy among others, the Allies insisted on German
reparations. Germany's payments would contribute to the price they
had to pay to the USA. It was a vicious circle. In 1922 the British
Government tried to break it by offering to remit all debts due to
Britain from her Allies in respect of loans, but as the USA insisted on
repayment, the British would still have to ask not for the whole debt

but sufficient to pay their creditors. The idea did not meet with approval. The French thought that all debts should be cancelled. After all, France had paid for the war in flesh and blood, the others could pay in cash.

In 1922 the USA demanded payment. President Calvin Coolidge was reputed to have said of war debts, 'they hired the money, didn't they?' Stanley Baldwin for Britain promised to pay over a period of sixty-two years, at three and a third per cent interest. The French and Italians later fixed their own terms with the USA. These events help to explain the determination of the Allies to make Germany pay. But in the end, neither reparations nor war debts were fully paid. By 1931 Britain had repaid nearly 2,000 million dollars. In return the USA lavished further loans on Europe. When the economic slump came in 1929 and the Americans called in their money, the European economies collapsed. Both reparations and war debts were forgotten in the resulting panic.

DISARMAMENT AND SECURITY

Although Germany had been forced to surrender her weapons and reduce her forces, the other Powers had not followed suit. France, disappointed by the failure to continue the wartime alliance, kept a large army. Britain and other Powers partially disarmed. Within the League, attempts were made to persuade nations to adopt a general disarmament policy, but with little success. Again the League was bypassed, the Powers seizing the initiative and negotiating independently with each other.

The Washington Conference, 1921

In the Far East, Japan had become the dominant Power. The German interests in China and the Pacific had fallen into Japan's lap in the peace treaties. The USA feared the extension of Japanese power in China, and pressed the nations to tie Japan down to formal agreements. In 1921 the USA invited Britain, Italy, France and Japan to send representatives to a conference at Washington. Other nations were also invited and at the end of a series of discussions three Treaties were signed:

1) The Four-Power Treaty signed by the USA, Britain, France and Japan, dealt with the Pacific, where they promised to respect each

other's rights and to solve any problems by consultation

2) The Five-Power Treaty signed by the same four, plus Italy. This agreement limited naval armaments but only of larger vessels, like cruisers and battleships. Quotas were fixed for each country. The ratios decided on were:

USA	GB	Japan	Italy	France
5	5	3	1·7	1·7

3) The Nine-Power Treaty by which nations promised to respect the integrity of China.

The decisions of the Conference were greeted with enthusiasm, for peace and control of armaments seemed assured in the Pacific. These hopes proved false, for Japan was secretly dissatisfied. The Japanese thought themselves insulted by not being given parity with the USA and Britain in shipping, and resented the control over their intrigues in China.

The Locarno Pacts, 1925

It was less easy to secure a measure of disarmament in Europe. The failure to achieve agreement over the Geneva Protocol led the nations seriously to reconsider alternative means to obtain security without arms. They fell back on interconnected regional pacts. In October 1925 at Locarno, their leading ministers reached agreement. The Pacts included:

(a) A Treaty guaranteeing the German-Belgian and the German-French frontiers, signed by Germany, France, Belgium, Britain and Italy

(b) A French-Polish and French-Czech Treaty for mutual assistance in case of German attack

(c) An agreement to allow Germany to enter the League of Nations

(d) Treaties guaranteeing arbitration in disputes between Germany and her neighbours, Czechoslovakia, Poland, France and Belgium.

Great Britain would not guarantee Germany's eastern borders, but even so, the limited Locarno agreements pleased France. They had not strengthened the League but had strengthened peace. Yet the Treaties contained the seeds of future troubles, for Britain's distinction between Germany's eastern and western frontiers made it obvious that France would have to stand alone in defending Poland and Czechoslovakia. But at Locarno Germany had entered into agreements voluntarily, in contrast to Versailles, and optimism and goodwill spread through Europe.

In 1926 Germany joined the League and took her place on the Council as a permanent member. Spain and Brazil, annoyed that they had not been given similar status, left the League.[1] The honeymoon period of good relations continued into 1927 when Briand proposed to the USA a pact in which the two countries would renounce war as an instrument of national policy. The American Secretary of State, Kellogg, agreed, but specified that war must be allowed in self-defence. He suggested that all nations be invited to sign. In August 1928 France, Germany, the USA, and Britain signed what became known as the Kellogg Pact. A host of other Powers, finally sixty-five in all, followed their example.

Men felt that this had strengthened the Covenant of the League, but although the Pact condemned all wars it did not say how aggressors were to be punished. The League was back where it had started, trying to find means to enforce peace. The Pact was an expression of moral principle, which it was one's duty to sign. Empty of force, it rested on trust and goodwill. Austen Chamberlain, Stresemann and Briand met frequently at Geneva and in their conversations improved relations between their countries, Britain, Germany and France. To prove this new-found friendship had real substance, in 1929 reparations payments were revised in the Young Plan. Germany had to pay over a period of fifty-nine years, but the total sum was reduced considerably, to £2,000 million. Chamberlain and Briand agreed to the withdrawal of all Allied troops from the Rhineland by June 1930, five years before the date fixed by the Treaty of Versailles.

THE DECLINE OF THE LEAGUE OF NATIONS

In the 1930s Fascism spread quickly throughout Europe. The failure of the elected governments to solve the economic problems of the period led men to turn to strong, ruthless leaders. Fascism was predominantly nationalist and in consequence the League, an international organisation, suffered a decline, like democracy. The situation in Europe changed suddenly in 1929. Stresemann died, leaving Germany in the grip of an economic crisis. Briand and Austen Chamberlain lost power in France and Britain. The peacemakers had gone, and with them one of the most calm periods in the history of the inter-war years. New threats to world peace loomed up almost immediately and the League of Nations was called on to handle its most difficult problems.

1. Spain returned in 1928.

Manchuria

The League's failure to deal decisively with the new dangers was clearly revealed in the Manchurian war. Japan was by tradition a militant and autocratic power. The difficulties of her economic position—an expanding population, overcrowded islands, the need to cultivate more food and export more silk and other goods—all these factors forced Japan towards aggression and territorial conquest. In 1931 her exports of silk fell considerably. Desperately, the Japanese looked to Manchuria, the large province to the north of China. An excuse was quickly engineered. The Japanese had since 1904 a right to station troops along the Manchurian railway. The Chinese were accused of having caused explosions along the railway. Later evidence revealed that Japan had plotted the whole affair. Without warning the Japanese army struck at and captured the key town of Mukden and in just over seven months overran most of the province. The Chinese Government appealed to the League. After a long delay the Council sent a Commission of Inquiry with Lord Lytton as its chairman. Japan maintained that she could not withdraw her troops until 'fundamental principles' were settled between herself and China. These principles were never explained to the League. The World Disarmament Conference was meeting in Geneva at the time, and the news of Japan's aggression caused other nations to think about reducing their armaments.

The Lytton Commission toured Manchuria, watched curiously by thousands of Japanese troops. The Commission's Report stressed the disorganised state of China as if this explained and excused the Japanese aggression. Japan suddenly and defiantly announced the creation of an independent state of Manchukuo, although it was quite clear to the Commission that the people of Manchuria had preferred their status before the invasion of 1931.

In 1933 the League of Nations finally issued a Report which said that Manchuria belonged to China; that the disorders should be peacefully settled; that Manchukuo was a puppet state of Japan, and that Japanese troops should be withdrawn from the province.

The Japanese Government then resigned from the League and launched air and land attacks on another Chinese province, Jehol. Far from being stopped, Japan had defied the League and went unpunished. Why did the League not take more drastic action at a decisive moment in its history? One must remember that the League was a group of separate nations, and each one had its own reason for remaining inactive. The Western Powers did not want war with Japan. Britain wished to retain Japan's friendship for strategic and economic reasons. Other nations saw no reason why they should fight in China in a dispute not of their making or their responsibility.

The European governments calmed their consciences by pointing out that a strong Japan would be a valuable barrier to Russian ambitions in the Far East. No one wanted to drive Japan from the League. The combination of these reasons meant that Japan escaped attack. The League lost dignity and effect—its decline accelerated after 1933.

The World Disarmament Conference

Meanwhile, the World Disarmament Conference of sixty-one nations drifted into stalemate. From its inception in 1932 the Conference faced grave problems, complicated by the world economic depression and Japanese aggression in Manchuria. Several plans were offered but none adopted. The Russian Foreign Minister, Litvinov, made the startling suggestion of complete disarmament. The Germans wanted equality in armaments, others hoped for the destruction of all but defensive weapons, and some suggested a League of Nations army. All plans were rejected. After 1934 the Conference ceased to meet; another nail had been driven into the coffin of the League.

After 1935 only those with more zeal than common sense put their faith for peace in the League of Nations. In the face of the Nazi revival of Germany, the French desperately increased their forces and strengthened their defences. Their efforts to surround Germany with a ring of alliances failed when the German-Polish Pact of 1934 was announced. One success for the French was the entry of Soviet Russia into the League in 1934 with a permanent seat on the Council. Yet Russia did not prove to be the doughty champion that France expected. The Russians suspected the Western Powers of trying to trick them into a war against Hitler, in which the British and French would remain neutral.

In 1935 the League conducted a plebiscite in the Saar. The people voted for return to Germany. However, the optimistic impressions of German cooperation with the League and the Allies were dissolved when Germany later repudiated the disarmament clauses of the Treaty of Versailles, introduced conscription and resigned from the League.

Abyssinia

In October 1935, Italian troops attacked Abyssinia. The Emperor, Haile Selassie, appealed to the League. Mussolini had earlier calculated that as the League had not taken action over the Manchurian War, he would be safe. Instead the Council of the League unanimously (except for the vote of Italy) declared that the Covenant had been broken. In the Assembly fifty out of fifty-four nations agreed that aggression had been committed, and set up a committee to arrange the application of sanctions against Italy. The acceptance of imports from, or sale of arms to, Italy was prohibited. Finally, a limited prohibition was put on exports and financial loans to Italy, although the exclusion of oil from the sanctions weakened the measures. The boycotting of Italy was not effective, although Article Sixteen of the Covenant said that members should 'undertake *immediately* the severance of *all* trade or financial relations.' Britain and France did not want to lose Italy's friendship: they needed Italy for the greater danger to the League contained in Germany's plans for rearmament. Consequently, Britain did not close the Suez Canal to Italian shipping and France maintained her exports of iron and steel to Mussolini.

Furthermore, Sir Samuel Hoare and Pierre Laval proposed a joint British-French Pact which would partition Abyssinia, granting Italy the greater share. By now (December 1935) the Council of the League followed the two Western Powers like children after the Pied Piper. But British public opinion was not as hypnotised: the outburst of anger against the Pact led to Hoare's dismissal.

With Mussolini now triumphant, sanctions seemed inessential. In July 1936 the League recommended that sanctions should cease. With the Abyssinian War the League reached a sad milestone in its history, for no one now saw it as the guarantee of international peace, save one or two optimists. By the end of 1936 Japan, Germany and Italy had left the League. Only Great Britain, France and Russia of the Great Powers remained to go through the motions of loyalty to the dying institution.

THE DRIFT TO WAR, 1936–39

Mussolini's defiance of the League encouraged Hitler to launch new assaults on the Treaty of Versailles. In March 1936 German troops marched into the Rhineland. Hitler's armies were not prepared for a war and firm action by Britain and France might have forced him to withdraw. Although the French were alarmed, they failed to persuade Britain of the danger, and nothing was done. In November 1936 Mussolini announced the creation of the Berlin-Rome Axis Pact and shortly afterwards the Anti-Comintern Pact united the two Fascist powers and Japan in an anti-communist front.

In 1936 also, General Franco, the Spanish Fascist leader, began his long struggle against the Republican government. The League declared for non-intervention, and Britain and France agreed, but Italy and Germany had no such intention. Italian aeroplanes bombed Republican-held cities, and German arms were smuggled to Franco. In reply, Soviet Russia gave aid to the Republicans.

The British and French governments, desperate to rescue some prestige for themselves and the League from the wreck of their hopes for peace, set up a non-intervention committee (including Germany, Russia and Italy) which in 1937 agreed in principle, although not in conduct, on a ban on the export of arms to Spain. Shortly afterwards, a German battleship was attacked by Spanish planes and so Italy and Germany withdrew from the committee. Mysterious submarine attacks were made on British and French shipping in the Mediterranean. In September 1937 at the Nyon Conference, called to discuss the sinkings, Britain and France decided to send out joint naval patrols. The attacks suddenly ceased. All this helped the Spanish Republicans very little, and by 1939 they had been defeated and driven from Spain.

The Japanese now seized the initiative, taking advantage of the paralysis affecting Britain and France. An incident between Japanese and Chinese troops in July 1937 led to more fighting. The Chinese found a new resolve to stand firm, but faced by superior Japanese forces, abandoned Peking to the invaders. The war flared up along several fronts with more Japanese victories. The Chinese Government appealed to the League of Nations which declared Japan to be the aggressor and called on other nations to aid China. In fact all that China obtained from her friends was words, not deeds. Although British commerical interests in Shanghai and Hong Kong were in some danger, no effective action was taken. Europe concerned the western Powers; China had to fight her own war, which dragged on until 1945.

In the years preceding the Second World War the League found itself ignored. Neville Chamberlain, the British Prime Minister from 1937, and Daladier, the French Premier, put their faith not in collective security but appeasement. Germany's and Italy's claims were to be met by 'reasonable concessions', in the hope that once the 'injustices' of the Versailles Treaty had been ended, peace would be guaranteed. Alongside this policy the two Allies re-armed, to deter the dictators from extreme acts of aggression. These policies ignored the fanatical aspect of German policy, which had no limit to its demands and its objectives. Once Hitler realised the Western Powers were on the retreat he demanded more and more concessions. In 1938 Austria, and in 1938–39 Czechoslovakia and Memelland, were seized and devoured by Germany. The League was hardly consulted. Britain and France handled these annexations by direct negotiation with Germany. The League remained a shadowy institution, ignored by the major Powers.

In 1939 Britain and France guaranteed Polish independence, and in September went to war because of the German violation of Polish territory. In December 1939 the League of Nations made its last impact on history when Finland appealed to it against a Russian attack. Russia was pronounced an aggressor and expelled from the League. The ILO and the Permanent Court of Justice survived the Second World War, to be absorbed into the United Nations in 1945. But to all intents and purposes the League died in 1939, a failure.

INQUEST

Why did the League fail? From the start, it had the handicap of being linked with the Treaties, especially the Treaty of Versailles, which the League had constantly to defend against those who wished to revise it. Germany, Russia, and Italy regarded the Paris Treaties as unfair; each nation in turn crossed swords with the League. Perhaps one should ask why the Treaties failed rather than why the League failed.

The men who drafted the Covenant assumed that after a terrible war, the nations would want peace and would work honestly and enthusiastically for it. They were unable to take into account the rise of the Fascist states, ready and willing to use war as an instrument of policy. Nor did the League have the power to deal with aggressors. Sanctions, when applied against Italy, were ineffective. The necessity for a unanimous decision in the Council and the Assembly on major issues was a paralysing factor in the League's history. With no army of its own, and no common policy between the nations, the League was disastrously weakened. The refusal of the USA to join, and the exclusion of Russia and Germany in its early days, gave the League the appearance of an Anglo-French alliance. Although eventually admitted to the League, the later resignations of Japan, Germany and Italy strengthened the dominance of Britain and France over events at Geneva. Instead of appearing as a truly international organisation, the League appeared to be an aide to Anglo-French policy.

Perhaps if given a stronger structure, with more power to the Secretary-General; if sanctions had been made automatic in case of aggression; if the Draft Treaty or the Geneva Protocol had been adopted; if a two thirds majority instead of unanimity had been applied to the voting procedure; all or one of these factors might have strengthened the League.

On the major issues—Manchuria, Abyssinia, the Rhineland and rearmament—the enemies of the League exploited its weaknesses. Quick military action, taken while a diplomatic smokescreen was put down at Geneva, presented the League with difficult problems. The Council and the Assembly seldom had the opportunity to act before aggression; presented with a 'fait accompli' the League could do little but protest.

These arguments indicate that the League failed because of bad management, bad faith, bad luck, and lack of strength. Beyond these factors lay the essential dilemma of the 1930s. People assumed that the existence of the League guaranteed peace. They assumed that the collective threat of war by a group of nations would deter an aggressor. After the horror of 1914–18 there could be no question of actual war, but threats would be sufficient. This was a hopeful, idealistic view of events. Statesmen did not dare disillusion people, by pointing out that the League had no life of its own, but was the common action of all the nations. That is, the League would only be effective if the nations *were* prepared to go to war. In the 1930s this collective will was missing. Japan, Italy and Germany all called the bluff of the League and the promises of the nations. Challenged by stronger wills, the League collapsed.

15

The Weimar Republic

THE REVOLUTION OF 1918

General Ludendorff's spring offensive of 1918 had ended in failure and retreat. The German armies were too exhausted to fight a rearguard action, and the Allied blockade of Germany had led to hunger and a demand from the disillusioned people for an end to the war. Ludendorff recognised the inevitability of defeat and advised the Chancellor, Prince Max of Baden, to bring Social-Democrat leaders into the government and to negotiate an armistice with the Allies before their troops invaded Germany. Finally, on 26 October, Ludendorff resigned his command. The first stage of the German revolution had ended with the replacement of the old imperial-army regime by parliamentary leaders.

The violent second stage came in November. The sailors of the German fleet had been restless for some time and mutinies broke out at Kiel and Wilhelmshaven. The rebels linked up with soldiers at Hamburg, and formed Workers' and Soldiers' Councils. They demanded the abdication of the Kaiser and an end to the war, although in the background some Communists hoped for a more violent socialist revolution on the Russian pattern. In Munich, Kurt Eisner, a socialist leader, proclaimed an independent Bavarian Republic. On 9 November, Prince Max resigned and Friedrich Ebert, the leader of the Social-Democrats, took over as Chancellor. The Kaiser fled into exile in Holland and later abdicated. At the same time the minor princes and kings of Bavaria, Saxony and other states abdicated and disappeared from Germany. Ebert then proclaimed the German Republic.

With Germany in a state of military and economic collapse Ebert had no alternative but to accept the Allied surrender terms on 11 November. The revolution was over. It had occurred because of defeat and hunger rather than any rush of genuine revolutionary spirit. Ebert wanted above all to restore order; the German people wanted peace. Consequently Ebert quickly and without conditions accepted the Allied terms and damped down the revolution to prevent it from spreading.

From the start the new Republic was thus saddled with the reputation of defeat and unrest. Nor could Ebert restore order immediately. For several months after November 1918 a dangerous revolutionary situation existed. Cold, hunger and anger created an atmosphere in which strikes, mutinies and disorder were everyday occurrences. Although the army was largely disbanded, some regiments remained in service to assist the police in maintaining order. In January 1919, after a general election, the new National Assembly met at the town of Weimar to escape the riots in Berlin. There they tackled the daunting problems facing the infant Republic.

THE RISINGS OF 1919

The Berlin riots had been engineered by the Spartacists[1] or, as they became in December 1918, the German Communist Party. In northern Germany the Communists had been quietly organising Workers' and Soldiers' soviets on the Russian pattern, planning and awaiting an opportunity for violent revolution. Led by Karl Liebknecht and Rosa Luxemburg, they accused Ebert of betraying socialism by maintaining the German High Command in power and by refusing to nationalise German industry. In December 1918 street fighting broke out in Berlin. These events divided the German socialists. Ebert and the Social-Democrats were prepared to work through the parliamentary system. They disliked the idea of violent Communism and were ready to use the army to crush Liebknecht. The third socialist group, the Independent-Socialists, favoured a temporary dictatorship until the immediate post-war problems had been solved. They advocated the introduction of parliament and socialism at a later date. As the Communists fought in the Berlin streets, three of the Independent-Socialist ministers resigned, rather than be connected with Ebert's harsh measures. The Minister of Defence, Noske, called on the army for help.

1. The Spartacists derived their name from a newspaper they published, *The Letters of Spartacus*, after the leader of a slave revolt against the tyrants of ancient Rome.

Liebknecht and Rosa Luxemburg were caught and shot. The rising collapsed. Of the three socialist groups, the Social-Democrats were now supreme, but only because of their reliance on the army.

In Bavaria, the unrest continued. Kurt Eisner was assassinated in February 1919 and a 'soviet' government seized power. Civil war followed. Eventually the capital, Munich, was captured by a combined army of regular soldiers and volunteers, called the Freikorps. Ebert had again to call on the army to restore order. Communists, pacifists and innocent reformers were rounded up and shot. In Munich resentment and hatred of the Social-Democrats burned deeply. The fact that some of the socialist leaders were Jews was given wide publicity and added to the general feeling that the Jews were the only people who had benefited from the war.

THE CONSTITUTION OF 1919

The new constitution, published in August 1919, gave Germany effective parliamentary government for the first time. At the head of the state was the President, elected every seven years by the votes of all the German people. The President chose the leading minister, the Chancellor. Unlike Bismarck's Germany, the Chancellor needed to command a majority in the Reichstag to form an effective government. The President was given extensive powers to deal with any crisis. For instance, he could rule by decree if there was no stable majority in the Reichstag able to form a government. In the final years of the Weimar Republic immediately preceding Hitler's seizure of power in 1933 these emergency powers came to be used regularly.

Parliament consisted of two houses. The Reichstag of 580 members was elected by all citizens over twenty, in a secret ballot, using the system of proportional representation. Under the working of this system, if a party obtained ten per cent of all the votes cast (electors voted for parties, not candidates) it obtained ten per cent of the seats (i.e. fifty-eight). The system favoured the small parties which dominated the Reichstag, but made it virtually impossible for any one party to gain a majority over all the others. Consequently, governments were formed by coalitions of the larger parties. A great deal of political manoeuvring went on behind the scenes before a government could be formed. Ministries tended to come and go in rapid succession if a section of the coalition disagreed and broke away. The Reichstag made the laws and dealt with questions of foreign policy, defence, police, finance and trade.

The other house, the Reichsrat, was composed of representatives from the 'Länder' (provinces) like Bavaria, Saxony, Prussia and Baden. The Reichsrat had little power, able only to delay legislation and reflect the views of the different areas of Germany. As in Bismarck's day these provinces retained some separate control over education, the law courts, and public health.

Other clauses of the new Constitution guaranteed all German citizens freedom of speech, freedom from arbitrary arrest, freedom of conscience, movement and association, and equality before the law. Altogether the Weimar Republic seemed on the surface to provide Germany with a perfect democratic system of government. Unfortunately the Constitution lasted only fourteen years and the faults within it helped to shorten its life. In addition, Germany had been introduced to democracy in the hour of defeat and civil war. Weimar—its politicians, its parties, its constitution—became suspect, tied to the acceptance of Versailles and imposed on Germany by the victorious Allies. Weimar had little chance of survival with these millstones around its neck.

THE ENEMIES OF THE REPUBLIC

Germany had taken no part in the negotiations at Versailles which led to the peace treaty of 1919. When the Treaty terms were published German public opinion was inflamed. The right-wing, nationalist groups denounced the Treaty as an insult to Germany and criticised the Weimar politicians for accepting it. The German people had been fed with propaganda during the war, convincing them that Germany was 'winning'. The German army was thought to be invincible, and consequently the legend was cultivated that the army had been stabbed in the back by the 'November Criminals' of the Weimar regime. On the day that the German representatives signed, Berlin newspapers appeared with a black mourning band across their front pages. The terms of the Treaty seemed vengeful and unjust. They imposed on the Germans a war-guilt they did not feel.[1]

1. The German people ignored the similarity of the Versailles Treaty to that which had been imposed on a defeated Russia by Germany in the Treaty of Brest-Litovsk in 1918. The Russians had been forced to surrender a quarter of their territory including a large slice of their industrial area.

The new Republic was assailed from all sides. In 1919 the main threat had come from the socialist Left. In March 1920 an attempt was made by the extreme Right to overthrow the government. The industrialists and landowners who had been left in possession of their factories and estates, and the officers of the new army (the Reichswehr) did not thank the Weimar politicians but took it to be their patriotic duty to support the young patriots of the Freikorps. The terms of the Versailles Treaty rubbed salt into the wounds. The Freikorps felt Germany had been betrayed by the politicians and Jews. They seethed with anger and when the Allies proposed to disband some units of the Marine Brigade, a Freikorps organisation, soldiers and marines under the leadership of Dr Kapp occupied Berlin and proclaimed a new regime. Dr Kapp proposed to overthrow the democratic constitution, suppress the trade unions and socialists, and fight the terms of the Versailles Treaty. Kapp hoped for support from the army leaders but, except for one or two fanatics like General von Lüttwitz who joined the rebels, the majority of the officers remained neutral and inactive, waiting to see the outcome of the struggle. The workers of Berlin fought back against the plot by refusing to run public transport, declaring a general strike and effectively bringing the life of the city to a stop. Dr Kapp's rising collapsed. He was arrested and imprisoned. Ebert, who had become Germany's first President, thus survived another attempt to unseat him, but the Kapp 'putsch' showed that the 'national-patriotic' groups of the Right had little to fear from Ebert, for the Freikorps went unpunished. During the next few years these young men, numbering up to 300,000, based themselves in Bavaria, where a right-wing government was in power. By demonstrations, marches, and assassinations of republican and socialist leaders, they showed Germany that militarism was far from being defeated.[1]

Reparations and Inflation

From 1919 to 1924 the Allies forced the terms of the Versailles Treaty on an unwilling Germany. When Upper Silesia was partitioned in 1921, another crisis faced the Weimar government. In the same year the Reparations Commission finally fixed Germany's debt at £6,600 million to be repaid by annual instalments of £100 million. At the London Conference of December 1922 the German delegation protested that they could not meet these demands. In January 1923 the French lost patience and their fiery Premier, Poincaré, moved French

---

1. Between 1919 and 1922 there were 376 political murders, including those of Erzberger, a Catholic leader and signatory to the Versailles Treaty, and Rathenau, the Jewish Foreign Minister.

troops into the Ruhr, to exact payments in iron, steel, and coal. The French occupation lasted eight months. Miners and steel workers downed tools and refused to work for the French. The French troops fought pitched battles with the German workers almost every day. Patriotic hysteria against the Allies rose to new heights. Finally, in September 1923 the French forces were withdrawn after a new German Government led by Gustav Stresemann had promised prompt repayment of reparations.

The German mark had been under pressure before 1923 but the paralysis of the Ruhr industry had dramatic results. The normal rate of exchange for the mark had been fifteen marks to £1. In the space of two years inflation produced this rate of exchange:

> January 1922: 760 marks to £1.
> January 1923: 72,000 marks to £1.
> November 1923: 16,000,000,000 to £1.

The Reichsbank employed 300 paper mills working twenty-four hours a day to provide the masses of paper money flooding Germany. Private savings became worthless overnight and workers carried away their wages in wheelbarrows, to find that they would purchase only a loaf of bread. The wild inflation was blamed on reparations, on the Weimar government and the Allies. The normally conservative middle class, ruined by the inflation, turned more and more to the desperate remedies of the nationalist groups, promising strong government and financial stability.

Adolf Hitler, taking advantage of the run-away inflation and a political crisis caused by a Communist attempt to seize power in Saxony, tried a 'putsch' in Bavaria. Hitler wanted to seize the city of Munich and then use it as a base for a march on Berlin to liquidate the 'November Criminals' and make himself head of the government. In November 1923 ex-General Ludendorff came out of retirement to join Hitler, who ordered his storm-troopers into Munich. As the Nazis approached the centre of the city they were met by a fusillade of shots from the Bavarian police, killing sixteen storm-troopers. The attack collapsed. Hitler was arrested, tried and imprisoned for five years although he served less than one year. At his trial Hitler used the opportunity to make anti-government speeches and bring attention to himself and his cause. Again, by trying to be fair and judicial, the Weimar politicians had allowed one of their most dangerous enemies both publicity and eventual freedom.

STRESEMANN IN POWER, 1923–29

Under Gustav Stresemann, who was Chancellor for a short time in 1923 and Foreign Minister from 1923 to 1929, Germany entered a period of stability after the earlier storms. He subdued the extremists of the Right and the Left, and reopened negotiations with the Allies on the question of reparations. In April 1924 General Dawes, an American working for the Reparations Commission, produced a Plan by which Germany was to pay reparations by annual instalments, graded to fit Germany's capacity to pay. The final figure and the length of time to be allowed for repayment was left unsettled. The French were persuaded to withdraw from the Ruhr and with the assistance of American loans Dr Schacht revalued the Reichsmark and stabilised the currency.[1] Stresemann had negotiated an international loan of 800 million marks to put German industry back on its feet. The loan was largely subscribed by American financiers who wished to see Germany recover and so again provide a valuable market for American goods and investment.

For five years Germany enjoyed a welcome prosperity. Many of the industrialists turned from the nationalists to support Stresemann, who had achieved the stability and American loans upon which the German prosperity depended. Yet the social effects of the inflation went deep. The German middle class had lost their savings, the trade unions their funds, and the wages of the workers had never kept pace with the increasing prices. Only the property-owners, the financial speculators and the industrialists with large debts had benefited. Although for a time the German people endured the Republic, they could not be trusted to be loyal to it. Weimar had earned few friends and vast numbers of disillusioned enemies.

Stresemann achieved a remarkable success in foreign affairs, for by 1926 Germany had re-entered the councils of Europe on equal terms with the other Powers. He encouraged the Allies to believe that Germany would fulfil her obligations under the Treaty of Versailles but his real aim was to end the Allied ring around Germany and to reverse some of the worst features of the Treaty. In 1925 the Powers met at Locarno in Switzerland to attempt to end the ill-feeling between Germany and the rest of Europe and to find a lasting peace. Various treaties were signed with the objective of ensuring that disputes over the frontiers of Germany should not cause war. The frontiers between

1. Between 1924 and 1929 Germany received loans totalling 25,000 million marks and paid out 8,000 million marks in reparations.

Germany and France and Germany and Belgium were recognised as permanent by the three nations, with Britain and Italy guaranteeing to defend them. This seemed to imply that any aggressor would have to face a European coalition including Italy and Britain. Germany was promised that no further invasions like that in the Ruhr would be made. At the same time, a more limited form of security was given to Germany's eastern neighbours. Stresemann indicated that although he did not regard Germany's eastern frontier as permanent he would not go to war to recover the lost provinces, Danzig, the Polish Corridor and Silesia. Treaties were signed between Germany, Poland and Czechoslovakia for the peaceful settlement of disputes, and France guaranteed the Poles and Czechs against a German attack. These complicated arrangements brought hope of a lasting peace, since Germany had voluntarily entered into international agreements and accepted Versailles for the time being. However, Locarno contained two major weaknesses. In the first place, Britain had refused to guarantee Germany's eastern frontier. This weakened the collective front against Germany, who came to believe that Britain would not oppose her expansion in this area. In addition, it became apparent that some nations were having second thoughts about the wisdom of Versailles, and so endangering the peace by giving hope to the Germans.

Locarno encouraged Stresemann to believe he could now pursue an independent German policy. In 1926 he extended the Treaty of Rapallo (1922) with Russia by negotiating a Treaty of Neutrality, which shocked the Allies. Germany was admitted to the League of Nations and given a place on the Permanent Council. In 1927 the Inter-Allied Commission, controlling German armaments, withdrew. In 1928 Stresemann was approached to sign the optimistic Kellogg-Briand Pact to outlaw war as an instrument of policy. Germany signed, but these peaceful moves did not convince the French who refused any further concessions to Germany. In 1928 Stresemann complained bitterly of the Allied intransigence and in return another committee of experts was appointed to study reparations. In 1929 they produced the Young Plan, which reduced the total amount of reparations to £2,000 million and fixed the term of repayment at fifty-nine years. At the same time, British and Belgian forces withdrew from the Rhineland to placate Germany.

At this point of success Stresemann died. He had been hounded in his last months by a combination of the nationalist parties. Hugenberg, the press tycoon and leader of the Nationalist party, had joined with Hitler and the Nazis in organising a monster campaign against the Young Plan. The late twenties had been lean years for the nationalist parties, but three weeks after Stresemann's death in 1929, newspapers announced the Wall Street crash and the situation dramatically changed.

THE ECONOMIC AND POLITICAL CRISIS OF 1929–33

World economic recovery following the depression reached its peak in 1929 when all previous industrial records were broken. Then overproduction and speculation led to the Wall Street crash in the USA, and its effects spread across Europe. The American financiers who had made generous loans and investments in Germany now reversed the process and recalled their money. Demand for German goods almost ceased in the world markets as every country tightened its belt. The great slump hit Germany harder than the inflation of 1923. Production cuts led to mass unemployment. In September 1929 there were 1,300,000 unemployed; In January 1933 the figure stood at 6 million, that is, a third of all adult males. The depression hit skilled and unskilled, agricultural and industrial workers alike.

The Weimar Republic was unable to deal with the economic crisis. Industrialists like Thyssen and Kirdorf turned to the Nazis, donating large sums to their funds. Hitler promised them he would stem the 'Red Tide' (in the 1930 elections the Communists won seventy-seven seats in the Reichstag), end Germany's repayments under the Young Plan, and restore economic stability. The Republic faced these dangers divided. Ever since 1919 no single party had been able to command a majority in the Reichstag. Three of the largest parties, the Social-Democrats, the Catholic Centre and the People's Party had maintained an uneasy but effective coalition. In 1930 a decision by the government to cut unemployment benefit and old age pensions did not pass the Reichstag because of socialist objections. The alliance between the republican parties dissolved, and Chancellor Brüning, of the Centre Party, had to ask President Hindenburg to use his emergency powers under the constitution to put laws into force.[1] Brüning faced protests in the Reichstag against the use of the emergency powers, so he dissolved the Assembly and ordered fresh elections. The Nazi representation rose from twelve to 107, although with 143 seats the Social-Democrats were still the biggest party. Brüning carried on, although he did not have a

1. Hindenburg had been elected in 1925 on the death of Ebert. In 1930 he was eighty-three years old and doddering.

majority in the Reichstag. More frequent use was made of President Hindenburg's special powers. Possibly only an economic boom might have saved the Republic but instead unemployment increased. The youth of Germany flocked into the SA[1] and the private armies of the Communists. The Nazi SA gave their troopers a uniform, food, and in street-fighting, an outlet for their energy. Hitler continued to rage against Weimar, Versailles and Brüning, and promised the German people, 'Ein Volk, ein Reich, ein Führer' (one people, one state, one leader). His picture of a united Germany working together for the glory of the Fatherland, destroying Marxists, Jews and all anti-Germans in the process, made a strong appeal to shrewd businessmen and visionary youth alike. Brüning had nothing to offer in exchange. Street fighting between Nazis and Communists occurred daily and tension grew.

In 1932 Hindenburg's term of office as President expired. In the resulting election the Communist Thalmann polled less than 4 million votes, Hitler 13 million and Hindenburg 19 million. Since the Catholic Centre and the Social-Democrats supported Hindenburg, Hitler's success had been extraordinary. Hindenburg's first action was to dismiss Brüning on the advice of General von Schleicher, leader of a group of army generals. The President formed a stop-gap administration with a wily politician, Von Papen, as Chancellor, and a Cabinet containing generals like Schleicher and industrialists. Schleicher opened up negotiations with Hitler to try to bring the Nazis into the Government in a subordinate role. Hitler refused power except on his own terms. The new Government's difficulties forced Von Papen to dissolve the Reichstag. Hitler felt that power was almost his. He flew in a private plane from town to town addressing monster rallies. In the July election the Nazis won 230 seats but were still short of the absolute majority necessary to give Hitler complete power. Von Papen's group was soundly defeated.

The political unrest continued throughout the autumn of 1932. Von Papen held fresh elections in November. Surprisingly, the Nazi impetus seemed exhausted for they won only 196 seats. Von Papen offered Hitler the Vice-Chancellorship and was rejected. Schleicher again intervened, persuading Hindenburg to dismiss Von Papen and make him, Schleicher, the Chancellor. Von Papen, who by then had joined the Nationalist party, was not to be dropped so easily. He persuaded Hindenburg that Hitler could be shackled by appointing Hitler as Chancellor but filling the Cabinet with Nationalist ministers. Hindenburg overcame his repugnance of the Austrian ex-corporal and

1. S.A. or Sturm-Abteilung (Assault Detachment).

on 30 January 1933 appointed Hitler as Chancellor, Von Papen as Vice-Chancellor, with Hugenberg and other Nationalists as Ministers.

WHY DID THE WEIMAR REPUBLIC FAIL?

The Weimar Republic was born in defeat, in the shadow of Versailles and under Allied pressure. The war-guilt clause, the loss of German territories and the inability to reverse one and recover the other weakened the Republic from the start. The German people lacked experience and affection for the methods of parliamentary government. They had been used to stern, disciplined regimes, to obeying orders given by 'natural' leaders, like Bismarck and the Kaiser. Germans found it difficult to obey the drab, quarrelling politicians of the Republic. No dominant leader emerged, save perhaps Stresemann and he died at a decisive time, in 1929. The peculiar character of German politics, with the fragmentation of parties and the bitter rivalry between them, added to the weakness. No one party emerged strong enough to dominate the Reichstag and, in any case, the nationalists of the Right and the Communists of the Left were bent on destroying the Republic.

Again, Weimar appeared to have failed to solve Germany's great problems, inflation, unemployment and the recovery of the lost provinces. The Republic appealed neither to the older generation of lawyers, teachers and civil servants nor to the younger generation, for whom the appeal of Hitler to throw off the yoke of the 1918 defeat and restore German prestige was an irresistible attraction. The young patriots of the SA and SS were convinced beyond reason that Hitler could, and would, destroy all that was weak, and purge Germany into a new virile force. Finally, the conversion of many of the army and industrial leaders to Nazism and the nerveless and fatal manoeuvrings of Von Papen, Hindenburg and Schleicher in 1932 allowed Hitler the opportunity to seize power on his own terms.

16

Hitler's Germany

✶✶

Adolf Hitler was born on 20 April 1889 at Braunau on the river Inn, in Austria. His father was a customs official who finally settled in Linz.[1] After school, the young Hitler moved to Vienna to study at the Academy of Fine Arts but failed the entrance examination. He stayed on, but poverty forced him to shelter in the doss-houses and seek a living selling post-cards. In 1913, already loathing the Jews and Slavs who, he thought, corrupted the German race, he moved to Munich, in Bavaria. In 1914 he enthusiastically supported the war and joined a Bavarian regiment. On the western front he fought in the first battle of Ypres, became a corporal, and received the Iron Cross, First Class. In 1918, temporarily blinded by gas, he moved into hospital, where he received a tremendous shock on learning of Germany's defeat. He passionately believed that Germany had been betrayed by its politicians. In 1919 he rejoined his unit in Munich and was selected to spy on the activities of socialist parties.

Hitler went to a meeting of the German Workers' Party, one of hundreds of similar groups operating in Bavaria. He joined the party as member number seven but by 1921 he had become its leader (Führer) and had established branch organisations in other parts of Bavaria. The party label was altered to the National Socialist German Workers Party, usually abbreviated to the Nazi Party. Hitler drew up a programme of twenty-five points, including demands for the cancellation of the Treaty of Versailles, union with Austria, and withdrawal of citizenship rights from the Jews. Added to these were a few socialist slogans, like the nationalisation of all department stores and the forfeiture of the gains made by war profiteers. As time passed, the Nazi party quietly dropped its socialist aspect, for the combination of

1. Hitler's father, Alois Schickelgrüber, had changed his name to Hitler in 1876.

nationalism and anti-semitism attracted greater support.

One feature of the Nazi movement was the outstanding success of Hitler as a speaker. From street corners he progressed to meeting halls where he addressed crowds of 2,000 or more. He lashed himself and his audiences into frenzied rage. He realised the value of mob control. 'To be a leader', he stated, 'means to be able to move masses.' He used his storm-troopers, the feared SA led by Captain Röhm, as rabble-rousers, cheering in the right place and ejecting hecklers with violence. When not employed in these activities, the stormtroopers raided meetings of other parties to wreck halls and bludgeon speakers. This mixture of mob oratory and violence built up a fanatic following for Hitler in Munich and raised the Nazis above all other parties. Hitler attracted men like Hermann Göring, an ex-fighter pilot, and Julius Streicher, the notorious Jew-baiter. In 1923 Hitler tried to seize control of Munich, but the affair ended in fiasco and the Führer's imprisonment in Landesberg prison.

In prison Hitler dictated *Mein Kampf* to his idolator, Rudolf Hess. The book was a mixture of autobiography, rage against the 'pestilence' of the Jews and Socialists, and Hitler's cures for German troubles. On his release from prison in 1924 he repaired the shattered remnants of his party and began to make himself nationally known. Fresh recruits joined the Nazi cause, although the Stresemann period of prosperity retarded Hitler's advance. One of the new men in the party was Dr Josef Goebbels, an embittered and crippled journalist who used the forces of propaganda for the Nazis. In his own words, 'any lie frequently repeated will ultimately gain belief.'

In the late twenties the Hitler Youth, Nazi newspapers, and the annual party rally added to Hitler's hold on public opinion. The rallies (Reichparteitag) were massive gatherings of Nazis from all over Germany. Military marches, torchlight processions, and violent, inspiring speeches from the Führer hypnotised thousands of brownshirts. When Hitler spoke at these rallies words poured from him in a torrent, deriding, boasting, challenging. His harsh voice and often ungrammatical sentences emphasised the violence of his opinions.

With the slump, Nazi fortunes flourished. In 1928 twelve deputies were elected to the Reichstag. By July 1932 their number had risen to 230. Finally, in January 1933 Adolf Hitler became Chancellor.

THE ESTABLISHMENT OF THE THIRD REICH, 1933

Hitler did not yet have a majority in the Reichstag, so he dissolved it and ordered fresh elections, for March 1933. The Nazis mobilised all their propaganda resources with money provided by Krupp, the iron and steel producer.

As the Nazis now controlled the government they used the radio and the press to publicise their policies. Göring, using his authority as Minister of the Interior in Prussia, conferred police status on his storm-troopers, using them to beat up and terrorise the Communists. Hitler did not suggest any schemes or plans. He merely stated vaguely that he would stem the 'Red Tide', and asked for a free hand to rule Germany.

The Reichstag Fire

One week before polling day, the Reichstag building in Berlin caught fire. The damage was not great, but the consequences were consider-able. The mystery of the fire-raisers has not yet been satisfactorily solved. A Dutch Communist, Van der Lubbe, was discovered in the building and arrested. He confessed, implicating other Communists. The Nazis used the fire to round up the leaders of the German Com-munists. One explanation is that the Nazis started the fire themselves, trapped Van der Lubbe on the premises, and so 'framed' the Com-munists. This story was recently shattered by an historian.[1] It appears that Van der Lubbe did it all alone. Hitler and the other Nazis were taken by surprise, but used the scare skilfully to their own advantage. At the trial Van der Lubbe made a pathetic, blundering figure and was finally executed. The other Communists, led by the Bulgarian, Dmitrov, who conducted his own brilliant defence, were acquitted for lack of evidence. Taking advantage of the situation, within twenty-four hours of the fire Hitler had persuaded Hindenburg to suspend the guarantees of freedom of speech, press, public meeting and from arrest contained in the Weimar constitution. On 2 March Hitler instituted 'protective custody' by which suspects could be rounded up and held without trial in concentration camps. A week's reign of terror pre-ceded the election. Even so, on polling day Hitler's Nazis secured only 43·9 per cent of the votes (288 seats). The Nationalist party obtained another fifty-three seats, so giving Hitler a very narrow majority in the Reichstag.

The Führer now prepared the Enabling Law. Under its application

1. Fritz Tobias: *Reichstagbrand* (1962).

the Reichstag could be dissolved by the Government, which could then assume the power to make laws and conclude treaties with foreign Powers. The Chancellor could draft the laws and he could use the emergency powers to maintain order. The Nazis declared that they wanted these extensive powers for a four-year probationary period. Any amendment to the constitution had to have a two thirds majority to pass the Reichstag. On the day of the vote for the Enabling Law the eighty-one Communist deputies were excluded from the building. The Enabling Law was passed, only the Social-Democrats voting against it.

The Terror

Hitler had suppressed liberty. He quickly crushed what opposition remained. By June no political party existed except the Nazis. Party members were promoted to fill the offices of central and local government. A special post, Minister of Propaganda, was created for Dr Goebbels. He abolished all freedom of the arts forcing the theatre, writers and artists to publicise and glorify Nazi views. Complete control of radio and press ensured that the German people were fed with Nazi boasts and lies. Non-Nazi newspapers disappeared. On May Day 1933 a public holiday was proclaimed. Hitler made a speech, stressing that he had drafted an ambitious Four-Year Plan, and called on all Germans to support the scheme. On the following day, storm-troopers occupied offices of the trade unions, confiscated their funds, arrested their leaders and absorbed the unions into one organisation called the German Labour Front. Its leader, Dr Ley, abolished strikes and forced employers and workers to cooperate in stepping up production. Wage rates were imposed by Dr Ley, who moved malcontents into the growing concentration camps.

The Four-Year Plan tackled the unemployment problem. Thousands of men were employed on slum clearance or on building new roads, houses and land reclamation. The expanding SA and the new SS accounted for many others.[1] The figure of six million unemployed in 1933 had dwindled to under a million by 1936.

In 1934 a scheme began by which all young Germans had to serve a compulsory year on the land or in industry. During this time they were indoctrinated with Nazi racial theories. Women were encouraged to stay at home; men took over their jobs wherever possible. Hitler's attitude to women was expressed in the phrase, 'Kinder, Kirche, Küche' (children, church and kitchen.)

Hundreds of musicians, writers, journalists and scientists fled from

1. SS—the Schutzstaffel, a specially selected and black uniformed elite of the Nazi party.

Germany. Among them were Einstein, Bertholt Brecht, and Otto Klemperer. To bring other critics to heel, Hitler tightened up the internal security of Germany. In 1933 Göring created the Gestapo, the feared new police.[1] They worked secretly, swiftly and ruthlessly, rounding up critics and non-Nazis of any importance. Under the Gestapo, the SS and the SA, Germany had become a police state.

Nevertheless the Nazis had gathered powerful mass support. Their dictatorship was not imposed by force against the consent of the German people, but accepted by them, at first with suspicion but with increasing approval as the economic problems of the early thirties were solved.

The Purges

Once in power Hitler dropped many of the former associates and ideas that he had shamelessly exploited. Gregor Strasser, who had helped to build up the party machine and had advocated more socialist measures, disappeared from the inner councils of the party. In June 1933 Hugenberg, the Nationalist leader, resigned. In 1934 Hitler detected mutterings from within the party against his authority. The Führer had deliberately created the SS and the Gestapo, both tied to him by oaths of personal loyalty, as efficient, disciplined guards. The SA on the other hand were more vocal, independent and critical. They expected a social revolution, in which the industrialists would be swept away and the SA rewarded with government posts. The boisterous elements in the SA thought they should replace the army generals. In this trial of strength Hitler backed the generals and the businessmen.

Captain Ernst Röhm, leader of the SA, sympathised with the disappointments of his men. He had expected to become Defence Minister and to have had the Army (the Reichswehr) fused into the SA. In April 1934 Röhm in a speech allowed himself to demand further socialist measures. Hitler decided that Röhm had to be stopped. He obtained the promise of the army generals to support him in a purge of the SA. On 30 June 1934 Röhm and other SA leaders were dragged from their beds and murdered by the SS. Simultaneously, arrests and executions in Berlin and other cities wiped out the major critics of Hitler. In the 'Night of the Long Knives', Gregor Strasser and General Schleicher were two of the distinguished victims, although as many as 400 others probably perished. Innocents suffered too: one man, a Munich musician, died because his name happened to be the same as another on the execution list. Leaderless, the SA revolt collapsed. No more demands

1. The Gestapo—Geheime Staatspolitzei (secret state police) eventually passed under the control of Heinrich Himmler who was also head of the SS.

were circulated for a social revolution. The SA were absorbed into the Army upon which Hitler now largely depended for his power. In all this, the German people played little part. A plebiscite had been held in November 1933 in which ninety-six per cent of the voters approved Hitler's dictatorial measures. After the Röhm purge the phrase was coined, 'the Führer knows best.' Germans, in return for their stake in the improved economic situation, closed their eyes and ears and accepted this nonsense. In August 1934 Hindenburg died. Hitler became not only Chancellor but President and Commander-in-Chief of all the armed forces. Every German serviceman had to swear an oath of loyalty to Hitler, including the words, 'I will render unconditional obedience to the Führer of the German Reich and People.'

Although Hitler drafted the main lines of German policy he left the details of administration to his subordinates. Consequently, Göring, Himmler, Ley and others created little empires for themselves which they ruled as despots.

HITLER'S IDEAS

Hitler changed his programme to suit the changing situation. But some ideas he never altered. For instance, as early as 1920 he demanded a 'Grossdeutsch' state, in which all Germans (including Austrians) would be united in a fanatical belief in Germany's mission. This was to be the Third Reich. This emotional idea attracted a remarkable number of solid Germans. Secondly, Hitler had always preached hatred of the Jews. In *Mein Kampf* he elaborated his theories of the racial superiority of the Aryans, although there is not a scrap of scientific evidence to prove his statements. The Aryans, in Hitler's view, had been the early Germans who had been defiled by contact with inferior races, like the Slavs and Jews. The Germans could recapture their purity by reducing the other races to the level of slave-labour and by forbidding inter-marriage. The German people, by discipline, training and a cultivated ruthlessness, could conquer the inferior races and dominate the world 'for a thousand years'.

Hitler favoured a dictatorship to accomplish these plans. Worlds were not won by democratic methods: he despised the parliamentary system of government and believed in the rights of the 'natural leaders' —such as himself. The people, the 'Volk', were to join in a common struggle, led by the Führer. In Germany Hitler applied these ideas. He made the laws, decided foreign policy, commanded the armed forces and through thirty-two Gauleiters and a myriad of lesser party officials completely centralised and disciplined his country. At other times, to win support, Hitler professed socialist beliefs, although he largely abandoned them after 1934. But above all, what Hitler was really interested in was power in all its forms.

The Jews

By 1934 Hitler had purged the civil service and the judiciary of liberal and fair personnel, replacing them with men loyal to the Nazis. Orders to the judges contained the instruction that their task was 'not to do justice, but to annihilate the enemies of National Socialism.' Most of these enemies were the Jews, who were allegedly responsible for losing the war and corrupting the Aryan race. Mixed with this was envy for the successful business ability of the Jewish people. Outbreaks of anti-semitism had occurred in pre-Hitler Germany and many people were not sorry to see Jews forced out of business and the professions.

In 1935 the Reichstag, specially recalled for the occasion, obediently passed the infamous Nuremberg Laws, which withdrew civil rights from the Jews, and forbade mixed marriages between Jews and Aryans. Julius Streicher, Heydrich, Eichmann and others set up concentration camps. Millions eventually perished in the gas-chambers of Auschwitz, Belsen, Dachau and other camps. Not only Jews but non-Germans, and countless opponents of the Nazis from socialists to Jehovah's Witnesses, were arrested without warning in the middle of the night and without trial hustled off to these camps. There they suffered torture, mutilation and death. Another function of the camps was to provide a supply of slave-labour in factories, quarries and mines. Given starvation rations and beatings, the prisoners could not last the pace. The Nazis terrorised the German people, using the camps as a warning of what lay in store for those who did not conform. All the Gestapo had to do was to enter a man's name on a form as 'an enemy of the state'. Arrest, torture and death followed in quick succession. The camps, ringed by electrified fences, were staffed by the SS. Later they became centres for medical 'experiments' on a constant flow of Jewish victims.

In November 1938 a young Jew shot a German diplomat in Paris. In revenge, Heydrich sent the SA and SS out to burn over a hundred synagogues, ransack Jewish shops and round up thousands for the concentration camps. By 1942 Hitler had ordered that 'the final solution' to the Jewish problem should be applied. This meant the extermination of all German Jews already in the camps and the herding of all non-German Jews into ghettoes where they were to be terrorised and eventually murdered.

The other churches were cowed, though not persecuted. Some pastors of the Lutheran Church supported the Nazis. Their leader, Pastor Müller, became a sort of Minister of Religion in 1933 and persuaded other churchmen to follow Hitler. Others, like Pastor Niemöller, a former submarine officer, denounced the cruelties of the Third Reich. He ended up in a concentration camp as a price for his courage.

The Roman Catholic Church made an agreement with Hitler in 1933 by which priests were not to meddle in politics and in return Hitler would not interfere with the Church. In fact, through his control of education, youth movements and newspapers, the freedom of action of the Catholic Church was severely restricted. Hitler himself, although a Catholic in his youth, had nothing but contempt for religion.

Youth Movements

Hitler wanted Germans to have large families because he feared that Germany would be out-numbered by the 'inferior' peoples of eastern Europe, like the Poles and Russians. New laws offered family allowances, reduced rents and financial grants for large families.

Within the Hitler Youth this new generation was to be indoctrinated. The organisation, divided into age-groups, concentrated on outdoor pursuits like hikes, camping and games. On the other hand, boys were told to despise international friendship and to prepare for the battle against the Jews, Slavs and Negroes. Boys had military training, strict discipline and regular lectures on Nazi policies. Yet the movement captured the imagination of the young. Some of the most fanatical Nazis grew up in the Hitler Youth, where they had sung, marched and saluted their loyalty to the Führer.

The organisation for boys between fourteen and eighteen had been founded in 1926. In 1928 two new movements appeared, one (the BDM[1]) for girls, and the other for boys of ten to fourteen. By 1934 the Hitler Youth had incorporated all other youth organisations and boasted a membership of 7 millions.

Entry to the university and the professions often depended on a career in the Hitler Youth. After the age of eighteen young Germans were expected to do from six months to a year on voluntary service in the Reich Labour Service before taking up employment. Beyond that lay the Party and the Army, with promotion to the respected and envied SS. The Nazi propaganda machine directed by Dr Goebbels

1 The *Bund Deutscher Mädchen*—the League of German Maidens.

insisted that within the schools absolute loyalty to the Führer should be taught. History text-books were re-written to emphasise the grandeur of the Third Reich and the futility of the Weimar Republic. At no period of his day or of his life was the German citizen outside the control of the Nazis. Watchful eyes covered every move.

ECONOMIC POLICY

The Nazis had based their campaign in 1930–33 on the promise to end the economic crisis. Unemployment was the biggest problem. Hitler discovered a solution, although it proved to be rather an artificial one, for the Army, the SA and the re-opened armaments factories absorbed the majority of the surplus labour force. Thousands more were taken into the Labour Front and employed on the roads, housing and factory schemes.

German workers found that the Nazis controlled rents, built houses for their families and organised cheap holidays at coastal resorts. In return for these material rewards the workers abandoned their claims to democratic freedom which under Weimar had only brought 'freedom to starve'.

Under the control of Dr Schacht, the President of the Reichsbank, the Government provided money to assist industry. Income tax concessions and state loans were provided for industrialists who replaced obsolete machinery. Industry was gradually pushed back on its feet. All these achievements, especially the wide, straight autobahnen impressed foreigners. In addition, the roads, factories and railways had a strategic purpose: they assisted the needs of Hitler's mechanised armies.

From 1935, once conscription had been introduced, Germany moved fast towards full employment. A patriotic drive to produce weapons and munitions of all kinds galvanised the factories into action. New aerodromes, barracks, hospitals and tanks were built. This expansion was financed by the issue of Government bonds, to which the German people subscribed, backed up with bank credits. Inflation did not occur because of the rigid Government control of wages and prices.

Hitler detested Germany's reliance on foreign countries for essential raw materials. He hoped to achieve, through a policy called Autarky, the economic self-sufficiency of Germany. *Ersatz* (substitute) materials produced by ingenious German chemists were used wherever possible in place of imported products. Substitutes for petrol, wool and rubber were made in large quantities although they were more expensive and less efficient. Imports were curtailed as far as possible. Products essential for Germany's expansion were the only ones to escape the Government's critical eye.

Dr Schacht tried to increase Germany's exports by providing incentives to exporters. He worked out a complicated system of currency manipulation by which the value of the mark was varied. For instance, foreign visitors obtained a generous rate of exchange to encourage them to spend more money in Germany. On the other hand obstacles were put in the way of foreign firms to prevent them taking their profits from the country. These methods resulted in 1935 in a small surplus of exports over imports. After this, the increasing export of German arms and ammunition, especially to South America, improved the German export figures. However, Germany never became entirely self-sufficient as Hitler had hoped.

In 1936 Hitler instituted the second Four-Year Plan to intensify agricultural production. Industry was given further grants and incentives. But in 1939 Göring's boast that the Plan would make Germany independent of foreign goods was proved false.

HITLER'S FOREIGN POLICY

From the outset, Hitler had clear objectives in his foreign policy. In the 1920s he had harped ceaselessly on the theme of the injustice of Versailles and demanded the revision of the Treaty. Ultimately, Germany's lost provinces, Alsace-Lorraine, Eupen-Malmédy, Upper Silesia, the Saar, Danzig and the Polish lands all must be regained. He had no list of priorities but waited for events and took advantage of them. Over the years he promised war and conquest but few believed him: the Allies counted it as bluster, the German generals thought it to be impossible. Hitler used war as a threat, knowing that the Western Powers would do anything to avoid its horrors. Occasionally he made pacific speeches himself, varying them with violent outbursts which kept the Allies guessing and his own intentions masked.

Beyond this, Hitler had more grandiose, although vague, ambitions. In his speeches he stressed the phrase 'Ein Volk, Ein Reich, Ein Führer', one people united under a single leader. By 1933 the German Reich under its Führer had come about, but the German people were still divided. Seven million German-speaking Austrians and over four million Germans in Czechoslovakia and Poland were still outside the Reich. Hitler hoped to unite them. He was encouraged by the arguments of his economists that 'lebensraum' (living space) was necessary to settle the expanding population and to grow sufficient food to accomplish Germany's self-sufficiency. Hitler looked to eastern Europe for 'lebensraum', apparently disregarding the fact that population density was high in these areas already, or perhaps he intended to make the Slavs into slave-peoples or expel them from these areas.

Hitler also wanted to recover the lost German colonies in the Pacific and Africa, and by extending them, establish an Empire which would rival Britain's. In 1933, however, his interests were European, to nibble away at the Versailles Treaty. Reparations had ceased to be paid before Hitler came to power, but other irksome restrictions remained. In 1931 Brüning had attempted to create a German-Austrian customs union, but his plan had been vetoed by France. Hitler had then seen the strength of the opposition to 'Ein Volk' and put his faith in deceit and military power to overcome it.

Rearmament

Under the Treaty of Versailles the German army was restricted to 100,000 men. Rearmament would challenge both the Treaty and the Allies but Hitler was prepared to take the risk, for his ambitions would ultimately depend on a strong army. It was a calculated risk, for the Allied statesmen were now divided, with many of them dubious about the wisdom of weakening Germany. Hitler cleverly played on their uneasy consciences, and offered Germany as a bulwark against Bolshevism. In 1933 at the Disarmament Conference in Geneva the German delegates asked the other Powers to disarm to Germany's level. The French, afraid to weaken themselves in the face of a revived Germany, opposed the suggestion. Britain proposed a compromise, that Germany should wait four years and then be given permission to rearm. Hitler took a chance. The League of Nations had already revealed its ineptitude over the Japanese invasion of Manchuria in 1931–33, and Hitler did not fear it. In October, the Führer dramatically announced Germany's withdrawal from the Disarmament Conference and the League of Nations and began to increase the German armed forces. This proved to be the first test of strength and nerve. The Allies dithered and finally did nothing. Hitler pressed home his advantage by holding a plebiscite by which the German people voted 40 million to 2 million in favour of his policies.

The Führer followed up with a series of speeches stressing Germany's peaceful intentions. In January 1934 he signed a Ten-Year Pact with Poland. In Europe, this Pact was interpreted as a sign of Hitler's good intentions, in that he had accepted the Polish frontiers of 1919. The Poles swallowed Hitler's promises and thought Germany would be a valuable ally against their enemy, Russia. For Germany, the move was designed to blind the Western Powers and to drive a wedge between them.

The German initiative revealed the differences that eventually paralysed the former Allies. In Britain it was felt that in some respects Versailles was wrong and there was a strong case for its amendment. Some British politicians felt that France, with a dangerously unstable political system, was weak and untrustworthy. Russia appeared to be a greater danger than Germany and many welcomed a strong Germany as a barrier to the Bolsheviks. The French feared Germany but felt powerless to stop her recovery. What could they do? March in? That would solve nothing. For the French, the Versailles Treaty needed to be strengthened, not weakened, yet they were powerless to do it. Of the other Allies, America had retreated into isolationism and Italy under Mussolini had imperial ambitions of her own. The distrust and suspicions among the former Allies were skilfully exploited by Hitler.

Even so, in 1934 the Powers huddled together for protection. In September, Soviet Russia joined the League of Nations and Litvinov, her representative at Geneva, made pleas for 'collective security', that is, a series of international agreements whereby an attack on one country would automatically bring in the others. But only France nibbled at the bait, for Russian intentions were still deeply suspected.

Austria, 1934

Hitler grew more daring. In the opening paragraphs of *Mein Kampf* he had stated, 'the reunion of these two German states (Germany and Austria) is our life task, to be carried out by every means at our disposal'. An Austrian Nazi party was formed, but at first made little impact. In July 1934 the Nazis struck. Dollfuss, the Austrian Chancellor, was murdered, and Nazis seized control of a radio station and announced that the National Socialists had assumed power. The move was defeated by the firmness of Dr Schuschnigg and other Austrian ministers, aided by the Army. The conspirators fled to Germany and appealed to Hitler. For a time it looked likely that the Germans would march on Austria. To forestall an invasion, Mussolini rushed troops to the Tyrol and declared that he would defend Austria's independence. Hitler had waited. He now hurriedly denied all knowledge of the plot and sent Von Papen to smooth the ruffled Austrians. For once he had been defeated by the resolution of his enemies.

Hitler needed a success to wipe out the bitter taste of this set-back. In January 1935 he obtained one when a plebiscite was held in the Saar. This gave a ninety per cent vote for return to Germany. The plebiscite had been provided for in the Versailles Treaty but the Nazis claimed it as a victory. In February, Pierre Laval the new French Foreign Minister obtained British and Italian agreement to submit the problem of disarmament to negotiation. Hitler's brutal answer to this peaceful move came in March 1935 when he reintroduced conscription, announced a target of 500,000 soldiers for Germany's peacetime army, and founded an airforce. Berliners cheered as Hitler paraded for their approval, flanked by ex-General von Mackensen, a relic of the war.

At Stresa, in Italy, French, Italian and British delegates censured Germany for the violation of the Treaty of Versailles, and guaranteed Austrian independence. At Geneva, the League of Nations laboriously copied their lead, and set up a committee to consider applying sanctions against Germany. Another committee discussed what the League's attitude would be on the next occasion that peace was endangered. In effect, nothing was done.

France, horrified by the German diplomatic victories, negotiated a Pact of mutual assistance with Russia. France had already created the 'Little Entente', a set of agreements linking her with Czechoslovakia, Poland, Rumania and Yugoslavia. Germany seemed to be surrounded by a host of enemies tightly bound together by treaties, but the apparent unity was misleading for there were strains both within the 'Stresa Front' and the 'Little Entente' which Hitler cleverly exploited.

The Anglo-German Naval Treaty, 1935

In June 1935 Hitler sent Ribbentrop to London. He negotiated an Anglo-German Naval Treaty, by which Germany was bound not to build beyond thirty-five per cent of Britain's naval strength. Submarines were excluded from this restriction, to Hitler's advantage, for the Germans built up a force of U-boats in the following years. The Treaty shocked Europe, for it was felt Britain had struck a blow against the Allies by making a private bargain with Hitler. The 'Stresa Front' against German rearmament was shattered, for Britain had tacitly consented to a breach of the Versailles Treaty by agreeing to even partial German rearmament, and without informing her friends.

Mussolini now took an independent line, by sending Italian troops to invade Abyssinia. The British Government, anxious to appease Hitler, went to the opposite extreme in its anger against Mussolini. Prime

Minister Baldwin strengthened the fleet in the Mediterranean and agreed to the imposition of sanctions against Italy. The French Government could not understand why Britain should turn a blind eye to the dangerous Hitler but punish the harmless Mussolini. The consequence was that the Italians sought a closer agreement with Hitler, turning away from their former friends in the 'Stresa Front'. The French struggled to prevent this by persuading Britain and the League of Nations not to impose sanctions ruthlessly. In so doing the Allies fell between two stools. They did not stop Mussolini from conquering Abyssinia, but merely brought themselves and the League into disrepute by their half-hearted, inconsistent actions. Hitler did not miss his opportunity: he invited the angry Italians to discussions on a possible pact with Germany.

With these diplomatic successes ringing in German ears, Hitler became even more confident of his powers and more contemptuous of the opposition. He was convinced he had a far keener grasp of political and military events than his generals or his diplomatic corps and he dazzled them with the startling success of his bold gambles.

The Rhineland, 1936

In March 1936 three battalions of the newly organised German army (the Wehrmacht) crossed the Rhine bridges and marched into the Rhineland, demilitarised since 1919. This flagrant violation of the Versailles Treaty and of the Locarno agreements was greeted with applause in Germany and the Rhineland but with stunned apprehension in Paris and London.

In 1936 the military strength of the Western Powers still far exceeded that of Germany. The goose-stepping Germans could have been hurled back across the Rhine: the German High Command uneasily expected at least the French to fight and had tried to prevent Hitler's aggressive policies. Feverish diplomatic activity in the Allied capitals produced no action. The paralysis affecting the Powers has been explained in terms of their divided, suspicious attitudes to each other. In addition, Britain was firmly launched along the road of appeasement. These alterations in the Versailles Treaty were looked upon in Britain as inevitable and in some cases necessary to redress the injustice of 1919. By allowing Hitler the Saar, the Rhineland and the right to rearm, Baldwin hoped that Germany would be satisfied. Hitler's speeches promising peace were still widely believed: the politicians of the West did not realise that each success led to further ambition.

Again, in the Rhineland Hitler's recklessness and strong nerve had brilliantly succeeded. Another plebiscite confirmed his actions by a massive vote of 98·8 per cent in favour. The Allies made a belated attempt to bring back Italy into their camp, but failed, for Mussolini was now hypnotised by Hitler. After a few weeks Britain and France tamely accepted the occupation and Hitler's promises of peace. One *Times* article was headed 'A Chance to Rebuild'. Optimism for the future cloaked the real danger to European peace. To allow Hitler's aggressive policies to go unchallenged was fatal. France had revealed her own inability to stop the German march and Britain had shown her motto to be 'safety first'.

The Rome-Berlin Axis Pact and the Anti-Comintern Pact

The Führer's next objective was Austria. Now that the Stresa powers were no longer united, the Austrians trembled for their independence. In July 1936 the Germans forced an Agreement on the unwilling Austrian Chancellor, Dr Schuschnigg, by which the imprisoned Nazis were released and Nazi sympathisers were accepted into the Austrian Government. Hitler in exchange recognised Austria's full independence. In the next eighteen months the Germans used the Agreement to lever further concessions and put increasing pressure on the unfortunate Dr Schuschnigg.

By these actions Hitler had placed his friendship with Mussolini in jeopardy, but the Duce was too impressed by German successes and strength to criticise. In the same month, July, Britain and France ended the sanctions placed on Italy. Mussolini remained unmoved and, when the Spanish Civil War began, cooperated with Hitler in assisting the Fascist forces of General Franco.

In Spain, Hitler's objectives were to overthrow the republican government, prolong the war, and acquire experience for his troops and airforce. The Nazi planes of the 'Condor Legion' learnt the tactics of massive bombing raids on undefended towns. Meanwhile, in Berlin in 1936 the Olympic Games had attracted thousands to marvel at the new wonders.[1] Diplomatically, Hitler was not idle. In October 1936 the vague agreement known as the Berlin-Rome Axis Pact came into existence, on the basis of cooperation in Spain and against Bolshevism. The Anti-Comintern Pact between Germany, Italy and Japan, directed against international Communism, followed in November 1936. This Pact did little more than promise co-operation between the three states to prevent the spread of Communism, but Hitler hoped that it would become the basis of a new military alliance, and the courtship of Mussolini continued unabated throughout 1937.

1. Hitler was most annoyed by the victories of the American Negro sprinter, Jesse Owens, over white athletes.

In *Mein Kampf* Hitler had stated that an alliance with Britain was necessary. He failed to achieve this, and was puzzled by Britain's role in world affairs. He could not understand the British reluctance to act forcefully in Europe and hoped that this meant Britain would co-operate with Germany. On other occasions he declared Britain to be 'decadent' and 'finished' but still feared her naval power. To win over the Conservative governments of first Baldwin, and from May 1937, of Neville Chamberlain, Hitler proposed a common front against Communism, an argument which gained some support not only in London but also in Paris. However, notes, inquiries and diplomats from Germany, France and Britain had little real effect. In November 1937 Neville Chamberlain, who hoped to be remembered as the great peacemaker of modern times, sent Lord Halifax, the Foreign Secretary, to see Hitler. Halifax was convinced of Germany's good intentions and let Hitler think Britain would accept some 'adjustment to new conditions' over German frontiers. Hitler decided that Britain would not intervene to prevent changes to Germany's eastern frontiers. Privately, he thought the British Government weak and cowardly. Later, he remarked, 'our opponents are little worms.' He was wrong, but correct in his belief that the British would do almost anything to avoid war. Chamberlain's faults were that he trusted his opponents: he believed he could make an honest bargain with Hitler. Events proved him wrong.

Austria, 1938

In January 1938 Chancellor Schuschnigg found evidence of another Nazi plot to overthrow the Austrian Government. He went to see Hitler, hoping to exact a German promise to end the intrigue. Instead, Hitler flew into one of his foaming rages and boasted that German soldiers would one day march on Vienna. Schuschnigg was faced with an agonising choice: he could resist Hitler's demands, fight, and hope for European support: alternatively, he could accept Hitler's demands and postpone the invasion. Choosing the latter course, he returned to Vienna and appointed the Austrian Nazi leader, Seyss-Inquart, as Minister of the Interior, as Hitler had demanded. Austria's economy was integrated with that of Germany. Hitler secretly told the Austrian Nazis to step up their campaign. Riots and demonstrations, encouraged by Seyss-Inquart with the police under his control, decided Schuschnigg on a last desperate attempt to save Austria. He arranged for a national plebiscite to be held on the question of union with Germany. On 11 March, two days before the poll, German troops appeared at the frontier posts. Hitler demanded that the plebiscite be cancelled. Schuschnigg agreed, but was then forced to hand over all power together with the office of Chancellor to Seyss-Inquart.

Some Austrian ministers wanted to fight: others, like Schuschnigg, did not want bloodshed and knew the result to be inevitable. A few minutes after he had broadcast his decision to surrender, he was arrested.[1]

Chancellor Seyss-Inquart then invited the Germans to enter Austria to restore order. On 12 March the Wehrmacht crossed the frontier. As Heydrich and Himmler rounded up over 80,000 opponents of the Nazis and moved them into concentration camps, Hitler re-entered his homeland and in a passionate speech announced the union of Germany and Austria. Next day, Seyss-Inquart resigned his office as Chancellor, handing over all power to the Führer.

It would be wrong to think that this seizure was accomplished in the teeth of Austrian opposition. Everywhere Hitler went he was met by excited, welcoming crowds. In a plebiscite held to confirm his action a vote of 99·75 per cent agreed with the Anschluss (union). Even allowing for the usual Nazi falsification of the votes cast, there is no doubt that the union with Germany proved widely popular, for some of the glamour and success of the Third Reich rubbed off on to the small battered state of Austria.

Again, the other European Powers and the League of Nations excused the aggression. They convinced themselves that Austria would benefit economically by the union, and were won over by Hitler's arguments that the Austrians desired incorporation in the Reich.

Czechoslovakia, 1938–39

One result of the annexation of Austria was that Germany now encircled Czechoslovakia on three sides. Czechoslovakia had been created at Versailles in 1919 on the basis of President Wilson's plea that national self-determination should be the principle applied in drawing up the frontiers of Central Europe. However, included with the Czech state were racial minorities, like the Slovaks, Ruthenes, and Poles, and in the Sudetenland over 3 million Germans. The Czech Government, headed by President Benes, had granted these minorities certain rights but the Germans in particular were dissatisfied and claimed further privileges. Konrad Henlein, the leader of the Sudeten Nazi party and a paid agent of Germany, kept up a barrage of agitation by demonstrations, marches and a press campaign against alleged Czech 'atrocities'.

Surrounded by enemies, Czechoslovakia at first sight seemed easy game. However, it had been one of the most successful of the post-war

1. Dr Schuschnigg was held in prison and concentration camps until liberated by the Allied armies in 1945.

democracies. The Czechs had an army of thirty-four divisions, strong mountain defences in the Sudetenland, the valuable Skoda armaments works, and defence agreements with Soviet Russia and France. The Czechs were unlikely to succumb without a struggle. Yet President Benes found that there were flaws in his defences. The British Ministers, Chamberlain and Halifax, persuaded the French and Czechs to make concessions to the demands of Henlein and Hitler. Benes discovered that each surrender on his part produced fresh German demands. As Britain had not committed herself to the defence of eastern Europe at Locarno, and the French were reluctant to stand alone against Hitler, Benes found his allies had feet of clay.

In April 1938 Henlein put forward demands for further rights for the Sudeten Germans. Hitler massed troops on the Czech border. The Czechs mobilised their armies and made a show of resistance. Hitler assured the Czechs that no aggression was intended, but the humiliation enraged him. In a directive to his generals he wrote, 'it is my unalterable intention to smash Czechoslovakia by military action in the near future.' In fact, he used the policy of diplomatic bluff and bluster to destroy Czechoslovakia. Instead of being heartened by the Czech resistance the British and the French Governments urged Benes to make further concessions to avoid war.

Obediently, the Czechs prepared a new law which proposed to grant the Sudeten-Germans all they asked. Henlein rejected these terms. In August 1938 Lord Runciman flew to Czechoslovakia to try to find a solution. His mission was a melancholy failure, for Hitler now wanted not improved conditions in the Sudetenland but the cession of the province to Germany and the destruction of Czechoslovakia.

On 12 September Hitler addressed the Nuremberg Rally. He denounced the Czechs, and demanded action. Then he waited. Next day, the Sudeten Nazi party led a revolt. The rising was crushed by the Czech armed forces in a few hours. Henlein fled to Germany where newspapers carried headlines claiming that the Czechs were persecuting the German minority.

At this point Neville Chamberlain decided to make a personal appeal to Hitler. On 15 September he met the Führer at Berchtesgaten, in Bavaria. Hitler ranted and Chamberlain listened. Hitler demanded the cession of the Sudetenland and Chamberlain believed that if the Czechs could be persuaded to surrender the territory, Hitler would be won over for peace. Chamberlain confidently returned to consult his colleagues. The French Premier, Daladier, agreed to abandon Czechoslovakia. On 21 September the Anglo-French proposals were presented to Benes. They provided for the surrender of border territories to

Germany without a plebiscite. An international commission would settle the details of the transfer of populations where no satisfactory national line could be drawn.

The Czechs accepted the proposals. Chamberlain immediately flew to Germany to meet Hitler at Godesberg. A shock awaited him, for Hitler announced the proposals to be insufficient and asked that all the Sudetenland be immediately ceded to Germany. Chamberlain returned to London faced with the choice of war or abject surrender. War preparations were made by both sides. In Britain, shelters were dug, gasmasks distributed and the armed forces alerted. Hitler had announced that he would march on Czechoslovakia on 1 October. However, when Mussolini suggested a Four-Power conference to discuss the issues, Hitler jumped at the opportunity to make further gains from the appeasers without war.

The conference met at Munich on 29 September. The Czechs and the Russians were not invited. The decisions were made by Hitler, Mussolini, Daladier and Chamberlain. The Munich Agreement contained little more than had been contained in the Godesberg proposals but the Germans were to be allowed to enter and occupy the Sudetenland on the following day. An International Commission would decide other questions by holding plebiscites, if necessary. The Czech delegates, kept waiting in an ante-room, were then informed of the terms. Deserted by their allies Russia and France, they surrendered. On 1 October German forces crossed the frontier unopposed and occupied the Sudetenland.

On his return from Munich Chamberlain was received with cheers, for his peace-seeking missions had won approval in Britain. Chamberlain brought with him a joint declaration signed by himself and Hitler including the Munich terms and indicating 'the desire of our two peoples never to go to war with one another again.' Chamberlain waved the paper aloft and later declared it to be a guarantee of 'peace with honour—peace for our time.' Chamberlain believed in Hitler's expressions of good faith; he still had his doubts about the wisdom of Versailles; he was convinced he had averted war. Apart from a few doubters, most people shared his optimism. Churchill, however, declared that 'the German dictator, instead of snatching the victuals from the table, has been content to have them served to him course by course.' In the House of Commons cries of 'Nonsense' greeted this criticism.

In Germany Hitler's grasp of politics had triumphed over his critics among the generals and the diplomats. His success dazzled the German people. He was not content with the Sudetenland alone, and preparations were made for fresh moves against the weakened Czechs.

Czechoslovakia, with her frontier fortresses in German hands, could not resist. On 10 October the Teschen district was ceded to Poland. In November, by the 'Vienna Award' a new Czech-Hungarian frontier was drawn by the Germans, to Hungary's advantage. The other racial minorities, the Slovaks and the Ruthenes, demanded new rights. Benes left the country and his successor, President Hacha, used stern measures against the Slovaks in a desperate bid to prevent his country from falling apart. In March 1939 Hitler used the Slovak grievances to push Czechoslovakia further into anarchy. Hacha travelled to Berlin and pleaded with Hitler to be left alone. In reply, Hitler disclosed his plans for an air assault on Prague. Hacha, in dismay, placed Czechoslovakia voluntarily in the hands of the Führer. On 15 March Hitler triumphantly entered his new inheritance and slept in the ancient castle at Prague. The Czech state was carved up. The provinces of Bohemia and Moravia were put under the protection of Germany, Slovakia became a separate, loyal, puppet state, and Ruthenia was ceded to Hungary. Czechoslovakia disappeared from the map. The British and French Governments did little but protest. After all, they had surrendered at Munich.

Memel, Danzig and War

After the occupation of Prague, another alarm followed in quick succession. Memelland, the former German province in the extreme north-east corner of East Prussia, had been ceded to Lithuania in 1919 although predominantly German in population. In March 1939 the people of Memel demanded incorporation in Germany. The Lithuanian Foreign Minister was called to Berlin and agreed to the immediate surrender of Memel.

The Poles, alarmed, feared that they were next. So far, Hitler had been reluctant to move against Poland, but the Danzig question now occupied his mind. Germany had deeply resented the loss of Upper Silesia and Danzig and the separation of East Prussia from the rest of Germany by the 'Polish Corridor'. Hitler had a good case for revision, but Chamberlain had by now decided to abandon appeasement. By March 1939 Hitler had been revealed as an aggressor, not as a reasonable peace-maker. On Danzig, Britain and France made their stand and gave an assurance to Poland that they would resist any threat to Polish independence. Hitler was checked for a time, although he did not believe that the Allied resolution had stiffened. He reckoned he could push Daladier and Chamberlain to concession over Danzig as he had over Czechoslovakia.

In April 1939 Hitler ended the 1934 Pact with Poland and the **Anglo-**

German Naval Agreement of 1935. Then he waited. But the Poles would not abandon their new alliance with Britain or concede a foot of territory in the Corridor or Danzig. In May, after Italy's seizure of Albania, the 'Pact of Steel' committing Italy and Germany to a military alliance was signed. It did not commit Italy to a war against Poland but it strengthened Germany's hand.

Russia remained the great mystery. Both sides made bids for Soviet support. In May, slow and tentative negotiations opened between Britain and Russia, but suspicion on both sides hampered progress. The Russians suspected that the British were deliberately trying to involve them in a war against Germany while Britain stayed neutral. Meanwhile, Germany moved fast. Hitler asked Stalin to sign a non-aggression pact. On 23 August Ribbentrop went to Moscow and drew up the terms. Apart from the non-aggression treaty, a secret agreement drew a line dividing eastern Europe into two spheres of influence. Hitler had a free hand in western Poland and Lithuania, while Russia was to exercise control over eastern Poland and the other Baltic states. The Russians signed the Nazi-Soviet Pact to purchase time to prepare their own defences; for Hitler it meant Poland was isolated in the east and the democracies had lost a powerful ally.

Hitler's war preparations proceeded. All along he expected the Polish and the British resistance to crack and Danzig and the Corridor to fall into his lap. On 1 September 1939 his troops invaded Poland. He believed Britain and France would, as with Czechoslovakia, accept the inevitable. Instead, on 3 September both Britain and France declared war on Germany.

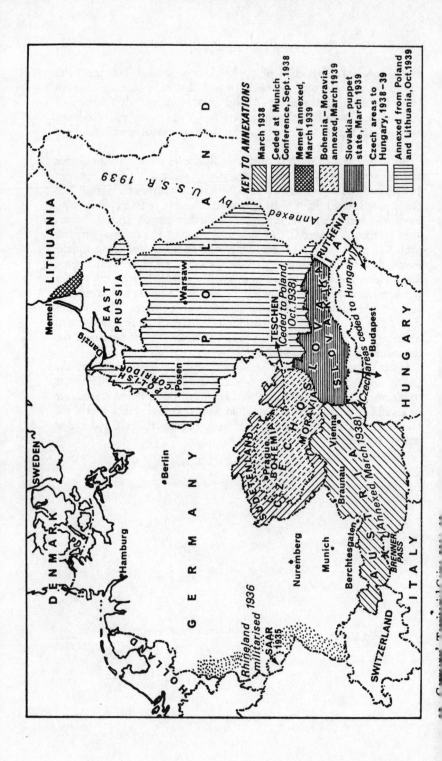

KEY TO ANNEXATIONS

- March 1938
- Ceded at Munich Conference, Sept. 1938
- Memel annexed, March 1939
- Bohemia – Moravia annexed, March 1939
- Slovakia – puppet state, March 1939
- Czech areas to Hungary, 1938–39
- Annexed from Poland and Lithuania, Oct. 1939

SWEDEN

DENMARK

•Hamburg

G E R M A N Y

•Berlin

Nuremberg

Munich

Berchtesgaten

Rhineland militarised 1936
SAAR 1935

A U S T R I A (Annexed March 1938)
Braunau
Vienna
BRENNER PASS
SWITZERLAND

I T A L Y

SUDETENLAND
•Prague
B O H E M I A
C Z E C H O S L O V A K I A
MORAVIA

Danzig
POLISH CORRIDOR
•Posen
EAST PRUSSIA
Memel
LITHUANIA

P O L A N D

•Warsaw

Annexed by U.S.S.R. 1939

TESCHEN (Ceded to Poland, Oct. 1938)

S L O V A K I A
RUTHENIA
Czech areas ceded to Hungary
•Budapest

H U N G A R Y

17

The Second World War, 1939-45

✳✳

POLAND INVADED, 1939

German tanks moved across the Polish frontier on 1 September 1939 from four separate directions, north, north-west, south and south-west. The Polish army fought fiercely and with incredible courage, but, out-numbered and out-gunned, their cause was doomed. Cavalry charges, no matter how brave, cannot hope to overwhelm machine guns. The German 'Blitzkrieg' swept eastwards: the Luftwaffe bombed towns, airfields, and barracks and the Panzer divisions then moved in with great rapidity to surround and destroy the dazed defenders. Britain and France could give no assistance: it took time for their own armies to be mobilised and with the German Air Force triumphant, supplying Poland proved impossible. In any case Poland fell before her allies had time to pull themselves together.

On 17 September Russia invaded and caught the Poles in a vicious pincer trap. The Polish Government escaped to Rumania. The city of Warsaw put up a heroic resistance but fell to the German soldiers on the 30th. In less than a month Poland had been conquered. The victors divided the spoils of war between them, as agreed in the Russo-German Pact. Himmler was made responsible for the deportation of Jews and Slavs from the provinces annexed by Germany. Elsewhere in Poland food and supplies were moved to Germany and eventually 'the final solution' to the Jewish problem was implemented at Auschwitz and other camps, in which over a million died.

THE 'PHONEY WAR'

All Europe waited uneasily for the next lightning blow to fall, but Hitler's armies remained inactive. The British Expeditionary Force moved to France and took up its positions along the French border on the left of the French line. In Paris it was believed that the Germans feared the Maginot Line; other nations waited to see the outcome of the struggle before deciding their actions. In Britain, hectic preparations for defence were made: shelters built, trenches dug, children evacuated to the country and all suspects were rounded up and interned. The British people then waited, confident, but, in reality, unprepared. Months passed without action. The period became known as 'the phoney war'. People had steeled themselves for a blow: when none fell, hopes rose. The British still hoped a major conflict would be averted. Rationing was not introduced until January 1940 and then only for butter and bacon. In the House of Commons, Kingsley Wood replied to the suggestion that German forests should be bombed, 'Are you aware it is private property? Why, you will be asking me to bomb Essen next.'

Germany delayed because Hitler thought that Britain and France, with the fate of Poland decided, might bid for peace terms. Hitler did not anticipate a war in the west. His immediate objectives attained, he expected the opposition to crumble, as at Munich. Nor did the German generals wish for a winter campaign for no one but Hitler expected an immediate break-through across the Maginot Line. Pleading insufficiency of ammunition and bad weather, the generals postponed their assault. The Allies did not want to cause bloodshed, and leaflets, not bombs, were dropped in 1939, urging the German people to overthrow Hitler.

The Führer waited impatiently for his generals to report their readiness. Events forced his hand. Stalin's armies attacked Finland in November 1939 and Britain asked Norway and Sweden for permission to move troops to Finland. Hitler was alarmed by this and by British naval exploits like the capture of the German supply ship, the *Altmark*, off the Norwegian coast. By April 1940 Admiral Raeder had come to the conclusion that the occupation of Norway was essential if only to protect German iron-ore supplies which came from Sweden. In addition, the coast of Norway would provide bases for German raiders and it might be possible to outflank the British blockade. Hitler agreed and a force of only five divisions overran Denmark and landed in

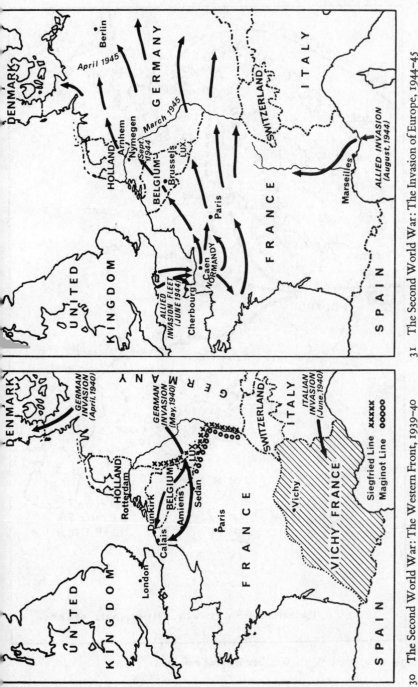

31   The Second World War: The Invasion of Europe, 1944–45

30   The Second World War: The Western Front, 1939–40

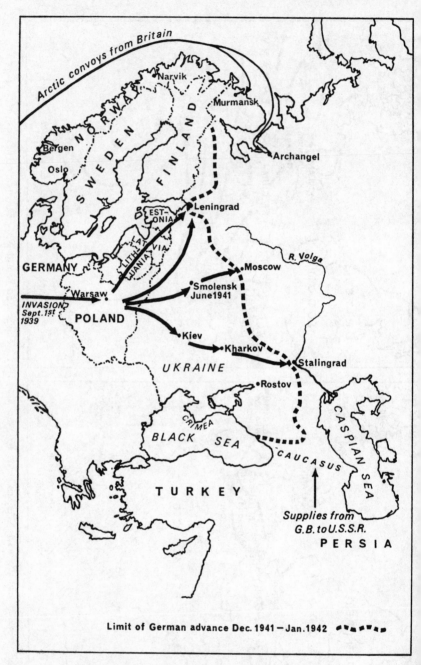

32 The Second World War: The Eastern Front, 1941–45

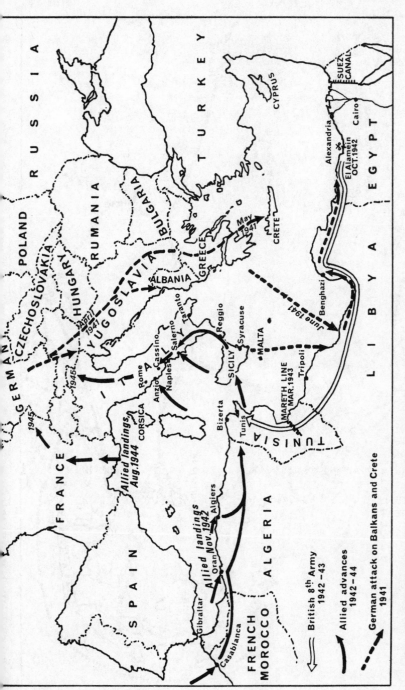

33 The Second World War: North Africa, Italy and the Balkans

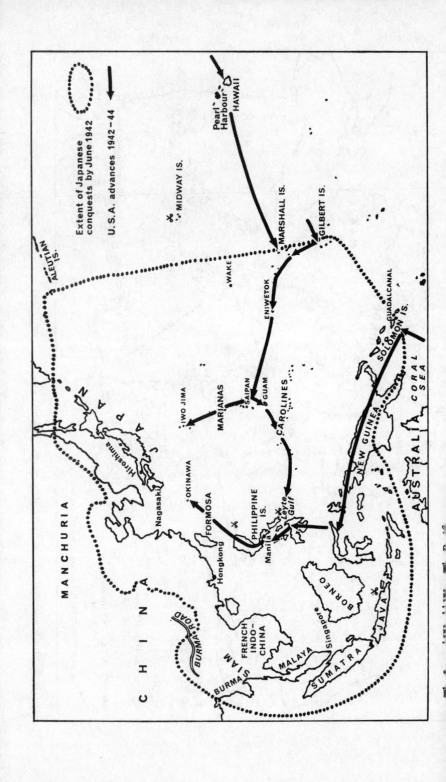

Norway. Within days the Germans had seized control of both countries. An Allied force landed in Norway but within three weeks had to withdraw. The 'phoney war' had ended.

Neville Chamberlain, the British Prime Minister, had no heart for the war. Parliament lost confidence in his handling of operations culminating in the disaster of Norway which caught the British Government utterly by surprise. On 10 May 1940 Chamberlain resigned and Winston Churchill took his place. At once Churchill infused Britain with a new spirit of resistance, of stubborn courage and a refusal to be beaten despite terrific odds. In an early speech to Parliament he said:

'I have nothing to offer but blood, toil, tears and sweat. We have before us an ordeal of the most grievous kind. We have before us many long months of struggle and suffering. You ask, What is our policy? I will say: it is to wage war by sea, land and air, with all our might and with all our strength that God can give us: to wage war against a monstrous tyranny.'

THE WAR IN THE WEST

On 10 May, the same day that Churchill became Premier, the main German army was launched against France and the Low Countries. The German attack bears a striking resemblance to the Schlieffen Plan of 1914. The forces were about equal, with roughly 136 divisions on each side. But the Germans had a heavy concentration of armour—tanks, armoured cars and artillery—in their centre, which crossed the difficult ground of the Ardennes, so by-passing the Maginot Line. The French had thought the Ardennes to be impassable for tanks.

Holland fell first to a swift assault by German paratroops and massed infantry. Rotterdam crumbled after heavy bombing by the Luftwaffe. In Belgium, dive-bombers spread panic among soldiers and civilians: refugees crammed the roads and impeded the troops. At Sedan in France the Germans broke through and advanced rapidly to take Amiens, and by 20 May they had reached and captured Calais and Boulogne. The Allied forces were cut in two. In Belgium, British, Belgian and French soldiers streamed towards the coast in retreat. The Belgian King surrendered on 28 May. In the south the demoralised remnants of the French army fell back on Paris.

At Dunkirk an apparent miracle took place. Hitler halted his armoured columns and harassed the British forces on the beaches with dive-bombers. He missed an opportunity to sweep the enemy into the sea, for 335,000 Allied troops were evacuated in hundreds of boats, great and small, by 3 June. The reasons for Hitler's hesitancy have never been satisfactorily solved. It may have been the result of a dispute between Göring and Rundstedt for the honour of finishing off the Allies. Göring's Luftwaffe was given the job but failed. As a result, although the troops had abandoned their equipment, virtually a whole army escaped to Britain to fight again. Yet nothing could lessen the magnitude of the disaster: the British had been driven ignominiously from Europe.

Within France, General Weygand tried to form a defence line north of Paris. Again German tanks drove through the French defences on the Somme. Mussolini, who could not control his impatience to be in at the kill, entered the war on the German side and invaded Savoy. On 14 June German vehicles rolled into Paris, which the French had decided not to defend in order to save it from destruction. Marshal Pétain, now eighty-four, was recalled from retirement to head a defeatist Government which soon sued for an armistice. Hitler divided France: the north and west, like Belgium and Holland, were occupied by German troops; the south was left in the hands of the government of collaborators, based on the town of Vichy. The French navy was to be disarmed and the costs of the German occupation were to be paid by the French government. General de Gaulle and others refused to accept defeat and formed a Free French Movement in London.

The Battle of Britain

Again, Churchill spoke to the British people: 'the battle of Britain is about to begin. . . . Let us brace ourselves to our duties and so bear ourselves that, if the British Empire and its Commonwealth last for a thousand years, men will still say, "This was their finest hour."'

Hastily, defences were strengthened, beaches mined, the Home Guard formed, concrete bunkers erected, aeroplanes and troops concentrated in the south-east. Hitler had no plans to invade Britain. The German navy could not establish control in the Channel. His submarines were too few. The Germans thought, rightly, that the key to invasion was control in the air. The German invasion force assembled in northern France, and the Luftwaffe was launched across the Channel to establish their superiority. The battle of Britain was fought in the blue skies over southern England throughout the summer of 1940. In July German bombers began to strafe air-fields and to harry the British fighters. Through August and September aerial battles went on daily. The *Spitfire* and the *Hurricane* held their own against the German fighters, and the invention of radar helped Fighter Command to spot enemy planes as they crossed the Channel. On 7 September the Luft-waffe changed their tactics and began night bombing raids on London. The 'Blitz' was a terrible shock but it indicated the end of the battle of Britain: Germany had failed to break the morale of the British people. The Germans had made one vital mistake: they had concentrated much of their power against London and not on airfields and radar stations. Above all, the British people had to thank the fighter pilots. In Churchill's words, 'never in the field of human conflict was so much owed by so many to so few.'

The battle had been a close thing. In September the RAF's Fighter Command had been stretched to the limit. Nor was it over. During the winter of 1940–41 Britain's cities were systematically bombed. 44,000 civilians died and the cities of London, Coventry, Hull and others like them suffered great damage.

In 1939 Britain had been unprepared for war. By 1941 her factories poured out armaments, and supplies from Canada and America added to the flow. Although the US Government under President Roosevelt did not wish to become directly involved in the war, it was no secret which side America wanted to win. Churchill negotiated a 'cash and carry' agreement by which the USA would sell military equipment if paid for and carried away by the purchaser. Britain had sufficient con-trol of the Atlantic Ocean to be able to take advantage of the offer. Even so, British shipping losses to the German U-boats and surface raiders were heavy. In 1940 the USA sold Britain fifty destroyers in exchange for the use of British bases stretching from Newfoundland to the Caribbean. In 1941 'Lend-Lease' supplied Britain with vast amounts of American supplies, to be paid for after the end of hostilities. The Royal Navy had again played an important part in defence. The Ger-man Navy had been bottled up in harbour, British destroyers blockaded the German coast, and mine-layers made the passage of German coast traffic a hazardous business. At Dunkirk, 200 naval vessels and 600 smaller ships had been able to run a shuttle service to England free from naval although not from air attack. The greatest menace proved to be the submarine, as in the First World War. On the first day of the war the liner *Athenia* was sunk and in October 1939 a daring U-boat pene-trated the defences of Scapa Flow to sink the battleship *Royal Oak*. In the Atlantic, merchant shipping had to run the gauntlet of U-boats, dive-bombers and cruising raiders. In December the British struck back by cornering the pocket-battleship *Graf Spee* at the mouth of the River

Plate and forcing her commander to scuttle his ship rather than surrender.

THE WAR WIDENS: NORTH AFRICA, GREECE AND RUSSIA

Hitler had never anticipated a long war against Britain. He had assumed that she would make peace, accepting Germany's gains. Once the battle of Britain had shown invasion to be impossible, he returned to his ideas of the 1920s—German expansion into the Balkans or even into Russia. The direction of Germany's assault was determined by the Italians. In September 1940 Italian troops from Libya invaded Egypt and advanced towards Alexandria. Quickly the British gathered forces from India, South Africa, Australia and New Zealand and under General Wavell this combined force struck hard at the Italians. The Allied forces swept on to Benghazi by February 1941 and aeroplanes crippled the Italian fleet as it lay in Taranto harbour. In East Africa British forces overran Mussolini's empire in Eritrea, Somaliland and Abyssinia. Emperor Haile Selassie returned to his capital to be restored to his throne.

Meanwhile, Germany had not been idle. Rumania and Bulgaria allowed German troops to occupy important positions and to build airfields. In October 1940 Italian troops had also attacked Greece, ruled by the dictator, General Metaxas, who fought grimly and drove out the Italians. Suddenly, on 6 April 1941 the Germans struck fast and furiously at Yugoslavia and Greece, using the victorious methods of the 'blitzkrieg'—dive-bombers, heavy artillery, and swift rushes by tanks and armoured vehicles. The triumphant Germans overran both countries, drove out a British force and immediately invaded Crete. By the end of May the German paratroops were masters of the island. The British troops had little air cover. Flying from their new airfields in the Balkans the German bombers, gliders and fighters overwhelmed the Allied forces, the remnants of which withdrew to Egypt.

In North Africa the Germans also came to the assistance of their now despised friends. From Sicily aeroplanes flew out the Afrika Corps, commanded by General Rommel. Wavell's forces, weakened by the loss of detachments sent to Greece, Syria and Iraq, were pushed back along the coast, although the garrison at Tobruk held out. Britain's control of the Mediterranean was questioned, for German planes inflicted severe losses on convoys and battered Malta.

On 22 June 1941, 138 divisions of the German army attacked Russia along a thousand-mile front. Churchill immediately offered Russia aid and cooperation. Britain no longer stood alone: she had gained a valuable ally, and Hitler, who had repeatedly spoken of the danger of two fronts, had deliberately gambled on a quick victory. The Germans despised Russia as a weak state and were confident of dealing a knock-out blow. They under-estimated the resilience of the 200 million Russian people and the vast areas their soldiers had to cover. Until 1945 two thirds of the German army were permanently engaged on the huge Russian front. At first the Germans advanced rapidly, overrunning the Baltic states of Lithuania, Latvia and Estonia. Eastern Poland fell; Smolensk, a town two thirds of the way to Moscow, fell within three weeks of the invasion. Leningrad was surrounded, although the Germans never succeeded in taking it. Their superiority in tanks and aircraft allowed them to sweep on into the outskirts of Moscow, but again, they failed to take the city. The Southern Army Group made even more spectacular progress through the Ukraine, capturing the key cities of Kiev and Kharkov. The Russians employed similar tactics to those used against Napoleon, retreating, drawing the Germans deeper and deeper into devastated country.

The Russians kept their armies intact, and waited for the winter to take its toll. Their factories were dismantled and moved to Siberia. Production increased and supplies were moved through Persia which Russia and Britain occupied jointly. Britain also sent equipment by the dangerous convoy route to Murmansk. As the winter of 1941 closed in, the Russians held on grimly. The Germans made the error of failing to destroy the enemy's forces or its industrial nerve-centres before the winter took its toll. Hitler had been torn between capturing Moscow, the great prize, and taking the Ukraine and the Caucasus with their vital economic resources. He captured neither. The Germans divided their forces into two: the northern and the southern armies. Both suffered from the Russian winter. Men reeling from frost-bite found their weapons and vehicles had seized up in the December ice.

On 6 December, Zhukov, the new Russian commander, hit back on the Moscow front. Hitler replaced any German general who advised retreat. The Germans hung on, hoping that in the spring they could recover the initiative.

THE ENTRY OF THE USA, 1941

F. D. Roosevelt and the Democrats, in power since 1933, had no sympathy for Nazism. However, their love of peace and reluctance to involve themselves in Europe were stronger emotions. As the European situation had worsened the USA had taken refuge behind Neutrality Acts (1935–37) which forbade American shipping and armaments from going to countries at war.

Most countries firmly believed in the Allied cause and welcomed 'Lend-Lease' as a means of providing Britain with munitions which did not have to be paid for immediately. Throughout 1941 more and more US factories moved over to war production. The Germans took reprisals by sinking American ships and in November 1941 Congress allowed US ships to fire at attackers. President Roosevelt and Churchill met on a battleship off Newfoundland in August and drew up the 'Atlantic Charter', a statement of their common principles based on the right of men to choose their own form of government, and containing guarantees of freedom from hunger, war, fear and tyranny.

Hitler had no wish to convert this open American antagonism into open war. The Japanese, however, had no such reservations. Japan hoped to exploit the war in Europe to extend her own Empire in the Pacific. Japanese troops had already occupied Indo-China. Beyond lay Malaya and the Pacific islands. The Japanese army was confident of capturing all these territories and of making the USA accept their conquests. Even so, one cannot quite understand the foolishness of the Japanese in attacking the USA: they might have taken British, Dutch and French possessions bit by bit, and without involving America. On 7 December 1941 they threw all caution aside. Japanese carrier-based planes launched a surprise attack on the American Pacific Fleet as it lay at anchor in Pearl Harbour, Hawaii. Within minutes eight battleships, three cruisers and three destroyers were either destroyed or severely damaged. On the following day the USA declared war on Japan but was totally unprepared to fight a major conflict in the Pacific immediately. The Japanese followed up this spectacular success by capturing the islands of Guam and Wake, and by sinking two battleships of the British fleet, the *Prince of Wales* and the *Repulse*. On 11 December Hitler declared war on the USA. Britain, loyal to her friend, declared war on Japan. The complexion of the war had altered radically by the end of 1941. No longer opposed by Britain alone, Hitler now found himself also at war with two Powers potentially far stronger than Germany. The Führer did not despair: he considered the USA decadent and Russia demoralised by the Communist purges. He had planned for a short successful war; now he was faced by the prospect of a long struggle of attrition. He thought his genius for dividing his enemies would rescue him. If not, he confidently thought the German army capable of even greater deeds.

While America began the vast build-up to wage war, the Japanese ran on from victory to victory. Their troops swept through Malaya, capturing the great naval base at Singapore. They occupied Hong Kong, the Philippines and the Dutch East Indies, and invaded Burma. America, forced to withdraw in face of the Japanese advance, used her only means of counter-attack, the navy. In May and June 1942 two great naval battles were fought, in the Coral Sea and Midway Island. Aircraft from carriers harried the Japanese fleet, sinking many ships and preventing an invasion of Northern Australia.

1942

During 1942 Japan and Germany still dominated the war. President Roosevelt decided that Germany looked the greater danger and that the United States' efforts should be concentrated in North Africa and Europe. In Africa General Rommel had swept all before him. He seized Tobruk and pressed on into Egypt to be halted at El Alamein. A massive German air assault on Malta failed to dislodge the British but their navy was driven from the island to take refuge in Egypt. The British commanders, Generals Alexander and Montgomery, spent the summer concentrating their forces—tanks, artillery, and fresh and rested infantry—in Egypt. Malta was reinforced in June, although only after heavy loss. Rommel's armies were suffering from exhaustion and the difficulties of a long supply line stretching from Libya. At El Alamein on 23 October, the Eighth Army attacked and heavily defeated the Germans, who were pursued by tanks along the coast of North Africa. On 8 November a combined British and American force under General Eisenhower landed in the French colonial territories of Morocco and Algeria. Rommel's armies were caught between the two advancing Allied armies which slowly closed the pincers.

In Russia, the Germans did not continue their victorious advance once the winter of 1941–42 was over. The severe cold stretched German morale and resources to the limit: their troops had not been provided with adequate winter clothing and their equipment did not function. Thousands of soldiers were put out of action with frost-bite, and the long lines of communication and supply were often cut by Russians operating behind the German lines. The German generals constructed huge supply dumps west of Moscow and repaired 16,000 miles of railway to keep their armies equipped. Only in the Crimea and on the Volga did the Germans make any progress in the spring of 1942. Hitler urged Von Paulus on towards Stalingrad in an attempt to cut the food and oil route running north from the Caucasus into central Russia. As the winter of 1942 closed in Von Paulus committed more and more men to the final assault on Stalingrad. A bitter struggle was fought in the ruins of the city. The Russians launched a series of counter-attacks. Von Paulus wanted to retreat. Hitler forbade it. Finally, in January 1943 the Russians surrounded the German army and forced it to surrender. Twenty-two German divisions (300,000 men) had been destroyed or captured in the fighting.

Germany had suffered two shattering blows—at Alamein and at Stalingrad. Hitler realised that the net would quickly close on him, and he stepped up the submarine offensive to stave off his enemies. At the end of 1941 Germany had only sixty U-boats but 300 were built in 1942. In this one year the Allies lost 6 million tons of shipping to the German submarine packs. By using radar, long-range aircraft and protected convoys, shipping losses were cut in 1943 and the rate of submarine sinkings rose. Dönitz, who replaced Raeder, even withdrew his submarines from the North Atlantic for a time.

1943-44, THE INVASION OF EUROPE

In January 1943 Churchill and Roosevelt met at Casablanca in North Africa. They decided that Germany must make an unconditional surrender and that invasion of Italy should precede an invasion of France. Stalin had demanded immediate Allied landings in France to relieve the pressure on Russia. When the Allies refused, Stalin became suspicious, believing that they hoped the Russians would be weakened in the war against Germany, and the Allies would take advantage to seize territory for themselves at the end of the war.

Ignoring Russian suspicions, the British and Americans gave priority to the expulsion of the enemy from North Africa. The Germans fought a brave and stubborn rearguard action. A large German force landed in Tunisia and seized Bizerta and Tunis. Rommel retreated from Libya and linked up. At the Mareth Line the Germans made their stand, but they crumbled against the sheer weight of the Allied armies. In May 1943, 250,000 Germans and Italians were taken prisoner, and the whole of the North African coast fell under Allied control.

The British and American governments decided to follow up their victory in Africa by invading Sicily and Italy. This displeased those who wanted an invasion of France but in 1943 the Allies needed time to mount a powerful offensive across the Channel. The heavy losses of the Commando raid on Dieppe in 1942 had revealed the strength of Hitler's fortress in Europe. Italy could first and more easily be knocked out of the war and German troops tied down, while the Allies made their preparations for an invasion of France.

On 10 July 1943 Allied armies landed in Sicily, covered by air support from Malta. Hundreds of landing craft carried the troops ashore. The landings were a brilliant success, for the port of Syracuse was seized on the second day, but the Germans fought stubbornly and were not expelled until late August. Italy's collapse was blamed on Mussolini who was arrested and imprisoned. Marshal Badoglio formed a government excluding the discredited Fascists and he negotiated an armistice in September, to the disgust of the Germans. In the same month the Allied armies made a series of landings on the Italian mainland. At Salerno bitter German resistance pinned down the Allies but Montgomery's Eighth Army advanced north from Reggio to relieve the pressure.

Naples fell in October, and Badoglio declared war on Germany. The Allied advance, at first so successful, ground to a stop in the winter because the Germans established a line of defences north of Naples. The old monastery of Monte Cassino was fortified and proved to be a key to the German defences. Mussolini was freed by German troops and returned to head a puppet Fascist government in northern Italy, under German dictation. In January 1944 the Allies landed at Anzio, behind the German lines, but they failed to break out until the summer.

In May, after a heavy build-up of their forces, the Allied armies commanded by General Alexander hammered at the German lines. Artillery fire, bombers and naval bombardments prepared the way for the infantry. After three days of fighting the Germans broke. The ruins of Monte Cassino fell at last, links were established with the Anzio troops and in June Rome capitulated.

The Russians, meanwhile, had not been idle. After the triumph of

Stalingrad they held the invaders and in the Caucasus forced the Germans to withdraw. Russian troops retook Rostov and thrust forward west of Moscow. In the spring of 1943 the Germans retaliated in the Ukraine. They advanced a few miles but again were forced into retreat.

In July the Russians mounted their major offensive. Kharkov, Smolensk, the Crimea and Kiev were all recovered. Desperate German attempts to stem the tide achieved only a temporary halt to the Russian advance. In January 1944 Leningrad was relieved, and the advance continued along the whole front. The Russians flung millions of men into the front line to sweep the Germans back by sheer weight of numbers. German transport, artillery and tanks, once technically superior to Russian, were now found to be inadequate. During 1944 the supplies sent from the Western Powers, added to the flow from Russian factories, meant that the Germans lost this superiority in armaments. Consequently, the tide moved nearer and nearer the frontiers of the Third Reich.

'D-Day'

The Allies spent the last quarter of 1943 preparing for the invasion of France. RAF and American bombers smashed industrial targets in Germany and occupied Europe, although they never succeeded in paralysing heavy industry, for Albert Speer worked miracles to increase German production. Night after night the bombers caused chaos and terror in German cities, making nonsense of Hitler's boasts that the Luftwaffe would never allow enemy aeroplanes to cross the frontiers of Germany.

Within conquered Europe the Resistance fighters continually harassed the German troops. In Yugoslavia Marshal Tito led a guerilla army which tied down German troops in fruitless searches for the partisans. From Poland to France resistance fighters derailed trains, blew up bridges, radioed information and assisted Allied agents to move around and eventually to escape.

In November 1943 Stalin, Roosevelt and Churchill met at Teheran. The Russian insistence that the Allies should land in France was met by a promise of an invasion in 1944. General Montgomery was withdrawn from Italy to lead the invasion and General Eisenhower was appointed supreme commander of all the Allied forces. The Germans had strengthened the coastal defences of France with concrete bunkers, heavy guns and mines, but they had to spread their forces along an extensive coastline stretching from Holland to the Spanish coast. The Germans made desperate efforts to anticipate the Allied landings but in the event were caught by surprise.

Southern England became a vast military camp for the armies of America, Britain and France. German installations in occupied Europe were bombed night and day. Railways, barracks, airfields, roads and bridges came under heavy attack. Finally, on 6 June (D-Day) an armada of 4,000 ships transported and protected an army of five divisions, supported by three airborne divisions which made the first assault. The place chosen proved to be a stretch of Normandy coast near Caen. Prefabricated ('Mulberry') harbours were towed across the Channel and put into position on the coast for the benefit of the transports. A pipeline under the ocean ('PLUTO') was laid from England across to the Allied positions and the resulting oil supply greatly assisted the mobility of their armies. The Germans had expected an attack across the Pas de Calais and had fortified the Channel ports. When the invasion took place the Germans were slow to move their troops to the battle area, for a violent air assault pinned their forces to the ground.

General Montgomery quickly established a bridgehead along fifty miles of the coast without great loss of life. By 25 June the town of Cherbourg fell to the American army. Thousands of troops poured into France. Rundstedt and Rommel fought desperately to curtail the Allied advance but inexorably the powerful Allied forces rolled eastwards.

RUSSIA, 1944

To coincide with the invasion of Normandy, the Russians mounted a major offensive in the east. The Germans resisted, losing heavily in dead, wounded and prisoners, but they could not stem the Russian advance along all fronts, from Latvia in the north to the Rumanian frontier.

In an attempt to save Germany from the wreck of Hitler's ambitions, a group of senior officers plotted an attempt on the Führer's life. On 20 July 1944 a bomb exploded at one of Hitler's military conferences. Hitler was badly shaken but survived to take a terrible revenge on the plotters. Anyone remotely connected with the officers was rounded up and shot. The chief conspirators were strangled with piano wire. Over 5,000 people died in the purges. Even Rommel did not escape the net: he was forced to commit suicide by the Gestapo on Hitler's orders.

Within Poland the Warsaw resistance staged a rising, hoping to gain the assistance of the advancing Russians or the RAF. The Germans crushed the revolt with great brutality, destroying the Jewish ghetto in the city at the same time. A few weeks later, the Russians captured Warsaw. During the winter of 1944–45 the advance continued into Rumania, Yugoslavia and Bulgaria. Often local resistance groups assisted the Russians.

1944–45, FINAL VICTORY

In France, once the Cherbourg peninsula had been cleared, the Americans broke through to Brittany. Brest fell quickly, and the mobile Allied forces swung round in an arc east to the Seine. The German retreat was continually harassed by air attack and in August the great prize of Paris fell into Allied hands. In the same month, on the fifteenth, another landing was made, in southern France. With Marseilles liberated, an advance was begun up the Rhône valley. In Italy, Florence fell to the Allies. In all parts of Europe, the Germans were on the retreat, their morale broken, their armies in disarray. Nevertheless, the war was not yet over. The Germans had decided to make a last-ditch fight to save the Fatherland, and to try to make the Allies give up their objective of an unconditional German surrender in favour of a negotiated peace.

The Allies had been flattered by their easy advance through France. Eisenhower had directed the move forward on a wide front, giving his subordinate commanders like Montgomery and Patton considerable freedom of action. By September 1944 northern France, Belgium and Luxemburg had been set free. The obstacle of the Rhine loomed ahead. Eisenhower planned to cross it on the Dutch border and then swing south behind the Siegfried Line. Arnhem and Nijmegen were key points and 10,000 troops were dropped or landed by gliders behind the German lines, to seize control of the bridges in these towns. The daring attempt failed due to faulty planning and strong German resistance. Few survived the slaughter.

Encouraged by their success the Germans struck another blow in December 1944. Rundstedt attacked in the Ardennes and for a time drove the Allied armies into retreat. The German advance was eventually held and turned. Hitler's plan to divide Russia from the West by negotiating a separate peace failed with the Ardennes offensive. Churchill had no wish to see Russia triumphant in eastern Europe but he was determined to crush Nazism utterly and at the same time be loyal to Britain's ally, Russia.

The Allied hopes of an early end to the war were shattered by the battle of the Ardennes. Germany was not yet beaten: she had still plenty of power and resilience. In her dying moments Germany produced new and dangerous weapons which indicated her ability to fight back. Flying bombs (V-1s) suddenly descended on London. When British troops captured their launching sites in northern France the Germans fired rockets (V-2s) against cities and military targets but again primarily at London. Fortunately for Britain the war was over before Germany could construct and fire many of these deadly weapons.

Nazi Germany's death-throes began in January 1945 as the Russians poured across Poland and into Germany. Austria was entered and Vienna fell to the Red Army. By April the Russians were hammering on the gates of Berlin itself. The Germans made a last desperate bid to stave off defeat by forcing the Russians to fight for every Berlin street.

British and American troops crossed the Rhine in March 1945 and soon reached the Elbe where they linked up with the Russians. The Fascist leaders were two of the last to die. Mussolini was seized and executed by partisans as he ran for Switzerland. Hitler committed suicide in the Chancellery bunker in Berlin. Admiral Dönitz, his successor, surrendered unconditionally to the Allies on 7 May. The war in Europe was over.

THE WAR IN THE PACIFIC

After the first shock of defeat had been absorbed by the British and the Americans in the Far East, the Japanese advance was eventually halted and the tide of war turned. In the spring of 1943 American troops and supplies flooded into the Pacific area. The Japanese were stopped in New Guinea. American troops invaded and captured Guadalcanal and other islands in the Solomons. From bases in Australia and Hawaii the American Air Force bombed Japanese installations in the north Pacific. When the island of Saipan in the Marianas was taken in February 1944 the new Super-Fortresses of the USAF began to attack Japan itself.

In Burma the enemy had also been held. Stubborn resistance throughout 1942 prevented a break-through to India. General Slim's

Fourteenth Army began the slow, exhausting task of driving the Japanese out of the jungle. By 1944 the British achieved control in the air and were able to drop supplies to Slim's army and to the patrols of Brigadier Wingate, operating behind Japanese lines. Fighting through dense jungle the British reopened the Burma Road to China in January 1945 and drew up plans to liberate Malaya and Singapore.

In 1944 General MacArthur's American offensive in the Pacific had two prongs. From New Guinea, Australian and American troops pressed towards the Philippines, which were invaded in October. The Japanese navy came out to prevent the American Army from landing. The major battle of the war, at Leyte, resulted in a decisive American victory. Japan lost three battleships, six aircraft carriers, and ten cruisers. American losses were slight, six ships in all. Manila, the capital of the Philippines, fell after fierce fighting.

The other prong of the offensive centred on the islands of the central Pacific—the Marshalls, the Gilberts, and the Marianas. Aeroplanes, ships and troops cooperated in a series of invasions, although the Japanese never surrendered without bitter fighting, and American losses were heavy.

Throughout 1944 and 1945, while the Americans leap-frogged from one island to another, Allied scientists were perfecting a new and terrible weapon, the atomic bomb. As the Americans considered its possible use, the battle for Okinawa was being fought. In April, troops landed on the island but it took three months to expel the Japanese. From airfields based on Okinawa bombers ranged Japan, spraying incendiaries and high explosives on Tokyo, Yokohama, and other cities. Although the British Fourteenth Army was steadily advancing in Burma, and had retaken Mandalay and Rangoon by May, the Allies realised that the invasion of Japan itself would result in heavy casualties. General MacArthur built up a powerful armada, but Roosevelt's advisers suggested that as the A-bomb was now ready, it should be used to bring Japan to submission. Roosevelt died in April 1945 and the new President, Truman, had to make the fateful decision of whether or not to use the bomb.

On 6 August the first atomic bomb fell on Hiroshima, killing 80,000 people and devastating the city. On the ninth a second bomb destroyed Nagasaki. On the fourteenth Japan surrendered, and the Americans occupied the country without a casualty.

PEACE TERMS

As the end of the fighting approached, the war-time Allies found their political differences widening. Churchill's warnings about the dangers of Communist coups in eastern Europe were remembered when the USSR set up pro-Russian governments in the liberated countries of Rumania, Bulgaria and Poland.

At a meeting of the 'Big Three' at Yalta, in Russia, in February 1945 Stalin had agreed to enter the war against Japan if Russia could be allowed to extend her influence in the Far East. He had also agreed 'to create democratic institutions of their own choice' for the liberated peoples of Europe. It became apparent that Stalin had no intention of implementing this promise. When the USA used the atomic bomb on Japan, Russia hurriedly entered the war and grabbed territory in Manchuria. In Europe, however, unrepresentative Communist dictatorships violated the terms of the Yalta agreements.

In April 1945 another conference, at San Francisco, drafted the terms of the United Nations Charter and agreed to the division of Germany into four military zones, to be occupied by the four major powers, the USSR, the USA, Britain and France. Berlin, an enclave within the Russian zone, was to be administered by the same four Powers and would be divided into four zones. The Russians later insisted on reparations and jumped the gun by transporting vast quantities of raw materials and machinery from the areas they conquered.

Once in control of Poland the Russians handed over, not to the Polish Government in Exile (in London) but to the Communist dominated Committee of National Liberation. Nor would Russia allow the Western Powers to supervise voting in Poland. The territories seized by Russia from Poland in 1939 were not surrendered. The Poles were compensated by the grant of eastern German borderlands.

When the war ended, a third meeting of the Allied leaders took place at Potsdam, near Berlin, in August 1945. However, only Stalin of the original 'Big Three' remained. Roosevelt was dead, and Truman appeared for America. Churchill, heavily defeated in the general election, gave way to Clement Attlee, the Labour leader, for Britain.

Again, agreements were few. Poland's seizure of German territory up to the Oder-Neisse Line was accepted, as was the movement of German minorities living in Hungary, Poland and Czechoslovakia. As for the peace treaties, a Council of Ministers was created to draw up draft treaties. Agreement ended there; the seeds of suspicion which led to the

Cold War of the late 1940s and the 1950s had already been sown by 1945.

Europe was a ruined, devastated continent. The Nazis had transported 7½ million foreigners to work as slave labour in Germany. Jews, the old, crippled and ill were executed. Countries like Poland had been looted and their economies subordinated to Germany. France, pillaged by Göring's agents, had paid huge reparations during the war years. A vast task of reconstruction faced the Europe of 1945, complicated by the political rivalry that had developed between the Communist powers and the democracies.

18

The Post-war World, 1945-70:
Eastern Europe

✕✕✕

THE END OF THE WAR

While the Second World War was in its final stages the Allied leaders met at Yalta, in February 1945. Stalin promised to come into the war against Japan and did so two days after the Americans destroyed Hiroshima in an attack with atomic bombs. In Europe, Stalin craftily kept his options open. He led the Allied leaders to believe that free, democratic states would be established in eastern Europe. Secretly, however, the USSR intended to set up communist or Russian-sponsored régimes in the liberated countries. The conflict of interests that divided East and West came to a head over Poland. At Yalta it was agreed that the frontiers of Poland should be moved westwards, up to the line of the rivers Oder and Neisse, territory that had formerly been part of Germany. Stalin supported the claims of the National Committee of Liberation which entered Poland side by side with the Red Army. The few liberals and democrats who had survived Nazi rule disappeared in the Warsaw Rising of 1944 or in the purges that accompanied the Russian occupation.

In July 1945 the Allied leaders reassembled at Potsdam, in Germany. President Roosevelt (who had died in April) was replaced by President Truman; Winston Churchill, overthrown in a General Election, was succeeded by Clement Attlee, the Labour leader; only Stalin remained of the original 'Big Three'. The main problem arose out of Germany's defeat. The leaders agreed to divide Germany (and Berlin) into four occupation zones. In Berlin the four commanders-in-chief of the major powers would constitute a Control Council to administer the city. Furthermore, it was agreed to bring about the complete disarmament of Germany; to bring all war criminals to trial; to destroy the Nazi party; to supervise the payment of reparations from Germany's industrial resources; and to make preparations for the return of a democratic form of government to Germany.

Stalin began to increase his demands in eastern Europe. The northern part of East Prussia was swallowed up in the USSR; Poland's frontiers to the north and west encroached upon former German territory, and American and British troops were persuaded to retire a hundred miles to the west, to allow the Russians to occupy their zone in eastern Germany. Furthermore, Stalin resisted all pressures to restore western forms of democratic government in Poland, and the Potsdam Conference broke up in some disarray, leaving outstanding questions to be discussed by the Foreign Ministers.

Clearly, then, the rifts that were to deepen into the Cold War had already appeared. Even now, one cannot be certain of Stalin's motives. He wanted Germany to be thoroughly weakened, so that there would be no threat to European peace from German militarism again. This explains the seizure of German territories and industrial equipment. As a defensive bastion against the West he resolved to extend Russia's frontiers into what had been Polish territory, compensating Poland at Germany's expense. Poland would provide a communist buffer behind which the USSR could shelter until the ravages of the war had been made good. The American possession of the atomic bomb; the capitalist nature of American society; the Russian military weakness and Stalin's instinctive suspicion of anyone not in accord with his own ideas all explain the deepening hostility in the post-war world.

Poland

In 1939 Britain entered the war against Hitler as a consequence of the German invasion of Poland, but the German military successes of 1939–42 prevented the British from giving the Poles any practical assistance. A Polish government-in-exile, headed at first by General Sikorski and after his death by Stanislav Mikolajczyk, made its headquarters in London. During the war Poles fought gallantly within the Allied armies and a vigorous resistance movement harassed the German forces inside Poland. The Poles feared the Russians as much as the Germans, and the discovery in 1943 of the bodies of 14,300 Polish officers in a mass grave at Katyn deepened Polish suspicions, for the Russians were widely believed to be the murderers. The brave rebellion in 1944 of the Warsaw partisans was cruelly suppressed by the Germans, while the approaching Red Army, acting, it was believed, on Stalin's orders, slowed its advance towards the city.

Stalin had no sympathy towards the London Poles, who he thought (correctly) were anti-communist and anti-Russian. However, he

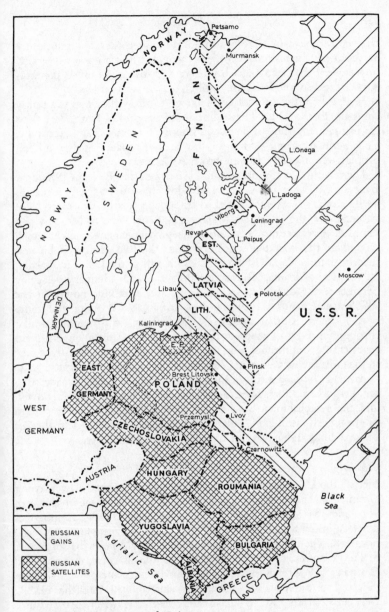

RUSSIAN
GAINS

RUSSIAN
SATELLITES

35　The USSR's Territorial Gains, 1945

allowed Mikolajczyk to return to Poland in June 1945, and reluctantly agreed to the inclusion of some of the exiled Polish leaders in a new government. For two years Mikolajczyk remained in office, continually harassed by the Russians, until in 1947 he was ousted.

At Potsdam, the Allied leaders agreed to allow the Poles to occupy lands up to the Oder–Neisse line (only fifty miles from Berlin) to compensate for the Russian acquisitions of former Polish territory. The German people living in this area (estimated at ten million people) were forcibly moved into East Germany.

The Czechs, on the other hand, welcomed the Russians. President Benes, exiled after the German invasion in 1939, had also made his headquarters in London, but throughout the war he was careful not to antagonise the USSR. In March 1945 Benes went to Moscow and joined the Czech communist leaders in a provisional government which took over the liberated territories from the Red Army. Stalin was successful, too, in establishing régimes friendly to the USSR in Finland, Yugoslavia, Albania, Rumania, Bulgaria and Hungary. Largely because of the overwhelming military and economic power of the USSR, these nations between 1945 and 1948 fell more and more deeply under Russian influence. The pattern was roughly similar throughout eastern Europe. A period of rule by coalition governments representing communist and non-communist parties usually ended in the Communists assuming control of the major departments of state —particularly the control of the armed forces, the police, broadcasting services and transport. Then came the communist seizure of total power, and the establishment of a single-party government on the pattern of the USSR. Rumania, Poland and Bulgaria succumbed to the last phase in 1947, Hungary and Czechoslovakia a year later.

Germany

In 1945 the USSR settled on a policy deliberately aimed at weakening Germany so that there would never be a repetition of the invasions of 1914 and 1941. In the Second World War the USSR had lost over nineteen million dead, and over thirty million people were made homeless. The horror of the German war would never be forgotten. Stalin did not hesitate to take his revenge: the disarmed, dismembered Germany of 1945 was a shadow of its former size and power. German industry in the east was dismantled and moved into the USSR; German scientists and technicians who had survived disappeared into Russian factories; and the Russian zone in east Germany was administered as a subordinate territory. The USSR demanded that western Germany should make considerable contributions to reparations in the shape of industrial equipment.

Austria received similar treatment. Four occupation zones were set up, and Allied troops remained in possession of the country until 1955. However, the Austrians were conceded the right to set up their own government, which by 1946 enjoyed a semi-independent status.

By 1948 the Western nations had come around to the idea that Germany might be reunited on the basis of free elections and a democratic government. But Stalin did not agree. The USSR's safety lay in German disarmament, in Germany's political and economic weakness. The whole question of Germany's frontiers might be raised, discussed and queried. Stalin countered the Western proposals by demanding permanent German disarmament and the increase of reparations to the USSR. In June 1948 the Russians cut the road and

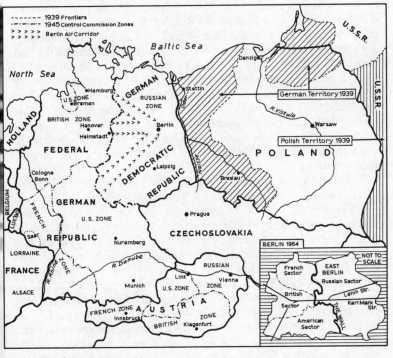

36   Central Europe, 1945–65

rail access to Berlin where Britain, France and the USA had rights of entry and administration. The Allies organised an expensive but effective air-lift. Hundreds of transport planes flew food, clothing and even coal into Berlin throughout the winter of 1948–9 until Stalin relaxed the pressure and reopened the road and rail links. The Berlin crisis of 1948 deepened the Cold War, which a year later entered a new phase when the USSR exploded an atomic bomb, and joined the nuclear powers.

Yugoslavia

By 1948 Stalin had apparently brought all the eastern European nations submissively to heel. In every state under Russian control the non-communists had been ousted and local communist parties, directed from Moscow, had established a harsh grip. In Yugoslavia, events took a different turn. Marshal Tito, the wartime resistance leader, had never depended on the Red Army. Tito was one of fifteen children of a peasant. In the First World War he joined the Austrian army and was captured by the Russians. In 1917 he enlisted in the Red Army and fought for the Bolsheviks. After the war he returned to Yugoslavia as a communist agitator. In 1937 he became Secretary of the Yugoslav Communist Party and during the Second World War brilliantly led the partisans in their resistance to the Germans. This independent man had no intention, in 1948, of allowing Yugoslavia to slip from the grasp of one tyrant into the pouch of another. In addition, he had an ambitious scheme in his head for a federation of Balkan nations.

Stalin, angered by Tito's forthright views, tried to bully and to oust the Yugoslav leader. He failed, for Tito, supported by the army and the Yugoslav people, broke away from the Soviet alliance. Stalin, angered by Tito's revolt, did not dare to invade Yugoslavia, for by 1948–9 Tito was accepting Western aid. Instead Yugoslavia was expelled from the Cominform, the international communist organisation. For the next twenty years Tito cleverly walked the tightrope between East and West. He erected a communist state in Yugoslavia, but entirely free of Moscow. Nevertheless, he did not allow his own followers the same independence. When Milovan Djilas tried to set up a breakaway socialist party in 1954, he and his followers were imprisoned. Tito made his own rules: in 1950 he abandoned the forcible collectivisation of agriculture. But he waited until 1963 to reform the constitution, allowing elections to be held in which not all candidates had to be communists. By then the breach with the USSR had been healed. With Stalin dead, Bulganin and Khrushchev visited

Yugoslavia in 1955, and in the following year agreed that each nation had the right to choose its own path towards socialism.

The Satellite States

After 1948 Stalin was determined that no other communist leader should follow Tito's example. The Red Army and the secret police cooperated in purging the communist parties of the dependent nations. In Hungary, Laslo Rajk, Minister of the Interior, was tried and executed; in Bulgaria, Traicho Kostov, a deputy Prime Minister, suffered the same fate. In Poland, Wladyslav Gomulka was arrested and imprisoned. In Czechoslovakia, Stalin had always disliked the coalition between President Benes and the Communists. In 1947 Benes opened negotiations with the USA for the possible supply of Marshall Aid. In so doing, he rang the tocsin for Czech democracy. First the civil service was 'purged' of those 'disloyal to cooperation with the USSR'. Klement Gottwald, the communist leader, became Prime Minister. In June 1948 Benes resigned and died a few months later. The popular Czech politician, Jan Masaryk, died as the result of a fall from a window, believed by many Czechs to be no accident. Gottwald, now in secure and unopposed control, emerged as a Stalinist: ruthless, determined and dedicated to the Moscow party line. All resistance crumbled as the security police silently moved in.

By the end of 1949 all the eastern states—Rumania, Bulgaria, Czechoslovakia, Poland, Hungary and Albania—were ruled by small cliques of communist politicians, with Russian advisers at their elbows. In Poland, for instance, Marshal Rokossovsky, the new Minister of Defence, was as Russian as vodka. The satellite states took their lead in economic matters, as in all else, from Moscow. The collectivisation of agriculture, Five Year Plans and the strangulation of consumer industries—all aspects of Soviet planning—invaded eastern Europe.

In September 1947 Stalin established the Communist Information Bureau (Cominform), designed to coordinate the policies of all communist parties, both within the Soviet bloc in eastern Europe and in France, Italy and other western states. From Moscow, the Cominform issued regular bulletins explaining Soviet policies and dictating the 'party line' to be followed by communist parties elsewhere. Side by side, more direct and secret orders were despatched from Moscow to all national communist parties.

In 1949 Stalin followed up by forming Comecon—the Council of Mutual Economic Assistance—an organisation designed to blend the economies of all the communist states: in effect it forced the weaker states to toe the line and to accept a role subservient to the USSR's needs. For anyone who questioned the role of the USSR, the NKVD or the equivalent force of security police in the satellite state was always hovering, ready to swoop and arrest any 'deviationist'. For a time it seemed that the Roman Catholic Church might lead the resistance to communism: however, when Cardinal Mindszenty of Hungary and Archbishop Stepinac of Yugoslavia were arrested and imprisoned, opposition fell silent.

THE USSR

In 1945 Stalin could not promise Russia any relief from the harshness of everyday life. The industrial progress brought about by the pre-war Five Year Plans had been destroyed in the flames of the Nazi invasion. Stalin, like a Mongol tyrant, drove the Russians to make even greater efforts. A new Five Year Plan, announced in 1946, concentrated almost all of Russia's energies on the repair of heavy industry—coal-mines, iron and steel mills, factories of all kinds but especially those that manufactured machinery. The Plans of 1946 and 1951 did not reach the ambitious targets set for them but by 1952 the USSR had reached the level of pre-war (1939) production. In agriculture, slower progress was accomplished: food prices remained high; there were regular shortages of essential foodstuffs, and peasants showed their reluctance to work on collective farms. Stalin ruthlessly used the resources of the satellites such as Rumanian oil, Hungarian wheat and Polish steel to plug the gaps in the USSR's production.

The NKVD, directed by Beria, rounded up and deported to labour camps all those thought to be critical or dangerous. Another party man, Zhdanov, made sure that artists, writers and film directors portrayed Stalin as the saviour of Russia. In these years (1945–53) life in the USSR was nasty, brutal and very often short.

The Death of Stalin, 1953

In his last years Stalin ruled the USSR with a hand as icy as a Siberian winter. Even the leaders of the Communist Party were not free from fear. Marshal Zhukov, the hero of the Second World War, was, like many other leading men, given a minor post. The Party was regularly purged, as it had been in the 1930s. Of Stalin's lieutenants, Zhdanov (who died in 1948), Malenkov and Khrushchev emerged as the possible heirs. Khrushchev's reputation arose out of his success in increasing the agricultural production of the USSR, largely by cultivating the huge 'virgin lands' of central and eastern Russia. Suddenly, in March 1953, as all Russia trembled, fearing another of Stalin's vengeful blood-lettings, the dictator had a stroke and died. He had ruled for twenty-five years. Stalin's critics have argued that the USSR would have developed into a major industrial power without him; that in the war with Germany he made colossal errors of judgement; and that the cruel dictatorship which caused death, imprisonment and unhappiness to millions of Russians was unnecessary. Bearing these opinions in mind, the USSR owed a huge debt to Stalin: his powerful will had taken the nation through a terrible war, and the Russia of today, for better or worse, is largely his creation.

Nikita Khrushchev, 1956–64

The manœuvrings for power began immediately after Stalin's death. At first Georgy Malenkov seemed most likely to succeed, but Khrushchev quickly replaced him as First Secretary of the Communist Party, an influential post. The man they all feared, Beria, head of the secret police, was arrested, tried and executed. By the end of 1956 Khrushchev had clearly emerged as the most dominating Soviet leader. Tough, resourceful and a clever organiser, Khrushchev won the struggle largely because of his tight hold on the Communist Party.

Feeling himself secure, Khrushchev startled a secret session of the Twentieth Party Congress of the CP in 1956 by launching into a fierce attack on Stalin, cataloguing the 'errors and crimes' (the execution of loyal Communists; mistakes in agricultural policies and in strategy during the war; responsibility for the quarrel with Yugoslavia, and above all the 'cult of personality'). Khrushchev's speech had a profound effect within and outside the USSR. Statues and portraits of Stalin toppled; Stalingrad became Volgograd, and the reputations of many who had been executed were restored. In Poland over 30,000 political prisoners were freed and in Czechoslovakia the evils of Gottwald's régime were denounced.

Revolts in eastern Europe

The anger of the poor, bottled up for so long, exploded with Stalin's death. In East Berlin the deep hatred of Walter Ulbricht's harsh régime, added to the shortage of food, clothing and housing, pushed people into open revolt in 1953. Russian tanks moved in to crush the insurgents.

Three years later, Khrushchev's speech opened the floodgates again.

Loyal Stalinists such as Ulbricht and Rakosi (in Hungary) were hard-pressed to prevent trouble, but they could not sit comfortably on their volcanoes for long. In June 1956 strikes and riots in the Polish city of Poznan were quickly crushed by troops. However, Gomulka (who had himself been released from a Stalinist jail in 1954) demanded that Poland should have more freedom to control her own affairs, and said that the riots in Poznan were due to poor living conditions which must be improved. Khrushchev flew to Warsaw to bully Gomulka, who threatened to use the army if Polish demands were not met. The Russians, with their hands full in Hungary, climbed down, recalled Marshal Rokossovsky to the USSR and left the Poles with their small victory. In the following years new economic policies increased the output of consumer goods, greater freedom was accepted in art, literature and the press and the dissolution of collective farms was allowed.

In July 1956 Rakosi, the Hungarian Prime Minister, resigned. In October, some students, encouraged by events in Poland, asked for political freedom and free elections. Imre Nagy, the new Prime Minister, formed an all-party government and announced a programme which included withdrawal from the Warsaw Pact, free elections and negotiations with the USSR for the release of prisoners. All the pent-up hatred of many years burst into flame in a violent uprising. On 4 November 1956 the Soviet Union moved tanks, troops and artillery into Hungary, massing for an assault on Budapest. Khrushchev had decided that the authority of Moscow and his own survival depended on the suppression of the revolt. The Hungarians fought bravely but were overpowered. Nagy fled to the Yugoslav embassy, but was later handed over and shot. Janos Kadar, the new First Secretary of the Hungarian CP, formed a new government, with Russian tanks on guard at the street corners. Distracted by the Suez crisis, the Western powers did nothing to help the Hungarians, apart from condemning the USSR's actions in the United Nations. 1956 had proved to be a bad year for Khrushchev, but worse for Hungary. The partial 'thaw' ended in a deep freeze, for many Communists within the USSR argued that if the satellite powers were allowed to taste the heady elixir of freedom, the whole communist system would be put in jeopardy.

Soviet Foreign Policy

In 1955 Bulganin and Khrushchev signed the Warsaw Pact with Poland, Czechoslovakia, Hungary, Rumania and Bulgaria, a defensive alliance which permitted Soviet troops to be stationed in these countries. Khrushchev followed up this diplomatic triumph by visiting Belgrade and resuming friendly relations with Yugoslavia.

Otherwise Soviet foreign policy changed very little after Stalin's death. The Russian leaders met President Eisenhower at a 'summit' conference in Geneva in 1955. No agreement could be reached on the German question, but an Austrian peace treaty was negotiated, guaranteeing the neutrality and independence of the country. As he grew more confident, Khrushchev's tactics changed. Tough and uncompromising hostility to the West alternated with olive-branch offers of peace and cooperation. He liked to apply pressure at a sensitive spot, squeeze and take full advantage of Western hesitation or weakness. In 1958, for instance, he demanded that all military forces should be withdrawn from Berlin, and when the Western Allies showed no sign of budging, he switched to a demand for another 'summit' conference to negotiate a treaty banning the testing of nuclear weapons. In August 1959 he visited the USA, and hopes rose throughout the world for a new initiative in East-West relations.

After two years of discussion, President Eisenhower, Mr Khrushchev, Mr Macmillan and General de Gaulle sat down at a meeting in Paris. A few days earlier an American reconnaissance plane, flying over the USSR, had been shot down. In Paris Khrushchev angrily denounced the USA and demanded that President Eisenhower condemn the actions of the air force, punish the men responsible and promise not to send any further U2 aeroplanes on spying missions. Eisenhower cancelled all further flights but rejected Khrushchev's other demands. After three days of desperate negotiations the conference broke up in confusion. All the high hopes of a settlement disappeared when Khrushchev left for Moscow.

The Russians switched their activities to the Congo, where a civil war had developed after the Belgian withdrawal. Khrushchev flew to the United Nations in New York to denounce Dag Hammarskjöld, the Secretary-General, as a colonialist, and to demand the end of all Western interference in the Congo. Khrushchev enjoyed the role of the aggressive, resourceful leader, keeping the Western powers on the hop. But he showed little pleasure when events nearer home weakened his diplomatic position. Such a setback came in August 1961. The number of refugees fleeing from East Germany into west Berlin was increasing daily, and the East Germans, possibly prompted by the USSR, erected a high wall which effectively sealed off west Berlin from communist East Germany.

The Cuban crisis of October 1962 brought the world nearer to the brink of war than at any time since the Korean war. The Soviet Union helped Fidel Castro in Cuba to build rocket sites. American intelligence reported to President Kennedy that these missile sites posed a direct threat to the safety of the USA. Kennedy demanded the removal of the installations and instructed the American navy to blockade Cuba. The Russian ships carrying missiles across the Atlantic were diverted, and eventually returned to the USSR. Later, Khrushchev agreed to the removal of all missiles and the dismantling of all sites in return for Kennedy's promise not to interfere in Cuban affairs.

The humiliation of the USSR in the Cuban crisis angered Khrushchev's colleagues, already perturbed by the worsening relations between the USSR and China. This rivalry had many causes, but Khrushchev did not help matters by bluster and threats. In 1960, following the USSR's refusal to share nuclear secrets, all Soviet technicians and scientists left China. After that, Mao Tse-tung and Khrushchev did not trust each other and the Chinese leaders refused to come to Moscow to discuss their differences.

Following the Cuban débâcle, Khrushchev became more friendly with the West, as if the threat of nuclear war had purged his rashness. In June 1963 a 'hot-line', a direct telephonic link between Washington and Moscow was opened, ensuring immediate communication between the two leaders. Two months later the long negotiations over a Test-Ban Treaty reached the final stages. The Treaty banned all atmospheric tests, and the USA, the USSR and Britain all signed.

The Fall of Khrushchev

Khrushchev's rule in Russia brought about a slow rise in living standards and a relaxation in international tension. Within the USSR he was able to use his powerful position as Prime Minister and First Secretary of the Party to bring changes in policy. He tried to increase agricultural production by offering incentives to collective farms and by spending large sums of money on the development of lands in the east. Progress proved to be slow, unlike the technological revolution, where spectacular successes dazzled the Russian people and the whole world. The triumph of the first 'Sputnik' in space in 1957 was followed by Yuri Gagarin's first manned orbit of the earth in 1961. The USSR justly claimed to be in the lead in space technology but lagged far behind the USA in living standards. By rigid censorship Khrushchev prevented the Russian people from recognising the vast differences in the quality of life. Novelists such as Boris Pasternak (author of *Dr Zhivago*, a novel set in the 1917 revolution), and Alexander Solzhenitsyn (who wrote a gripping novel of life in a Stalinist labour camp) were persecuted for their candid opinions of life in the USSR.

The murmurings against Khrushchev's leadership came to a head in the autumn of 1963. A considerable fall in grain production (partly brought about by a summer drought) could be plugged only by importing grain from Canada and other western countries. The deepening quarrel with Mao Tse-tung was blamed on Khrushchev's abrupt and angry retorts to Chinese complaints. In October 1964 Khrushchev's colleagues plotted his overthrow within the Central Committee of the Communist Party, which Khrushchev had considered to be safely under his thumb. He was out-manœuvred, out-voted and forced to resign. He went into reluctant retirement in the country and the leadership of the USSR passed into the hands of new men.

The USSR, 1964-70

After Khrushchev's fall, Alexei Kosygin became Prime Minister and Leonid Brezhnev succeeded as First Secretary of the Communist Party. A calmer, more considered atmosphere prevailed in Soviet counsels, but when Kosygin visited the USA to consult President Johnson in 1967, the two sides could find little in common. Mao Tse-tung visited Moscow but failed to resolve the disputes between China and the USSR, and the Eastern European countries soon found that attempts to follow more independent paths were very quickly blocked by the Soviet leaders. The change in leadership in 1964 brought little benefit to either the Russian people or the satellite states, a factor made clear in the Czechoslovak crisis of 1968.

Czechoslovakia, 1968

The improving economic situation in the eastern European states encouraged some Communists to ask for greater freedom from the USSR. The Rumanians, for instance, more openly criticised the Warsaw Pact and Soviet policy in the Middle East and demanded that Rumania should be allowed to negotiate trade pacts with the West. The Russian leaders gave way on some minor points, but in August 1968 the whole of the communist alliance was imperilled by the situation in Prague. Czechoslovakia, like East Germany, had given Moscow little cause for complaint in the years since 1948. Antonin Novotny, the Czech communist leader, had been a loyal servant. In 1968 a group of Communists engineered Novotny's overthrow. Alexander Dubcek and Oldrich Cernik, his successors, released radio, television and the newspapers from censorship and set free many political prisoners. Czechoslovakia suddenly exploded. The long-subdued wrath against the USSR now found voice and the Russians were asked to loosen their grip on the economy, political affairs and the army. Dubcek and his colleagues wanted Czechoslovakia to move towards a more independent, but strictly communist role, similar to the Yugoslav regime. The Soviet leaders, perturbed by the rising opposition to the USSR throughout eastern Europe, acted forcefully to quell the dangerous rising. At first they tried threats, enlisting the support of Polish, East German and Hungarian communists to caution the Czechs to reverse their policies. When the Czechs refused to come to heel, Kosygin and Brezhnev sent in Russian tanks and troops. The Czech army capitulated, but Prague radio and newspapers continued to criticise the Russian actions, until they were closed down. The Russians announced to the rest of the world that they had intervened to protect lives and property. Dubcek was hustled off to Moscow for consultations, and returned a beaten man. Censorship was reimposed and the proposed changes in government withdrawn. The Rumanians were firmly warned not to rock the boat.

In 1969 Dubcek and Cernik found themselves on the run. Changes in leadership saw Dubcek shifted to a minor position, as Ambassador to Turkey, but in 1970 he was recalled to Prague and expelled, like Cernik, from the Communist Party. Czechoslovakia, crushed, returned to the Soviet sheepfold. Elsewhere in communist Europe resentment at both the heavy hand of the Soviet Union and the continuing failure to match the economic progress of the Western nations showed itself in occasional skirmishes. In December 1970, for instance, riots in Gdansk and other Polish ports arose out of rising food prices and anger at Gomulka's failure to deal effectively with economic problems. A change of leadership, with Gomulka replaced by a new man, Edward Gierek, calmed the rioters, but the unrest was an indication of the bitterness smouldering below the surface.

19

The Post-war World, 1945-1970: Western Europe

In 1945 the states of Western Europe faced the arduous task of reconstruction, both political and economic. To begin with, parliamentary democracy was restored in France, Holland, Belgium and Italy. Only in the neutral countries of Spain and Portugal did dictatorship survive the war. But economic recovery proved to be more difficult. The immediate problem of feeding, clothing and housing thousands of homeless families and refugees was tackled by the *Relief and Rehabilitation Administration of the United Nations* (UNRRA) which between 1944 and 1948 distributed twenty-two million tons of supplies to seventeen countries. Three-quarters of the money and aid came from the USA. The devastation in Germany could not be remedied by swift measures: twenty-five per cent of all houses had been destroyed or badly damaged and many roads, railways, ports and factories were in ruins. To a lesser degree the rest of Europe mirrored the devastation in Germany. Britain, for instance, had not suffered occupation by the Germans but the cost of the war had sapped the national wealth by a quarter; over four million homes had been damaged or destroyed, and industry was severely dislocated by war production. For a time the European nations struggled alone, helped by UNRRA, but, too weak to withstand both the pressure of depressed economies and the advancing power of communism, the western European nations turned to the USA for help.

THE COLD WAR

As the Red Army triumphantly crossed eastern Europe, the Russians erected communist régimes in the liberated states. Poland, Bulgaria, Rumania, Albania, Hungary and East Germany all succumbed to direct Russian control. The British and Americans, in turn, liberated France, the Low Countries, Norway, Denmark and Italy. In July 1945 East and West stared at each other, with Germany the hub between them. Relations grew cooler and cooler until in March 1946, Winston Churchill, speaking at Fulton, in Missouri, said that 'from Stettin on the Baltic to Trieste on the Adriatic an iron curtain has descended across the Continent'. On one side of the iron curtain stood the powerful legions of the USSR: on the other were mustered the armies of the Western Allies, protected by the USA's atomic power.

The expression 'the Cold War' described the tension that existed between these two adversaries. The war never became 'hot', that is, open warfare. The 'fighting' was confined to the conference table and other diplomatic exchanges but even so the divisions that separated the two sides were sufficiently dangerous to make many people fear that war might occur. What, then, were the causes of this Cold War between former allies?

Fear and suspicion were two important factors. The American possession of the atomic bomb frightened the Russians, who knew that they could not manufacture such a terrible weapon for some years. To Stalin, distrusting even his closest colleagues in the USSR, it seemed more than possible that the USA would use the bomb to crush the Communists. To try to balance the USA's advantage, Stalin kept six million men in arms, backed by 50,000 tanks, a growing navy and 20,000 aircraft. At the same time, in 1945–6, the USA and Britain drastically reduced their forces: the Americans maintained only 500,000 men in Europe.

Once the German war ended, the two sides realised their essential differences: the USA was a capitalist power and the USSR communist. Stalin had often declared that communists must seek to overthrow capitalism at every opportunity, and the communist parties of Italy, France and other nations looked to Moscow to give a lead. On the other hand, the USA and Britain felt that the defence of democracy lay in their care.

The nearest that the Cold War came to open conflict was in Greece. In

1944 the newly formed coalition government proposed to disarm the Communists, who had fought against the Germans. The Communists resisted and the British, who had entered Athens in October 1944, found themselves caught up in a civil war. In 1946 elections for a new government resulted in the return of right-wing parties. Again the Communists fought back and established a guerrilla outpost in northern Greece, assisted by Bulgarian and Albanian sympathisers. The British supported the Greek monarchy and the Athens government but found the financial strain an intolerable burden. The USA came to the rescue with both money and military aid and by 1949 the Communists were defeated.

The Truman Doctrine and Marshall Aid

The Greek civil war made it clear to President Truman that the USA must be prepared to move her vast resources into Europe if aggressive communism was to be contained. In March 1947 the President published a statement which came to be known as the *Truman Doctrine* in which he declared that American assistance would be offered to help 'free people to maintain their free institutions and their national integrity against aggressive movements that seek to impose upon them totalitarian régimes'. All those who were suffering from 'hunger, poverty, desperation and chaos' were eligible. The initiative passed to General Marshall, the American Secretary of State, who invited the European nations to a meeting in Paris to discuss the question of the aid required and how it should be used. The Russians were invited, and Molotov, the Soviet Foreign Minister, joined the Paris talks, held in June 1947. However, he refused to support the Marshall Plan which he argued the USA was using to interfere in the internal affairs of the European nations, and the USSR put pressure on Poland, Czechoslovakia and Hungary to refuse Aid.

Once the Plan had been agreed, the USA swung into action. The first immediate effect was the supply of arms to the Greek government and the return of American servicemen to Europe. Congress voted 5,300 million dollars for the first year's Aid. In April 1948 a European planning unit, the *Organisation for European Economic Cooperation* (OEEC), consisting of sixteen nations, was established to administer the programme. American money, medical supplies, arms and food poured into Europe: by the end of 1951 the USA had contributed 12,000 million dollars. The Americans believed that a prosperous Europe was the most effective method of preventing the Communists in Italy, France and elsewhere from obtaining power. Within three years (by 1951) industrial production in the OEEC countries increased by sixty-five per cent, and agricultural production by thirty-five per cent, justifying American optimism. To some extent Marshall Aid deepened the crisis of the Cold War: American influence in western Europe increased, hardening Russian suspicions of a capitalist plot, and the USSR took strict action to weed out people sympathetic to Western ideas and replace them in positions of power by men loyal to Moscow.

The Military Alliances

In March 1948 Britain, France, Belgium, Holland and Luxemburg signed the *Brussels Treaty* which guaranteed the assistance of all powers if one of their number was attacked. American policy had been gradually hardening against the USSR and the twin victories of Mao Tsetung in China and the Communists in Czechoslovakia launched President Truman on a course to 'contain' further Soviet expansion. In April 1949 the five Brussels powers were joined by the USA, Canada, Denmark, Norway, Iceland, Italy and Portugal in the *North Atlantic Treaty Organisation* (NATO), a military pact which provided for mutual support against aggression. No member would stand alone against an enemy, for all the resources of NATO would be thrown into a struggle. In 1951 Greece and Turkey joined the alliance.

A common strategic plan and unity of command was the ultimate objective. For a start, a permanent central organisation was set up in Paris, with the military command, the Supreme Headquarters Atlantic Powers in Europe (SHAPE), nearby in Versailles. The USA set a target of fifty divisions for NATO, a figure never attained, despite the American reinforcements that poured into Western Europe. Two famous soldiers were appointed to command this force, General Eisenhower as Supreme Commander and General Montgomery as his Deputy.

The USSR retaliated in 1955 by forming the *Warsaw Pact,* a military alliance of eastern European countries, guarded by Russian troops who under the terms of the Pact were allowed to occupy the territory of the member states. No war or military confrontation ever took place between the two armed juggernauts but the existence of a unified army in Western Europe, supported by the USA, deterred Stalin and later Khrushchev from embarking on any forays. Germany for a time remained separate from the alliances but in 1954 West Germany entered NATO and East Germany joined the Warsaw Pact. It was agreed by the NATO powers that Germany would not be allowed to manufacture chemical, bacteriological or atomic weapons, bombers or warships. After 1955 some of these restrictions were removed and West Germany became an integral partner of the NATO alliance.

After 1950 the USA constructed another, more deadly, military force. Bases in Britain, Spain, Libya and Turkey were built for the United States' Strategic Air Force which was equipped with nuclear bombs. Nuclear defence was the West's ultimate deterrent against a Soviet attack, with NATO as a 'forward' defence post, armed with conventional weapons. The USA and the USSR tried to outstrip each other in a nuclear arms race. In 1954 the USA developed hydrogen bombs. The USSR soon followed suit and elaborate radar warning systems, rockets and high-flying aeroplanes were all added to the armouries of the two 'super-powers', so creating what became known as the 'balance of terror'. A new dimension was added in 1957 when the Soviet Union put a *sputnik* into orbit.

The threat of war was never far away and in 1950, in Korea, the Cold War warmed up. Communist forces from North Korea attacked the independent Republic of South Korea. The USA appealed successfully to the Security Council of the United Nations and General Mac-Arthur assumed command of a UN army (largely composed of American troops) which pushed the North Koreans back to the thirty-eighth parallel, the border zone. When Chinese forces entered the struggle, MacArthur called for the nuclear bombing of China and he was dismissed. In July 1953 an armistice was negotiated and the war ended. After this the United States increased the number of troops stationed in Europe which again became an arsenal.

After the death of Stalin the need for a strong NATO became less of a priority. Britain and France developed their own nuclear weapons and the USA fitted submarines with Polaris missiles, which could strike into the heart of the USSR. The Europeans, alarmed by the increase of nuclear strength on both sides of the iron curtain, tried to find ways out of the jungle of armed might. Count Rapacki, the Polish Foreign Minister, suggested that Poland, Czechoslovakia and the two Germanies should form a 'clean' zone, free from nuclear weapons. The Western powers interpreted this as the withdrawal of West Germany from NATO and rejected the Plan.

In the 1960s NATO seemed to be weakening. General de Gaulle favoured an independent role for France and NATO headquarters was moved to Brussels. Britain tried to persuade the West Germans to accept a greater share of the defence costs. Then, suddenly, the Russian invasion of Czechoslovakia in 1968 made it clear that Western Europe still needed a combined, alert military force in case of Soviet aggression on a similar scale.

EUROPEAN UNION

In the post-war world several attempts were made to bring closer European cooperation. *The Council of Europe*, formed by eighteen countries in 1949, aimed at achieving 'greater unity between its members'. But as soon as the delegates began to discuss the form of political unity, disagreements emerged. Britain rejected a suggestion of a 'supra-national' authority (that is, one in which the national governments would surrender some of their authority to a controlling body). Instead, the Consultative Assembly, which meets three times a year in Strasbourg, is similar to a national Parliament, with delegates from the member-states, but it cannot pass laws. Delegates discuss major issues of European importance and in this sense the Council is an open debating chamber.

Many enthusiastic Europeans disliked the slow progress towards European union and the increasing influence of the USA and USSR in continental affairs. In May 1950 Robert Schuman, the French Foreign Minister, suggested placing the whole of Franco-German coal and steel production under one organisation. This led, in 1952, to the *European Coal and Steel Community*, composed of France, Germany, Belgium, Luxemburg, Holland and Italy. The coal and steel industries of the Community were administered by a High Authority of nine men, assisted by a Council of Ministers, a Court of Justice and an Assembly.

The next stage, Schuman felt, was a common defence policy. In the same year, 1952, the *European Defence Community* (EDC) came into operation, designed to replace national armies with a multi-national European army. Under the terms of the Treaty no single country was to have an army greater than 12,000 men and on this point the plan floundered, for the French National Assembly did not wish to restrict the size of France's army or to surrender control of their defences to non-Frenchmen. And yet it was essential to bring Germany into an alliance. In 1954 the EDC was abandoned and in its place the *Western European Union* (WEU) was set up, with Britain a member. A year later Germany entered the NATO alliance.

In 1955 discussions began on the full-scale economic integration of the six states within the Community. The Foreign Ministers thrashed out the thorny problems that eventually led to the Treaty of Rome which was signed by the 'Six' in March 1957. The Treaty

established the *European Economic Community* (EEC) and at the same
time a separate treaty set up the *European Atomic Energy Community*
(EURATOM). The functions of EEC (or 'the Common Market'
as it is popularly called) were to plan for full economic union by the
gradual abolition of all trading restrictions between the members,
and by replacing national tariffs by a common external tariff. Side by
side, the Community planned to abolish restrictions on the free
movement of workers and to devise common policies for agriculture,
transport and foreign trade. To administer it, the EEC has a High
Commission, a Council of Ministers, a Court of Justice and an Assembly.
Progress was quickly made in welding the six countries into a single
economic unit. Difficulties did arise in reaching a compromise on
difficult problems: in agriculture, for instance, the French fought
hard to obtain good terms for their farmers. Little progress has been
made towards Robert Schuman's dream of political unity: discussions
are proceeding and a Common Parliament still remains the ultimate
aim, but by 1970 it was the remarkable progress and prosperity of
the Community in finance and trade that provided the success story.
In the first five years (1958–63) the Community's external trade increased by forty-five per cent, and internal trade rose by one hundred
and thirty per cent.

   In 1955 Britain did not apply to join the European Economic
Community. Even Winston Churchill, who had spoken so firmly
in favour of a 'united Europe', saw Britain as a sponsor and not a
member of EEC. In 1958, worried by the prospect of exclusion from
European trade, Britain proposed the reduction of tariffs, but wanted
each nation to be free to decide on its own external tariff policy. The
'Six' rejected Britain's plan which, after all, was designed to protect
the Commonwealth. Britain therefore turned to the other nations
excluded from EEC—Austria, Switzerland, Denmark, Norway,
Sweden and Portugal—and, in 1960, established the *European Free
Trade Area* (EFTA). The EFTA nations aim to create among themselves a free trade area. Unlike EEC, however, EFTA does not intend
to introduce firm rules of conduct and political federation. In EFTA
each country retains its right to decide its own tariff policy although
restrictions on trade within the 'Outer Seven' nations have virtually
gone. To some extent EEC and EFTA are rivals and serious attempts at
'bridge building' between the two groups of nations have failed.
After the failure of Britain to obtain entry to EEC in 1963 and 1967
attempts were made to strengthen EFTA. At the time of Britain's
application President de Gaulle considered that Britain's links with
the Commonwealth and the USA prevented her from becoming a

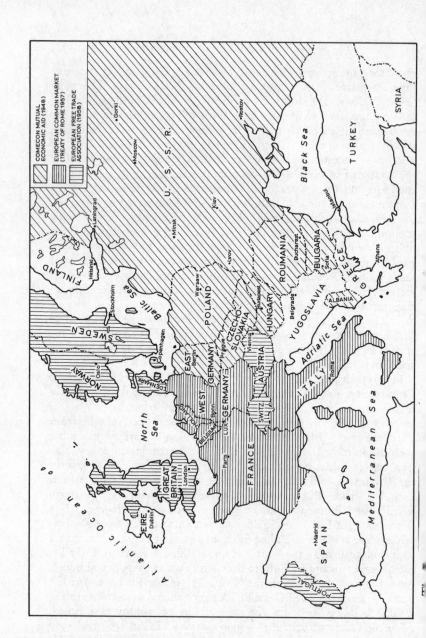

wholly European partner. In 1970 negotiations began for the third time, and the future composition of both EFTA and EEC is uncertain.

FRANCE 1940–70

After the fall of France in June 1940, Marshal Pétain set up a Government at Vichy. The Germans controlled northern France and the Channel and Atlantic coastlines. For a time it seemed possible for France to exist in a state of precarious neutrality alongside Nazi Germany, but when both the USSR and the USA entered the war, Pétain, Laval, Darlan and the other collaborators found themselves relying more and more on German support. The Vichy government cooperated fully: the press was strictly censored, trade unions were abolished and a special type of French security police assisted the Gestapo in capturing Resistance fighters and in rounding up young men for forced labour in Germany.

Outside France General de Gaulle, who had fled to Britain in 1940 after bravely leading a French tank division in the battle for France, organised his survivors into the Free French Movement, to which some colonial territories (such as the Cameroons and Chad in Africa) allied themselves. In 1942 the Allies invaded Algeria and Tunisia. The Germans promptly occupied the whole of France which became indistinguishable from other captured territories. In Britain, de Gaulle came to be recognised as the national French leader, but during the war he was often slighted and ignored by the Americans and the British, insults he took to heart and never forgot. In 1944 the Free French movement in exile declared itself to be the Provisional Government of the Republic. De Gaulle, as leader, worked closely with the Resistance movement inside France and in 1944 triumphantly received the accolade of liberated France.

The Government of National Unanimity accepted de Gaulle as its leader, mobilised an army to assist him and, after 1944, began the mammoth task of feeding and housing thousands of war victims. By June 1945 when 1,200,000 Frenchmen were in uniform, de Gaulle's efforts received recognition for France became one of the five permanent members of the Security Council of the United Nations and assumed responsibility for an occupation zone in Germany.

In France itself, while the work of reconstruction progressed, private revenges were exacted. Frenchmen who had fought in the Resistance, or who had joined de Gaulle in exile, sought retribution against those who had collaborated with the Germans. Pétain, aged 89, was tried and sentenced to death, but later his punishment was commuted to life imprisonment. Pierre Laval, however, was executed. Thousands of others were punished, or mysteriously disappeared. De Gaulle disliked this vengeful persecution of the former pro-Germans, but he could not halt it. Besides, he had other problems to contend with. Railways, bridges, rolling stock, roads, ports and houses had to be repaired and rebuilt. The supply of food to the big cities caused problems: food in Paris was expensive and in short supply, while rural France had plenty. In this situation the 'black market' flourished.

The Fourth Republic, 1946–58

In October 1945 a referendum revealed that few people wanted a return to the old constitution of the Third Republic. A Constituent Assembly elected in the same month contained almost equal numbers of Communists (158), Socialists (142) and a new party, the MRP (Mouvement Républicain Populaire), with 152 seats. De Gaulle continued as head of the Cabinet which contained members of all three parties. He quickly became disillusioned with petty politics.[1] Suddenly, in January 1946, he resigned from office and retired to his country home. He fully expected France to run into difficulties without him, and when the politicians turned to him he would be able to dictate his own terms. In 1947 he launched the RPF (The Rally of the French People), a new party which by 1952 was the biggest single group in the Assembly but was not strong enough to carry de Gaulle back into power. The call to office never came and in disgust de Gaulle dissolved the RPF and retired further into the shadows. In the same year Maurice Thorez led the Communist Party into opposition.

The Constituent Assembly produced a constitution for the Fourth Republic, which, in effect, operated in much the same way as the ill-fated Third Republic. In the space of twelve years there were three general elections and twenty-five separate governments, the longest of which lasted fourteen months. The three major groups, Radicals, Conservatives and Socialists, juggled power between themselves and this led to constant political manoeuvring and changes of government. All governments came from shifting coalitions of the major parties and a government could be overthrown if one group went into opposition. There were from time to time newcomers on the edges of power.

1. 'Do you think I saved France for a handful of dried peas?' he asked in exasperation at one Cabinet meeting called to discuss the food problem.

In 1956 the supporters of Pierre Poujade who campaigned for lower taxation, the reform of the constitution and an imperialist policy, obtained 52 seats in the Assembly. But the Poujadists made little impact on government and Frenchmen cynically came to accept the brevity of governments. After all, the same pack of politicians was shuffled to produce a fresh government, and an efficient Civil Service saw to it that continuity of policy was maintained.

Despite France's political weakness, the country made a remarkable recovery. Jean Monnet, a brilliant economist, produced a series of Plans for the modernisation of industry. The success of the Plans for transport, the iron and steel industry and fuel led to further developments and schemes to improve education and the social services. Progress was achieved despite labour troubles (especially after 1947 when the Communists tried to disrupt industry), rising prices and political instability. The formation in 1952 of the European Coal and Steel Community, in which Monnet played a leading part, helped France. By 1957 French industry and agriculture was producing goods at a rate unequalled in her history.

Colonial Problems

Two politicians, Georges Bidault and Robert Schuman, directed French policy with far-sighted wisdom. They both enthusiastically supported the idea of European defence and cooperation. Less successful was France's handling of her colonial territories. By and large, the imperial possessions of the European powers had become financial burdens. Belgium hurriedly left the Congo to a disastrous civil war; the Dutch failed to hold on the to East Indies, and in Africa and Asia Britain gave way to demands for independence.

Indo-China

When the Japanese withdrew from Indo-China in 1945 the French set up three states—Laos, Cambodia and Vietnam—all under French protection. The communist leader in north Vietnam, Ho Chi-minh, demanded the union of north and south Vietnam in an independent Republic. The French, who had valuable trading and financial interests in Saigon and the south, resisted the nationalist claims. In December 1946 Ho Chi-minh led the communist Vietminh forces in a rising against the French. For eight years the French fought a costly and unpopular war. The fall of the fortress of Dien Bien Phu in May 1954 was the last straw. The French called it a day and Prime Minister Mendès-France agreed to a settlement, decided at Geneva. Laos and Cambodia became independent and Vietnam was partitioned at the

17th parallel into two states, the communist North and non-communist South. Shortly afterwards the USA took up the protection of the south Vietnamese and inherited France's war.

Algeria

Rather than risk long wars in Tunisia and Morocco, the French government granted independence to these states, despite the opposition of French settlers. Algeria could not be evacuated so easily. Algeria contained over a million French settlers, linked by loyalty and family to mainland France. Indeed, another half million French-Algerians were employed within France. In 1952 the discovery of large deposits of oil and natural gas in the Sahara added to Algeria's economic value. However, the nine million Arabs and Berbers, led by the FLN (the Front de la Libération Nationale), demanded total French withdrawal and the grant of independence. The French settlers (*colons* or *pieds noirs*) controlled Algerian politics and had vocal sympathisers, not only throughout the French army, but also in Paris. The French government therefore decided to fight to retain Algeria and by 1954 over 500,000 French troops were trying to stamp out the terrorism and guerrilla warfare mounted by the FLN.

Both sides lost heavily in the Algerian war. Over 200,000 Algerians and some 14,000 French soldiers were killed or wounded. Despite these losses many French officers were determined that there should be no retreat as in Indo-China. These officers, fearing that the Paris government would betray the *colons*, organised their own political group, led by Jacques Soustelle and General Massu. In May 1958 Pierre Pflimlin, a man known to favour concessions to the FLN, became Prime Minister. The Algerian settlers took the law into their own hands and set up a Committee of Public Safety which assumed the powers of an independent government in Algeria. General Salan put the city of Algiers under the control of the army. After fifteen days, Pflimlin resigned. All sides turned to de Gaulle to bring France out of the crisis. The *colons* expected the General to overthrow the constitution and establish firmer rule in France; the army looked to him to safeguard their rights, and the politicians of the Fourth Republic hoped that they might be brought into his government. There was a danger that if de Gaulle did not act quickly the *colons* or the army would seize power in Paris and would set up a military dictatorship.

De Gaulle made a number of ambiguous announcements which seemed to suggest to all groups that he was their man. The Algerian settlers felt certain that he would protect their interests and howled for his return. On 15 May 1958 de Gaulle announced that he would 'assume the powers of the Republic'. All the political parties rallied to him, except the extreme left-wing parties. President Coty invited the General to become Head of the Government. The Assembly granted him full powers for six months and asked him to reform the constitution. After twelve years in the wilderness, de Gaulle had triumphed.

The Fifth Republic

President de Gaulle had no party to rely on. Indeed, he tried to avoid dependence on any one group by forming his new government from all the major parties, except the Communists. Michel Debré, Prime Minister from 1958 until April 1962, was one of the very few open Gaullists in the government. But all this changed within a year, when a new Gaullist party, the UNR (Union for the New Republic) swept to victory in the elections.

As he saw it, de Gaulle felt his immediate task to be threefold: to reform political institutions; to restore authority, and to solve the Algerian problem. Work quickly began on drafting the new constitution of the Fifth Republic. In September 1959 79 per cent of the voters in a referendum approved the constitution. The powers of the National Assembly were considerably reduced. For instance, if the Assembly held up legislation containing financial clauses for more than seventy days, the government could rule by decree. Where the Assembly lost powers, the President gained. He had the authority to dissolve the Assembly and order new elections; he appointed the Prime Minister and ministers and could assume emergency powers in time of internal unrest. In the elections, the old system of proportional representation was swept away and each member of the Assembly was to represent a constituency.

The effects of the new constitution were made clear in the first elections. The Communists mustered only ten seats in the Assembly and the Socialists, forty. The UNR, which won 188 seats, joined up with the MRP and the Independent Conservatives to provide de Gaulle with a substantial majority in a right-wing National Assembly.

The second of President de Gaulle's tasks—the restoration of law, order and prosperity—took longer. In 1958, with his prestige at its height, he asked France for a 'patriotic loan'. In seven weeks Frenchmen donated 140 tons of gold and subscribed 320,000 million francs. Between 1958 and 1963 over 300 decrees were passed, dealing with the stock exchange, finance, rents, justice and education. The franc was devalued, a move which helped to boost exports but which also stimulated a rise in prices. De Gaulle checked the dangerous inflationary situation by direct government action to control wages and prices. Dramatically, by 1963 industrial production and French gold reserves were on the increase.

French Foreign and Colonial Policy, 1958–70

On 4 June 1958 de Gaulle flew to Algiers. He told a vast, cheering crowd that *Je vous ai compris* (I have understood you). No one quite knew what de Gaulle meant, but in the following months it became clear to the army and the *colons* that the General was not to be their puppet. First, General Salan, the commander-in-chief in Algeria, was removed from his command. Next, ignoring the objections of the settlers, de Gaulle offered all Algerians full French citizenship, but the FLN rejected this offer and another in 1959 that would have given Algeria self-determination in four years. A year later the President declared that an independent Algerian republic was inevitable. The army and the diehard settlers could not stomach this and in April 1961 a military revolt, led by General Salan, locked Algiers in another crisis. De Gaulle made a stirring appeal on radio and television and in four days the revolt collapsed. The rebels took to terrorist plots both within Algeria and France and on two occasions de Gaulle narrowly avoided assassination. Finally, in July 1962 Algeria became an independent state; the French army withdrew to France and the *colons* had to decide to stay in Algeria or return to France, which they did in their thousands.

De Gaulle dismantled the remaining parts of the former French Empire. He offered to make special arrangements for the former colonies to allow them to remain within the French Community. In 1960 Madagascar, Senegal and Mali obtained their independence and shortly afterwards Mauritania, Dahomey, Gabon, the Ivory Coast and other territories became sovereign states. But these new states preferred outright independence and de Gaulle's idea of an association within the Community floundered in the 1960s.

In foreign affairs President de Gaulle supported the Western alliance but he became increasingly determined that France should follow an independent policy. This was made clear in his attitude to the NATO alliance. He rejected all schemes which would have placed French troops under NATO or non-French control. He pressed on with the formation of an independent striking command, the *force de frappe*, and he continued to develop atomic weapons, exploding nuclear devices in the Sahara. He believed that France had a right to belong to the 'nuclear club' both for her own defence and for international prestige. He refused to sign the nuclear Test-Ban Treaty and put pressure on NATO to move its headquarters from Paris to Brussels. At the same time he stressed that France would remain a loyal member of the alliance, but on her own terms. Although he showed friendship towards the USSR, visiting both Moscow and Warsaw, he revealed in the Cuban crisis of 1963 that his sympathies lay with the USA.

France's dominant position in the Common Market and in European trade provided de Gaulle with a strong diplomatic base. In the Common Market the President insisted on the best terms he could obtain for French farming interests. On two occasions, in 1963 and 1967, he vetoed Britain's application to join the Common Market on the grounds that Britain's close friendship with the USA and her Commonwealth ties prevented her from being a truly European power. He feared the total subjection of Europe to American dominance and was unafraid to criticise American policies in Vietnam and the Middle East. In 1964 he gave diplomatic recognition to Communist China and three years later, on a visit to Canada, he startled the world by his clarion-call of *Vive Québec Libre!* which seemed to be direct encouragement for the French-Canadian extremists.

Perhaps the greatest triumph of French policy in these years was the friendship with West Germany. The two states worked closely in the development of the Common Market and in 1963 a Franco-German Friendship Treaty was signed by de Gaulle and Adenauer.

In May 1968 President de Gaulle was forced to hurry home from a state visit to Rumania to deal with widespread unrest. Students and workers combined forces in a massive protest against the conservative nature of de Gaulle's internal policies. The President weathered this storm and was given a massive vote of confidence a few months later. He followed up by proposing to reform local government and the Senate and declared that if he did not obtain a majority in a referendum on these issues, he would resign. By now there was considerable opposition to de Gaulle's policies which many Frenchmen believed were stagnant and unambitious. A forty-eight per cent share of the vote was not enough: de Gaulle resigned in disgust in April 1969 and lived quietly in retirement until his death in November 1970. The new President, Georges Pompidou, did not make any radical changes in policy, except to allow Britain to reopen negotiations to enter the Common Market. De Gaulle's greatest achievement (which his successors recognised) was to pass a stable and prosperous France to a new generation.

ITALY, 1945-70

After the Potsdam Conference the victorious powers left the settlement with the defeated nations (Italy, Rumania, Bulgaria and Hungary)
to the Council of Foreign Ministers which by 1947 had decided on
solutions to the major problems.

Italy was in a special position: the three years at the side of Nazi
Germany had been followed by eighteen months as her enemy.
Considerable destruction had been caused in Italy during the fighting,
although the northern industrial region escaped the worst of the
damage. As recovery started, King Victor Emmanuel III, who had
appointed Mussolini in 1922 and dismissed him in 1943, abdicated in
favour of his son, Umberto. In a plebiscite ten million voted for the
monarchy and twelve million against it, and Umberto, after a reign
of thirty-four days, went into exile.

In the first elections the Christian Democrats secured 207 seats in
the Constituent Assembly, but strong Socialist (115) and Communist
(104) representation revealed the power of the left-wing parties in
Italian politics. The Communists under their energetic leader, Palmiro
Togliatti, secured a tight hold on local government and it was feared
there would be a communist seizure of power similar to the Czechoslovak *coup*. The leader of the Christian Democrats, Alcide de Gasperi,
was in command of the government at this time and it was largely
because of his skilful manœuvring (in which the clergy were his allies)
that the Communists were held at bay. In May 1947 Togliatti took the
Communists out of the coalition government and into permanent
opposition: de Gasperi then became Prime Minister, remaining in
office for six years.

Italy turned eagerly to the proffered hand of Marshall Aid. Despite
the communist-inspired strikes and demonstrations that affected
industrial life, Italian production increased. De Gasperi willingly
cooperated with Germany and France in the Coal and Steel Community
and in the formation of the Common Market. Italian products such
as scooters, motor-cycles, cars, refrigerators and electrical goods made
a considerable impact in world markets. Unfortunately, southern
Italy did not share in this prosperity.

When de Gasperi retired in 1953, Italian politics lost their stability.
The Christian Democrats continued to win the greatest share of the
votes in elections, but they had to rely on support from other groups

to form coalition governments. Despite these political uncertainties, Italy prospered and proved to be a flexible and valuable member of the Common Market and NATO.

GERMANY, 1945–70

Germany in 1945 was a wasteland. Her cities, from Hamburg to Munich lay in ruins. The *New York Times* reporter wrote of Berlin, 'it is only a geographical location, heaped with mountainous mounds of debris'. To add to the confusion eight million people, freed from concentration camps or forced labour camps, flooded in. Shortages of food and clothing were quickly remedied by UNRRA, but clearly swift economic recovery was essential.

The USSR demanded, as a price of defeat, that Germany should pay reparations to the Allies. The USA, France and Britain decided not to plunder Germany but Molotov, the Soviet Foreign Minister, demanded 10,000 million dollars in goods, raw materials and equipment. In 1946 the Allies reluctantly agreed to allow the Russians to take supplies from the western half of Germany, to the tune of ten per cent of capital equipment in exchange for Russian products. A year later the USA was reversing the process, supplying Germany with money and goods through the agency of Marshall Aid.

After 1945, four occupation zones were created, administered by the USA, the USSR, France and Britain. Berlin had four zones too. The Allies assumed that the occupation would be temporary, pending a final settlement at a peace conference. In the meantime a Control Commission composed of the four commanders-in-chief, meeting in Berlin, took responsibility for government. A start was made at reducing Germany's frontiers: a large slice of the east (including much of East Prussia) landed in Poland's lap; Sudetenland was returned to Czechoslovakia, and Austria again became a separate state. The Poles and Russians, unofficially, expelled people from Germany's former eastern territories. Possibly as many as ten million Germans moved westwards in 1945–6. These people had to be fed, housed and clothed, and the early efforts of the Control Commission were directed into this work.

Strains soon began to appear in the Allied control of Germany. The Russians who had suffered German invasions twice in thirty years did not intend to forgive and forget, and they saw in the division of Germany a guarantee of her weakness. The French, too, were not keen to see Germany united.

In 1946 the Russians merged all the communist and socialist parties into one group, the Social Unity Party, which formed a government in East Germany, directly under Soviet control. A year later the British and American zones were formed into one economic unit and in 1948 at a London conference the three Western powers agreed to form a separate government for western Germany. Two parties, the Christian Democrats and the Social Democrats, were allowed to function.

Side by side with this political change, the Allies intended to introduce a reform of the German mark, to help revive trade and industry. By now the Russians were thoroughly alarmed by the Western proposals and declared that currency reform and political unity were expressly forbidden by the Potsdam agreements. In June 1948 the USSR closed the corridor to Berlin from the west. The Allied powers took this as a blockade designed to winkle them from Berlin and launched a massive relief operation by means of an air-lift of supplies to the city throughout the winter of 1948–9. In May 1949 the Russians reopened the rail and road links and the danger of open warfare receded. By now Germany was the focal point in the Cold War and the Western powers went ahead with the formation of the Federal Republic of Germany. In the first elections Dr Konrad Adenauer's Christian Democrats gained a majority and formed a government in what had been the three zones occupied by the Western powers. In the east, the USSR formed the German Democratic Republic with a Socialist, Otto Grotewohl as Prime Minister. In a short time, Walter Ulbricht, a Communist, took over as Prime Minister. In 1949, then, Germany was divided into two halves by the iron curtain that separated the communist east from the capitalist west.

Adenauer's Germany

In 1949 Dr Adenauer became the first Chancellor of West Germany. Currency reform, Marshall Aid and a rebuilding programme had started the process of recovery, but the resilience and the hard work of the German people worked an 'economic miracle' that proved to be one of the wonders of the post-war world. Industry expanded so quickly that all the refugees from the east and the unemployed were by 1956 absorbed into factories and workshops. Adenauer presided over this recovery. He had been Mayor of Cologne as long ago as 1917, and had been a minor politician in the days of Weimar. During the Hitler period he lived in retirement, occasionally harassed and imprisoned by the Gestapo. After the war he helped to build up the Catholic party, the Christian Democrats, and at the age of seventy-four, in 1950, became Chancellor.

Adenauer worked closely with the Western powers to hurry on Germany's recovery. Dr Erhard, the Economics Minister, directed Germany's amazing economic boom, while Dr Adenauer handled the diplomatic exchanges. West Germany eagerly cooperated with France in forming the Coal and Steel Community, the European Defence Community, and in 1957 Adenauer negotiated the Treaty of Rome by which the European Economic Community (the Common Market) was created.

Many Germans thought that Dr Adenauer did not press forcefully enough for the reunification of Germany and the return of the lands lying to the east of the Oder–Neisse line. Adenauer did his best. In the Berlin Conference of 1954, however, the dividing lines between East and West were made very clear. The Americans proposed for Germany free elections, a new all-German government and the freedom for Germany to choose her own allies. The USSR, on the other hand, wanted a provisional government with equal numbers of representatives from East and West Germany, and a peace treaty which would decree that Germany would form no alliances and be neutral. The failure of the Berlin Conference led directly to the recognition by the Western powers of the complete independence of the German Federal Republic. Dr Adenauer guaranteed that West Germany would not seek to reunite Germany or extend her frontiers by the use of force.

In 1956 West Germany obtained her own army and entered NATO. From here, Dr Adenauer went on to his greatest triumphs—the deepening friendship with France which led to the Friendship Treaty in 1963, and earlier, the negotiations that preceded the Treaty of Rome and the formation of the Common Market. In 1958 Khrushchev made another attempt to bridge the gap. He suggested that Berlin should become a Free City, and threatened that if the Allied powers did not agree the USSR would recognise the GDR as a sovereign state in East Germany. The Western powers rejected the suggestion and the position lay in stalemate until in August 1961 the East Germans suddenly erected a wall along the dividing line between the eastern and western sectors of Berlin. The flow of refugees from the east ceased at a stroke. Khrushchev sharply replied to protests that as the West had failed to agree to terms for the two Germanys, the border between them should be marked. After 1961 the two divided halves of Germany went their separate ways and there seems no immediate prospect of reunification.

In 1963, Dr Adenauer, then eighty-seven years of age, retired from public life. His party had suffered setbacks in the elections and his successor (Dr Erhard) relied on the support of a small group, the Free Democrats, to retain power. In December 1966 Dr Erhard, deserted by his allies, lost office as Chancellor to Kurt Kiesinger the leader of the Christian Democrats. Kiesinger and Willy Brandt, the Social Democrat, governed Germany in an uneasy alliance until in 1969 Brandt himself became Chancellor.

THE UNITED NATIONS ORGANISATION

In April 1945 the representatives of fifty-one nations met at San Francisco and signed the Charter of the United Nations. Article 1 of the Charter declared the purpose of UNO was 'to preserve international peace and security'. To achieve this, a permanent organisation, with its headquarters in New York, was set up, and all the member nations promised to observe certain rules, such as the non-intervention of one power in the internal affairs of another.

The *General Assembly* supervises the whole work of the organisation. The Assembly, which meets annually, reviews the work of committees, commissions and the Secretary-General, and decides on matters of urgency. Decisions can be taken in the Assembly by a simple majority or a two-thirds majority, depending on the importance of the issue. Every member state is represented in the Assembly.

In 1945 the Allied powers believed it necessary to retain reserve powers in the hands of the leading nations, and by Article 24 of the Charter a *Security Council* was formed with, originally, eleven members. Five powers (Britain, USA, USSR, France and Nationalist China) received permanent seats on the Council. The remaining six places (increased to ten in 1965) went to nations elected by the General Assembly to serve for two-year terms. The function of the Council is to take action in an emergency, acting on behalf of the Assembly which is only in session for a few weeks in the year. Within the Council the approval of all five permanent members is necessary before any action can be taken. Any one power, therefore, can exercise a veto. In the first eight years of the United Nations, the USSR used this veto on over a hundred occasions. But the USSR failed to prevent the Security Council from authorising the intervention of UN forces in Korea in 1950, because at that time the Russians were boycotting meetings of the Council. To manœuvre around the regular use of the veto, which paralysed the Security Council, the Assembly in 1950 devised a new procedure. A special meeting of the Assembly can be called at any time for an emergency debate, and decisions formerly taken in the Council could be decided by the Assembly. Subsequently, in the crises over Suez (in 1956) and Czechoslovakia (in 1968) the General Assembly took the initiative.

Other important councils and commissions of the United Nations are: the *Economic and Social Council* (which considers the supply of financial and economic aid to nations); the *Trusteeship Council* (which supervises the administration of the various trust territories); the *International Court of Justice* at The Hague, in Holland; the *Food and Agriculture Organisation*; the *Educational, Scientific and Cultural Organisation* (UNESCO) and many other special agencies. At the helm of the United Nations is the *Secretary-General* and his staff. The first holder of this office was Trygve Lie, a Norwegian. In 1953 Sweden provided his successor, Dag Hammarskjöld, who was killed in an air-crash in Africa. For the third Secretary-General the UNO turned away from Europe and chose U Thant, of Burma. The duties of the Secretary-General are to supervise the running of the UNO, and to report on any dangers to peace.

In the course of its history since 1945 the United Nations changed in both its composition and its functions. By 1965 the original fifty-one members had increased to 122, with over half of that number drawn from Africa and Asia. To settle problems of peace and war the United Nations relied on negotiation and persuasion. The UN does not possess its own army, but relies on the supply of contingents from its members to man its peace-keeping forces. United Nations troops (supplied by the USA, Britain, Turkey and other nations) fought in Korea and served as observers in India, Indonesia, Jordan, Egypt, Palestine, the Congo and Cyprus.

The success of the United Nations in political matters depends on the cooperation of the major powers, and therefore the Cold War has seriously limited its effectiveness. Despite the rivalry of the Great Powers, the UN has acted effectively in many disputes—notably in the Suez War of 1956, in the Congo and in Cyprus. But the UN's greatest achievements have been shown in economic and humanitarian work in the underdeveloped countries, where there has been close cooperation between countries on both sides of the Iron Curtain.

20

Europe, 1960–1980

✳✳

During the twenty years from 1960 to 1980 the political situation in Europe remained static. There were no major wars between the European nations, no dramatic shifts in alliances, no outward weakening of the two power blocs: the USSR and the Warsaw Pact countries behind the Iron Curtain, and the NATO and EEC countries in western Europe.

These twenty years, however, did see a number of dangerous flashpoints, both in Europe itself (such as the rebellion in Czechoslovakia in 1968), and caused by American–communist rivalry beyond Europe (as in the USA's involvement in the Vietnam War). In these years the economic gap between East and West widened, too. Economic recovery and the growth of international trade—which favoured the western nations—brought material prosperity, and this contrasted with the food shortages and slower recovery and economic development of the eastern European nations.

In these twenty years, too, Europe ceased to be the main stage for American–Soviet rivalry. Troubles in other parts of the world such as the Middle East, Africa and the Far East diverted the world's attention from the political situation in Europe. There were wars in Africa, and in the deserts between Israel and her Arab neighbours; there were risings and rebellions in the Caribbean islands; revolutions in South America; a long and bitter war in Vietnam; and a Russian invasion of Afghanistan. These events took world attention from Europe. However, in 1981 Europe, the USSR and the USA faced one of the great problems of the time; a problem which, if it was not solved, could destroy civilisation. This was the arms race, the steady build-up of more and more powerful weapons of war which the nations brandished at each other. In 1981, as in 1951, talk between the nations was of disarmament: how could it be achieved, and how could the spread—and possible use—of nuclear weapons be prevented?

THE USA AND EUROPE

In January 1961, John F. Kennedy, the new President of the USA and at 43 the youngest in American history, made a famous inaugural speech.

'Let every nation know,' he said, 'whether it wishes us well or ill, that we shall pay any price, bear any burden, meet any hardship, support any friend, oppose any foe to assure the survival and success of liberty.'

In Europe, Kennedy pressed the western powers to work more closely together in pursuit and defence of this liberty. He wanted them to share with the USA the burdens of defence and to offer a stronger bulwark against the USSR. The western leaders agreed with his aims, but differed on the means to accomplish them. President de Gaulle, for instance, did not want France to be subordinate to the USA or Britain, and he opposed British entry to the EEC, while demanding an independent role for France's armed forces, separate from NATO. President Kennedy did not have time to develop his strategy before the danger was upon him.

The Berlin Wall

In June 1961 Kennedy journeyed to Vienna to meet Khrushchev, the Soviet leader. Kennedy realised that the Russians were anxious about the flow of refugees from East Berlin to the west, and he would make no move towards an agreement about Germany. Two months later the grim barbed-wire obstacle of the Berlin Wall was built. For the next twenty years the Wall remained a barrier, a constant reminder of the Cold War. A few East Germans escaped across it; others died trying to make the crossing.

President Kennedy visited Berlin to see the Wall. In a speech he made it clear that the USA stood solidly behind her NATO allies. Within the USSR, Khrushchev was criticised for his 'weak' policy, and so he began a new series of nuclear tests ending with the explosion of a hydrogen bomb, 3000 times more powerful than the bomb which destroyed Hiroshima in 1945. Kennedy could not ignore these warlike gestures and in 1962 the USA resumed the testing of nuclear weapons.

Cuba and the hot-line

In 1962 the Russians again tested the nerve of the western leaders. In August, an American U2 spy-plane photographed missile bases on the island of Cuba in the Caribbean. Other photographs showed rockets, launch pads and Soviet planes. The Cuban crisis (see page 296) brought the danger of the Third World War very near. For a short time Kennedy considered using weapons to destroy the bases, but wisely decided against this step. Instead he ringed Cuba with warships, standing in the path of a convoy of twenty-five Russian ships heading towards the island. On Thursday 25 October 1962 the world came close to war. Khrushchev waited, letting his ships steam on, and then announced a change of plan. The convoy turned back, and in the following weeks the Russian rockets and planes were withdrawn and the sites ploughed over.

Afterwards, Cuba continued to be a problem for the USA, passing completely under Russian political direction, but no diplomatic incidents occurred as a result of the Russian control. The two leaders, Kennedy and Khrushchev, then agreed to share a 'hot-line'. This was a direct telecommunications link between the Kremlin and the White House. Ever since then, the leaders of the USA and USSR have been able to talk direct to each other.

In another way, too, the Cuban danger brought a benefit. Both sides saw that if they continued to build great arsenals of nuclear weapons, they would damage their economies and add to the dangers to world peace. In 1963 the USA, USSR and the UK signed a Test-Ban Treaty agreeing to ban tests of nuclear warheads, except those done underground.

After this easing of tension, both men disappeared from the world scene. In January 1963 President Kennedy was assassinated at Dallas, and was replaced as President by Lyndon B. Johnson. In October 1964, Nikita Khrushchev was ousted from power and put into retirement. Alexei Kosygin and Leonid Brezhnev took over in the USSR and remained Russia's leaders throughout the 1970s.

PRESIDENT JOHNSON AND THE VIETNAM WAR

Johnson, who was President from 1963 to 1968, spent most of his time in office wrestling with the Vietnam War. Thus, again, the spotlight moved away from Europe. The British, German and other European leaders had supported Kennedy in his stand against the USSR, but in the 1960s they, like the people of Europe, grew anxious and restless at Johnson's policies.

In 1962, Kennedy had 10,000 military 'advisers' in Vietnam, helping the South Vietnamese in their struggle against the Communists of the North. By 1968 there were half a million American soldiers in Vietnam and the war was costing the USA over two billion dollars a week. Johnson's policy was to prop up the pro-western but corrupt governments of South Vietnam, and to bomb the North Vietnamese in attempt to destroy their bases and stop the guerrillas from moving south. However, regular supplies of arms and equipment were sent to the north from China and the USSR, and the bombing only seemed to strengthen the resistance and determination of the Communists.

In the USA, Johnson became very unpopular. In Europe, his allies were anxious about the American involvement but did nothing to embarrass him. However, ordinary people showed their anger by demonstrations and marches against American policies in Vietnam.

Finally, in 1968, Johnson decided not to stand for re-election and Richard Nixon became President. His policy was called 'Vietnamisation': that is, he built up the strength of the South Vietnam army with money and weapons, while American troops slowly withdrew to the US. However, the war spread to neighbouring Cambodia and Laos, and Nixon stepped up the bombing of North Vietnam. Early in 1973 a ceasefire was negotiated. More American troops went home. Then, in 1975, the South Vietnam defence collapsed; the Communists swept into the capital, Saigon, and the whole of south-east Asia was abandoned by the USA. By this time Nixon, disgraced by the Watergate scandal, had resigned as President and had been replaced by Gerald Ford.

The American disasters in Vietnam had substantial effects in Europe. In the first place, the war put a strain on the western alliance. Secondly, the USA's embarrassment helped the USSR, whose leaders made great play in eastern Europe, in Africa and in the non-aligned countries about American aggression against smaller nations.

No one doubted that in their sphere of orbit the Russian leaders would use force to crack down on any satellite country which showed signs of rebelling against Moscow's iron grip. This had been shown in Hungary in 1956 and was seen again in 1968 when Russian tanks moved into Prague to crush the Czechoslovak rising (see page 297). A new pro-Moscow government took over in Prague, and in the other states the Communist leaders took care not to be too daring in their dealings with the Russians.

THE 1970S—TOWARDS DÉTENTE

Ever since 1945 the USA and the USSR had glowered and abused each other without coming to blows. Their rivalry spread to the Middle East, to South America (where in 1970 a marxist leader, Allende, became President of Chile until he was overthrown with the help of US agents), and to Africa. In space, too, the Americans and Russians were rivals. The USA overhauled and passed the Russians in technical achievements, and an American, Neil Armstrong, was the first man on the moon, in 1969.

In their nuclear arsenal, the USA had Polaris missiles capable of being launched from beneath the sea, and both power-blocs had 'first-strike' and 'second phase' aerial rocket forces capable of attacking planes and ships and ready to destroy cities with a swift shower of missiles. The USA had planes permanently in flight carrying rockets with nuclear warheads. The Soviet counterweight in the 'balance of terror' was a large force of intercontinental missiles, capable of being launched from underground shelters against European and American targets. In addition, the USSR kept a large army in East Germany and Poland, ready to use against the allied forces in the west. Faced with these terrible dangers to peace, the USA and USSR again tried to find means of reducing tension. This process of trying to relax the strain and of moving closer towards an agreement was called 'détente' or 'disengagement'.

The USA, meanwhile, was suffering agonies of leadership. Nixon's replacement, Gerald Ford, lasted only two years and did not show any kind of dynamic leadership. In November 1976 the American electors chose Jimmy Carter, an unknown politician from Georgia, as President. Carter promised honesty and fair dealing, and he was willing to talk to the Soviets. After much discussion, the USA and USSR designed the Nuclear Non-Proliferation Treaty, by which they attempted to stop the spread of nuclear weapons to other nations. In Europe, all nations signed except France. In 1978, too, new discussions called SALT (Strategic Arms Limitation Talks) had some success. However, both sides remained heavily armed and suspicious of each other.

President Carter had successes in other fields of foreign policy. He brought President Sadat of Egypt and Mr Begin, the Israeli leader, to the USA for talks and moved them a long way towards a peaceful agreement after many years of Arab–Israeli conflict. However, in 1980 the American people again decided on a change of leader, and Ronald Reagan was elected as President. SALT and other discussions about nuclear détente and disengagement were set up in Geneva and elsewhere, but no fundamental changes were made to the balance of power—or of terror.

FRANCE

After the retirement of President de Gaulle, Georges Pompidou was France's new leader. He favoured British entry to the EEC and worked hard to achieve it. However, in 1974 he died and was succeeded by Valéry Giscard D'Estaing. A member of the aristocracy, D'Estaing brought a relaxed style to government, although he was just as determined as De Gaulle had been that France's independent spirit would not be submerged in the NATO alliance. He built up France's armaments and in 1976 added nuclear weapons to the armoury. D'Estaing developed a close working relationship with Helmut Schmidt, the West German leader, and between them the two men brought stability to Europe at a time when America had problems elsewhere in the world.

Inside France, D'Estaing lowered the voting age to 18 and introduced laws to give workers a greater voice in industry. The oil crisis affected France, causing high prices for fuel and bringing economic problems. In addition, like other countries, France suffered from acts of terrorism by groups on the far right and far left of politics. There were occasional bombings and shootings on French streets, although the great mass of people, enjoying the prosperity which came from the long membership of the Common Market, did not suffer from the terrorist attacks. In 1981, in the presidential elections, D'Estaing was narrowly defeated by a socialist, François Mitterand, and France entered a new period of change.

WEST GERMANY

In May 1974 Willi Brandt, the socialist Chancellor of the Federal Republic of Germany, suddenly resigned. He was succeeded by Helmut

Schmidt, whose skilful economic policies added to Germany's wealth
and won the support of the German people. His skill in foreign policy
earned him the respect of western leaders and also of Brezhnev, the
Soviet President, who saw him as a go-between in negotiations with
the USA.

One of the features of Europe in the 1970s was the continuing
prosperity of West Germany. Inflation did not rise above six per cent
at a time when prices were jumping much higher elsewhere in Europe.
The investment in new industries was paying off, and unemployment
never moved beyond one and a half million. Modest pay claims and a
buoyant export trade kept Germany prosperous while France, Italy
and Britain were struggling to control high wage claims and rising
unemployment.

THE EXPANSION OF THE EEC

Negotiations for British entry to the European Economic Community
began after de Gaulle's retirement, and in January 1973 the 'Six'
became the 'Nine' with Britain, Ireland and Denmark joining the
original members. The long-drawn-out negotiations over Britain's
entry did not end there, for when the Labour Party came to power in
1974 it was decided to revise the terms of entry and hold a referendum
(vote) on the terms. The British people voted two to one to stay in
the EEC.

By 1981 it was estimated that fifty per cent of Britain's trade was
going to EEC countries. Similarly, the economies of the other members benefited. Conscious of the need to help poorer nations, the EEC
set up a Regional Development Fund to provide money and aid for
investment in new industry and in agriculture. In a move to help the
poorer nations of the Third World, the Lomé Convention of 1975
declared that forty-six countries which had once been colonial territories should be able to sell industrial and agricultural goods to EEC
countries without paying import duties.

People were puzzled by the Common Agricultural Policy (CAP) of
the EEC. In most of the six original member countries, and France in
particular, farmers were used to being government-supported. To help
their farmers, the French demanded that food prices should be high.
Each year, the EEC fixed prices, and kept out cheaper supplies of food

from non-EEC countries. Surplus food—butter, wine, milk—was stored, in order to be used or sold later. As a result of this policy, in the 1970s the EEC paid out large sums of money called 'subsidies' to farmers. They in turn produced more and more food which was stored in 'mountains' of beef, sugar and wheat, and 'lakes' of wine. In the end, this excess food was used as animal foodstuffs or sold at very low prices elsewhere in the world. However, despite these policies, the EEC was responsible for many important economic advances, and in 1980 applications for membership were received from other countries who wished to share the advantages of belonging to the EEC.

EASTERN EUROPE—THE USSR

The leaders of the Soviet Union from 1964, Brezhnev and Kosygin, were cautious men. They changed little within the USSR. The Government and the Communist Party exerted tight control over the economy and over what people were told about events inside and outside Russia. A constant problem was growing enough food to feed 258 million people. Efforts continued to use more land in the east, but grain failures (as in 1976) meant the USSR was forced to buy from abroad, particularly from Canada. The Soviets also continued to develop industry, putting a large proportion of government spending into armaments, defence and the space programme. From 1970 greater efforts were made to produce more consumer goods, but by strict control of the Press the Soviet leadership disguised from the people the fact that there was a wide gap between the standard of living and the range of consumer goods in the USSR compared with western countries.

Some brave people in the USSR spoke out against the Government. They were called 'dissidents'—men and women who criticised and opposed the Communist Party. In 1966 two writers, Siniavsky and Daniel, were sent to a labour camp for having their novels and essays published in the west. In 1980 Andrei Sakharov, a famous nuclear physicist, protested at the injustice in the Soviet system. He was moved from Moscow to a town in the east.

Perhaps the most famous victim of Russian repression was the writer Alexander Solzhenitsyn. He served in the army, and was then imprisoned in a forced labour camp. He wrote about his experiences in a powerful novel called *One Day in the Life of Ivan Denisovich*. The Soviets had never admitted that these camps existed, and so the novel caused a sensation. Solzhenitsyn was awarded the Nobel Prize for Literature in 1970. He continued to write, and in 1974 was expelled from the USSR, moving to France.

The USSR and China

Shortly after Khrushchev retired, China exploded its first nuclear device. The Chinese were irritated by the USSR's interference in Vietnam, India and (in 1980) by the Soviet invasion of Afghanistan. Relations between the two communist countries grew steadily worse after 1964 until there were clashes between troops along the Manchurian border. The Chinese leaders do not see the USSR as a 'true' communist state at all: they say the Russian leaders are not supported by the people and rule by fear. The quarrels between the two largest communist countries brought its own dangers to peace, for China would not negotiate with the USA and the west while American soldiers were in Vietnam. Today, China is seeking closer trade ties with western countries and this may help world peace.

Poland

Noting what happened to rebels in Hungary (1956) and Czechoslovakia (1968) the communist leaders of satellite states such as Bulgaria, Rumania, Poland and East Germany were careful not to annoy Brezhnev and the Russians. But the people of these countries jealously guarded their independence and by guile and cunning their leaders were able to survive. In Poland, however, resistance took firmer root. The Poles were encouraged by the election of a Polish Cardinal as Pope John Paul II. Before this, in the late 1970s, the workers in the main cities of Poland had shown they were restless. In 1980, led by shipyard workers, the Polish unions protested at the food queues, the low wages, the absence of goods in the shops and the regime of Edward Gierek, the communist leader. A new political movement called Solidarity, with Lech Walesa as leader, was enthusiastically supported by the vast majority of Poles. Gierek resigned and Poland went through several crises while the Russians anxiously watched and waited.

PROBLEMS IN BRITAIN

One cause of political strife in Britain in the 1970s was the state of the economy. Unable to galvanise British industry or to stop the flow of foreign imports, each successive government, Labour and Conservative, struggled to find a solution. However, as the 1970s wore on, inflation and unemployment caused major problems which no government could solve.

Another feature of British politics was the growth of the immigrant population. The Commonwealth Citizenship Act of 1947 allowed a citizen of any independent Commonwealth country the right to enter and settle in Britain. Asians and West Indians came to Britain to find work and in the 1950s they were welcomed. The Immigration Act of 1962 and laws passed in 1968 and 1971 changed things, allowing in only the families of adults already settled in Britain. The immigrants concentrated in towns near to places of possible employment such as south London, Bradford and Birmingham, and this caused tension. All governments, however, were united in their opposition to all forms of racial intolerance.

Ireland

In 1920, the British gave a regional government and parliament to Northern Ireland. In these six counties, called Ulster, the Protestants outnumbered the Catholics by two to one. For the next fifty years, power at Stormont (the parliament) was totally in the hands of a Protestant party, the Ulster Unionists. Catholics were discriminated against: at local levels many did not even have the right to vote, and Protestants were favoured for jobs and council houses.

In 1967 a Civil Rights Association was formed, which organised peaceful protest marches. Fighting broke out on the fringe of the marches and the Catholics defended their flats in the Falls Road district of Belfast against police raids. Unrest grew worse when the British government sent in troops to keep order. In 1970 the Irish Republican Army came into the open to defend Catholic areas in Londonderry and Belfast. Both 'wings' of the IRA, the 'Officials' and the 'Provisionals' fired at the troops and the death roll mounted. In 1972 the British Government ended the rule of the Stormont parliament and took over completely. However, throughout the 1970s the murders continued. Camps and prisons were fortified to hold terrorist captives, and the

IRA moved their campaign to mainland Britain in a series of bomb attacks which killed and maimed many innocent people. All attempts to find a political solution to Northern Ireland failed and the conflict between the two sides, with the British troops in the middle, seemed to have no end.

EUROPE IN THE 1980S

At the beginning of the 1980s, the Iron Curtain still divided Europe as it had in the 1950s. The USSR showed no sign of relaxing its hold on eastern Europe, although in Poland unrest came to the surface. In the western countries there was anxiety about defence, particularly as the USA and the USSR continued to stockpile nuclear weapons.

The twin spectres of unemployment and inflation affected all countries. Europe was heavily dependent on oil imported from the Middle East and Africa. When the Arab states doubled and trebled the price of oil in the 1970s, the economies of European nations creaked. The discovery of oil reserves in the North Sea helped Britain, but fuel costs for everyone, including industry, were high. Rising prices for food and other necessities also affected everyone, and the poor were worst hit.

Unemployment, too, caused unrest. The decline of older industries such as coal-mining and steel-making, which had employed thousands of people, was one cause. Another was high wages, which forced companies to dispense with workers. In some countries, such as Germany, Governments had taken the precaution of investing in newer industries such as electronics. In others, such as Britain, the cost of paying for unemployment and for special schemes for young people was a heavy burden. The political and economic outlook for Europe in the 1980s, therefore, was very uncertain.

Index